AMERICA'S TEACHERS

AMERICA'S TEACHERS
An Introduction to Education

Joseph W. Newman

University of South Alabama

Longman

New York & London

America's Teachers: An Introduction to Education

Longman, 95 Church Street, White Plains, N.Y. 10601
A division of Addison-Wesley Publishing Co., Inc.

Associated companies:
Longman Group Ltd., London
Longman Cheshire Pty., Melbourne
Longman Paul Pty., Auckland
Copp Clark Pitman, Toronto

Executive editor: Naomi Silverman
Production editor: Ann P. Kearns
Cover design: Thomas William Design
Production supervisor: Joanne Jay

Library of Congress Cataloging-in-Publication Data

Newman, Joseph W.
   America's teachers.

   Bibliography: p.
   Includes index.
   1. Education—United States—History.   2. Teachers—
Vocational guidance—United States.   I. Title.
LA217.N49   1990   370'.973   89-8311
ISBN 0-582-28682-4

ABCDEFGHIJ-MA-99 98 97 96 95 94 93 92 91 90

For Dorothy and Beth,
Corinne and Joe

Contents

PART I

Teaching as an Occupation

CHAPTER 1

Deciding to Teach and Finding a Job

MOTIVES FOR TEACHING

Talking with prospective teachers about why they want to teach is an excellent way to begin a discussion of teaching as an occupation. For more than ten years I have asked the students in my introduction to education classes to write down their major motive for teaching. Comparing their responses with the results of similar surveys conducted around the nation, I see several clear patterns. Why do you want to be a teacher? Almost certainly you can give several reasons, but try to narrow them to just one: your major motive for wanting to teach. Now compare your response with those in Table 1.1. If your motivation centers on *students*, you have plenty of company. With remarkable consistency, about half the prospective teachers in my classes link their desire to teach directly to young people. If *academics*—the love of a particular subject or of learning in general—prompts you to teach, you are also in good company. Approximately one-fifth of the future teachers in my survey have academic reasons as their major motive. Surveys conducted throughout the nation show the same patterns: student-centered motives almost always top the list, with academic motives usually running a distant second place.[1]

Other motives for teaching (and the rounded percentages of my prospective teachers who put them in first place) include *job advantages* (10%), the *social value* of teaching (10%), and the *influence of other teachers* (5%). These patterns, too, are consistent with the results of other surveys. The brief statements quoted in Table 1.1 are representative of the ways in which future teachers summarize their motives.

TABLE 1.1. WHY DO YOU WANT TO BE A TEACHER? MOTIVES OF PROSPECTIVE TEACHERS

1. Students
   "I love children."
   "I like working with young people."
   "I want to help students."
2. Academics
   "I enjoy a particular subject."
   "I love learning."
3. Job advantages
   "I like having my summers off."
   "My hours as a teacher will match my children's hours in school."
   "Teaching is a good job for people on their way to something else."
4. Social value
   "Teaching is society's most important job."
   "I can improve society by teaching."
5. Influence of other teachers
   "Some of my teachers helped me so much, they made me want to teach."
   "Some of my teachers hurt me so much, they made me want to teach."

(*Sources: This profile is based on my ongoing survey of prospective teachers at the University of South Alabama and on J. Marc Jantzen, "Why College Students Choose to Teach: A Longitudinal Study,"* Journal of Teacher Education 32 [*March–April 1981*]: 45–48; Cassandra L. Book and Donald J. Free-man, "Differences in Entry Characteristics of Elementary and Secondary Teacher Candidates," *Journal of Teacher Education 37 [March–April 1986]: 47–51; and National Education Association,* Status of the American Public School Teacher, 1985–86 [*Washington: NEA, 1987*], pp. 55–58.)

Considered as a whole, studies of motivation pay future teachers genuine compliments. Teachers are altruistic; they want to help. Most of them enter the occupation with the welfare of others in mind, and they believe they can make a difference in their students' lives. Some prospective teachers have been helped—or in a few cases hurt—so much by their own teachers that they feel motivated to teach. Some extend their concern for others to society as whole. Now notice what the surveys do *not* say. People do not go into teaching for the money—with good reason, as we will see in the next chapter. Nor do people choose teaching for the prestige. Americans respect teachers, but it is a peculiar respect—the kind accorded to outsiders, to people set apart from the mainstream of society.[2]

Can we take what prospective teachers say about their motives at face value? Aren't some of their statements too good to be true? Based on my work with future teachers, I am convinced that their altruism and idealism are real. But based on what they say outside of class, informally and off the record, I am also convinced that the perceived advantages of the occupation pull more people into teaching than the surveys indicate. Notice the job advantages listed in Table 1.1. Teacher education students often joke that "teaching has three main bene-fits: June, July, and August." Of course the summer vacation is attractive, but should it be someone's major reason for wanting to teach? Prospective teachers who admit that it is, along with others who are reluctant to confess, should consider that some school systems have already moved to a year-round schedule and the summer break is closer to 10 weeks than to 12 in most systems. Taking graduate and inservice courses during the summer further reduces time off for teachers. So does "moonlighting." Fourteen percent of teachers work an evening or weekend job outside their school systems during the school year, and 19 percent have outside employment during the summer.[3]

Another perceived advantage of teaching is the daily schedule it offers. As more nontraditional (age 25 and older) students, many of them women, go to college to pursue the degrees they did not obtain when they were younger, more students talk frankly about choosing a career that will allow them to spend time with their own children. As a parent I can appreciate this motive, but should it be first on a prospective teacher's list? Although the nontraditional students in my classes usually have realistic expectations for the occupation, they often underestimate the demands that teaching will make on their time during the evenings and weekends.[4]

Finally, there is the perception that teaching is a good temporary job for people who have other career and life plans in mind. As one student told me recently, "I want to be a lawyer, but I think I'll teach for a while. After all, teaching is easy to get into and easy to get out of." Actually, this is an old notion. Historical studies going back to the colonial era show that some teachers (mostly males) have used the occupation as a stepping stone to other careers, while other teachers (most of them females) have used it as a way station en route to marriage and family.[5]

Americans view teaching as women's work. The feminization of the occupation began in the mid-1800s as school boards turned increasingly to women to fill teaching positions. Females had two advantages over the males who had dominated the occupation earlier: the character and personality of women were regarded as better suited to working with young children, and women constituted a cheap, reliable labor force. These nineteenth-century perceptions are with us still. Today women are 69 percent of all teachers and 86 percent of elementary school teachers, and the percentages are even higher in areas of the nation where highly traditional views of sex roles prevail.[6]

"I love children." Since prospective teachers choose these words so often to express their motivation for teaching, we would expect employed teachers to reflect the same sentiment. But the evidence is curiously mixed. Contemporary and historical studies of teachers' letters and diaries reveal few discourses on loving chidren. Instead, teachers discuss how demanding teaching is, or they focus on matters unrelated to their work. In the letters and diaries, teaching comes across mainly as a job, something people do for economic survival. Yet for a century and a half, society has been sending women the message that they should teach because they love children. They should *want* to be teachers— obviously not for the money but for the children. It is almost as if women, trying hard to please by saying what society expects, have repeated "I'm going to teach because of the children" so often that they have come to believe it.[7]

Perhaps this discussion is too harsh. Teachers *should* care about students, and the evidence suggests that most of them do. When asked why they stick with their demanding jobs, most teachers answer, "the students." What gives teachers their greatest intrinsic satisfaction? They reply, "reaching the students."[8] For convincing evidence of how student-centered teachers are, read the "People" section of almost any issue of *NEA Today*, a newspaper for members of the National Education Association (NEA). "I genuinely like and respect young people . . . and look for the best in them," says a 14-year veteran. "I encourage them to stretch in reaching for their goals." A teacher with 21 years of experience puts it this way: "I do love teaching. I'm working with these kids who want to learn, and telling them about the world, and getting paid for it!" A teacher whose career spans six decades (!), a veteran with "no qualms about using the word *love*," says the best teachers "exult when children succeed—and bleed when they hurt."[9]

Admittedly, teaching is no job for people who do not care about young people, but personal concern is not the only quality that teachers need. A logician would say that caring about students is a necessary but not sufficient qualification for teaching. The job involves interpersonal skills, but much more. Teachers who enter the occupation motivated solely by their good feelings can be bitterly disappointed when students do not return their affection. To be blunt, some students do not want your love. Think twice about becoming a teacher just because you care.

Also reconsider if you believe you will be teaching students whose socio-economic backgrounds are similar to yours. A demographic profile of prospective teachers shows that they are overwhelmingly female, middle class, and white. More than 80 percent grew up in suburbs or rural areas and want to return to teach students like themselves. Only 9 percent—and the percentage is shrinking—want to teach in big cities, where teacher shortages are often acute. As we will see in Chapter 8, the demographic profile of America's students is strikingly different. One in four students is from a family living in poverty. Twenty percent of students are in large school districts with enrollments of more than 40,000. By the turn of the century, as many as 40 percent of the nation's students will be black, Hispanic, or Asian—yet the percentage of prospective teachers who are minorities is decreasing, as Chapter 3 points out.[10]

These trends suggest a serious and increasing mismatch between America's teachers and their students. We will return to the changing demography of teachers and students in other chapters, but the point here is that future teachers are increasingly unlikely to find jobs teaching Dick-and-Jane kids. Instead, more teachers may find themselves identifying with "Here I Was, a New Teacher," a moving account of a teacher's first year in the New York City schools, published in the June 22, 1988, issue of *Education Week*.

Future teachers not only need to consider the kind of students with whom they will be working; they need to think seriously about the kind of work they will be doing. Some prospective teachers, not particularly fond of any academic subject, may gravitate toward elementary, early childhood, or special education, where they believe the emphasis will be on "getting along with the kids." Much of the school day will be filled with games and activities, they think. The human side of teaching will be fun and rewarding. As for the academic side, surely they will know more than their students. Besides, a number of people— including some teachers and administrators—have told them that you do not have to be very smart to be a teacher. They may even have heard that being too bright can hurt.

Let me dispel several myths about teaching. In spite of all the publicity on teacher burnout, some people cling to the belief that teaching is a fun job. It is not. Getting through to students can certainly be rewarding, but reaching them takes hour upon hour of effort. Fun is not the right word. Notwithstanding the public outcry over academically incompetent teachers, some people believe another myth: rudimentary literacy is the only academic qualification that teachers of the youngest or least able students must have. It is not. This belief, another holdover from the past, finds no support in the research on teacher effectiveness, but it dies hard nevertheless.

Perhaps such beliefs appeal to a basic antiintellectual streak in the American character. When taken to the extreme of "the smarter you are, the worse you will do as a teacher," this myth has disastrous effects on the occupation. On college campuses it crops up in the guise of professors who steer bright students away from elementary teaching and toward secondary teaching, or toward college teaching, or out of teaching entirely. In school systems it appears in the form of administrators and personnel officers who are wary of teacher applicants with excellent grades and test scores because they believe such people will not be patient with slower students. Despite the lack of evidence to support this myth, some school systems search diligently for teachers whose academic ability is mediocre. After all, they will probably be less likely to leave teaching for another career.[11]

Yes, this discussion is harsh. To put things more positively, the best teachers strike a balance between their concern for academics and their concern for students. They do not emphasize one to the exclusion of the other. Today the scales of the occupation are out of balance, however, tipped heavily toward the concern for students. In recruiting teachers, society in effect asks college students who care about young people to step forward. After minimal academic requirements screen out a few candidates, many of the remainder become teachers.

Suppose society sends a different message: Will people with excellent academic skills please step forward? Of these, the candidates who care about students *and* are able to help them learn can become teachers. To balance the scales in this way will require a complete restructuring of teaching as an occupation—major improvements in teacher salaries and working conditions no less than teacher education. Make no mistake about it. These are radical changes. As we will see in the following chapters, however, the odds that they will occur are better today than in previous years. Despite the many problems we will discuss in the next section and throughout this textbook, there are good reasons to be cautiously optimistic about teaching as an occupation.

SATISFACTION WITH TEACHING

Ask currently employed teachers how they feel about their jobs. Listen carefully to their answers, for they are speaking volumes about teaching as an occupation. Since 1961 the NEA, the nation's largest teacher organization, has asked teachers the ultimate question about job satisfaction: If you could make your decision again, would you become a teacher? The trends in their answers, collected by the NEA at five-year intervals and reported here in Table 1.2, are troubling. Throughout the 1960s and into the early 1970s, at least three-fourths of the teachers responded that they probably or certainly would teach again, with fewer than 15 percent saying they probably or certainly would not. As late as the mid-1970s, more than 60 percent said they would enter the occupation again, while fewer than 20 percent said they would not. These changes in job satisfaction, though, were an early sign that something was going wrong in the occupation. The survey conducted in 1980–81 left no doubt. Only 47 percent gave their occupation a vote of confidence, while more than a third said they probably or certainly would choose another career. The qualified good news from the latest poll is that slightly more teachers, 49 percent, say they would be willing to teach again, while those who say they would reject the occupation have decreased to 31 percent. Still, the latest figures show that teachers hardly give their jobs a rousing endorsement.[12]

What has happened to teaching? Teachers answer that several essential qualities have become scarce in the public schools, where about 90 percent of them work. According to recent Gallup Polls of teachers, the top four things the schools lack are parental interest and support, public financial support, student

TABLE 1.2. IF YOU COULD MAKE YOUR DECISION AGAIN, WOULD YOU BECOME A TEACHER? TEACHERS' RESPONSES

Response	Percentage of Teachers					
	1961	*1966*	*1971*	*1976*	*1981*	*1986*
Certainly would	50	53	45	38	22	23
Probably would	27	25	30	26	25	26
Chances are about even	13	13	13	18	18	20
Probably would not	8	7	9	13	24	22
Certainly would not	3	2	4	6	12	9

(*Source: National Education Association,* Status of the American Public School Teacher, 1985–86 [*Washington: NEA, 1987*], pp. 58–59. Reprinted by permission of the publisher.)

interest, and student discipline. Adding insult to injury, from the teachers' points of view, is the fact that the general public sees the problems of the schools differently. While Gallup Polls at least show a public consensus that discipline and money are lacking, most citizens seem unaware of—perhaps they are even unconcerned with—the problems caused by the lack of parental support and student interest. That hurts.[13]

These problems sting teachers all the more because they are who they are. Most of them, as we have seen, go into teaching for the students. They want to work with students, to help them. Other teachers are attracted to a subject or the learning process. These teachers, along with others whose motives are equally idealistic, enter the occupation only to discover that their work always demands much and often returns little. Teachers care, but they say that too few of their students do. It is even more upsetting to teachers that so few parents care.

What keeps teachers in the occupation, then? To put the situation in the most positive and complimentary light possible, many teachers are so strongly committed to their work that they are able to overcome the problems they face. The perseverance of these teachers is all the more admirable because they rarely receive the praise and recognition they deserve. Another positive but seldom mentioned factor is that some teachers work in schools that have the healthy vital signs other schools lack: supportive parents, adequate financial resources, and interested, well-behaved students.

Burnouts and Dropouts

But we must also acknowledge a far less pleasant reality. The economic risks of changing careers, combined with teachers' doubts about their ability to succeed in other lines of work, keep many of them on the job. Teachers who remain in spite of their desire to leave are candidates for *burnout*. Typically they begin by missing a few days of class; then their absences increase. When they report to school they go through the motions of teaching, but their commitment has gone. They may want to care, they may try to care, but they cannot. The very quality that brought most of them into teaching, their concern for others, has dissipated. They are exhausted, physically, mentally, and emotionally.[14]

Teachers are not the only workers who must cope with burnout, of course. People who work in the helping professions—which include medicine, nursing, social work, psychology, and child care as well as teaching—are all highly susceptible to burnout. Helping professionals have jobs that are stressful by their very nature, and their working conditions often aggravate the stress. Fortunately, the workers in some helping professions are able to manage stress by controlling their jobs, and some workers have jobs with incentives that encourage people to cope. Other helping occupations, by contrast, leave their workers feeling demoralized and powerless, almost as if the jobs were perversely designed to burn people out.[15]

Compare two occupations within the field of health care. Both doctors and nurses help the sick, but their jobs differ in several important ways. In the first place, doctors have more *autonomy,* more control over their work. As we will see in Chapter 4, autonomy is the right to make decisions and use judgment. Doctors have a great deal of autonomy—more, in fact, than the members of any other occupation. Being in control helps them manage the stress of their work. But while doctors are in a position to give orders, nurses must take orders. Serving as the buffers between those in control and those who need medical help, nurses experience the frustration that comes from knowing what to do but lacking the authority to do it.[16]

In the second place, doctors have a greater sense of *self-esteem.* As members of America's most prestigious occupation, they receive a great deal of respect and admiration. Society regards doctors as full professionals but nurses as *semi*professionals. Several steps lower in the health care hierarchy, nurses feel their work is underrated and underappreciated. They go home feeling far less positive than doctors about their contributions to their patients.[17]

Finally, as everyone knows, doctors earn substantially more than nurses. We do not have to be crass to understand that the *extrinsic rewards* of income can go a long way toward encouraging workers to cope with occupational demands. Doctors work hard and receive high monetary rewards; nurses feel they work just as hard, but their incomes are only a fraction as high.

Teachers have more in common with nurses than with doctors. It may sound flattering to call teaching "a noble profession," but teaching, like nursing, is a semiprofession. In fact, teachers have recently become less like doctors and more like nurses. Teachers have never had the autonomy accorded to full professionals, but since the late 1970s teachers have watched their informal control of the classroom slip away. As American education went back to basics by way of standardized testing, teachers lost control over how to teach, how to test, and how to grade. Today, school board members and school administrators hand down these policies, and teachers have to carry them out whether or not they believe they are in the best interest of students. A barrage of public criticism has wounded the self-esteem of teachers. Their salaries are often not high enough to make coping with job stress seem worthwhile. So why try?[18]

The picture does have a brighter side. Chapter 4 points out encouraging signs that the tide may be turning, that teachers themselves are trying to take charge of their occupation and move toward professionalism. But when the public wants to know why many teachers are unhappy with their jobs, the only honest way to answer is to talk frankly about such things as autonomy, self-esteem, and extrinsic rewards.[19]

People who have left teaching for greener pastures point to the importance of these three factors again and again. A recent poll of "teacher dropouts" conducted for the Metropolitan Life Insurance Company by Louis Harris and Associates has received a great deal of play in the news media—it made the front page of *USA Today.* The survey gives straight answers to the public's questions about teaching. Why do people leave teaching? Sixty percent of the former teachers say their main reason was low pay. Thirty-six percent fault working conditions in the schools, criticizing such things as excessive paperwork, nonteaching duties (cafeteria and hall supervision, bus duty, and so forth), and a lack of involvement in making decisions. The latter complaint is especially significant. The former teachers had definite ideas about how to improve the schools, but they lacked the autonomy to put their ideas into practice.[20]

What about stress? Fifty-seven percent say they were under "great stress" as teachers; only 22 percent find the stress as great in their new careers. Self-esteem? Sixty-four percent say the respect they received as teachers was less than they had expected. Do they miss teaching? Fifty-eight percent say yes, but 83 percent doubt they will ever return to the classroom, for almost all of the teacher dropouts are satisfied with their new careers.[21]

When currently employed teachers are polled about their work, their answers are much the same. Metropolitan Life surveys show that more than one-fourth of teachers say they are "very likely" or "fairly likely" to leave within the next five years, and more than half have thought seriously about quitting. Sadly, teachers who have stuck with the occupation echo the complaints of their colleagues who have left.[22]

The Critical Years Ahead

For your sake as a prospective teacher, I am trying to paint a realistic picture of the career you are considering. I prefer to call it realistic rather than negative, for there certainly are positive aspects of teaching as an occupation. In the chapters that follow we will see that teaching may indeed be on the verge of real progress and that the next few years will be critical. A major reason is that America's teaching force is greying: the median age of teachers is now 40 years, up from 33 in the mid-1970s, and the median length of teaching experience is 15 years, almost double the 8 years of the mid-1970s. Given the fact that a substantial percentage of currently employed teachers will soon retire or resign—the annual turnover rate rose from 6 percent in the 1960s to more than 9 percent in the 1980s—people who become teachers in the 1990s will be in an excellent position to shape the occupation's future.[23]

Some of the best news for prospective teachers is that their chances of finding a job have been steadily improving. Overall, teachers face the most favorable job market they have seen in 20 years. The news for students, parents, and other citizens can be just as good, *if* they listen to teachers and make long-needed changes in the occupation. Mary Futrell, president of the NEA, puts it this way: "I think what the teachers are saying and what they are crying out for is that they want to be treated like professionals and want to be paid like professionals." Albert Shanker, often at odds with the NEA as president of the rival American Federation of Teachers (AFT), in this case heartily agrees: "We have to quit treating teachers like they are hired hands in a factory and start treating them more like partners in a law firm." Otherwise, the leaders caution, the nation will be forced to replace a large number of its teachers with "illiterate baby sitters."[24] Fair warning.

THE TEACHER JOB MARKET

Your main interest in the job market understandably revolves around your own prospects of employment. Articles in academic journals as well as the popular press offer contradictory views of the odds you face. "Teacher Shortage Looms." "Teacher Shortage a Hoax." "No One Wants To Be a Teacher." "College Students Show More Interest in Teaching." Whom do you believe?

Always consider the source. Keep in mind that many people have a vested interest in shaping public opinion on the job market. At one end of the spectrum of opinion are teacher organizations, who are trying their best to convince the nation that a major shortage of teachers is just around the corner. The NEA and AFT hope that, with teachers in short supply, school systems will compete for their services by raising salaries (which *are* getting better, as we will see in the next chapter) and improving working conditions. Taxpayers will have to cooperate, of course, and teacher organizations want them to believe that better salaries and working conditions offer the only hope for easing the shortage. Obviously currently employed teachers stand to profit, but if these improvements attract more capable people into the occupation, as the NEA and AFT promise, the entire nation will benefit.

At the other end of the spectrum are conservative politicians committed to holding down taxes and social spending. They insist that throwing money at educational problems will not solve them, adding that teachers are better paid and more satisfied than their unions admit. These politicians argue that the way to attract more *and* better teachers is to open the occupation to college graduates who have not been trained in teacher education programs. Obviously the conservatives have a sharp eye on the bottom line—they want to ease the teacher shortage without raising the taxpayers' ante for public education—but their desire to improve the academic quality of the teaching force seems sincere.

I will organize our discussion of the job market around the *demand* for teachers and the *supply* of teachers. In both areas I will rely heavily on demography, the study of population characteristics and population trends.

The Demand for Teachers

Every discussion of the teacher job market must take account of the *baby boom*. Often called the postwar baby boom because it began when World War II ended, this demographic bulge of more than 70,000,000 people continues to throw its weight around in American schools and society. Actually the word "postwar" is misleading, for although the number of births in the United States started to climb in 1946, the peak year for births was 1957, and the number of births remained high through the early 1960s. Thus the baby boom was a phenomenon that lasted almost 20 years. The early baby boomers, the children born from the mid-1940s through the early 1950s, took American education by surprise. The young people who would come of age in the era of Vietnam, civil rights, and social change strained their schools at the seams. Many of them attended elementary school on double sessions and found high schools and colleges unprepared for their arrival.[25]

The children of the late baby boom, those born from the mid-1950s through the early 1960s, those who would become young adults during the malaise of the 1970s, found American education in a better state of physical if not academic readiness. These students strained the schools in other ways. Academic standards fell as drug use and discipline problems increased. School officials, now paying more attention to demography, breathed a sigh of relief as the last baby boomers graduated from high school.

The officials were aware that the number of births had fallen sharply from the early 1960s through the mid-1970s. As the students born during this era made their way through the schools, their much smaller age cohort picked up the unfortunate label *baby bust*. Understandably, they hope the label will not stick. These students saw their schools go back to basics as the national mood grew more conservative in the late 1970s and 1980s. The oldest students in this group became adults during the Reagan era; their youngest peers will graduate from high school in the early 1990s.[26]

The demand for teachers rose and fell in response to these trends in student enrollment. As the baby boomers entered school and enrollment went through the ceiling, the demand for teachers outstripped the supply. Teacher shortages developed, hitting elementary (K–8) schools during the 1950s and spreading to secondary (9–12) schools during the 1960s. Prospective teachers found excellent employment opportunities throughout this era.[27]

But the favorable job market did not last into the 1970s. As Table 1.3 indicates, elementary school enrollment peaked in 1969 and then decreased with the baby bust until 1984—15 years of virtually unbroken decline. Enrollment in secondary schools reached a peak in 1976, then decreased until 1990—14 years of decline. The total number of students in grades K through 12 decreased from 1972 through 1984. As enrollment dropped, the demand for teachers fell, and the job market turned sour.[28]

Fortunately, the outlook for prospective teachers is much better today. In 1976 the United States entered the era of the *baby boomlet*, a phenomenon that has also been dubbed the "echo" of the baby boom. At first the nation greeted the echo with little fanfare, but demographers now recognize it as a major trend. The number of births has been climbing since 1976, not because of a significant increase in the *fertility rate* (which demographers define as the number of children born per year per 1,000 women), but simply because the baby boomers

TABLE 1.3. ENROLLMENT IN ELEMENTARY AND SECONDARY SCHOOLS: 1965 THROUGH 1990 (in millions)

Year	Elementary (K–8)	Secondary (9–12)	Total (K–12)
1965	35.5	13.0	48.5
1966	35.9	13.3	49.2
1967	36.2	13.7	49.9
1968	36.6	14.1	50.7
1969	36.8	14.3	51.1
1970	36.6	14.6	51.3
1971	36.2	15.1	51.3
1972	35.5	15.2	50.7
1973	35.1	15.4	50.4
1974	34.6	15.4	50.1
1975	34.2	15.6	49.8
1976	33.8	15.7	49.5
1977	33.1	15.6	48.7
1978	32.1	15.6	47.6
1979	31.6	15.0	46.6
1980	31.7	14.7	46.3
1981	31.3	14.3	45.6
1982	31.4	13.9	45.3
1983	31.3	13.8	45.1
1984	31.2	13.8	45.0
1985	31.3	13.8	45.1
1986	31.7	13.7	45.3
1987	32.2	13.4	45.6
1990 (estimated)	34.1	12.5	46.6

(*Source: U.S. Department of Education, Center for Education Statistics,* Digest of Education Statistics, 1987 [*Washington: U.S. Government Printing Office, 1987*], p. 8. Figures show combined enrollment in public and private schools in the fall of each year.)

have entered their prime child-bearing years and are having children. Their families are small, but there are so many families.[29]

As a result of the baby boomlet, enrollment in elementary schools turned around and started to climb in 1985; enrollment in secondary schools will do the same in 1991. At both levels, the number of students will increase well into the 1990s. As the children of the boomlet move through the educational system, the demand for teachers is rising once again.[30]

The echo of the baby boom is loudest in the nation's Sunbelt. In general, school enrollment will climb most steeply in the West, followed by the South, the Midwest, and then the Northeast. In fact, demographers predict that between 1980 and 2000, almost three-fourths of the nation's increase in children under age 14 will be concentrated in five Sunbelt states: California, Florida, Texas, Arizona, and North Carolina. High birth rates among blacks and Hispanics will accentuate the trend.[31]

Factors other than births and school enrollment also have an effect on the demand for teachers. We have already discussed the teacher turnover rate—it has increased and may rise higher as the teaching force greys. Pupil/teacher ratios also affect teacher demand. Overall, the ratios have fallen in both elementary and secondary schools since the 1960s, although recently there has been a disturbing increase in the percentage of students in classes of 35 or more. Some school systems facing financial insolvency have tried to balance their budgets by raising class sizes to levels unheard of in systems with more taxpayer support. Many public school teachers in my community, to cite a personal example, are struggling to teach classes of 40 to 50 students.[32]

On balance, though, the news on the need for teachers is good. The indicators point to strong, continuing demand. Now we turn our attention to the supply side of the ledger.

The Supply of Teachers

The information on this side is far more speculative. While demographers can confidently predict elementary school enrollment into the mid-1990s and secondary enrollment into the next century by counting children who have already been born, there are no comparable sources of demographic information on the supply of teachers. A large number of hard-to-estimate variables enter the equation. In the first place, how many people will *want* to teach during the 1990s? The answer to that question hinges on a wide range of social, political, and economic factors, forces at work both inside and outside the occupation. We simply do not know how high teacher salaries will be in five years, for example, nor how attractive those salaries will be in the economy of the mid-1990s. In the second place, how many people will society *allow* to teach? That answer depends in part on trends in teacher education and certification; and once again, social, political, and economic variables make it impossible to answer precisely.

We can attempt to answer, however, for we have reliable information on the past answers to such questions. We know that as the baby boom swelled elementary and secondary school enrollments, the news that teaching jobs were available traveled fast. College students responded by preparing to teach in larger numbers. Teacher education, long the most popular program at many colleges and universities, did even bigger business from the mid-1950s through the early 1970s. Teacher educators swung the gates open wide in an effort to meet the demand for new teachers; there was little concern for standards and selectivity. The public wanted teachers in those classrooms, and teacher educators were more than happy to deliver.

As the early baby boomers reached college in the mid-1960s, the gap between teacher supply and demand began to close—with astonishing speed. "Major in education and you'll get a job," the students were told, and many took the advice. The number of bachelor's degrees in education climbed steadily and peaked in 1972–73 at 194,000. Education majors earned 21 percent of all the undergraduate degrees awarded that year. But recall that elementary school enrollment turned down after 1969 and secondary school enrollment declined after 1976. As these trends came together, the unhappy result was the teacher surplus of the 1970s. Teacher educators had helped close one gap—now the nation had enough teachers—but they had opened another. Now many prospective teachers could not find jobs. Almost overnight, or so it seemed, the job market was flooded with applicants in search of teaching positions that simply were not there. College students responded by turning away from teacher education. After 1972–73, the number of bachelor's degrees awarded in education fell by roughly 10,000 per year through the rest of the decade. Given the size of the teacher surplus, though, the numbers did not fall nearly fast enough.[33]

In 1982–83 the number of bachelor's degrees awarded in education bottomed out at 98,000—about half the number granted 10 years earlier. But then the situation changed, once again so rapidly that it caught many people off guard. *A Nation at Risk* (1983) and the flood of reports that followed called attention to problems in the schools. Suddenly education was in the news almost every day. School reform became one of the hottest political issues of the 1980s. In state after state, legislators put together reform packages, raising teacher salaries along with teacher education standards. At about the same time, as we have seen, the echo of the baby boom sent more students to school, pushing up the demand for teachers. In the fall of 1983, teacher educators on many college campuses found that interest in teaching was growing again—a trend that continued throughout the rest of the decade.[34]

The Politics of Teacher Supply and Demand

It is far from certain, however, that colleges and universities will turn out larger and larger numbers of teachers during the early 1990s. It is even less certain that the supply of new teachers will satisfy the demand. The National Center for Education Statistics of the United States Department of Education has projected the supply of "new teacher graduates" into the early 1990s. New teacher graduates include, in addition to education majors, arts-and-sciences majors and other students who have taken the education courses required for teacher certification. The Center for Statistics has made three alternative projections based on the proportion of all bachelor's degree recipients who are expected to qualify to teach. The high projection assumes that an increasing proportion of bachelor's degree recipients will qualify to teach; the intermediate projection assumes that a constant proportion will qualify; and the low projection assumes a decreasing proportion.[35]

Under all three projections, the nation faces a teacher shortage. The question is how severe it will become in the 1990s. Consider the outlook for the 1993–94 school year. Even if the high projection proves to be accurate, the supply of teachers will satisfy just 90 percent of the demand. Under the intermediate projection, the supply will fill 63 percent of the demand. Under the low projection, the supply will satisfy only 45 percent of the demand.[36]

These projections seem all the more significant when we consider the source, the United States Department of Education. During the Reagan administration, Secretary of Education William Bennett joined other federal officials in downplaying the possibility of a teacher shortage. How did Mr. Bennett propose to avoid the shortage?

"I believe that, generally, the key to bringing more and better teachers to our schools is to open up the profession," he maintained. "We should not bar capable men and women from our schools because they do not possess this paper credential or that."[37] This position represents one end of the spectrum of opinion on the job market. Teacher organizations, who advocate vigorous enforcement of teacher education and certification standards, are at the other end of the spectrum. Most teacher educators position themselves toward the teacher organizations' end, while state education officials move back and forth across the spectrum in response to trends in supply and demand.

All of this makes a fascinating case study in the politics of education. Teacher shortages have been the rule rather than the exception in this century, and as we will see in Chapter 3, state education officials have been quite willing to bend teacher education and certification standards to help alleviate the shortages. The plain truth is that academic standards have taken a back seat to market demands. During the 1950s and 1960s, for example, state legislatures and state boards of education opened the occupation to large numbers of persons who had little or no formal training in education. When local school boards exhausted the supply of certified teachers, state officials simply issued temporary licenses and emergency certificates.[38]

What else could they have done, politicians and school officials ask? Raise salaries and improve working conditions to make the occupation more attractive, teacher organizations answer. To be sure, salaries did rise, if slowly, during the 1960s, but the immediate response of the states was to put uncertified people into classrooms. State officials also called on certified teachers to teach out of field—that is, to teach academic subjects outside their areas of expertise—when local school boards ran short of personnel certified in particular subjects, most frequently science and math.[39]

Now we are witnessing a replay of the 1950s and 1960s, albeit on a smaller scale thus far. Faced with "spot" teacher shortages in some parts of the country and in certain academic fields, state officials are once again bending education and certification standards. Likewise, the percentage of teachers who spend at least part of their time teaching out of field is increasing. In 1961 the percentage stood at 31. By 1980 it had fallen to 16, but in 1986 the percentage was 17 and rising. The news media and popular press sometimes call this phenomenon "education's dirty little secret."[40]

Opinions on how the nation should respond to teacher shortages are hardening—on both ends of the spectrum. Teacher organizations are now adamant about enforcing education and certification standards, convinced that keeping new teachers in short supply and prohibiting out-of-field teaching will pressure school officials to improve salaries and working conditions. Despite their criticisms of teacher education programs, the NEA and AFT are using their considerable political clout to defend the principle that teaching requires specialized training. The two organizations are working to gain more control over the licensing process themselves, and the last thing they want to see is eased entry into teaching. Chapter 4 points out how these efforts are part of the NEA's and AFT's drive to make teaching a profession controlled by its practitioners, classroom teachers.

Some politicians are just as determined to open up the occupation, in effect trying to make the emergency and temporary provisions of the past standard practice. They argue that many people with degrees in the arts and sciences, people trained in such fields as physics, mathematics, history, and English, would make excellent teachers. Some arts-and-sciences graduates would choose teaching immediately after college. Others, already employed, would be willing to trade their present jobs for teaching positions. Here, then, is one way to head off the teacher shortage: allow arts-and-sciences majors as well as graduates of business, engineering, and other programs to bypass teacher education and proceed directly from the college campus or world of work into the classroom. Once on the job, the new teachers take a compressed version of coursework in education during their first year of teaching. The state of New Jersey, spurred by an education commissioner with a low opinion of teacher education, pioneered this road into teaching in 1985. At least 17 other states have followed New Jersey's lead, and we will discuss their efforts in Chapter 3.

The important point for this chapter is that constantly shifting political winds combined with social and economic changes make it difficult to forecast the supply of teachers, and thus the job market. In addition to the factors we have discussed, there is a reserve pool of teachers to be reckoned with. This potential source of supply includes people who qualify to teach but never try to enter the occupation—as many as 25 percent of each year's new teacher graduates fall into this category—and teachers who have left the occupation. Estimates of their numbers run as high as several hundred thousand. What would it take to pull a higher percentage of new teacher graduates into the job market? What reforms would lure more former teachers back into the classroom? No one can give definite answers to such questions.[41]

Trends in the Job Market, Field by Field

What we can do is look at the success prospective teachers are having in their search for jobs. The Association for School, College and University Staffing (ASCUS), which has been tracking teacher supply and demand for two decades, offers the reassuring assessment that "dependent upon subject area preparation and geographic location, the marketplace for teachers has improved substantially since the early 1980s."[42] Table 1.4 is a status report on the job market. Every year ASCUS surveys teacher placement officers throughout the United States and produces a rank-ordered list of teaching fields based on the balance between teacher supply and demand in each field. Table 1.4 also shows job market trends in each field—changes in the supply/demand balance from 1985 through 1989.

This table is a valuable guide to the job market in the nation as a whole. To locate more specific information, talk with university faculty members, local and state school personnel officers, and others who are familiar with market conditions where you would like to teach. Even in the five fields with considerable shortages of teachers, the market varies from region to region. The same is true of fields whose rankings are low. The job market for elementary teachers, for example, is most favorable in the Southeastern, South Central, and Western states, where the baby boom is echoing loudly.[43]

As many prospective teachers view the job market, however, it is not national or regional but local. Teachers tend to be less willing to move to obtain a job than, for example, lawyers or accountants. The financial payoff from a move is less for teachers, and many have family and personal ties that make them reluctant to leave a given area. Teachers who *are* willing to relocate—even within their region—can improve their job prospects dramatically. New York teachers, for example, can improve their chances if they are willing to teach in New York City or a rural upstate county rather than a suburb. Teachers in most other states can follow the same guidelines. In general, the school systems that have the greatest difficulty filling their vacancies are in central cities and rural areas.[44]

To try to solve this problem, some states are broadening their market by holding job fairs in the spring or summer. The state of Florida is leading the way with an annual fair called "The Great Florida Teach-In," which draws large numbers of prospective teachers, most of them from the Southeast but many from outside the region. In the words of one teacher who recently attended, "It's great to be wanted for a change. The Florida recruiters made me feel I have an important contribution to make to their state as a teacher." California has launched a recruitment drive with the slogan "A Class Act: Be a Teacher." This campaign has the support of school officials, colleges and universities, and teacher organizations. Even Madison Avenue has gotten into the act. "Reach for the Power—Teach" is the slogan of a national advertising campaign conducted by Recruiting Young Teachers, Inc. A toll-free number flashes on television screens across the nation as Americans learn that no other occupation ". . . has this power. The power to wake up young minds. The power to wake up the world. Teachers have that power. Reach for it. Teach."[45]

Some local school systems around the nation are encouraging teachers to relocate by giving them recruitment bonuses, finding them apartments and paying the first month's rent, offering discounts on bank loans and credit cards, and in other ways trying to make teachers feel appreciated. As welcome (and over-

TABLE 1.4. THE JOB MARKET FOR TEACHERS: OUTLOOK IN 1989 WITH FIVE-YEAR TRENDS

Teaching Field	Trend in Market, 1985–89
Considerable shortage of teachers	
1. Bilingual education	More favorable
2. Special education—behavior disorders	More favorable
3. Special education—mental handicaps	More favorable
4. Special education—learning disabilities	More favorable
5. Speech pathology/audiology	More favorable
Some shortage of teachers	
6. Special education—multiple handicaps	Little change
7. Science—physics	Less favorable
8. Special education—deaf	More favorable
9. Science—chemistry	Less favorable
10. Special education—gifted	Little change
11. Mathematics	Less favorable
12. School psychologist	More favorable
13. Modern language—Spanish	More favorable
14. Computer science	Less favorable
15. Library science	Little change
16. Data processing	Less favorable
17. Reading	Little change
18. Science—earth	Little change
19. Modern language—French	More favorable
Balanced supply and demand	
20. Science—general	Little change
21. Modern language—German	More favorable
22. Counselor—elementary	More favorable
23. Science—biology	Little change
24. Counselor—secondary	Little change
25. Music—instrumental	Little change
26. School social worker	More favorable
27. Music—vocal	Little change
28. English	Little change
29. Industrial arts	Less favorable
30. Speech	Little change
31. Agriculture	Little change
32. Business	Less favorable
33. Journalism	Little change
34. Driver education	Little change
Some surplus of teachers	
35. Elementary—primary	Little change
36. Elementary—intermediate	Little change
37. Home economics	Little change
38. Art	Less favorable
39. Health education	Little change
40. Social science	Little change
Considerable surplus of teachers	
41. Physical education	Little change

(*Source: Adapted from James N. Akin,* Teacher Supply and Demand in the United States: 1989 Report [*Addison, IL: Association for School, College and University Staffing, 1989*], *with permission.*)

due) as this treatment is, we should realize that it is a product of the current job market rather than human kindness and good will. We should also remember that most teachers have yet to receive such treatment. Returning to a job market flooded with job seekers would be a step backward, but a market in which candidates are sought after and highly prized helped move medicine, law, and other occupations down the road to professionalism. Optimistically, the same thing may happen to teaching.[46]

ACTIVITIES

1. Conduct your own survey of teacher motivation. After talking with prospective teachers about their motives, ask currently employed teachers why they chose the occupation. Play the role of a friendly critic in your interviews.
2. Talk with principals and personnel officers about what they look for when they hire teachers. Ask about the relative importance of personal qualities versus academic skills.
3. Interview a variety of currently employed teachers—female and male, experienced and inexperienced, elementary and secondary, urban, suburban, and rural—about their job satisfaction. Conduct similar interviews with former teachers and make comparisons.
4. Use the information and suggestions in this chapter to begin your job search. Consider as wide a range of school systems as possible, and take advantage of the services provided by your institution's placement office. If you have the chance to attend a job fair for teachers, by all means do so.

SUGGESTED READINGS

Teachers speak out on the positive and negative sides of their occupation in Dan C. Lortie's *Schoolteacher: A Sociological Study* and Dee Ann Spencer's *Contemporary Women Teachers: Balancing School and Home* (see notes 2 and 7, below). A study that offers a 25-year perspective on teaching is the NEA's *Status of the American Public School Teacher, 1985–86* (see note 1). The best single source of current information on the job market is each year's *Teacher Supply/Demand Report* by the Association for School, College and University Staffing, 301 S. Swift Road, Addison, Illinois 60101 (312/495-4707).

NOTES

1. My study of teacher motivation, which began in the fall of 1977, includes information on more than 2,500 prospective teachers at the University of South Alabama. Compare J. Marc Jantzen, "Why College Students Choose To Teach: A Longitudinal Study," *Journal of Teacher Education* 32 (March–April 1981): 45–48; Cassandra L. Book and Donald J. Freeman, "Differences in Entry Characteristics of Elementary and Secondary Teacher Candidates," *Journal of Teacher Education* 37 (March–April

1986): 47–51; and National Education Association, *Status of the American Public School Teacher, 1985–86* (Washington: NEA, 1987), pp. 55–58.

2. Linda Darling-Hammond and Arthur E. Wise, *A Conceptual Framework for Examining Teachers' Views of Teaching and Educational Policies* (Santa Monica, CA: Rand Corporation, February 1981). Two landmark studies of teachers, their attitudes, and their status in American society are Willard Waller's work *The Sociology of Teaching* (New York: Wiley, 1932), and Dan C. Lortie's *Schoolteacher: A Sociological Study* (Chicago: University of Chicago Press, 1975).

3. Lortie, *Schoolteacher*, pp. 30–37; National Education Association, *Status of the American Public School Teacher*, pp. 68–69.

4. Lortie, *Schoolteacher*, pp. 31–32.

5. To gain a historical perspective on teaching as an occupation, begin your reading with Willard S. Elsbree's classic, *The American Teacher: Evolution of a Profession in a Democracy* (New York: American Book Company, 1939).

6. Elsbree, *The American Teacher*, ch. 17; National Education Association, *Status of the American Public School Teacher*, pp. 76–77.

7. Nancy Hoffman, *Woman's "True" Profession: Voices from the History of Teaching* (Old Westbury, New York: Feminist Press, 1981); Dee Ann Spencer, *Contemporary Women Teachers: Balancing School and Home* (New York: Longman, 1986); Joseph W. Newman, "Reconstructing the World of Southern Teachers," *History of Education Quarterly* 24 (Winter 1984): 585–595.

8. Lortie, *Schoolteacher*, ch. 4; Robert B. Kottkamp, Eugene F. Provenzo, Jr., and Marilyn M. Cohn, "Stability and Change in a Profession: Two Decades of Teacher Attitudes, 1964–1984," *Phi Delta Kappan* 67 (April 1986): 559–567; Lortie, "Teacher Status in Dade County: A Case of Structural Strain?" *Phi Delta Kappan* 67 (April 1986): 568–575; Spencer, *Contemporary Women Teachers*, pp. 9–10.

9. See "People," *NEA Today* (May 1986), p. 18, and (April 1988), p. 18; and "Meet: Will Hays," *NEA Today* (December 1987), p. 11.

10. Blake Rodman, "Teacher-Training Enrollment Surging Upward, Poll Finds," *Education Week* (March 2, 1988), pp. 1, 26; "Today's Numbers, Tomorrow's Nation," *Education Week* (May 14, 1986), p. 14; U.S. Department of Education, Center for Education Statistics, *The Condition of Education, 1987 Edition* (Washington: U.S. Government Printing Office, 1987), p. 64; Patricia Albjerg Graham, "Black Teachers: A Drastically Scarce Resource," *Phi Delta Kappan* 68 (April 1987): 598–605.

11. Arthur E. Wise, Linda Darling-Hammond, and Barnett Berry, *Effective Teacher Selection: From Recruitment to Retention* (Santa Monica, CA: Rand Corporation, 1987), pp. 58–59; Phillip C. Schlechty and Victor S. Vance, "Do Academically Able Teachers Leave Education? The North Carolina Case," *Phi Delta Kappan* 63 (October 1981): 106–112.

12. National Education Association, *Status of the American Public School Teacher*, pp. 58–59.

13. Alec Gallup, "The Gallup Poll of Teachers' Attitudes Toward the Public Schools," *Phi Delta Kappan* 66 (October 1984): 104–105.

14. Barry A. Farber and Julie Miller, "Teacher Burnout: A Psychoeducational Perspective," *Teachers College Record* 83 (Winter 1981): 235–243, and Mark C. Shug, "Teacher Burnout and Professionalism," *Issues in Education* 1 (1983): 133–153.

15. Shug, "Teacher Burnout and Professionalism," pp. 137–140.

16. See Joseph Benton Howell and David P. Schroeder, *Physician Stress: A Handbook*

for Coping (Baltimore: University Park Press, 1984), and Marlene Kramer, *Reality Shock: Why Nurses Leave Nursing* (St. Louis: Mosby, 1974).

17. An excellent study of the semiprofessions is Amitai Etzioni, *The Semiprofessions and Their Organizations: Teachers, Nurses, and Social Workers* (New York: Free Press, 1969).

18. Ibid.; Linda Darling-Hammond, *Beyond the Commission Reports: The Coming Crisis in Teaching* (Santa Monica, CA: Rand Corporation, July 1984), pp. 13–16; Arthur E. Wise, *Legislated Learning: The Bureaucratization of the American Classroom* (Berkeley: University of California Press, 1979).

19. Patricia Ashton and Rodman B. Webb analyze the current situation and suggest ways to improve it in *Making a Difference: Teachers' Sense of Efficacy and Student Achievement* (New York: Longman, 1986).

20. Louis Harris and Associates, *The Metropolitan Life Survey of Former Teachers* (New York: Metropolitan Life Insurance Company, 1986); Nanci Hellmich, "Teachers Give Up on the Classroom," *USA Today* (March 14, 1986).

21. See note 20.

22. Louis Harris and Associates, *The Metropolitan Life Survey of the American Teacher* (New York: Metropolitan Life Insurance Company, 1986).

23. National Education Association, *Status of the American Public School Teacher*, pp. 19, 73–74; Linda Darling-Hammond, "What Constitutes a 'Real' Shortage of Teachers?" *Education Week* (January 14, 1987), p. 29.

24. Quoted in Hellmich, "Teachers Give Up on the Classroom."

25. U.S. Department of Education, National Center for Education Statistics, *Projections of Education Statistics to 1990–91*, vol. 1 (Washington: U.S. Department of Education, 1982), pp. 7–14.

26. Phillip Kaufman, "Trends in Elementary and Secondary Public School Enrollment," in U.S. Department of Education, Center for Education Statistics, *The Condition of Education, 1986 Edition* (Washington: U.S. Government Printing Office, 1986), p. 141.

27. U.S. Department of Health, Education, and Welfare, National Center for Education Statistics, *Projections of Education Statistics to 1986–87* (Washington: U.S. Government Printing Office, 1978), pp. 49–50, 55–60.

28. U.S. Department of Education, Center for Education Statistics, *Digest of Education Statistics, 1987* (Washington: U.S. Government Printing Office, 1987), p. 8.

29. U.S. Department of Commerce, Bureau of the Census, *Fertility of American Women* (Washington: U.S. Government Printing Office, 1985), pp. 1–7.

30. U.S. Department of Education, *The Condition of Education, 1987 Edition*, p. 60.

31. Brad Edmondson, "The Education of Children," *American Demographics* 8 (February 1986): 26–29, 51–52, 54.

32. National Education Association, *Status of the American Public School Teacher*, pp. 33–34.

33. U.S. Department of Education, *The Condition of Education, 1986 Edition*, p. 104.

34. U.S. Department of Education, *The Condition of Education, 1987 Edition*, p. 104; National Commission on Excellence in Education, *A Nation at Risk: The Imperative for Educational Reform* (Washington: U.S. Department of Education, 1983); Robert Rothman, "Proportion of College Freshmen Interested in a Career in Teaching Up, Survey Finds," *Education Week* (January 20, 1988), pp. 1, 5.

35. U.S. Department of Education, *The Condition of Education, 1986 Edition*, pp. 62–65.

36. Ibid.

37. Quoted in Hellmich, "Teachers Give Up on the Classroom."

38. See Michael Sedlak and Steven Schlossman, *Who Will Teach? Historical Perspectives on the Changing Appeal of Teaching as a Profession* (Santa Monica, CA: Rand Corporation, November 1986), and Donald R. Warren, "History and Teacher Education: Learning from Experience," *Educational Researcher* 14 (December 1985): 5–12.

39. National Education Association, *Status of the American Public School Teacher,* p. 65.

40. Ibid., p. 29.

41. Darling-Hammond, "What Constitutes a 'Real' Shortage of Teachers?"

42. ASCUS Research Committee, *Teacher Supply and Demand in the United States: A Look Ahead* (Addison, IL: Association for School, College and University Staffing, 1989), p. 7.

43. James N. Akin, *Teacher Supply and Demand in the United States: 1989 Report* (Addison, IL: Association for School, College and University Staffing, 1989), p. 2.

44. Lynn Olson and Blake Rodman, "Is There a Teacher Shortage? It's Anyone's Guess," *Education Week* (June 24, 1987), pp. 1, 14–16; Darling-Hammond, "What Constitutes a 'Real' Shortage of Teachers?"; Cindy Currence, "Shortages of '85 Vanish as Schools Hire Uncertified Teachers," *Education Week* (September 25, 1985), pp. 1, 16.

45. Pat Ordovensky, "The Bait Is Set to Lure Teachers," *USA Today* (May 22, 1986); "New Ad Campaign to Tell Youths: 'Reach for the Power—Teach,' " *Education Week* (February 24, 1988), p. 2.

46. Ibid. In Chapter 4 we will examine supply and demand in the context of professionalism.

CHAPTER 2

Earning a Living and Living with Evaluation

Can you make a decent living as a teacher? "It depends on what you call decent," the students in my introduction to education classes invariably respond. Although every prospective teacher's answer to this question will be personal and subjective, examining the facts and figures on teacher salaries will make your answer better informed. This chapter surveys salaries as they are, have been, and may be, with the future contingent on the success of current reforms that promise teachers better wages. We will compare salaries of teachers to salaries of workers in other occupations. We will also look at the controversies over *merit pay, accountability*, and *evaluation*—issues that will directly affect your career as a teacher.

The chapter concludes with a discussion of *career ladders*, which are designed not only to raise teacher salaries but to restructure teaching into an occupation with different levels of expertise and responsibility. The influential reports of the Carnegie Forum on Education and the Economy and the Holmes Group envision a national career ladder that would enable some teachers to earn salaries of $70,000 or more. As much as teachers would welcome that kind of income, not everyone shares the Holmes and Carnegie vision. Reflecting divisions within the teaching force, the NEA and AFT disagree on how to reward teachers and to reform teaching. Still, the most recent news about salaries is encouraging. It may even change your mind about how well you can live as a teacher.

TABLE 2.1. AVERAGE TEACHER SALARIES ACROSS THE NATION (ranking of states from highest to lowest)

All Teachers 1987–88		Percentage of Increase for All Teachers in Constant Dollars 1977–78 to 1987–88		Beginning Teachers 1987–88	
1. Alaska	$40,424	Connecticut	27	Alaska	$26,880
2. D. Columbia	34,705	Virginia	19	California	21,900
3. New York	34,500	New Hampshire	18	Connecticut	20,703
4. Connecticut	33,487	Georgia	18	New York	20,650
5. California	33,159	Delaware	17	New Jersey	20,500
6. Michigan	32,926	S. Carolina	15	Michigan	20,100
7. Rhode Island	32,858	Minnesota	15	Minnesota	19,625
8. Maryland	30,933	Ohio	13	Florida	19,500
9. New Jersey	30,720	Kentucky	13	Maryland	19,478
10. Massachusetts	30,019	Vermont	13	Georgia	19,400
11. Minnesota	29,900	Wisconsin	12	Arizona	19,300
12. Illinois	29,663	Rhode Island	12	D. Columbia	19,116
13. Delaware	29,575	Kansas	11	Delaware	19,100
14. Pennsylvania	29,174	Texas	11	Wyoming	19,000
15. Wisconsin	28,998	Colorado	11	Massachusetts	18,800
16. Hawaii	28,785	Indiana	11	Texas	18,800
17. Colorado	28,651	Missouri	11	Iowa	18,721
18. Washington	28,116	Oregon	10	Hawaii	18,698
19. Oregon	28,060	Pennsylvania	10	Nevada	18,523
20. Ohio	27,606	Arizona	9	Virginia	18,439
21. Nevada	27,600	Michigan	9	Pennsylvania	18,400
22. Virginia	27,436	Alabama	9	Wisconsin	18,332
23. Arizona	27,388	New Jersey	9	Alabama	18,200
24. Indiana	27,386	Tennessee	9	Oregon	18,022
25. Wyoming	27,260	Maine	9	Washington	17,905
26. Georgia	26,177	Mississippi	8	New Mexico	17,897
27. Texas	25,655	Massachusetts	7	Illinois	17,804
28. Florida	25,198	Florida	7	Missouri	17,717
29. N. Carolina	24,900	Nebraska	7	S. Carolina	17,609

(Continued)

TEACHER SALARIES, STATE BY STATE

In 1987–88 the average salary of public school teachers in the United States was $28,044. As the first column of Table 2.1 indicates, teacher salaries vary considerably around the nation. In 10 states the average salary exceeds $30,000; in one state it is below $20,000. Salaries tend to be highest in the Northeast, followed by the West, the Midwest, and the Southeast, but notice the many exceptions to this pattern. Alaska's teachers rank first with an average salary of $40,424: they are well paid, even considering their high cost of living. Down at the other end of the column, the low salaries paid by several states in the Midwest, West, and Northeast are beginning to make teachers in the Southeast feel better about their wages.[1]

TABLE 2.1. (CONTINUED)

All Teachers 1987–88		Percentage of Increase for All Teachers in Constant Dollars 1977–78 to 1987–88		Beginning Teachers 1987–88	
30. Iowa	24,867	Maryland	6	N. Carolina	17,600
31. Missouri	24,703	Arkansas	6	Kansas	17,377
32. Kansas	24,647	N. Carolina	6	Rhode Island	17,302
33. New Mexico	24,351	New York	5	Indiana	17,300
34. Kentucky	24,274	California	5	New Hampshire	17,300
35. S. Carolina	24,241	Nevada	5	Tennessee	16,970
36. New Hampshire	24,019	Wyoming	5	Colorado	16,813
37. Montana	23,798	N. Dakota	4	Mississippi	16,600
38. Tennessee	23,785	Oklahoma	4	Oklahoma	16,432
39. Maine	23,425	D. Columbia	3	Ohio	16,374
40. Vermont	23,397	Idaho	3	Kentucky	16,150
41. Alabama	23,320	New Mexico	3	Arkansas	15,996
42. Nebraska	23,246	Montana	2	Maine	15,863
43. Utah	22,621	Iowa	1	Nebraska	15,595
44. Idaho	22,242	Illinois	1	Utah	15,266
45. Oklahoma	22,006	S. Dakota	−1	N. Dakota	15,218
46. W. Virginia	21,736	W. Virginia	−2	W. Virginia	15,055
47. N. Dakota	21,660	Alaska	−2	S. Dakota	15,020
48. Louisiana	21,209	Utah	−14	Louisiana	14,966
49. Mississippi	20,669	Washington	−5	Vermont	14,966
50. Arkansas	20,340	Louisiana	−8	Idaho	14,793
51. S. Dakota	19,750	Hawaii	−12	Montana	NA
U.S. Average	28,044		7		18,557

NA = not available. (*Sources: First and second columns: National Education Association,* Rankings of the States, 1988 *(Washington: NEA, 1988), pp. 20–21. Third column: American Federation of Teachers,* Survey and Analysis of Salary Trends, 1988 *[Washington: AFT, 1988], p. 45.*)

Now examine the second column of Table 2.1, which shows how much teacher salaries have increased, in constant dollars, from the late 1970s through the late 1980s. Notice that when inflation is taken into account, teachers in the nation as a whole have increased their real earnings by 7 percent. Given the double-digit inflation that eroded the purchasing power of workers in every occupation during the late 1970s and early 1980s, the news that teachers in most states have come out ahead in real income is most welcome. On the other hand, some Americans believe that teachers have realized handsome gains in purchasing power since the 1970s. They have not.[2]

In many states, teacher salaries have risen steadily since 1983. With the release of *A Nation at Risk* and a barrage of other reports on the schools, state legislatures and boards of education went into action. The result was round after round of school reform. Some of the reforms, as we will see in later chapters, seem threatening to teachers—the test-driven "cookbook curriculum" that takes classroom decisions out of the teachers' hands may be the most upsetting. On the other hand, teachers find it hard to fault the efforts of many states to attract better teachers by offering better salaries. Now that the enthusiasm for reform may be cooling off a bit, teacher organizations are working to insure that the trend toward higher salaries continues.

Compare the first and second columns of Table 2.1. Some of the states that have traditionally paid teachers the lowest salaries—several Southeastern states in particular—are making the most impressive strides toward improving salaries. On the other side of the coin, some of the states that have paid teachers relatively well—Alaska, Illinois, California, and New York, for example—are in danger of letting their good reputations slip, for their salaries have changed little, in constant dollars, since the late 1970s.

The third column of Table 2.1 shows starting salaries for teachers. Comparing it with the first column, we can see that several of the states that rank below the national average in salaries of all teachers have raised salaries of beginning teachers to above the national average. Florida, Georgia, Arizona, and Texas—all in the Sunbelt, not coincidentally—are prime examples of states that have "front-loaded" teacher salaries, packing the greatest rewards (relatively speaking) into the first few years. Salary schedules set up this way appeal to beginning teachers and may help these states avoid teacher shortages—or so their state legislatures and boards of education hope. But front-loaded schedules become discouraging as teachers gain experience, for once people are in the occupation they have nowhere to go, financially. Such schedules offer poor incentives to make teaching a career.[3]

The patterns and trends in teacher salaries, like those in the teacher job market, are constantly changing. Just as you should investigate the job opportunities in your teaching field in as wide a geographic area as possible, you owe it to yourself to conduct the same careful investigation of salaries.

The information in Table 2.1 should be only the beginning of your study, for variations in the cost of living make teacher salaries far more attractive in some places than others. Housing is the most important cost-of-living variable to consider. As a rule, the costs of buying or renting housing are higher in the states near the top of the first column of Table 2.1 than in the states near the bottom, but variations *within* states are just as important. Housing tends to be more expensive in cities and suburbs than in small towns and rural areas, and the higher salaries that city and suburban school systems offer may not be enough to offset the difference. The "average" Illinois teacher whose salary is $29,663 may own a home and live comfortably in small-town Taylorville, while a teacher earning several thousand dollars more in an affluent suburb of Chicago may be hard pressed to make ends meet, much less move out of an apartment and make payments on a home.[4]

A PROFILE OF AMERICA'S TEACHERS

Who is the "average" teacher? The demographic profile in Table 2.2 helps answer the question. In America as a whole, the average teacher is a woman, white, 41 years old, married with two children. She holds a graduate degree and has been teaching for 15 years. When you ask yourself whether you can make a decent living as a teacher, put yourself in this teacher's shoes—or at least put yourself well into your career. How would you like to earn $28,044 (or the average salary for the state where you would like to teach) after earning a graduate degree and spending 15 years in the classroom?[5]

You should consider that the average teacher has a spouse who contributes to the income of their family. In fact, the average household income for all teachers in 1986 was $43,413, and now the figure is approximately $50,000. A household income of $50,000, fifteen years into a teaching career, is certainly a more pleasant prospect than an individual salary of $28,031. With the sum of $50,000 in mind, a middle-class lifestyle, owning a home, and college for the two kids all seem within the realm of possibility. If we compare the aver-

TABLE 2.2. A PROFILE OF AMERICA'S TEACHERS

Gender	
Female	69%
Male	31%
Race	
Black	7%
White	90%
Other	3%
Average age	*41 years*
Age distribution	
Under 30	11%
30–39	38%
40–49	30%
50 and over	21%
Marital status	
Married	76%
Single	13%
Widowed, divorced, separated	11%
Teachers with children	*72%*
Average number of children	*2*
Teachers with employed spouses	*65%*
Highest degree	
Bachelor's	48%
Master's or specialist's	51%
Doctor's	1%
Average teaching experience	*15 years*

(*Source: National Education Association,* Status of the American Public School Teacher, 1985–86 [*Washington: NEA, 1987*], pp. 11, 14, 73, 80. *Reprinted by permission of the publisher.*)

age American household income of $24,897 in 1986 with the average teacher's household income of $43,413 in 1986, teachers seem to be doing well indeed.[6]

The first time I discussed household income in my introduction to education classes, my students' reactions took me by surprise. I was being unfairly (and uncharacteristically) positive, the students said. They pointed out that household income also includes the moonlighting that many teachers do outside the school system (see Chapter 1) as well as the additional duties they take on at school—coaching and summer teaching, for example. Yes, I admitted, almost half of all teachers find it necessary to supplement their household income in these ways. Several students also reminded me, referring to the profile in Table 2.2, that one out of every four teachers is *not* married. It is small consolation to the single teacher who lives on one income that the average teacher has a household income of $50,000. Nor is that figure of much comfort to the divorced teacher who is trying to raise several children on one income.[7]

Thus I joined my students and concluded that although it may be helpful to know the average household income of an occupation's members, using household income to make individual salaries seem more acceptable can be deceptive. Prospective teachers who say, "Teaching provides a good second income" or "I'll never earn much as a teacher, but if I get married I'll be alright financially," are apologizing for their chosen occupation before they enter it. This defeatist attitude continues to hold teaching back. Teachers who regard their salaries as secondary may think of their work as secondary—as something less than a "real" career.

"We are teaching for a living, not a hobby," teacher organizations constantly remind politicians and the public, and the facts about teaching support this view of the occupation. In the public school teaching force as a whole, the salaries of male teachers provide almost two-thirds of the income in their households, while the salaries of female teachers account for more than half of their household income. In most teacher households, the income from teaching is primary, not secondary. Every chapter in the first part of this textbook emphasizes that teaching has the potential to become a full profession, evolving as medicine, law, and a few other occupations have during this century. For this change to occur, public attitudes toward teaching must change, with the attitudes of teachers themselves changing first.[8]

COMPARING SALARIES IN TEACHING AND OTHER OCCUPATIONS

Income is an important measure of worth in our society, one estimate of how much society values a particular kind of work. How do salaries of teachers compare with salaries of workers in other occupations? In the comparisons that follow, remember that in 1987–88 the average starting salary of public school teachers was $18,557, while the average salary of all teachers in the public schools was $28,044. (Private school teachers, who make up about 15 percent of the nation's teaching force, earn considerably less. As a rule, elite independent schools are the only private schools that pay salaries comparable to those in public schools. See the last chapter of this book for more about private schools.)

The Labor Department's *Occupational Outlook Handbook, 1988–89 Edition*, provides information we can use to compare salaries. If we begin with social work and nursing, two female-dominated occupations that society views, like teaching, as semiprofessional, we see that teaching fares reasonably well. Starting salaries for social caseworkers with BSW (Bachelor's in Social Work) degrees average $16,700. Casework supervisors with MSW (Master's in Social Work) degrees start at $21,500. The average compensation for experienced social workers in medical centers and hospitals is $27,300 and, for all social workers employed by the federal government, $31,800. Turning our attention to nursing, we find a field struggling with a shortage of trained workers, a shortage even more widespread and acute than the one in teaching. Hospitals, medical schools, and medical centers have been trying to cope with the shortage by raising the salaries of beginning registered nurses, which has pushed their average starting pay up to $20,400. Experienced registered nurses in medical institutions earn an average of $27,800, with experienced head nurses earning $35,000. The average salary of all registered nurses, however, is just $23,900, and for those who work for the federal government, only $26,100. Nurses, like teachers, find that once they are in the occupation, there is relatively little room for financial advancement.[9]

Teaching looks less competitive—although it is still in the running—compared with business and management, fields in which women are now receiving almost half of the bachelor's and one-third of the master's degrees. Accountants with bachelor's degrees have starting offers that average $21,200; with master's degrees, they receive offers of $25,600. Average earnings of all nonsupervisory accountants are $31,800. Chief management accountants earn considerably more: an average of $54,700. Purchasing agents and managers start at $21,200 in the private sector; with experience their compensation ranges between $26,400 and $33,600, while senior agents earn an average of $41,300. Financial managers who work in banks, industry, and similar settings often start with salaries below $20,000, but their wages climb to an average of $30,400.[10]

Looking at salaries in scientific and technical fields makes it clear why there is a shortage of science and math teachers. Quite simply, people with such skills must be willing to make a financial sacrifice if they want to teach. Engineers with bachelor's degrees go to work in the private sector for starting salaries of $27,900; with master's degrees, their entry-level job offers average $33,100. Mid-level, nonsupervisory engineers have average earnings of $42,677, while their senior supervisors earn $79,021. Mathematicians have starting salaries of $24,400 and $30,600 with bachelor's and master's degrees, respectively, while the average wages of all mathematicians are $38,100. Chemists start at $23,400 with bachelor's degrees and $28,000 with master's degrees. Mid-level, nonsupervisory chemists earn an average of $41,500, and senior supervisory chemists have salaries of $74,600. Women workers are still underrepresented in scientific and technical fields. In engineering, for example, women are earning only 15 percent of the new undergraduate degrees.[11]

Turning finally to the two occupations that Americans consider most professional, law and medicine, we can see the substantial financial rewards that accompany high occupational status. Beginning attorneys in private practice can anticipate earning about $31,000, while the most experienced attorneys in private practice may have incomes of more than $100,000. Physicians also have great earning potential. As residents they receive stipends of only $20,000 to $24,000, but on entering private practice their incomes climb steeply. General practitioners earn an average of $72,840; pediatricians, $84,340; general surgeons, $122,370; and all physicians, $106,300. On an encouraging note, women are now earning 30 percent of the medical degrees and 39 percent of the law degrees.[12]

Barring a drastic reordering of our nation's social and economic priorities, teachers will never command the average incomes of doctors or lawyers. Having said that, we should not despair of the possibility of major improvements in teacher salaries. The career ladders that several states have built offer "master teacher" salaries of more than $40,000. The Holmes Group and the Carnegie Forum on Education and the Economy would like to build a national career ladder for America's teachers. The Carnegie Forum in fact has established a national teacher certification board that may enable some of the nation's best teachers to become "lead teachers" with salaries of $42,000 to $72,000.

Before analyzing the promises and perils of these innovations conceived by the school reformers of the 1980s to improve teaching in the 1990s and beyond, we can encourage ourselves with the fact that the most experienced, most highly educated teachers in some school systems are *already* earning $50,000—on regular salary schedules. Or we can just as easily discourage ourselves with the fact that, in other systems, teachers who have taught for 30 years and earned graduate degrees have salaries of $25,000 or less—on regular salary schedules.

TEACHER SALARY SCHEDULES

Tables 2.3, 2.4, and 2.5 illustrate the diversity in teacher pay throughout the United States. Notice that, as different as the salaries on the three schedules are, however, they have several key features in common. These schedules, like most in the nation, are based on just two factors: experience and education. These schedules make no distinctions among teachers by subject or grade level, nor do they reward teachers according to their competence and performance. On each schedule, a teacher who has five years of classroom experience and a bachelor's degree earns exactly the same salary as every other teacher with five years and

TABLE 2.3. A TEACHER SALARY SCHEDULE WITH "PERVERSE INCENTIVES"

	Track		
Step	Bachelor's	Master's	Specialist's
1	$15,000	$17,000	$19,000
2	15,200	17,200	19,200
3	15,400	17,400	19,400
4	17,000	19,000	21,000
5	17,200	19,200	21,200
6	17,400	19,400	21,400
7	17,600	19,600	21,600
8	17,800	19,800	21,800
9	18,000	20,000	22,000
10	18,200	20,200	22,200

a bachelor's degree. Schedules like these bring a sense of security and predictability to teaching as an occupation.

For the first half of this century, teacher organizations fought hard for salary schedules with these features. School boards must treat all teachers alike, the organizations insisted; teacher salaries must be based strictly on experience and education. In system after system, state after state, teacher organizations won these battles, and gradually school boards quit paying secondary teachers more than elementary, male teachers more than female, and most recently, white teachers more than black. School boards adopted *single salary schedules* that

TABLE 2.4. A TYPICAL TEACHER SALARY SCHEDULE

	Track					
Step	Bachelor's	Bachelor's +20 hours	Master's	Master's +20 hours	Specialist's	Doctor's
1	$18,500	$18,500	$19,500	$19,500	$20,000	$21,500
2	18,700	18,900	20,200	20,600	21,500	23,000
3	19,100	19,800	21,100	21,800	23,100	25,100
4	21,000	21,700	23,000	23,700	25,000	27,000
5	21,500	22,200	23,500	24,300	24,700	27,800
6	22,000	22,700	24,000	24,900	26,400	28,600
7	22,500	23,200	24,500	25,500	27,100	29,400
8	23,000	23,700	25,000	26,100	27,800	30,200
9	23,500	24,200	25,500	26,700	28,500	31,000
10	24,000	24,700	25,000	27,300	29,200	31,800
11		25,200	26,600	28,000	30,000	32,700
12			27,200	28,700	30,800	33,600
13			27,800	29,400	31,600	34,500
14			28,400	30,100	32,400	35,400
15			29,000	30,800	33,200	36,300

Teachers who reach the top of the master's, master's + 20 hours, specialist's, and doctor's tracks qualify for longevity raises of 3% every two years.

TABLE 2.5. AN EXCEPTIONALLY GOOD TEACHER SALARY SCHEDULE

			Track			
Step	Bachelor's	Bachelor's +20 hours	Master's	Master's +20 hours	Specialist's	Doctor's
1	$24,000	$24,000	$25,000	$25,000	$25,500	$26,000
2	24,200	24,500	25,700	25,900	26,600	28,000
3	24,600	25,400	27,100	27,600	28,600	30,000
4	26,600	27,400	29,100	29,600	30,600	32,100
5	27,400	28,200	30,100	30,600	31,700	33,300
6	28,200	29,000	31,100	31,600	32,800	34,500
7	29,000	29,800	32,100	32,600	33,900	35,700
8	29,800	30,600	33,100	33,600	35,000	36,900
9	30,600	31,400	34,100	34,600	36,100	38,100
10	31,400	32,200	35,100	35,600	37,200	39,300
11		33,000	36,200	36,700	38,400	40,600
12			37,300	37,800	39,600	41,900
13			38,400	38,900	40,800	43,200
14			39,500	40,000	42,000	44,500
15			40,600	41,100	43,200	45,800
16				42,100	44,500	47,200
17					45,800	48,600
18					47,100	50,000
19					48,400	51,400
20					49,700	52,800

Teachers who reach the top of the master's, master's + 20 hours, specialist's, and doctor's tracks qualify for longevity raises of 3% every two years.

put teachers with equal experience and education on equal footing. Another battle the organizations won—or hoped they had won—involved merit pay, the practice of basing salaries on evaluations of competence and performance. Teacher organizations have consistently and for the most part successfully opposed merit pay, but this old battle keeps breaking out on new fronts.[13]

The operation of single salary schedules like those in Tables 2.3, 2.4, and 2.5 is easy to understand. New teachers with bachelor's degrees start at the first step on the bachelor's track and advance one step each year. When teachers qualify for another track by taking graduate work, they move laterally to the right—they do not return to the first step on the new track. On schedules like the one in Table 2.3, teachers who move through all the tracks and take all the steps reach maximum salary well before retirement—a sad commentary on the way some school boards view teaching as a career. For teachers in this situation, an across-the-board raise granted by the state or local board offers the only hope for a higher salary. Schedules like those in Tables 2.4 and 2.5, however, provide longevity raises for career teachers, as the notes at the bottom of the schedules explain.

There are many other obvious differences among the three salary schedules. The schedule in Table 2.3 is the kind that, to be blunt, offers discouragingly low salaries, bottom to top—to beginners with bachelor's degrees as well as to veterans with graduate degrees. This kind of schedule is standard in the states that rank low in the first *and* third columns of Table 2.1. Pointing to one such state in each region as a prime example, we might choose Vermont, Arkansas, South Dakota, and Idaho. As the salaries in Table 2.1 suggest, however, these states are certainly not the only ones in which this kind of salary schedule appears. One bright spot is that even in the states ranked consistently low in Table 2.1, a few wealthier suburban and city systems may add enough local revenue to the minimum salary schedule established by the state board of education to offer teachers somewhat better wages. And, to be sure, the lower cost of living in some areas may make the schedule in Table 2.3 look fairly attractive to some prospective teachers.

Enough excuses and apologies. This schedule abounds with what economists call "perverse incentives." With its starting salary of $15,000, yearly step raises of $200, and top salary of $22,200, this schedule gives people strong incentives *not* to become teachers and, even if they do, to leave the occupation after just a few years. Teachers can look forward to a raise exceeding $200 on just three occasions: when they become tenured, which occurs in most states after three years; when they receive a graduate degree; or when the school board or state legislature grants a cost-of-living raise to all teachers. Imagine how veteran teachers must feel. After spending a large part of their adult lives in the classroom and going back to school for advanced degrees, they earn only a few thousand dollars more than the novice teachers down the hall. What kind of people does this salary schedule attract? What kind does it keep in the occupation? To be complimentary for now, we can say truly dedicated people, but the next chapter balances this answer with a less flattering one.

The other two schedules offer a better outlook. Table 2.4 shows a schedule representative of systems that pay average salaries to both beginning and experienced teachers. With its starting point of $18,500 and a ratio of about 2:1 between its highest and lowest salaries, this schedule is fairly typical for America's teachers. Common in the Northeast, West, and Midwest, the schedule stands out as exceptional primarily in the Southeast and in a few states outside that region where top and bottom salaries are compressed into a narrower range.

Salary schedules like the one in Table 2.4 are often the product of collective bargaining between teacher organizations and school boards, a practice we will discuss in Chapter 4. Significantly, collective bargaining is relatively well established in every region but the Southeast. Where bargaining occurs, teacher organizations usually negotiate for less compressed schedules similar to this one, which offer relatively good salaries to the experienced teachers who make up most of the organizations' membership. This schedule gives teachers incentives to stick with the occupation and make it a career. Experienced teachers with graduate degrees can be expensive to school boards, however, and without the pressure of collective bargaining, boards often opt for front-loaded salary schedules. A cold, harsh fact of life makes front-loaded schedules more attractive than the schedule in Table 2.4 to some board members. Front loading produces higher rates of teacher turnover, driving out experienced teachers but attracting a steady stream of lower-paid recruits who are eager to fill the vacancies. What experienced teachers see as a perverse incentive, some board members see as good business.[14]

Fortunately, the salary schedule in Table 2.4 has a fairly respectable high end of $36,300. Notice that this schedule contains more steps and more tracks than the first one we examined. As teachers move down the tracks, they are encouraged to find that the later steps bring higher raises than the earlier steps. Notice, too, that the additional tracks provide more immediate incentives for teachers to pursue master's and specialist's degrees, since they reward progress toward the degrees.

The salary schedule in Table 2.4 acknowledges the fact that some classroom teachers are interested in and capable of obtaining doctoral degrees. School officials in systems that have salary schedules similar to the one in Table 2.3, by contrast, sometimes justify the lack of a doctoral track by asserting that anyone smart enough to earn a doctorate is too smart to be an elementary or secondary school teacher. Considering the salaries that the schedule in Table 2.3 offers, it seems that the officials may have a point.

If all teachers worked in systems with salary schedules like the one in Table 2.5, this chapter—possibly this entire book—would have a different tone, for teaching would be a different occupation. Without question, different would mean better, for we know that the small number of school systems that actually pay teachers top salaries in the neighborhood of $50,000 can afford to be more selective in hiring, more careful about granting tenure, and more supportive of people who make teaching their career. Most such systems have collective bargaining between teachers and school board members, but the emphasis at the bargaining table is on cooperation rather than on confrontation. Labor relations specialists call this a "win-win" approach to negotiations. Teachers win, the board wins, and most importantly, students win, because all concerned can work together without having to fuss over money.[15]

A visit to a public school system with such a salary schedule and the financial resources that make it possible—try Palo Alto, California, Winnetka, Illinois, or a suburb of Washington, D.C.—would convince most teachers that although money is not a panacea, it can certainly make a difference. The catch, of course, is that most of the school systems paying top salaries of $50,000 or more are located in wealthy communities where local support for public education, financial and otherwise, is quite high. These systems are by no means typical. We will take a closer look at school finance in Chapter 9, but obviously it would take quite a commitment from the federal, state, and local governments to put all 2,275,209 of the nation's public school teachers on salary schedules resembling the one in Table 2.5.

But suspend disbelief for a moment. Giving America's teachers an across-the-board, 50 percent raise would make the average teacher's salary more than

$42,000. This reform would put the average teacher on a salary schedule similar to the one in Table 2.5, and it would give teachers in such low-wage states as South Dakota and Arkansas salaries comparable to those that Massachusetts and Illinois paid in 1987–88. The prospect of such a reform is exciting. How much would it cost? America spends a total of about $160 billion on public elementary and secondary education every year, with about $65 billion going directly into teachers' paychecks. Considering such additional costs to school systems as retirement, insurance, and social security contributions, we can estimate that giving teachers a 50 percent raise would mean increasing the nation's annual spending for public schools by about $40 billion. Although this reform is too expensive to implement in a single year, it can still serve as a goal for teachers to work toward over several years.[16]

Albert Shanker, president of the AFT, believes the goal is out of reach. The nation will never increase its real spending on public education by such a massive amount, he argues. As an alternative, Shanker and his union have been edging warily toward the concept of paying much better salaries to some teachers than to others. Shanker understandably bridles at the words "merit pay" because they call up bitter memories of bias and favoritism, but he and the AFT are cautiously embracing an updated version of merit pay as part of a plan to make teaching a *differentiated* occupation, one that would recognize different levels of expertise and responsibility. Shanker's ideas closely parallel the proposals of the Holmes Group and the Carnegie Forum on Education and the Economy, which we will examine in the last section of the chapter. Why is the AFT, a teacher union that has fought merit pay with do-or-die determination for most of this century, now softening its position? And why is the rival union that Shanker refers to as the "other organization," the much larger NEA, sticking to its guns against merit pay?[17]

MERIT PAY: THE BIRTH OF "SOUND AND CHEAP"

The answer lies in the organizations' differing views of the past, present, and future of merit pay. The NEA's position is that merit pay has failed miserably in the past and that today's experiments are faring just as badly. To the NEA, merit pay for teachers is an inherently flawed concept. Opinion polls show that more than 60 percent of teachers are opposed to merit pay. Why, the NEA asks, should teachers change their minds and support a bad idea?[18]

The AFT agrees that merit pay has an unsavory past, but it clings to the hope that the idea can be salvaged. Frankly, the AFT feels that with polls showing more than 60 percent of all Americans in favor of merit pay, pressure from the general public and especially the business community may force teachers to live with some version of the concept. Trying to cope with what it sees as a new political reality, the AFT wants to take the lead and develop the fairest merit pay plans possible.[19]

At least the two teacher organizations agree on the past. Educational historians have documented the record of merit pay, and a most unimpressive record it is. Forty to 50 percent of the nation's school systems tried merit pay in the World War I era and during the 1920s. "Scientific efficiency" was all the rage in business management, and school boards jumped on the bandwagon with a variety of plans to base teachers' salaries on evaluations of their ability and performance. Scientific efficiency as applied to public education was, in theory, an attempt to make the schools "both sound and cheap." Teachers discovered that, in practice, the emphasis was on cheap.[20]

A typical merit pay plan involved arranging a school system's teachers in a pyramid-like hierarchy based on their evaluations. For example, "Rank 5" teachers were those judged to be the best, "Rank 4" teachers were the next best, and so on down to the "Rank 1" teachers who received the worst evaluations. Each rank carried a different salary schedule, with Rank 5 teachers earning the highest salaries and Rank 1 teachers the lowest.[21]

All well and good, some teachers thought. Then, as now, there was undeniable appeal in the principle that the better you are at a job, the greater your rewards should be. But then, as now, there were tremendous difficulties in defining what "better" meant and deciding which teachers fit the description. Relying on two techniques that were becoming fashionable in business management, school boards required administrators and supervisors to evaluate teachers in the classroom and required teachers to take tests. Neither technique was new in public education; what was different was that under merit pay plans, evaluations and test scores affected salaries.

Teachers objected strongly. School boards that had grown accustomed to quiet, complacent employees suddenly faced storms of teacher protest. Across the nation teachers banded together and formed local organizations, sometimes taking the radical step of affiliating with the AFT, the national teacher organization that dared to call itself a union. The NEA and the state teacher associations, the "professional associations" that were dominated by administrators and college professors, also expressed reservations about merit pay, albeit more politely than the AFT. The major battles against merit pay, however, were fought by local teachers in local school systems.

The complaints against classroom evaluations often centered on bias and favoritism. Teachers charged that administrators and supervisors used the evaluations to reward their friends and punish their enemies. Evaluators brought their political views, religious beliefs, and social preferences into the process, teachers claimed. Sometimes an especially controversial evaluation turned into a local newspaper sensation that had the entire community up in arms and taking sides: a Protestant principal's unfavorable evaluation of a Catholic or Jewish teacher, or a Democrat's low ranking of a Republican teacher, or a male principal's alleged partiality toward the attractive woman who taught fourth grade. Merit pay could be the perfect topic for community gossip and debate.

The checklist evaluation instruments used during the 1910s and 1920s invited controversy because they were so subjective. Often the evaluator rated teachers on such items as "Teacher moves around frequently," "Teacher is neat and well groomed," and "Teacher has pleasant demeanor." Beyond the room that such items left for evaluators to inject their own biases, teachers complained that the items had no necessary connection to good teaching. It was just possible that students might be able to learn from rumpled, fussy teachers who seldom stirred from their desks as well as teachers with the traits that the checklists favored. The use of such evaluation instruments, slanted toward teachers who dotted their i's and crossed their t's, could penalize teachers who were unconventional but nevertheless commanded the respect of students, parents, and peers.[22]

Teacher testing, which we will examine in greater detail in the next chapter, was also controversial. Although it alternately amuses and irritates the public that the people who give tests to students complain so much about having to take tests themselves, the consistency of teachers' complaints over the years deserves our attention. The essence of their criticism has been that many of the questions on teacher tests are irrelevant to the work that teachers do. When school boards in the 1910s and 1920s mandated questions covering the *general knowledge* that was considered the mark of any well-educated person, teachers argued that translating passages from Latin or identifying capitals of foreign countries (yes, such items were frequently on the tests) were things that most teachers rarely, if ever, had to do. As for *pedagogy*, the art and science of teaching, the complaint was that questions about teaching could not measure the ability to teach. Questions covering the *subject matter* for which teachers were responsible—English or mathematics, for example—were somewhat more acceptable, but teachers often criticized these questions, too, as unrepresentative of the knowledge that they actually used in the classroom. There was also controversy over how much English or math or science the elementary teacher, a generalist, had to know. Surely not as much as the specialized secondary teacher, but how much?[23]

Administrators and supervisors often joined the protest against merit pay. Many of them were no more comfortable conducting the evaluations than teachers were being evaluated. Merit ratings proved to be divisive, pitting teachers against administrators and one teacher against another. Running a merit pay system was a bureaucratic nightmare, administrators complained, as a host of new responsibilities competed for time on their already crowded schedules. The last straw broke when it became clear that many school boards were using merit pay to reduce the budget for salaries. A favorite ploy was refusing to approve any teachers for the highest rank, regardless of their evaluations and test scores. Sound and cheap? Transparently cheap.

The battles over merit pay were mercifully short in most school systems. Teachers took their case to the local communities, calling on newspaper editors and politicians to help win the sympathy of parents and other citizens. In the face of determined opposition, school boards threw up their hands and decided that having a merit pay plan wasn't worth the trouble. Tried and rejected by almost half of the nation's school systems, by the 1930s and 1940s merit pay had been declared a dead letter.

THE ACCOUNTABILITY MOVEMENT: MERIT PAY REBORN

If much of the above sounds familiar, it should, because in one sense the arguments over merit pay have changed very little. Merit pay has a habit of reappearing in slightly different incarnations, with each new, improved model promising to correct the defects of the older ones. It revived briefly during the 1950s, died again during the 1960s, and has been trying to come back to life since the 1970s as part of the accountability movement. Accountability is a concept with a positive sounding name and a great deal of surface appeal. Who would dare argue that educators should *not* be accountable? Accountability is a response to the popular perception that the costs of public education have soared while the quality has plummeted. The accountability movement promises taxpayers "more bang for the buck." No more vague promises—school boards have found new ways to measure student achievement, and now the pressure is on teachers to be accountable for how much their students learn.[24]

Accountability has changed the way Americans think about public education. As we will see in Chapter 10, standardized achievement tests with their aura of scientific respectability have become the accepted means of measuring student achievement. Releasing news about test scores—preferably *rising* test scores—has become the accepted way for school boards to reassure the public that students are learning. A few school boards have tried to take accountability to the limit by using the concept as the latest twist in merit pay. Why not reward those teachers whose students have the highest achievement? In other words, why not base teacher salaries on student test scores?[25]

From a business management point of view, the idea sounds good. Follow the logic of a school board member with a background in business. Just as the high tech assembly-line worker who turns out better silicon chips than the other workers deserves a financial pat on the back, so does the teacher who turns out better students. After all, the board member reasons, a school is like a business. Educated students are the products of the business, and teachers, the workers in the business, must be accountable for the quality of the products. If teachers complain about the subjectivity of classroom evaluations and the irrelevance of teacher tests, then surely teachers will have no objections to using student test scores as an index of how well they are doing their jobs. What could be more relevant and objective?[26]

Schools are not like businesses, teachers respond—often angrily—because students are not like silicon chips or any other tangible "product." Students are human beings, not inanimate objects. The education of a human being is far more complex than the production of a silicon chip. High tech workers, operating in a sterile environment, have almost complete control over their chips. Teachers have no such environment and no such control. Teachers are responsible for teaching, to be sure, but students are responsible for learning. Countless factors, both inside and outside the school, influence the teaching-learning process.

Teachers have been fighting various versions of the business or factory model of education since before the Civil War, but the model has become more threatening than ever with the added feature of merit pay based on student test scores. Teacher organizations have drawn the line over the issue. School boards trying to implement merit pay plans based on accountability have faced determined opposition from teachers, with teacher organizations sometimes going to court to block the plans.[27]

Picture a courtroom with a school system's director of testing on the stand. The director is using the example of a third-grade teacher and her class to explain accountability-based merit pay. "The school system administers standardized tests to measure the achievement of the teacher's students at the start of the school year and again at the end of the year," the director testifies. "We attribute the difference between the two sets of test scores—an increase, we hope!—to the teacher, even though we know that other factors also affect the scores. To control for some of the other factors, we compare the test scores of this teacher's students with the scores of other students from similar socioeconomic backgrounds. Then the teacher gets a merit raise if her students' scores have increased more than the scores of comparable third-grade students. That's the essence of accountability-based merit pay."

Now listen as a witnesses for the teacher organization, a professor of educational measurement and evaluation, takes the stand. "The fundamental problem with such a plan," the professor begins, "is that the third-grade teacher is not the only influence on her students' test scores, as the previous witness admitted. We can divide the factors that affect test scores into two groups: school influences and nonschool influences. School influences include not just the one teacher but other teachers, and also other students, administrators, textbooks, the temperature in the classroom, and countless other factors, many of them beyond the teacher's control. The list of nonschool influences is even longer, ranging from parents to peers, from exercise to diet, from magazines to television, virtually *all* of them beyond the teacher's control. We know that the combined nonschool influences on achievement test scores are two-to-three times stronger, statistically speaking, than the combined school influences. Trying to isolate the influence of one teacher to use as the basis of merit pay is little more than a guessing game."

The opposition of teacher organizations to accountability-based merit pay—adamant opposition up through the mid-1980s—forced school boards to develop other strategies. The NEA remains adamant, but the AFT has indicated a willingness to accept the use of student test scores as *one* factor in experimental merit pay plans. Albert Shanker is keeping his fingers crossed, hoping that this gamble will pay off for his union and for teaching as an occupation.

BEHAVIORAL EVALUATION OF TEACHERS

Meanwhile another form of teacher evaluation has taken center stage in the merit pay controversy. It represents a return to the old idea of evaluating teacher performance in the classroom, but with a new emphasis on student achievement. This *behavioral* approach is the most important form of teacher evaluation in many of the career ladder plans we will examine in the last section of this chapter. Developed by such advocates as Madeline Hunter and the research team of Medley, Coker, and Soar, the basic methodology of behavioral evaluation is disarmingly straightforward. It involves breaking down teaching into as many small, discrete behaviors as possible; deciding which behaviors are indicators of effective teaching: observing teachers to determine the degree to which they exhibit these behaviors; evaluating teachers on the basis of the observations; and rewarding teachers accordingly.[28]

Observers—who may be administrators, supervisors, or teachers themselves—are trained to look for the behaviors in the classroom and code them on computer scanning sheets. As the observers watch a teacher in action during a period of 45 minutes or so, they repeatedly mark the scanning sheets, "bubbling in" the ovals that correspond to the behaviors they see. Does the teacher "begin instruction promptly"? "Handle materials in an orderly manner"? "Give specific academic praise"? "Emphasize important points"? "Maintain instructional momentum"?[29]

These behaviors are 5 of the 124 "effective indicators" of competent teaching on the Florida Performance Measurement System. The developers of such systems boast that their methodology is "noninferential," that it does not require the evaluator to pass judgment on a behavior, but only to recognize the behavior and record the frequency with which it occurs. Moreover, the developers carefully use the term "observer" rather than "evaluator" in order to threaten teachers as little as possible. The actual evaluation comes later, when administrators review the observations and advise teachers on how to improve their work in the classroom. To put things positively, helping teachers improve is the most important purpose of the evaluation.[30]

But evaluation also involves the difficult and often unpleasant task of making decisions about salaries, promotions, and careers. Behavioral evaluation

systems provide quantitative data; they produce averages, curv
ations, and cutoffs. These systems make evaluation seem sci
From the administrator's point of view, they have the virtue
responsibility for tough decisions away from people and towar
teacher barely misses the cutoff for a merit raise, the administrato.
the teacher's problems on the observation sheets: a failure to ͟ ͟conduct
beginning/ending review," perhaps, or a loss of "instructional momentum."

What do teachers like about the behavioral approach? That it is specific. It
lets them know exactly what is expected of them and provides clear pointers on
how to change. What do they dislike? That it is mechanical. It pressures them to
teach in a certain way and encourages game playing.[31]

Already teachers are asking critical questions about behavioral evaluation.
Standing in front of a mirror at home on the night before an observation,
practicing the approved repertoire of behaviors, and trying to exhibit as many of
them as possible in 45 minutes—is that the best way for a teacher to improve?
Is it the best way for a teacher to qualify for a raise or promotion? Consider the
goal of making teaching a profession. How would doctors or lawyers react to
such a system of evaluation? Would anyone dare define the competent practice
of medicine or law with a set of 124 "effective indicators"?

We are taking a close look at teacher evaluation as the basis of merit pay
because it is so often overlooked—by the public and by prospective teachers if
not by the teachers whose jobs are actually affected. As one teacher told me
recently, "When *your* career is on the line, you pay more attention to the fine
print." Some of the merit pay plans we will examine here are admittedly
attractive. At best, they offer the hope of pulling teaching as an occupation out
of a financial rut. Remember, though, that the plans are no better than the
evaluation systems on which they rest.

CAREER LADDERS AND OTHER PLANS:
MERIT PAY, LATEST VERSIONS

The Second Mile Plan

The representative plans we will study range in scope from local to state to
national. Perhaps the best-known local approach is the Second Mile Plan developed by one of the nation's largest systems, the Houston Independent School
District. Initiated in 1979, the Houston plan has received a great deal of media
attention as a modern pioneer of merit pay, for it predated *A Nation at Risk* and
the reform movements of the 1980s. In another sense, the Second Mile Plan is
just another square on the checkered history of merit pay. It ceased operation in
1987.[32]

Although it was touted as an attempt to "move beyond traditional lockstep
salary schedules," the Second Mile Plan, like most merit pay plans, actually
supplemented a traditional single salary schedule. Teachers who went the second

mile could receive extra pay. Six categories of service qualified for "bonus stipends": teaching in a school with "a concentration of educationally disadvantaged students"; teaching in a field with a staff shortage; compiling an outstanding attendance record; completing approved in-service and university courses; teaching in a school where the "academic gain (as measured by standardized tests) is greater than the mathematically predicted school achievement goal"; and teaching at a special school for exceptional or vocational students.[33]

Based on our earlier discussion, you should be able to guess the reactions to the Second Mile Plan. School officials said it accomplished its mission admirably by raising test scores, attracting more teachers to schools with large numbers of disadvantaged students, alleviating the shortage of teachers in certain fields, and making teaching a more rewarding career. Some teachers shared the officials' enthusiasm for the plan. On the positive side, more than two-thirds of Houston teachers received annual bonuses ranging up to several thousand dollars. The school system made a strong financial commitment to the plan. From the teachers' point of view, at least, "cheap" was not the problem.[34]

What bothered many teachers was using student test scores as a factor in awarding merit pay. In addition to the statistical problems we have discussed, teachers complained that the emphasis on raising test scores put pressure on them to "teach the tests." Teaching and learning did not improve, they argued, but teachers and students certainly learned to play the testing game. We will examine this complaint, a common one in school systems across the nation since the late 1970s, in Chapter 10. Teachers also questioned the wisdom of paying bonuses for teaching certain subjects or teaching in certain schools. This practice sent the divisive message that the work of some teachers is more valuable than the work of others. Teacher organizations have argued for years that the high school physics teacher is worth no more and no less than the kindergarten teacher and that teaching in the central city and teaching in the suburbs are of equal value. Teacher organizations charged that the Second Mile Plan did not supplement the single salary schedule—it violated everything the hard-won schedule stood for. Faced with teacher opposition, increasing costs, and a downturn in the Texas oil economy, Houston phased out the plan after an eight-year trial.[35]

Merit Pay Plans That Last

Any merit pay system, of course, violates the principle that only seniority and education should determine teacher salaries. To make teachers more willing to compromise the principle, researchers who have studied merit plans suggest four strategies for winning teacher approval:

1. Define merit pay as "extra pay for extra work" rather than as a reward for outstanding performance.
2. "Make everyone feel special" by awarding merit pay to almost every teacher.

3. "Make merit pay inconspicuous" by making participation voluntary and keeping rewards relatively small.
4. Involve teachers in designing the plan.

A fifth suggestion might be: Start with a school system where "nearly everything seems to work well"—a system with strong community support, hard working students, and happy, well-paid teachers. All the merit pay plans that have survived for more than a few years have been in such systems. These suggestions support the NEA and AFT's contention that merit pay would make better sense if teachers had decent salaries and working conditions to begin with.[36]

Career Ladders

Whether the nation will heed this advice remains to be seen, but several states are trying to overhaul the entire structure of teaching by building career ladders. Teachers have long complained that teaching is not a *scaled* or *staged* occupation, that responsibilities and earnings increase relatively little over the course of their careers. In many other occupations, workers feel a satisfying sense of progress as they move through the ranks; salaries rise and titles change as people get better at their work and take on new duties.

Teachers, by contrast, face the same old routine, year after year. Some teachers who want more responsibility and more money become administrators, to be sure, but not every teacher is suited for administration. Besides, this limited path of career mobility leads many of the best and most ambitious teachers out of the classroom and into the office, depriving students of contact with superb instructors. Shouldn't it be possible for talented teachers to stay in the classroom yet increase their responsibilities and earnings as their careers progress?

Answering this question affirmatively, several states have developed career ladders to restructure teaching as an occupation. Tennessee led the way in the mid-1980s, followed quickly by several other Southeastern states. The movement spread to Missouri, Nebraska, and Utah, and by the late 1980s more than one-third of the states in the nation had career ladders in place or under construction. The first career ladders were statewide ladders, but now the trend is toward local ladders supported by the state but designed by individual school districts.[37]

Most careers ladders consist of four or five rungs. Typically, teachers enter the occupation on an *Apprentice* rung where they are evaluated frequently, with special help and guidance provided during their first year. Most career ladders are designed to bring new teachers into closer contact with experienced teachers, enabling veterans to serve as mentors to novices. Without such planned assistance, new teachers usually have to sink or swim on their own. New teachers often complain that teacher education programs do not prepare them well for their first year; they want on-the-job training. Apprenticeships may give teachers a way to pass the lore of their occupation from one generation of practitioners to the next.

Apprentices remain on the first rung of the ladder for three to five years. When they qualify for tenure, they step up to the *Staff* level. Staff teachers have passed the most intensive screening; they are fully certified teachers with the job security that tenure provides. As Chapter 5 explains, tenured teachers are entitled to continuing employment as long as their work remains satisfactory. On most career ladders, teachers can stay at the staff level indefinitely if they wish—moving up is voluntary. Staff teachers, like other teachers, draw their wages on a traditional salary schedule, but those who choose to climb the career ladder can qualify for incentive (that is, merit) raises.

In the states that already have career ladders, most teachers are trying to move up. The higher rungs may have such titles as (in ascending order) *Career Level I, Career Level II, and Career Level III*, with the latter sometimes also called *Master Teacher*. (Tennessee, however, dropped the Master Teacher designation after teachers protested the implication that only top-rung teachers had mastered their craft.) Teachers must serve a certain period of time at each level—typically five years—before they are eligible to apply for the next level, and they must receive favorable evaluations in order to qualify.

Teachers who reach the top two rungs may sign 10- to 12-month contracts and take on such new responsibilities as working with apprentices, evaluating other teachers, and developing curricula. In some cases they may teach the equivalent of four periods per day, spending the rest of the time on their additional duties. The quasiadministrative nature of these tasks leads critics to charge that career ladders are actually "job ladders" that lure people out of teaching and into administration. The architects of career ladders reply that top-rung teachers are just that, teachers, for most of the day. The goal of the ladders is to keep outstanding teachers in the classroom while allowing them to use their talents and experience in other ways. Advocates also call attention to what may be the most attractive feature of career ladders: the extra pay that comes with extra work. The annual pay incentives that teachers can earn as they move up the ladders range from $1,000 or so at Career Level I to $7,000 or more at Career Level III.[38]

How do teachers feel about career ladders? The most extensive evidence comes from Tennessee, the state with the oldest ladder. Despite the favorable publicity it has received, the Tennessee career ladder has been shaky from the start. The Tennessee Education Association (TEA), the state affiliate of the NEA, complains that classroom teachers have had too little involvement in designing the ladder. Teachers are evenly divided over whether it should be torn down. The evaluation system, based on behavioral evaluation as well as such other factors as a student questionnaire, a principal questionnaire, and a written test, is especially unpopular with Tennessee teachers. Eighty-five percent of teachers in one poll stated that the evaluation system could not work fairly and effectively, particularly in distinguishing excellent teachers from good teachers.

Many teachers are also frustrated that the top two rungs of the ladder have been difficult to reach.[39]

On the other hand, Tennessee school officials continue to refine the evaluation system, and they defend the system's selectivity. To be sure, selectivity is something that teachers are not used to—it has been sorely lacking in the occupation. Tennessee's average teacher salary of $23,785 ranks it 38th in the nation, and some teachers say just the opportunity to compete for an income of $40,000 is a major step forward. Many teachers also welcome the chance to help one another. This attitude is most encouraging, for as we will see in Chapter 4, teachers themselves must take more responsibility for their occupation if it is ever to become a profession.[40]

But troubling questions remain. So far, state-wide career ladders have appeared almost exclusively in states that pay teachers salaries below the national average. Will the ladders raise salaries substantially and make teaching a more attractive occupation in these states? Or will the ladders give good salaries to a few teachers without significantly raising average salaries—an updated version of sound and cheap? The effects of career ladders on teacher morale and collegiality are also open to question. Some teachers frankly do not want to make their schools more like corporations or even law firms. They chose teaching as an occupation precisely because teachers are equals among equals, not climbers on their way past stallers. They like the fact that teachers do *not* compete with one another for slots on a bureaucratic hierarchy. How will these teachers react to a new game with new rules? With salaries and promotions at stake, will career ladders strengthen or weaken the spirit of cooperation?[41]

HOLMES, CARNEGIE, AND A NATIONAL CAREER LADDER

As answers to these questions emerge, reformers are hard at work laying the groundwork for what could well become the ultimate career ladder: a national ladder designed for a national teaching profession. Two reports issued in 1986 drew up the blueprints: *Tomorrow's Teachers: A Report of the Holmes Group*, by a consortium of education deans and chief academic administrators from major research universities, and *A Nation Prepared: Teachers for the 21st Century*, by the Carnegie Forum on Education and the Economy. Although the proposals in the two reports differ in some respects, both advance the idea that teaching should be a *differentiated* occupation whose members have clearly defined levels of expertise, responsibility, and compensation. These reports call for fundamental reforms. If the nation follows their lead, the days of equals among equals will soon be over. The occupation will frankly recognize that some teachers know more, can do more, and therefore should earn more than others.[42]

We will examine the Carnegie and Holmes reports in several chapters of this book, but our major concern here is with the occupational ladder they support. The Holmes Group envisions three ranks of teachers. *Instructors*, bright people who want to teach but do not have a career commitment, will hold five-year nonrenewable certificates. *Professional Teachers*, the "backbone" of the occupation, will have graduate training in education, full certification, and tenure. *Career Professionals*, veterans of proven competence who excel at teaching students as well as working with adults, will plan curricula, conduct research, supervise Instructors, and carry out other such responsibilities.[43]

These levels, similar to those found on existing career ladders, will probably have many of the same strengths and weaknesses. Notice, however, the clear recognition that some people can make a contribution to teaching without making teaching their career. The Holmes Group hopes that the rank of Instructor, open to college graduates with degrees in the arts and sciences but little or no training in education, will insure a constant flow of talent into teaching. This provision also has a powerful economic rationale. Since Instructors will earn considerably less than teachers in the two higher ranks, the occupation will have a new way to concentrate its financial resources on career teachers.[44]

This provision has won the praise of Albert Shanker and the AFT, but it represents a radical break with the history of teaching. Too radical, apparently, for the NEA, which sees merit pay written all over such proposals. When the Carnegie Forum on Education and the Economy asked the NEA and AFT to endorse a very similar set of recommendations, Shanker pledged his union's "full support," while NEA President Mary Futrell offered support "with reservations." As Futrell explained, the idea of putting some teachers in charge of others "suggests that some teachers are more equal than others." To her, creating a hierarchy of teachers sounds suspiciously like "the flawed and failed merit-pay and job-ladder plans."[45]

Nevertheless, Carnegie and Holmes are moving ahead. The Carnegie Forum has established a National Board for Professional Teaching Standards, a majority of whose members are classroom teachers. The board will begin issuing teaching certificates in the early 1990s. Certification will be voluntary, much like national board certification for physicians, but the Carnegie Forum believes that national teaching certificates will become so prestigious that teachers will seek them and states will recognize them.

Carnegie foresees a four-level teaching force consisting of *Licensed Teachers* who have state licenses and are preparing for national certification; *Certified Teachers*, the majority of the force, who have passed the written and observational evaluations that the national board is now developing; *Advanced Teachers* who have passed even more rigorous evaluations; and *Lead Teachers,* elected by teachers from among the advanced teachers, who would serve as the "instructional leaders" of their schools. Expertise, responsibility, and compensation will increase as teachers move up a national career ladder.[46] In exchange, teachers will have to be more accountable. The Carnegie report endorses merit pay based in part on student test scores, even though it admits that "no method that we know of for measuring student performance and connecting it to teachers' rewards is yet satisfactory."[47]

The Carnegie Forum is more specific than the Holmes Group about teacher salaries. Recognizing that local, state, and regional variations will continue, Carnegie recommends that licensed teachers earn from $15,000 to $25,000; certified teachers, $19,000 to $39,000: advanced teachers, $26,000 to $46,000; and lead teachers, $42,000 to $72,000. Compare these figures with the current salaries in Table 2.1 and the salary schedules in Tables 2.3, 2.4, and 2.5. Prospective teachers will hardly stand up and cheer about their immediate prospects under the Carnegie proposal, but long-term rewards will be potentially greater for those who make teaching a career.[48]

The Carnegie Forum's *A Nation Prepared* and the Holmes Group's *Tomorrow's Teachers* have become the hottest topics of discussion among educational reformers since *A Nation at Risk*. A vision of better-paid teachers is in all three reports, and so is a vision of better-educated teachers. The Holmes and Carnegie reports, however, make several forthright recommendations about teacher education that *A Nation at Risk* only hints at between the lines. Holmes and Carnegie call for eliminating undergraduate degrees in education, requiring all prospective teachers to major in the arts and sciences, and moving teacher education to the graduate level.

The battle lines are drawn. These recommendations are generating even more controversy than the proposals for changing the structure and compensation of teaching—probably because people are taking the recommendations on teacher education even more seriously. The next chapter explains why.

ACTIVITIES

1. Request salary schedules from the school systems in which you are most interested in teaching. Compare their schedules with the three representative schedules in this chapter. Inquire about state and local career ladders and other forms of merit pay.
2. Talk with a variety of currently employed teachers about merit pay, accountability, evaluation, and other issues discussed in this chapter. Interview retired teachers and compare their opinions.
3. Broaden your interviews to include political officials, particularly local and state school board members, state legislators, and others who have influence on teacher salaries.

SUGGESTED READINGS

For more of the kind of information presented in Tables 2.1 and 2.2, information that will be useful as you talk with people about teachers and public education in the United States, consult the NEA's *Rankings of the States* and the AFT's *Survey and Analysis of Salary Trends*, both of which are updated annually (see notes 1 and 3, below). For two views of teaching as a differentiated, better-compensated occupation, read *A Nation Prepared* by the Carnegie Forum and *Tomorrow's Teachers* by the Holmes Group (see note 42).

NOTES

1. National Education Association, *Rankings of the States, 1988* (Washington: NEA, 1988), p. 20.
2. Ibid., p. 21.
3. American Federation of Teachers, *Survey and Analysis of Salary Trends, 1988* (Washington: AFT, 1988), p. 45.
4. For state-by-state information on variations in the cost of living, see ibid., pp. 9–10, 18, 20.
5. NEA, *Status of the American Public School Teacher, 1985–86* (Washington: NEA, 1987), pp. 11, 14, 73, 80.
6. Ibid., pp. 69–71; U.S. Department of Commerce, Bureau of the Census, *Statistical Abstract of the United States: 1988* (Washington: U.S. Government Printing Office, 1987), p. 423.
7. NEA, *Status of the American Public School Teacher, 1985–86*, pp. 68–69.
8. Ibid., pp. 69–71.
9. U.S. Department of Labor, *Occupational Outlook Handbook, 1988–89 Edition* (Washington: U.S. Government Printing Office, 1988), pp. 101–104, 150–53.
10. Judy Mann and Basia Hellwig, "The Truth about the Salary Gap(s)," *Working Woman* (January 1988): 61–62; U.S. Department of Labor, *Occupational Outlook Handbook, 1988–89*, pp. 14–16, 43–45, 24–25.
11. U.S. Department of Labor, *Occupational Outlook Handbook, 1988–89*, pp. 51–53, 68–69, 78–79; Mann and Hellwig, pp. 61–62.
12. U.S. Department of Labor, *Occupational Outlook Handbook, 1988–89*, pp. 84–87, 129–132: Mann and Hellwig, "The Truth About the Salary Gap(s)," pp. 61–62.
13. Don Cameron, "An Idea That Merits Consideration," *Phi Delta Kappan* 67 (October 1985): 110–112.
14. Blake Rodman, "Teachers Spurn an Unsolicited Starting-Pay Proposal," *Education Week* (February 19, 1986), p. 14. See also Randall W. Eberts and Joe A. Stone, *Unions and Public Schools: The Effect of Collective Bargaining on American Education* (Lexington, MA: Heath, 1984), and Anthony M. Creswell and Michael J. Murphy with Charles T. Kerchner, *Teachers, Unions, and Collective Bargaining in Public Education* (Berkeley, CA: McCutchan, 1980), ch. 11.
15. Roger Fisher and William Ury, *Getting to Yes: Negotiating Agreement without Giving In* (Boston: Houghton Mifflin, 1981).
16. National Education Association, *Estimates of School Statistics, 1987–88* (Washington: NEA, 1988), p. 6.
17. Albert Shanker, "The Making of a Profession," *American Educator* 9 (Fall 1985): 10–17, 46, 48.
18. Alec Gallup, "The Gallup Poll of Teachers' Attitudes toward the Public Schools," *Phi Delta Kappan* 66 (October 1984): 103.
19. Gallup, "The 17th Annual Gallup Poll of the Public's Attitudes toward the Public Schools," *Phi Delta Kappan* 67 (September 1985): 39.
20. For analysis of merit pay and its historical context, see Richard J. Murnane and David K. Cohen, "Merit Pay and the Evaluation Problem: Understanding Why Most Merit Pay Plans Fail and a Few Survive," *Harvard Educational Review* 56 (February 1986): 1–17; Susan M. Johnson, "Merit Pay for Teachers: A Poor Prescription for Reform," *Harvard Educational Review* 54 (May 1984); 175–185: and Raymond E.

Callahan, *Education and the Cult of Efficiency: A Study of the Social Forces That Have Shaped the Administration of the Public Schools* (Chicago: University of Chicago Press, 1962), ch. 5.

21. The discussion in this section is based in part on case studies of the Atlanta Public Schools. See Joseph W. Newman, "A History of the Atlanta Public School Teachers' Association, Local 89 of the American Federation of Teachers, 1919–1956" (Ph.D. dissertation, Georgia State University, 1978), ch. 1, and Wayne J. Urban, "Progressive Education in the Urban South: The Reform of the Atlanta Schools, 1914–1918," in Michael H. Ebner and Eugene M. Tobin, eds., *The Age of Urban Reform:. New Perspectives on the Progressive Era* (Port Washington, New York: Kennikat Press, 1977), ch. 9.

22. Arthur C. Boyce, "Methods of Measuring Teachers' Efficiency," *Fourteenth Yearbook of the National Society for the Study of Education, Part II* (Bloomington, IL: Public School Publishing Co., 1915); Lloyd Young, *The Administration of Merit-Type Teachers' Salary Schedules* (New York: Teachers College, Columbia University, 1933).

23. Arvil Sylvester Barr, "Measurement and Prediction of Teaching Efficiency: Summary of Investigations," *Journal of Experimental Education* 16 (June 1948): 203–283.

24. A highly influential book by the father of the movement is Leon M. Lessinger's *Every Kid a Winner: Accountability in Education* (New York: Simon & Schuster, 1970). For an opposing point of view, read Don T. Martin, George E. Overholt, and Wayne J. Urban, *Accountability in American Education: A Critique* (Princeton, NJ: Princeton Book Company, 1976).

25. Joel Spring, *Conflict of Interests: The Politics of American Education* (White Plains, NY: Longman, 1988), pp. 18–19, 126.

26. The discussion in this section is based on Donald M. Medley, Homer Coker, and Robert S. Soar, *Measurement-Based Evaluation of Teacher Performance: An Empirical Approach* (White Plains, NY: Longman, 1984), ch. 3.

27. Blake Rodman, "Rating Teachers on Students' Test Scores Sparks Furor, Legal Action in St. Louis," *Education Week* (September 17, 1986), pp. 1, 18.

28. The behavioral evaluation model developed by Medley, Coker, and Soar is widely used, as is the Madeline Hunter/Clinical Supervision model. See Noreen B. Garman and Helen M. Hazi, "Teachers Ask: Is There Life after Madeline Hunter?," *Phi Delta Kappan* 69 (May 1988): 669–672.

29. B. Othanel Smith, Donovan Peterson, and Theodore Micceri, "Evaluation and Professional Improvement Aspects of the Florida Performance Measurement System," *Educational Leadership* 44 (April 1987): 16–19.

30. Ibid; Medley, Coker, and Soar, *Measurement-Based Evaluation of Teacher Performance*, pp. 41–45.

31. Garman and Hazi, "Teachers Ask," 670–672.

32. A good survey is Frederick S. Calhoun and Nancy J. Protheroe, *Merit Pay Plans for Teachers: Status and Descriptions* (Arlington, VA: Educational Research Service, 1983).

33. *The Second Mile Plan* (Houston: Houston Independent School District, n.d.); Elaine Say and Leslie Miller, "The Second Mile Plan: Incentive Pay for Houston Teachers," *Phi Delta Kappan* 64 (December 1982): 270–271: Calhoun and Protheroe, *Merit-Pay Plans for Teachers*, pp. 51–52.

34. See note 33.

35. See note 33.

36. Murnane and Cohen, "Merit Pay and the Evaluation Problem," pp. 12–15.

37. Lynn Olson, "State Ladder Plans in Several Places Moving Forward," *Education Week* (May 7, 1986), pp. 1, 6, and "Performance-Based Pay Systems for Teachers Are Being Re-Examined," *Education Week* (April 15, 1987), pp. 1, 16–17.

38. Samuel B. Bacharach, "Career Development, Not Career Ladders," *Education Week* (March 12, 1986), p. 28; Russell L. French, " 'Misconceptions' in Critique of Career Ladders," *Education Week* (May 14, 1986), p. 42.

39. Lynn Olson, "Pioneering State Teacher-Incentive Plans in Florida, Tennessee Still Under Attack," *Education Week* (January 15, 1986), pp. 1, 24–25, and "Performance-Based Pay Systems," pp. 16–17.

40. Carol B. Furtwengler, "Lessons from Tennessee's Career Ladder Program," *Educational Leadership* 44 (April 1987): 66–69.

41. Lynn Olson, "Performance Pay: New Round for an Old Debate," *Education Week* (March 12, 1986), pp. 1, 18–20: Susan J. Rosenholtz, "Education Reform Strategies: Will They Increase Teacher Commitment?" *American Journal of Education* 95 (August 1987): 534–562.

42. Holmes Group, *Tomorrow's Teachers:. A Report of the Holmes Group* (East Lansing, MI: Holmes Group, 1986); Carnegie Forum on Education and the Economy, *A Nation Prepared: Teachers for the 21st Century. A Report of the Task Force on Teaching as a Profession* (New York: Carnegie Forum, 1986).

43. Holmes Group, *Tomorrow's Teachers*, pp. 10–13.

44. For analysis of the Holmes Group's proposals, see the Spring 1987 issue of *Teachers College Record*, reprinted as Jonas F. Soltis, ed., *Reforming Teacher Education: The Impact of the Holmes Group Report* (New York: Teachers College Press, 1987).

45. Carnegie Forum, *A Nation Prepared*, p. 117.

46. Ibid., pp. 55–69, 87–95.

47. Ibid., p. 92.

48. Ibid., pp. 95–103.

CHAPTER 3

Learning to Teach and Proving Your Competence

The education of America's teachers has always been controversial, as a brief look at its history readily shows. In the early years of the nation, before teachers undertook special training for their work, some citizens argued that teachers obviously needed help. Teachers lacked both knowledge and skill, a Massachusetts school reformer complained in 1826: They "know nothing, absolutely nothing, of the complicated and difficult duties assigned to them." "Literary and scientific" training, he later suggested, could help people learn what and how to teach.[1] Not so, other citizens countered. Any intelligent person who had been to school had already learned "the art of instructing others," and "if intelligence be wanting, no system of instruction can supply its place." Bright people can teach naturally, according to this argument, and dull people who try to teach are just asking for trouble—and dismissal.[2]

We can still hear arguments on both sides of this debate. In fact, the two opposing positions weave in and out of this chapter as themes. The advocates of formal teacher education have generally had the upper hand in the debate, but today the issue of how teachers should prepare for their occupation is lively once again.

The first public teacher training institution, a quasisecondary school called a *normal school*, opened in Lexington, Massachusetts, in 1839, and very gradually the idea of teacher education caught on. In Chapter 6 we will see that teacher education was one of the goals of the common school reformers who succeeded in building statewide public school systems throughout the nation. Yet in 1900 the typical elementary school teacher was a woman who felt lucky if she had finished high school, much less received any formal training for her work. The typical secondary teacher was a man with some college credit, a smattering of which may have been in *pedagogy*, the art and science of teaching, which was just developing as a university subject.[3]

What combination of knowledge and skill should form the content of teacher education? In what kind of institution should it take place? Does teacher education have anything to offer bright people? Can it turn average people into competent teachers? The search for answers to such questions continued into the twentieth century as universities assumed more responsibility for teacher education, expanding their programs for high school teachers and developing programs for elementary teachers. Normal schools made a bid for status by transforming themselves, first into teachers colleges, then into colleges, and finally into full-fledged universities. State boards of education began requiring teachers to obtain state certificates that corresponded to higher levels of education.

But university degrees and state credentials have not put the arguments over teacher education to rest. On the contrary, the arguments have recently intensified. Many students who enroll in a college or department of education expecting, reasonably enough, to learn how to teach do not realize that they have stepped into the middle of a controversy. They soon find out, however, when they pick up an issue of *Time* or *Newsweek* and read a cover story that is critical of teachers and scornful of teacher educators, or when they talk with business, engineering, or arts and sciences majors who ask, "What? You're taking education courses? Why would an intelligent person who has other options go into teaching?" As a prospective teacher, you undoubtedly have your own answers to such questions, but this chapter will give you a better understanding of *why* teacher education programs and their graduates generate so much controversy.

Just as Chapters 1 and 2 of this textbook offer hope as well as criticism, this chapter suggests that the arguments over teacher education and teacher competency may have a positive outcome. As I have said before, there are signs that the occupation may be changing for the better. We will survey the content of teacher education, taking a close look at the three areas that make up teacher preparation programs. We will examine current attempts to reform teacher education, ranging from the near elimination of specialized courses for teachers to the "professional" programs advocated by the Holmes Group and the Carnegie Forum on Education and the Economy. Depending on whose opinion we accept, reforms like these may prove to be either the best or the worst developments ever in teacher education.

The trend toward higher standards in teacher education programs also deserves our attention. Raising standards, the watchword in teacher education today, generally means requiring teachers to take more standardized tests. A response to the public's latest discovery of the teacher competency issue, admission and certification tests have become extremely controversial. Will more testing produce better teachers? Or are the tests keeping capable and deserving people, minorities in particular, out of the occupation?

THE CONTENT OF TEACHER EDUCATION

Despite the talk of reform in the air, there remains a remarkable sameness to teacher education in the United States. Visiting colleges and universities and talking with professors of education around the county, I notice variations in such things as course titles, sequences, and credit hours; I see different professors using different approaches; and I hear administrators boasting that their teacher education programs put more emphasis on, say, clinical and field experiences than other programs. But beneath these differences lies a framework that varies little from program to program and campus to campus.

About 70 percent of America's prospective teachers are undergraduates majoring in education. They are working on bachelor's degrees in education in their college or university's department, division, school, or college of education. The other 30 percent of prospective teachers fall into one of two categories. Most of them are undergraduates pursuing bachelor's degrees in fields other than education, usually arts and sciences disciplines, and also taking the education courses required for state teacher certification. A small but growing number of people who want to teach, however, are people who already have bachelor's degrees in other fields, have worked in other occupations for several years, and are back in school seeking teacher certification. Later in this chapter we will examine the alternate routes that many states, worried about teacher shortages, are opening to help these people change careers and get into teaching as quickly possible.[4]

First, though, we will take a more general look at teacher education, dividing its content into three broad areas:

1. *liberal education* in the arts and sciences;
2. the *teaching field* (or fields) for which teachers will be responsible in the classroom—the "what" of teaching; and
3. *professional education* in methods and foundations—the "how" and "why" of teaching.

Although the names and specific content of these areas have changed over the years, teacher education programs have consisted of the same three areas since the days of normal schools. For a century and a half Americans have argued over how much emphasis each area should receive, with the debate usually centered on the trade-off between the third and the first two areas. In 1847 the principal of the State Normal School of Albany, New York, one of the nation's first teacher training institutions, spoke of the trade-off in terms that have changed little: "To be a teacher, one must first of all be a scholar. So much stress is now placed on method, and on the theory of teaching, that there is great danger of forgetting the supreme importance of scholarship and culture." Keep the concept of trade-off in mind as we survey each area in turn.[5]

Liberal Education

This area consists of courses in the arts and sciences, the core of any college education. These courses are liberal in the sense that they are designed to liberate the mind from provincial thought, opening it to a variety of viewpoints. The arts and sciences transmit a common culture: knowledge that educated people deem valuable, organized into such disciplines as history, English, foreign languages, mathematics, biology, and chemistry. These disciplines are more than just bodies of knowledge, however; they represent different ways of knowing. Think for a moment about how differently historians and biologists organize and use knowledge, or how differently philosophers and mathematicians solve problems.

Theodore Hesburgh, a former president of the University of Notre Dame, suggests that liberal education enables people "to think clearly, logically, deeply, and widely"; to express themselves with the same facility; "to evaluate, to have a growing sense of moral purpose and priority"; and "to cope daily with the ambiguities of the human situation."[6] Although the case for liberal education is not primarily vocational, I could argue that of all citizens, teachers have the greatest need *in their work* for the skills that Hesburgh describes. As the Holmes Group states in *Tomorrow's Teachers,* "Teachers must lead a life of the mind. They must be reflective and thoughtful: persons who seek to understand so they may clarify for others, persons who can go to the heart of the matter."[7]

But Hesburgh, the Holmes Group, and other professors and organizations in both education and the arts and sciences recognize that liberal education is imperfect. It, too, cries out for reform. Fragmentation, excessive specialization, poor teaching—prospective teachers encounter these problems far too often in liberal education courses. Professors of the arts and sciences are not always the academic exemplars that some of them claim to be. For years a rivalry has raged between education and the arts and sciences. Many teacher educators, battle-weary and defensive, are reluctant to share any more of the teacher education program. Today, depending on the particular program and institution, liberal education accounts for one-third to one-half of the content of undergraduate teacher education. Is that enough? What is the trade-off with the other two areas?[8]

The Teaching Field

This area involves preparation in the subject or subjects that prospective teachers will convey to their students. One-fourth to one-third of the courses in teacher education programs are in the teaching field, and that range encompasses even more variation than the fractions suggest. Consider first the case of prospective secondary teachers, some of whom (about 60%) major in secondary education while others (about 40%) major in the arts and sciences. All secondary teachers take their teaching field courses in the arts and sciences, with English teachers studying in the English department, math teachers in the math department, and so forth. Secondary teachers who major in the arts and sciences take about one-third of their total programs in the teaching field. Those who major in secondary education, however, take about one-fourth of their total programs in the teaching field, trading off three or four semester courses in the teaching field in order to take three or four more courses in education. From an arts and sciences point of view, secondary education majors learn too little about the "what" of teaching, their academic subjects. The secondary education majors, of course, can reply that they learn more about the "how" and "why" of teaching.[9]

Aggravating the argument is the requirement in many states that secondary science and social studies teachers hold certification in at least two teaching fields. This requirement, designed to ease staffing problems in the schools by producing "switch hitters," as one of my colleagues in secondary education recently explained, sacrifices mastery of a single subject for coverage of two or more subjects. The National Science Teachers Association and, to a lesser degree, the National Council for the Social Studies have expressed concern over the situation. Can a secondary science major learn enough to teach biology *and* chemistry from five or six semester courses in each subject? What about the secondary social studies major struggling to cover history, sociology, *and* economics in three or four courses each?[10]

The teaching fields for elementary education, special education, and physical education majors deserve separate consideration. These students receive about two-thirds of the bachelor's degrees in education, with elementary majors alone accounting for more than one-third. Where within the college or university should they take their teaching fields? We could argue that prospective elementary teachers, who must be responsible for many subjects, should take a sampler of courses in the arts and sciences. Special education teachers might go to the psychology department, while physical education teachers could concentrate in physiology in the biology department. In some teacher education programs, to be sure, these teachers do go to arts and sciences for at least part of their teaching fields. Far more often, however, they take their teaching fields in the college of education, where they enroll in courses with such titles as "Sports Physiology," "Behavior Modification of Emotionally Conflicted Children," and "Math for Elementary Teachers."[11]

Many teacher educators argue that this practice is both logical and academically sound. They claim that teaching field courses designed for teachers and focused on the classroom are more useful than courses designed for arts and sciences majors. The critics, when they are in a polite mood, argue that such courses take future teachers out of the academic mainstream, cutting them off from professors and students who are working in the disciplines. Less politely, the critics throw around words like "Mickey Mouse." Name calling hurts, of course, and it often diverts attention from the real questions: How valuable to a second-grade teacher is a math course in algebra or number theory? How many professors of biology know or care much about sports physiology? Do arts and sciences professors in general understand the academic world in which future elementary, special education, and physical education teachers will work?

Professional Education

This is the most controversial area in teacher education programs. Here "Goofy" joins "Mickey Mouse" in the critics' stock of cartoon-character insults. In a more serious vein, the report *A Nation at Risk* sets forth a common complaint: "The teacher-preparation curriculum is weighted heavily with courses in 'educational methods' at the expense of courses in subjects to be taught."[12] Notice again the idea of a trade-off, and notice the use of "methods" as a generic description of virtually everything that colleges and departments of education try to do. In fact, the professional education courses that make up one-fourth to one-third of teacher education programs are considerably more varied and complex.

Even the shorthand distinction I made above—"how" courses in methods versus "why" courses in foundations—does not do justice to the array of education courses found in college and university catalogs. Courses in methods of teaching are the most numerous, to be sure, and they are designed to be practical and helpful. In foundations courses, students use such disciplines as history, philosophy, sociology, and political science to study the relationship between school and society. The distinction between methods and foundations courses is clear enough, but other education courses deal with both hows and whys. Courses in evaluation and measurement, among the most technical in teacher education programs, can also raise questions of rationale and purpose, as can courses in educational psychology. Curriculum courses bring together knowledge of how, why, and what. Student teaching, the culmination of teacher education programs, *ideally* puts a prospective teacher's entire repertoire of knowledge and skill to the test.

"Ideally" is a word that symbolizes the problem with teacher education, according to the critics. Teacher education programs abound in wishful thinking, they charge. Education professors, well meaning but out of touch with elementary and secondary schools, teach courses that run together in a blur. Students waltz in and glide through. Field experiences and student teaching offer a taste of the real world, but after graduation new teachers must literally teach themselves to teach in order to survive. Education professors rarely talk about discipline, but out in the schools it becomes the first and often the only priority. Education courses that seemed fun at best and boring at worst turn out to be useless. Voicing feelings of frustration verging on bitterness, experienced teachers give their education courses low marks. Many teachers say the only worthwhile part of their professional education was student teaching.[13]

If the last paragraph seems harsh, it is intended to. Just as I tried to be honest about teacher satisfaction in the first chapter and teacher salaries in the second, I owe you an objective look at teacher education in this chapter. As the author of a teacher education textbook, however, I obviously believe that professional education is valuable, and we professors of education do have our defenders. Susan Ohanian, a veteran third-grade teacher whose writing about teaching has won her a reputation for pulling no punches, contends that

> teachers must stop asking education professors for the whole house. I know plenty of teachers who are disappointed, indignant, and eventually destroyed by the fact that nobody has handed them all four corners. But the best we can expect from any program of courses or training is the jagged edge of one corner. Then it is up to us to read the research and collaborate with the children to find the other three corners.[14]

There are no "stir-and-serve recipes for teaching," Ohanian insists. "We do not need the behaviorist-competency thugs to chart our course." Teachers deserve education courses that are intellectually challenging—and too many are "stupid," she acknowledges—but "much of the training must be self-initiated." Professors of education should open teachers' minds and give them a sense of purpose and direction. But Ohanian concludes that the only way to learn how to teach is to teach.[15]

REFORMING TEACHER EDUCATION

Longtime observers of American education say they have seen it all before: the 1980s were a replay of the 1950s. In both decades the public became convinced that public education had gone soft, and in both decades the public insisted that the schools get back to basics. The finger of blame for the nation's educational problems pointed first at incompetent teachers and then at the teacher educators who had obviously mistrained them. Faced with a teacher shortage, Americans resolved to reform teacher education. During the 1960s, however, the nation turned its attention to other matters; teacher educators won favor by pitching in to help solve the teacher shortage; and the critics went away for awhile. The 1990s, according to the veteran observers, will be like the 1960s. When the smoke clears, teacher education will be doing business as usual.

The current wave of reforms *may* make more lasting changes in teacher education, however, if only because many of today's reformers are more politically astute than their precedessors. The new reformers are doing their homework in universities and legislatures, developing programs and pushing through bills that may indeed change the way teachers prepare for their work. The details of the reform packages vary, but three themes stand out.

1. Cut back professional education. Professional education has *some* value, the reformers seem to be saying, but not enough to take up one-fourth to one-third of an undergraduate program.
2. Strengthen the teaching field. America needs teachers who know their subjects.
3. Raise standards. This theme has a variety of meanings, but most often it is a call for brighter teachers with higher test scores. Remember the words of the nineteenth-century critic: "If intelligence be lacking, no system of instruction can supply its place."

As put into practice by today's reformers, the first two themes are crowding professional education out of bachelor's degree programs and reshaping it into a variety of post-baccalaureate programs, which we will examine in this section of the chapter. The third theme reflects the controversy over teacher competency and teacher testing, which we will analyze in the next section.

Holmes and Carnegie

Reformers in the Holmes Group and the Carnegie Forum on Education and the Economy have elaborate visions of a teaching profession whose members receive their specialized training at the graduate level. Both *Tomorrow's Teachers* by the Holmes Group and *A Nation Prepared* by the Carnegie Forum call for the elimination of undergraduate degree programs in education. People with degrees in the arts and sciences but no formal preparation for teaching would be able to enter the occupation, but all fully certified teachers would have master's degrees in teaching. Much, perhaps most, professional education would take place at "clinical sites." Here Carnegie and Holmes draw analogies to the teaching hospitals used to train medical doctors. Indeed, Carnegie speaks specifically of "interns" and "residents." Both reports envision clinical programs conducted jointly by teacher educators in the universities and experienced teachers in the schools. At the top of the new profession would be veteran teachers with doctorates in teaching, some of whom would hold adjunct appointments as university faculty members.[16]

These reforms would change teacher education radically, but it might well become an even more important part of the work that universities do. Holmes and Carnegie like to put things positively. They prefer to say that teacher education would be lengthened to five years rather than cut back to one year.

As we saw in the last chapter, the Carnegie Forum has established a National Board for Professional Teaching Standards, the majority of whose members are classroom teachers. The board is hard at work developing tests and other evaluation procedures to be used in awarding national teaching certificates. Because the Carnegie Corporation's prestige and powers of persuasion are formidable, the content of the tests may shape the content of teacher education programs—not necessarily a pleasant prospect, according to criticism we will examine. Carnegie's *A Nation Prepared*, better known and more widely discussed outside of education circles than the report of the Holmes Group, has already been a factor in the decision of several state legislatures to phase out undergraduate degree programs in education.[17]

The impact of the Holmes Group, however, has been more immediate and emotional. Just mentioning its name is enough to start an argument in most colleges and departments of education. The Holmes strategy is to reform teacher education from the top down, by concentrating on the universities at the top of the academic pecking order. The Holmes Group is a consortium of teacher education deans and chief academic officers at approximately one hundred major research universities. Their vision of a teaching profession is far reaching, as we have seen, but the goal of eliminating bachelor's degree programs in education has been the lightning rod for controversy. Several member institutions have already shifted their professional education programs almost entirely to the graduate level, leaving only a course or two at the undergraduate level for students who plan to teach. But about thirty universities that were invited to become charter members of the group declined, and several others have withdrawn. Eliminating undergraduate education programs, among the top moneymakers on some campuses, is a move that even large research universities will not make lightly. In smaller state universities and four-year public and private colleges, the change could touch off a riot. Why, it would threaten faculty jobs. It would deprive undergraduates of a popular major. It would . . .[18]

Some teacher educators, even in Holmes Group institutions, are outspoken opponents of the reforms.[19] Professors of elementary education, special education, and physical education complain that they would be forced to compress or simply eliminate much of the professional education curriculum. The Holmes Group recommends a five-year preparation program for elementary teachers that includes "area concentrations" in language and literature, mathematics, science, social science, and the arts. The undergraduate major would be in one of these areas; the other four areas, each "roughly equivalent in time commitment to a minor," would take up most of the remaining program.[20] Counting up the time left for instruction in methods, foundations, curriculum, evaluation, educational psychology, and other traditional areas, some professors contend that the job simply cannot be done.

Without question, the Holmes Group reforms break with tradition. If they catch on, teacher education will have to change. Doing business as usual will not be possible, and, according to the Holmes Group, that is precisely the objective.

The Texas Squeeze Play

While Holmes and Carnegie have their visions of a new profession, other reformers are advocating plans that, if less elaborate, have a simplicity that plays well politically. The Texas state legislature is attracting national attention by simply squeezing teacher education at the bachelor's level rather than shifting it to graduate level. As of 1991, Texas will abolish bachelor's degree programs in education, and prospective teachers will take *no more than* 18 semester hours of undergraduate course work in professional education. This reform marks the first time a state legislature has set maximum rather than minimum requirements for teacher education. Given a bare-bones allocation of six hours of "core" education courses, six hours of methods, and six hours of student teaching, teacher educators in Texas are wondering how they will do their work.[21]

The Texas plan raises numerous questions. Will elementary teachers simply choose an arts and sciences major, or will colleges and universities develop interdisciplinary majors? Curiously, the legislature is allowing the state board of education to exempt teachers of early childhood education, reading, special education, bilingual education, and English as a Second Language from the 18-hour limit. Does that imply that their professional education courses are more worthwhile? More complex? These teachers too, however, will have to major in something other than education. Which arts and sciences fields will they choose? How will these reforms affect the six Texas universites that are members of the Holmes Group? Will their five-year programs have any appeal in a state where a person can earn a teaching certificate in only 18 semester hours?[22]

The New Jersey Shortcut

As the dust settles in Texas, at least 18 other states are opening alternate routes into teaching that allow people with bachelor's degrees but no formal preparation for teaching to try their hands at the occupation. Without question the alternate routes are primarily a response to teacher shortages. As we saw in Chapter 1, state legislatures and state boards of education have proven themselves more than willing to bend teacher education and certification standards in order to put warm bodies in front of the classrooms. In New Jersey, California, Massachusetts, and other states that have recently approved alternate routes, many state legislators have again been talking "sound and cheap," and you know by now what that means. Alternate routes give state legislatures a way to turn yesterday's emergency provisions into today's standard practice. In all fairness, however, the developers of the plan in New Jersey are trying to put people who can teach as well as traditionally prepared teachers into those classrooms. And the plan may be succeeding.[23]

Under the New Jersey plan, which went into effect in 1985, a person with a bachelor's degree in an academic subject can become a provisional teacher by passing a test in that subject. A major goal of the plan is to encourage math majors to become math teachers and science majors to become science teachers, and about a third of the alternate route teachers are doing just that. About 40 percent, however, are people with degrees outside of education who want to teach elementary school. After passing a more general test covering several academic fields, into the schools they go.[24]

All of New Jersey's provisional teachers take a compressed version of professional education course work during their first year of teaching, much of it within the first few weeks. They also work with experienced teachers who serve as mentors, spending their first month under supervision before assuming full responsibility for teaching. If the alternate route teachers like their jobs, receive satisfactory evaluations, and make satisfactory scores on the National Teacher Examinations (NTE), they become fully certified teachers.

Amid dire predictions of failure from teacher educators, the New Jersey program has gotten off to a good start. In the late 1980s about 20 percent of the state's new teachers were coming into the occupation via the alternate route. Provisional teachers are receiving evaluations as good as those of regularly prepared teachers, and the plan itself is getting good reviews from its "graduates." Their complaints, ironically, are more embarrassing to traditional teacher education than to the alternate route. Provisional teachers rate working with their mentors as more beneficial than taking courses from teacher educators and school administrators who, according to the provisionals, have "little knowledge of the day-to-day demands of a classroom, and little to offer in the way of practical lessons or advice." Adding insult to injury, the alternate route teachers are making higher scores on the NTE than graduates of traditional teacher education programs.[25]

Are alternate route programs the beginning of the end for formal teacher education? Rather than traveling the Holmes and Carnegie route to a teaching profession, which will be expensive, America may decide to take the New Jersey shortcut. The temptation will be to make deeper and deeper cuts in professional education, using the justification that teachers who do not take education courses perform as well as people who do. Teacher educators will fight back, of course, and in their corner will be the NEA and AFT, for the last thing teacher organizations want is an occupation that almost anyone with a bachelor's degree can stroll into. A showdown is coming in the 1990s.

A Tale of Two Occupations

Several times each year the media carry the story of someone who has been discovered practicing medicine without a license. Usually the ersatz doctor has a degree in biology or chemistry, a reassuring bedside manner, but no formal training in medicine. Doesn't the fact that such persons are often able to practice successfully for years, completely undetected, cast doubt on the necessity of going to medical school? Shouldn't we allow biologists and chemists to take a few courses in medicine, work with mentors, and then see how well they can do as physicians?

Of course not. Most Americans believe that medicine is too complex and important to treat in such a careless way. Medicine is a profession, after all, and we quite rightly insist that professions maintain high standards. Teaching, however, receives different treatment, as we will find in the concluding section of this chapter and in the chapter that follows.

RAISING STANDARDS IN TEACHER EDUCATION

Rediscovering Teacher Incompetency

Americans rediscovered teacher incompetency in the late 1970s, and the mass media joined academic journals in tracing the problem back to teacher education. Prospective teachers were among the poorest students in colleges and universities, Americans heard repeatedly. At a time when many citizens were upset with declining scores on college entrance examinations, they learned that the test scores of future teachers had fallen even faster than the scores of other students. Ranked against other undergraduates by their Scholastic Aptitiude Test (SAT) and American College Testing (ACT) program scores, teacher education students consistently came in near the bottom, ahead only of students majoring in such fields as agriculture and home economics. Professors of education bore much of the blame, the media charged, for they had lowered their standards during the 1970s in response to declining enrollment in teacher education programs. *A Nation at Risk* captured the mood of the early eighties when it stated that "not enough of the academically able students are being attracted to teaching" and "too many teachers are being drawn from the bottom quarter of graduating high-school and college students."[26] How could teacher educators have let the nation down?

Many news stories and journal articles left the impression that there was once a golden age of teaching, a time when teachers, if not exactly well paid, were uniformly bright and well educated. Educational historians tell a different story. The mid-to-late 1800s were certainly not golden years. School officials could not afford to be selective in hiring teachers—the problem was finding enough teachers to staff the rapidly growing common schools. Recall our discussion of turn-of-the-century teachers and their modest educational credentials. During the 1920s and 1930s, as researchers began administering standardized tests of academic ability, their studies showed that prospective teachers, many of whom were enrolled in normal schools and teachers colleges, ranked low when compared with the full range of college students. In some studies, teachers even ranked below high school seniors. At four-year colleges and universities, "eddies" and "aggies" had to put up with jokes about their shallow interests and weak intellects.[27]

Throughout this century as well as the last, teacher educators have complained that more prestigious, better paying occupations were luring bright people away from teaching. Teacher educators documented their complaints in academic journals and books, waiting for the next public discovery of the teacher competency issue. Close on its heels, they knew, would be another round of criticism of teacher education. The late 1940s and 1950s brought an especially strong media attack, the harshest since "muckraking" journalists uncovered poor teaching in turn-of-the-century schools. The fifties critics lashed out at teachers and teacher educators, writing such scathing books as *And Madly Teach* and *Quackery in the Public Schools*. Newspapers, news magazines, radio, and television joined the attack. And recently, since the late 1970s, Americans have taken up the teacher competency issue again.[28]

History is more than cycles and repetition, however. The social changes of the last three decades have affected teaching as an occupation in ways that we are just beginning to understand. In particular, the feminist and civil rights movements have been powerful influences. The history of America's teachers, as we will see in Chapter 6, is largely women's history. It is the story of women who have worked hard for little compensation. Since the 1960s, with the reduction of discrimination against women in higher education and in many occupations, teacher education programs have suffered a "brain drain" of bright, career-oriented students. It makes many Americans uncomfortable—even resentful—to realize that they can no longer buy teachers of the same quality for the same price, nor even for a higher price. Teaching is a better-paid occupation than ever before, but the bright women who once formed a captive employment pool for teaching, nursing, and social work now have other options.[29]

To a degree, the same is true of minorities, especially black Americans. Many of the brightest black students, women and men, once became teachers. Discrimination placed such severe limits on their chances of education and employment in other fields that teaching reaped a bounty of talented blacks. At the turn of the twentieth century, black teachers in many Southern cities had more years of schooling and held higher degrees than their white counterparts. Well into the 1960s, school systems did not have to worry about attracting talented black college students, for after graduation they had few choices. Like the brightest women, the brightest black students are now going into the full professions. But in contrast to women, the percentage of black students going to college fell throughout most of the 1980s. Moreover, new teacher education requirements, particularly standardized tests, are making it more difficult for black students who want to teach to enter the occupation. Blacks, unlike women, are not moving into higher-status fields in sufficient numbers to justify the consoling explanation that teaching's loss is law and medicine's gain.[30]

No, there never was a golden age of teaching, not even when teaching attracted a larger share of the brightest women and minorities. Even then, the overall intellectual quality of the teaching force was not very impressive. Even then, teacher competency was a serious concern. It is unfair and inaccurate, however, to paint teachers with a single brush. Teaching has always attracted a wide range of people, some of whom have been among the nation's most intelligent individuals. I hasten to add that the public has always gotten better teachers than it has paid for. But the average American teacher, compared with all college students, has ranked low on standardized tests of academic ability as long as there have been standardized tests.

If test scores meant nothing, as some argue, we might not need to be concerned. But there *is* a teacher competency problem, and it manifests itself in many other ways. Parents know something is wrong when teachers send home notes with grammatical and spelling errors in every sentence. Students worry when teachers routinely make mistakes in simple arithmetic on the board. These concerns are legitimate. In teaching, of all occupations, there can be no excuse for weak literacy skills, for these skills are the tools of the teacher's trade.

Literacy is only one aspect of teacher competency. We cannot afford to take literacy for granted, but teachers must be more than literate. The three areas in teacher education programs suggest other areas in which teachers must be competent: general knowledge, knowledge of the teaching field, and knowledge of professional education. The ultimate test of teacher competency, of course, is performance in the classroom. Can the teachers teach? As we saw in the last chapter, however, evaluating teaching skills is difficult and controversial. The other aspects of teacher competency, if no less controversial, lend themselves to an easier form of evaluation: pencil-and-paper testing.

Until the late 1970s, state boards of education did in a sense take it for granted that college graduates who had completed teacher education programs were competent. State boards issued teaching certificates to virtually everyone who finished a state-approved program, with no questions asked. Then, as the public rediscovered the teacher competency issue, state boards and state legislatures began asking questions. Soon they mandated standardized tests as a check on the quality of teacher education. Today more than half the states require prospective teachers to take tests for admission to teacher education programs, and almost every state requires or will soon require tests for teacher certification. Only three states—Arkansas, Georgia, and Texas—require currently employed teachers to take competency tests. Now we will take a closer look at the various forms of teacher testing.[31]

Literacy Tests

Most of the tests for students seeking admission to teacher education measure nothing more than simple literacy. Perhaps the "nothing more" is inappropriate, for it is essential that all teachers have the ability to use "our two principal symbol systems, words and numbers," as the former director of testing for the Dallas public schools so aptly states.[32] Perhaps it is time to stop apologizing for the emphasis that teacher education programs are putting on literacy tests. Stressing literacy is putting first things first. The adjective "simple" does seem appropriate, however, since the admission tests are slanted toward such lower-level literacy skills as word recognition, punctuation, and basic computation. Moreover, the *cutoff* scores that prospective teachers must make to pass the tests are usually set very low—in some cases, embarrassingly low.[33]

In the process of setting the cutoffs, testing companies often *norm* the tests by administering them to various groups of people: for example, to large samples of eighth graders, tenth graders, twelfth graders, and college freshmen. The average score of each group is that group's *normal score* or *norm*. Teacher education officials or state board of education members can then decide which norm to use as the cutoff score for admission to teacher education.[34]

One thing the public has generally overlooked in its latest discovery of teacher incompetency is that cutoff scores for admission to teacher education programs are usually set at the equivalent of tenth to twelfth-grade norms. That is, the average tenth or twelfth grader could pass the tests. For obvious reasons, teacher educators and state board members do not go out of their way to publicize the cutoffs, but, when pressed, they justify them in several ways. First, they want to maintain enrollment in teacher education programs. Raising the cutoffs, they believe, could cause enrollment to fall, worsen the teacher shortage, and put teacher educators out of work. Second, they cannot agree on the level of literacy necessary for teaching. Third, they want to be fair to prospective minority teachers, who do not score as well on the tests as prospective white teachers.[35]

All of these justifications are controversial. To demonstrate that they have some basis in experience, however, we need only consider what has happened in school systems administering their own literacy tests to applicants for teaching positions. Setting cutoffs at the tenth-grade norm, the Dallas Independent School District screened out more than half of its applicants in the late 1970s and early 1980s—people who held bachelor's degrees and teaching certificates. With cutoffs set as low as the sixth-grade norm in Pinellas County, Florida, 15 to 30 percent of the applicants failed. In both systems, minorities failed at much higher rates than whites, an issue to which we will return later in this chapter. Other school systems using literacy tests have had similar results. The good news is that applicants for teaching positions have been doing better on the tests, in part because teacher education programs have been putting more emphasis on literacy.[36]

But teacher educators are proceeding with caution. "America cannot afford any more teachers who fail a twelfth grade competency test," the Holmes Group says.[37] Easier said than done. With the low cutoffs that teacher education programs currently use, the rate of failure on admission tests throughout the nation averages 28 percent. If every program moved the cutoff to the equivalent of a college freshman norm, about half of all college freshmen would immediately become ineligible for admission. (Since the norm is the average score of the group being tested, by definition about half the group falls below the norm.) Even more seriously, as many as 80 to 90 percent of all black college freshmen would be ineligible. Teacher educators could boast that they had raised standards, but would they have raised the right standards?[38]

On the one hand, empirical research on the relationship between teachers' scores on literacy tests and their students' scores on achievement tests is inconclusive. Some studies show a modest correlation; others do not. Thus some teacher educators argue that emphasizing the literacy standard may keep potentially good teachers out of the occupation. These teacher educators make the same argument on SAT and ACT scores. Research does not show a definite link between the SAT and ACT scores of teachers and the achievement test scores of their students. Why, then, should teacher education programs turn away students with below-average scores on these tests? Doing so is arbitrary and discriminatory, some professors argue, and doing so can land you in court.[39]

On the other hand, we found in the last chapter that the entire area of research on measuring teacher influence on student test scores is fraught with problems. Because so many other factors inside and outside of schools outweigh the influence of teachers on student achievement, it is difficult to measure the effect of *any* teacher characteristic or behavior on student test scores. Frankly, this kind of research may never give teacher educators much guidance in setting standards. Professors in other areas of higher education express amazement that teacher educators spend so much time agonizing over standards and grasping for empirical studies to justify every change. Medical schools and law schools do not base their high admission standards on studies showing that doctors and lawyers with higher test scores perform better operations and win more cases. Professors of medicine and law do not even conduct such studies. In setting standards, they simply state the obvious: doctors and lawyers must be highly literate, for their jobs demand it.

Surely professors of education can make the same case for teachers. When they have done so in court, they have won, for the courts emphasize "job-relatedness": the demonstration of a *reasonable* relationship between what the test measures and what the job requires. Even in cases involving the testing of currently employed teachers in Arkansas, Georgia, and Texas, courts have accepted the job-relatedness of literacy. It is only reasonable that people who constantly use literacy skills in their work, people whose jobs involve raising the literacy of others, be highly literate themselves.[40]

Tests of General Knowledge, the Teaching Field, and Professional Education

The strong emphasis I give literacy in this chapter reflects the attention it is receiving in teacher testing, but teacher competency obviously involves more. By far the most widely used teacher certification tests are the NTE developed by the Educational Testing Service (ETS) of Princeton, New Jersey. The largest testing company in the world, ETS also produces the SAT, the Graduate Record Examinations (GRE), and numerous other standardized tests. Several states have contracted for teacher certification tests with National Evaluation Systems (NES) of Amherst, Massachusetts, or other testing companies.[41]

The controversy over literacy tests is mild compared with the arguments over teacher certification tests. The NTE currently consists of a "core battery" covering communication skills, general knowledge, and professional knowledge, and a set of "specialty area" tests tailored to various teaching fields. The content of the NES examinations is similar. Disgruntled teachers and prospective teachers, often with the backing of the NEA, have challenged each part of these tests in court. The arguments revolve around a deceptively simple question: What do teachers need to know?[42]

In the area of general knowledge, prospective teachers sometimes complain that the test items are obscure, trivial, or irrelevant to their future jobs. I can tell when my students have taken the NTE or NES exams, for some of them invariably return with questions like these: "Why do I need to recognize the musical notation for the opening notes of the *Fifth Symphony*? Who cares who discovered radium? Where are the Alleghenies, anyway?" Students whose social and educational backgrounds have not prepared them for such questions may charge that the tests are culturally biased, and minority students are not the only ones who raise this issue. As we will see in Chapter 8, the issue is one of social class as much as race and ethnicity.[43]

From one point of view, the questions above betray an appalling ignorance of—and indifference to—matters that should be common knowledge, at least to people with college degrees. Those who take this point of view throw up their hands in despair at the thought of teachers whose knowledge is so thin and spotty. There *is* cultural bias in the tests, these people argue, but the bias is toward a culture they want the schools to transmit. It is unfortunate and unjust that the schools do not expose every student to that culture, but every prospective teacher has an obligation to acquire it.

From another point of view, however, there is no longer a consensus on the knowledge that educated people should have in common, if indeed such a consensus ever existed. The best selling books *Cultural Literacy: What Every American Needs to Know* (1987) by E. D. Hirsch, Jr., and *The Closing of the American Mind* (1987) by Allan Bloom have sparked a vigorous debate, one that we will hear in more detail in Chapter 10. Some educated Americans do not believe that it is possible to make a list of essential knowledge—which is exactly what Hirsch attempts in his book. If Hirsch's list is nothing more than arbitrary, they suggest, then so is any test of general knowledge.[44]

Tests in the teaching field are less controversial, but they too involve debates over what teachers need to know. We have already seen the disagreements over the teaching fields for elementary education, special education, and physical education teachers. Consider the difficulty involved in constructing a teaching field test for elementary teachers in, say, mathematics. If the testing company asks classroom teachers, professors of education, and professors of mathematics for advice on the test, they are likely to make different suggestions—especially in math, the subject that most elementary teachers like the least. The advisors must decide which areas of mathematics the test will cover, how broad and how deep the coverage will be, and so forth. Then a different group of advisors must repeat the process for every other subject in the elementary curriculum.[45]

Still to come is the highly technical work of actually constructing the test. Item writers compose the questions. Theirs is a critical job, for in multiple-choice testing, the options listed are the only acceptable answers. A multiplication problem has only one correct answer, to be sure, but in most academic fields, specialists often disagree over "right" and "wrong" answers. The more you know about literature, for example, the more likely it is that several answers to a question about a children's story—or no answers—may appear to be correct. Thus all standardized tests reflect the "biases" of a variety of people, academic advisors as well as technicians at the testing company. Finally, the company field-tests the questions on a sample of elementary teachers, conducts statistical analyses of the results, and makes revisions in the test. Teacher education officials and state board members, of course, have the ultimate power to determine who passes and who fails, since they establish the cutoff scores. Keep in mind that, next to literacy tests, teaching field tests are the most straightforward.[46]

The least straightforward tests, as you must realize by now, are tests of professional education. Teacher certification tests should reflect the *knowledge base* for teaching—what teachers need to know in order to do their work. Actually, the content of teacher education programs and teacher certification tests shows that there are multiple knowledge bases for teaching, which we have called liberal education, the teaching field(s), and professional education. Rivalries and competition among the knowledge bases are common, as we have seen, giving many prospective teachers the feeling that they have been caught in an academic tug of war. As if that were not enough, teacher educators still disagree over what should constitute the professional knowledge base for teaching—the specialized knowledge that belongs to the occupation alone. Once again the question comes around: What do teachers need to know?[47]

Here is the problem. Because teacher educators disagree among themselves, not only on the areas that constitute the specialized knowledge base but on important issues within each area, the professional education questions on teacher certification tests are: (a) obvious; (b) confusing; (c) theoretical; (d) common sense; (e) all of these. The correct answer is "e." Please understand that I am not insulting teacher educators and test developers. I am only suggesting that the lack of consensus about professional education makes testing teachers in that area most difficult.

Linda Darling-Hammond, director of the Rand Corporation's Education and Human Resources Program, has analyzed the professional knowledge section of the NTE. Based on a sample test provided by ETS, her analysis reveals the following breakdown of questions. Ten percent of the questions require knowledge of testing and assessment; 25 percent involve school law and administration; and fewer than 10 percent, surprisingly, demand "knowledge of theory, research, or facts pertaining to teaching and learning." More than half of the questions, then, tap other kinds of knowledge and skills. Fifteen percent, according to Darling-Hammond, require only "careful reading or knowledge of simple word definitions"; 25 percent call for "agreement with the test's teaching philosophy," which she describes as "liberal" and "highly individualized"; and 15 percent require "agreement with the test's definition of socially or bureaucratically acceptable behavior," which at least one item on the test itself characterizes as "nonthreatening."[48]

By her count, about 40 percent of the questions have no "right" answer. One question on techniques of "effective teaching," for example, includes several answers that are supported by different bodies of research. Prospective teachers can mark an answer that favors mastery learning or one that endorses whole-group instruction. Both of these approaches have support in the research, and both have their advocates among teachers and teacher educators. These answers are "wrong," however. Only the test-takers who opt for the answer that favors individualized instruction and pacing get the item right. The questions on school law and administrative procedures, on the other hand, are more clear-cut: "The United States Supreme Court decision against permitting prayer in the public schools was based on which of the following?" Perhaps ETS gravitated toward this area, which occupies one-fourth of the test, in search of reasonably clear rights and wrongs. Law and administration, however, account for nothing like one-fourth of the content of professional education.[49]

Faced with mounting complaints and lawsuits, ETS has announced that it is phasing out the NTE. By 1992 the company plans to market a successor, a teacher assessment program that it promises to develop with the goal of eliminating cultural and racial bias. The new program will have three stages. The first will be administered during or after a prospective teacher's sophomore year to measure basic academic skills. The second stage will be given on the completion of a teacher education program to assess the candidate's knowledge of the teaching field(s) and professional education. The third stage, administered after a period of supervised teaching to evaluate classroom teaching skills, may involve interactive video, computer simulations, and portfolios of the teacher's work.[50]

The NES is also facing problems with its teacher certification tests. The state of Alabama settled a challenge to the NES exams out of court in 1985, then decided in 1988 to drop the entire NES certification testing program. Lawyers for a group of teachers who had failed the NES exams claimed that the tests were racially biased as well as poorly constructed.[51]

Teacher Testing and Minority Teachers

Fairness to minority teachers is one of the most difficult issues in teacher testing. The issue is part of a larger question: How can the nation's schools continue to attract qualified minority teachers? The Holmes Group and Carnegie Forum recognize the urgent need to find answers. Academic journals feature articles with titles as alarming as "The Desperate Need for Black Teachers" and as hopeful as "Minority Teachers Can Pass the Tests."[52] Even if there is room for hope, there is broad agreement that the current situation is precarious. At a time when the percentage of minority students in elementary and secondary schools is increasing, the percentage of minority teachers is decreasing. Already 23 of the 25 largest city school systems are "minority majority," and by the turn of the century as many as 40 percent of all the students in the nation will be black, Hispanic, or Asian-American. In the public schools, the percentage of black students has risen to more than 16 percent, yet the percentage of black teachers has fallen, slowly but steadily, for three decades—from 8 percent in 1970 to 6 percent in 1990. If this trend continues, only 5 percent of America's teachers will be black in the year 2000. The outlook for Hispanic teachers is similarly bleak.[53]

What can be done? Almost everyone agrees that making teaching a more attractive occupation will help. As every chapter in the first part of this book points out, there is certainly hope for the occupation. Attracting more black teachers while raising standards, however, presents special problems. Even though the percentage of black students going to college may be stabilizing after several years of decline, only about 29 percent of black high school graduates are going to college, in contrast to 33 percent of white graduates. Blacks who do get to college tend to have lower SAT and ACT scores than whites. The black-white gap on the SAT, although closing, is still almost 200 points. Among the highest scoring black students, fewer than 1 percent say they want to be teachers.[54]

Thus it is not surprising that teacher testing hits prospective teachers who are black harder than those who are white. The passing rate on Louisiana's teacher certification test in the mid-1980s was 78 percent for white candidates but only 15 percent for black candidates. In Georgia the figures were 87 percent for whites and 34 percent for blacks. Other states have produced narrower gaps, but they seem to have done so by setting lower cutoffs on the tests rather than by improving the education of black teachers. In Texas, more than 99 percent of currently employed teachers, including 95.4 percent of blacks and 98.9 percent of Hispanics, passed a controversial literacy test that the Texas State Teachers Association had tried unsuccessfully to block in court. The cutoff, however, was apparently the equivalent of an eighth or tenth-grade norm. After Alabama agreed to lower the cutoff on its certification test to produce the same success rate for black and white students, 98 percent of all the candidates passed the test. At that point the state decided the test was not worth the trouble and expense.[55]

In states with large minority populations, teacher testing has brought forth bitter accusations. Teacher testing is a racist ploy, some teachers contend—the latest chapter in a long record of discrimination. No, it is a necessary step in improving the occupation, others reply—the real ploy is using the race issue to block higher standards.

Teacher education must find a way out of this dilemma, even if doing so proves to be difficult and expensive, as it certainly will. Listen to the counsel of Patricia A. Graham, dean of the Graduate School of Education at Harvard:

> The problem cannot be solved simply by raising the cutoff scores on tests, by ignoring the tests, by calling them racially biased, or by declaring them inappropriate for future teachers. The tests may contribute to the problem, but they are not central. The central problem is that blacks in the U.S. are not getting as good an education as whites are—and the education that whites are getting is not good enough. [56]

Graham's major recommendation is improving elementary and secondary education. She also suggests recruiting more blacks as college students and helping them succeed once they enroll. Graham points to the record of Grambling State University, a historically black school in Louisiana that is "fighting the scores instead of the tests." The performance of Grambling's students on Louisiana's teacher tests has improved substantially. Grambling has chosen not to challenge the tests, nor is it "teaching the tests," as so many institutions try to do for both black and white students. Instead, Grambling has tried to improve every area of its teacher education program. Graham also argues that the nation needs to invest more money and imagination in attracting bright black college students to teaching. Noting the influx into teaching of people who are dissatisfied with their present jobs, Graham calls for the recruitment of more blacks at mid-career or even later. She specifically mentions government workers and military retirees. [57]

Cautious Optimism about Teacher Education and Teacher Testing

Working in a rapidly changing context, the Holmes Group, Carnegie Forum, and other reformers are pressing ahead. Carnegie's National Board for Professional Teaching Standards is in place, and teachers themselves—two words I will use often in the next chapter—are taking the lead in developing national certification tests. On a most encouraging note, Carnegie's *A Nation Prepared* admits that "the assessment techniques used will have to go far beyond multiple choice examinations." [58] Such tests, all too popular at every level of education, are suited to some but not all kinds of evaluation. To find out whether a prospective teacher has mastered factual information, multiple-choice exams are helpful. Medicine, law, and other full professions make use of them. But the essay format is far more flexible, for it can allow candidates to analyze classroom situations and justify their choices of action. Within certain limits, there can be several "right" answers. Carnegie also has great hope for performance evaluations "based on observation of the candidate's actual teaching over a substantial period." [59] The National Board for Professional Teaching Standards is working closely with the ETS as the testing corporation designs a three-stage teacher assessment program to replace the NTE.

Optimistically, teaching may now be where medicine was in the 1870s— just beginning to develop a professional knowledge base that *actually works*. In medicine, it took several decades for the new scientific knowledge base to prove its worth. Only then, in the early 1900s, were medical educators and the American Medical Association able to drive out quacks and improve medical practice. Only then could they use examinations based on scientific medicine to raise standards.[60]

Teaching is still an occupation in search of a specialized knowledge base. Giving teachers themselves a major role in finding it, as Carnegie has, is a great step forward. But before any national board can develop fair examinations, teachers and teacher educators must reach a consensus on how to evaluate answers on the tests and performance in the classroom. Otherwise a least-common-denominator pseudoscience of education—a teach-by-the-numbers approach—will freeze into place, and the occupation will splinter into teachers who go along with it and teachers who see through it and reject it.

ACTIVITIES

1. Invite several professors of education and professors of arts and sciences into your class for a panel discussion of the content of teacher education, especially the trend toward five-year, "Holmes-Carnegie" programs.
2. Talk with a public school administrator and an administrator in your college or university's teacher education program about the effects of raising standards on the quality of the teaching force. Be sure to discuss admission and certification tests and their effects on minority teachers.
3. Ask currently employed teachers for their views on the issues in this chapter, especially the strengths and weaknesses of teacher education programs.

SUGGESTED READINGS

To catch the spirit of the "professional" reformers in teacher education, read *Tomorrow's Teachers* by the Holmes Group and *A Nation Prepared* by the Carnegie Forum on Education and the Economy (see notes 7 and 16 below). Both reports are concise and well written. You may find it interesting to compare the suggestions that James B. Conant, a president of Harvard University, made several years ago in *The Education of American Teachers*. See note 13 for information on Conant's book and several other critical studies of teacher education.

NOTES

1. James G. Carter, *Essays on Popular Education* . . . (1826), and *Outline of an Institution for the Education of Teachers* (1866), in David B. Tyack, ed., *Turning*

Points in American Educational History (Waltham, MA: Blaisdell, 1967), pp. 153, 428.

2. Report of the Committee on Education of the Massachusetts House of Representatives (1840), in Rush Welter, ed., *American Writings on Popular Education: The Nineteenth Century* (Indianapolis: Bobbs-Merrill, 1971), p. 94.

3. Tyack sketches a brief history of teacher education on pp. 412–420. See also Donald R. Warren, "History and Teacher Education: Learning from Experience," *Educational Researcher* 14 (December 1985): 5–12. A recent book edited by Warren may become the definitive historical study: *American Teachers: Histories of a Profession at Work* (New York: Macmillan, 1989). This book, which includes chapters by Tyack and other major educational historians, will take its place beside Willard S. Elsbree's classic *The American Teacher: Evolution of a Profession in a Democracy* (New York: American Book Company, 1939).

4. U.S. Department of Education, Center for Education Statistics, *The Condition of Education, 1987 Edition* (Washington: U.S. Government Printing Office, 1987), p. 48.

5. David Page, *Theory and Practice of Teaching: Or, the Motives and Methods of Good School-Keeping* (1849), in Tyack, p. 412.

6. Theodore M. Hesburgh, "The Future of Liberal Education," *Change* 13 (April 1981): 38–39.

7. Holmes Group, *Tomorrow's Teachers: A Report of the Holmes Group* (East Lansing, MI: Holmes Group, 1986), p. 47.

8. See *The Humanities in American Life: Report of the Commission on the Humanities* (Berkeley: University of California Press, 1980). I base my estimates of the amount of course work allocated to each area of teacher education on an examination of college and university bulletins.

9. U.S. Department of Education, *The Condition of Education, 1987 Edition*, p. 48.

10. Robert Rothman, " 'Startling' Data Upset Certification Program for Science Teachers," *Education Week* (September 24, 1986), pp. 1, 15, and "Teachers Asked To Seek Certification," *Education Week* (October 15, 1986).

11. Diane Ravitch, "Scapegoating the Teachers," in *The Schools We Deserve: Reflections on the Educational Crises of Our Times* (New York: Basic Books, 1985), p. 95.

12. National Commission on Excellence in Education, *A Nation at Risk: The Imperative for Educational Reform* (Washington: U.S. Department of Education, 1983), p. 22.

13. For contemporary criticism of teacher education, see C. Emily Feistritzer, *The Making of a Teacher: A Report on Teacher Education and Certification* (Washington: National Center for Education Information, 1984), and Reginald G. Damerell, *Education's Smoking Gun: How Teachers Colleges Have Destroyed Education in America* (New York: Freundlich Books, 1985). A well-balanced "inside" critique by two professors of education is *Ed School: A Brief for Professional Education* by Geraldine Joncich Clifford and James W. Guthrie (Chicago: University of Chicago Press, 1988). Two classic studies from the 1960s are James Bryant Conant's *The Education of American Teachers* (New York: McGraw-Hill, 1963) and James Koerner's *The Miseducation of American Teachers* (Boston: Houghton Mifflin, 1963). See also earlier studies cited in note 28.

14. Susan Ohanian, "On Stir-and-Serve Recipes for Teaching," *Phi Delta Kappan* 66 (June 1985): 701.

15. Ibid., pp. 697, 699, 700.
16. Holmes Group, *Tomorrow's Teachers,* pp. 3–20, 61–68; Carnegie Forum on Education and the Economy, *A Nation Prepared: Teachers for the 21st Century* (New York: Carnegie Forum, 1986), pp. 55–78.
17. Lynn Olson, "Carnegie Unveils Makeup of National Teacher Board," *Education Week* (May 20, 1987), pp. 1, 14–15, and "With Board in Place, Broader Agenda Looms," *Education Week* (May 27, 1987), pp. 1, 16.
18. Lynn Olson, "Indiana University's Status in Holmes Group Uncertain," *Education Week* (November 26, 1986), and "Holmes Group Reflects on How To Sustain Its Momentum," *Education Week* (December 9, 1987), p. 6.
19. "Teachers," *Education Week* (October 28, 1987), p. 5.
20. Holmes Group, *Tomorrow's Teachers,* p. 95.
21. Lynn Olson, "Texas Teacher Educators in Turmoil over Reform Law's 'Encroachment,' " *Education Week* (December 9, 1987), pp. 1, 19.
22. Ronald A. Lindahl and Jorge Descamps, "Texas Reforms Endanger Teacher Effectiveness," *Education Week* (November 11, 1987), pp. 28, 22.
23. Lynn Olson, "Alternative-Certification Routes Praised," *Education Week* (March 11, 1987), p. 5.
24. Blake Rodman, " 'Alternate Route' Said a Success," *Education Week* (February 24, 1988), p. 7.
25. Ibid. For a spirited exchange between a critic and the chief developer of the New Jersey plan, see Martin Haberman, "The 'New Jersey Model': Biases, Not Facts," *Education Week* (August 28, 1985), and Saul Cooperman, "Critique of the 'New Jersey Model' Falls Short in Its Predictions," *Education Week* (October 2, 1985), p. 17.
26. National Commission on Excellence in Education, *A Nation at Risk,* p. 22. Two of the most widely discussed articles in education journals were W. Timothy Weaver's "In Search of Quality: The Need for Talent in Teaching," *Phi Delta Kappan* 61 (September 1979): 29–32, 46, and Victor S. Vance and Phillip C. Schlechty's "The Distribution of Academic Ability in the Teaching Force: Policy Implications," *Phi Delta Kappan* 64 (September 1982): 22–27. For criticism in the popular press, see "Teachers Are in Trouble," *Newsweek* (April 27, 1981), pp. 78–79, 81, 83–84.
27. Several chapters in Warren's *American Teachers: Histories of a Profession at Work* highlight these points.
28. Mortimer Smith, *And Madly Teach* (Chicago: Regnery, 1949); Albert Lynd, *Quackery in the Public Schools* (Boston: Little, Brown, 1953).
29. Weaver, "In Search of Quality"; Vance and Schlechty, "The Distribution of Academic Ability in the Teaching Force"; Michael Sedlak and Steven Schlossman, *Who Will Teach? Historical Perspectives on the Changing Appeal of Teaching as a Profession* (Santa Monica, CA: Rand Corporation, November 1986).
30. Joseph W. Newman, "Reconstructing the World of Southern Teachers," *History of Education Quarterly* 24 (Winter 1984): 585–595; Patricia Albjerg Graham, "Black Teachers: A Drastically Scarce Resource," *Phi Delta Kappan* 68 (April 1987): 598–605.
31. Office of Educational Research and Improvement, U.S. Department of Education, *What's Happening in Teacher Testing: An Analysis of State Teacher Testing Practices* (Washington: U.S. Government Printing Office, 1987), pp. 1, 11–14.

32. Richard Mitchell, "Testing the Teachers: The Dallas Experiment," *Atlantic Monthly* (December 1978), pp. 66–70.
33. Office of Educational Research and Improvement, U.S. Department of Education, *What's Happening in Teacher Testing,* pp. 5, 7, 36–37.
34. William A. Mehrens and Irving J. Lehmann, *Measurement and Evaluation in Education and Psychology*, 3d ed. (New York: Holt, Rinehart and Winston, 1984), ch. 13.
35. Office of Educational Research and Improvement, U.S. Department of Education, *What's Happening in Teacher Testing,* p. 5.
36. William J. Webster, "The Validation of a Teacher Selection System," paper presented at the annual meeting of the American Educational Research Association, Boston, April 1980; Thomas S. Tocco and Jane K. Elligett, "On the Cutting Edge: The Pinellas County Teacher Applicant Screening Program," *The Board* (Winter 1980): 5.
37. Holmes Group, *Tomorrow's Teachers*, p. 4.
38. See Carnegie Forum, *A Nation Prepared*, pp. 79–87.
39. Phillip C. Schlechty and Victor S. Vance, "Institutional Responses to the Quality/Quantity Issue in Teacher Testing," *Phi Delta Kappan* 65 (October 1983): 101, and "The Distribution of Academic Ability in the Teaching Force," pp. 25, 27.
40. Patricia M. Lines, "Testing the Teacher: Are There Legal Pitfalls?" *Phi Delta Kappan* 66 (May 1985): 618–622; W. James Popham and W. N. Kirby, "Recertification Tests for Teachers: A Defensible Safeguard for Society," *Phi Delta Kappan* 69 (September 1987): 45–49; Office of Educational Research and Improvement, U.S. Department of Education, *What's Happening in Teacher Testing,* pp. 15–17; and Blake Rodman, "Testing Practicing Teachers: The Battle Nobody Really Won?" *Education Week* (March 16, 1988), pp. 1, 13.
41. For a critical look at the ETS, read Allan Nairn and associates, *The Reign of ETS: The Corporation That Makes Up Minds* (Washington: Ralph Nader Report on the Educational Testing Service, 1980). The board of trustees of ETS defends the organization in *1984 Public Accountability Report* (Princeton, NJ: ETS, 1984).
42. George F. Madaus and Diana Pullin, "Teacher Certification Tests: Do They Really Measure What We Need To Know?" *Phi Delta Kappan* 69 (September 1987): 31–38.
43. See Martha L. Bell and Catherine V. Morsink, "Quality and Equity in the Preparation of Black Teachers," *Journal of Teacher Education* 37 (March–April 1986): 17–18.
44. E. D. Hirsch, Jr., *Cultural Literacy: What Every American Needs To Know* (Boston: Houghton Mifflin, 1987); Allan Bloom, *The Closing of the American Mind* (New York: Simon and Schuster, 1987).
45. Office of Educational Research and Improvement, U.S. Department of Education, *What's Happening in Teacher Testing*, 135–138.
46. David Owen critiques multiple-choice testing in *None of the Above* (Boston: Houghton Mifflin, 1985).
47. To appreciate the struggle, read Lee S. Shulman, "Knowledge and Teaching: Foundations of the New Reform," *Harvard Educational Review* 57 (February 1987): 1–22, and Hugh T. Sockett, "Has Shulman Got the Strategy Right?" *Harvard Educational Review* 57 (May 1987): 208–219.
48. Linda Darling-Hammond, "Teaching Knowledge: How Do We Test It?" *American Educator* 10 (Fall 1986): 18–21, 46.

49. Ibid.
50. Lynn Olson, "E.T.S. To Initiate Anti-Bias Effort in Teacher Tests," *Education Week* (May 28 1986), pp. 1, 17, and " 'Different' Tests of Teaching Skill Planned by Firm," *Education Week* (November 2, 1988), pp. 1, 27.
51. Blake Rodman, "Alabama Board Expected to Appeal Ruling in Teacher-Testing Case," *Education Week* (December 10, 1986), pp. 5, 11; "Board Dumps Teacher Test," *Mobile Register* (July 13, 1988), p. 2B.
52. John Hope Franklin, "The Desperate Need for Black Teachers," *Change* 19 (May/June 1987): 44–45; Barbara J. Holmes, "Do Not Buy the Conventional Wisdom: Minority Teachers Can Pass the Tests," *Journal of Negro Education* 55 (Summer 1986): 335–346.
53. Graham, "Black Teachers," pp. 599, 605.
54. "New Data Show More Minorities Going to College," *Education Week* (March 9, 1988), p. 15; Graham, "Black Teachers," pp. 605, 602.
55. Graham, "Black Teachers," p. 600; "Update," *Education Week* (September 10, 1986), p. 23; "Board Dumps Teacher Test."
56. Graham, "Black Teachers," p. 601.
57. Ibid., pp. 603–604; Blake Rodman, "At Grambling: 'Fighting the Scores instead of the Tests,' " *Education Week* (November 20, 1985), p. 13.
58. Carnegie Forum, *A Nation Prepared*, p. 66.
59. Ibid.
60. For an insightful essay comparing the development of professionalism in medicine and teaching, see William R. Johnson, "Empowering Practitioners: Holmes, Carnegie, and the Lessons of the Past," *History of Education Quarterly* 27 (Summer 1987): 221–240.

CHAPTER 4

Joining a Teacher Organization and Empowering a Profession

In the first three chapters, I have tried to paint a realistic picture of teaching as an occupation. As you can see, the picture is not exactly rosy. America's teachers have their share of problems. The idealism and commitment that new teachers bring to their work can vanish in the face of low salaries, poor working conditions, public doubts about teacher competency, and lingering questions about teacher education. As I keep pointing out, however, a realistic assessment of the occupation does not have to be a hopeless assessment. Taking an honest look at their mutual problems encourages many teachers to seek solutions by working together in teacher organizations.

One of the first decisions you will make as a public school teacher will be whether to join one of the two major organizations, the National Education Association (NEA) and American Federation of Teachers (AFT). This chapter opens with a look at their similarities and differences and continues with a discussion of their strategies. Both the NEA and the AFT use *collective bargaining* and *political action* in their efforts to upgrade teaching as an occupation, and therein lies one of the great controversies of public education.

If you talk with people about the AFT and NEA, you will find that few teachers (or other informed citizens, for that matter) have a neutral opinion about them. The reason is that the organizations have a clear vision of what they want, and they pursue their vision aggressively. The AFT and NEA have helped shatter the "Miss Dove" and "Mr. Chips" images of teachers as beloved servants. They would like to replace it with an image of teachers as competent professionals. No popular characters from books or the electronic media have completely captured that image, for teachers are still in the process of creating it.

Bringing the professional teacher to life will require a complete restructuring of the occupation, and that exactly is what the NEA and AFT are trying to do. They do not use the word *professional* lightly. They want to win for teachers the rights and responsibilities that society now reserves for doctors, lawyers, and members of a few other occupations. To some people, making teaching a profession represents the best hope for improving the public schools; to others it is educational heresy. In the conclusion of this chapter we will explore why the goal of professionalism is so controversial and why it has eluded teachers for so many years.

NEA AND AFT

Throughout most of this century, the NEA and AFT have been in competition to organize America's teachers. Until the 1960s the two groups were quite different. The NEA was a large, mild-mannered "professional association" that was better at collecting information, issuing reports, and talking about teachers' problems than taking action to solve them; the AFT was a small, scrappy "union" that was trying hard but making little progress toward improving teachers' salaries, benefits, and working conditions. Things changed during the 1960s and 1970s as the long-standing rivalry between the two organizations intensified. The AFT's militant tactics began making sense to more teachers, its membership figures soared, and the NEA's "tea sipping" ways seemed behind the times. Since then the organizations have become much more alike— that is to say, the NEA has become militant too—but several key differences remain, differences that have been significant enough to keep the two from merging.[1]

Before we look at how the organizations differ, though, it is important to emphasize how much they have in common. Today both the AFT and the NEA are unions whose major goals are increasing the economic security of public school teachers and improving their working conditions. Both groups pursue these goals by looking after teachers' interests in the political area and, in most states, by representing teachers in collective bargaining sessions with school boards. Both are also professional associations that take stands on a variety of issues that affect students, teachers, and public education generally, and the issues range from academic standards to teacher education to the federal budget. Convinced that a stronger teacher voice in *all* educational decisions can only improve the schools, both groups believe in teacher power. Above all, the AFT and NEA say they are trying to make public school teaching a true profession.

But these similarities obscure important differences. First there is the matter of size. The NEA has about 1,900,000 members, the AFT about 700,000. The NEA, the largest union/employee organization/professional association of any kind in the world, argues that its size gives it more clout; the AFT, pointing to its dramatic recent growth—more than 10 times as large today as in 1960—claims to represent the wave of the future. Both recruit members from outside the ranks of teachers, encouraging paraprofessionals, support personnel, college professors, and others who work in the field of education to join, but more than 70 percent of the members in both organizations are classroom teachers. Overall, the NEA has organized about 60 percent of America's public school teachers, the AFT about 20 percent.[2]

Whether you join the AFT or NEA (or neither) may well depend on where you teach, for the second difference between the two organizations is their geographical strength. The AFT is essentially a big-city union, while the NEA dominates in suburban, small-town, and rural America. The AFT, as a member of the American Federation of Labor-Congress of Industrial Organizations (AFL-CIO), the umbrella labor organization in the United States, has always been most successful where the labor movement is strongest and best established—in such major cities as New York, Chicago, Pittsburgh, Cleveland, Detroit, and St. Louis. Even though the AFT now has about 2,500 local affiliates or "locals" (a good union word) and 22 state federations, there are so few members in some school systems—indeed, in some entire states—that the organization has virtually no power there.

The NEA, by contrast, has state associations in every state and more than 10,000 local affiliates, most of which now call themselves locals. The NEA boasts of its grass roots strength throughout the United States, proud that it has brought together more than half of the nation's highly diverse teaching force in one organization. Doing so has been no easy task. While the AFT has always required teachers to become local, state (if possible), and national members, the NEA has required "unified" membership only since the 1970s. Some of the NEA's state and local associations are well over a century old, and many teachers maintain stronger loyalties to their state and local associations than the national. Some NEA members try to distance themselves from the national association, complaining that the NEA's politics are "too liberal" or its policies "too militant." The unified NEA is powerful, to be sure, but the diversity of which it is so proud can be a source of weakness as well as strength.[3]

The third difference between the organizations lies in their official positions on key issues. Although both make policy democratically—delegates elected in the locals come together in national summer conventions to confer, debate, and vote—since the mid-1970s the NEA has been more willing than the AFT to take stands on broad social and political issues that, while not strictly educational, have an impact on the schools. These "human and civil rights issues" range from family planning to gun control to nuclear war. Most of the NEA's stands are considered liberal, which is ironic since the NEA has historically had the reputation of a moderate-to-conservative association while the AFT has been the liberal-to-radical union.[4]

Before the 1960s, for example, the NEA dragged its feet on race relations; it did not merge with the all-black American Teachers Association until 1966, and some of the NEA's state and local affiliates in the South remained segregated until the late 1970s. The AFT, on the other hand, went on record in support of desegregation well before the landmark *Brown* decision (1954) and required its locals to desegregate in 1956. Standing history on its head, today's NEA is one of the nation's strongest advocates of minority rights—including affirmative action—while the AFT is moving to the middle of the road.[5]

On educational issues, the two organizations agree far more often than they disagree, but during the 1980s several important differences emerged. As the conservative tide that swept the nation reached the schools, the NEA dug in its heels and stuck to its long-standing opposition to merit pay and competency tests for currently employed teachers, while the AFT has been willing to compromise. As we saw in the last chapter, the AFT is more supportive of the Carnegie and Holmes recommendations on how to restructure teaching as an occupation. Regarding trends in the public school curriculum, the NEA has been sharply critical of the heavy emphasis on standardized testing, arguing that it denies a quality education to many students—especially those "at risk." The AFT accepts more emphasis on testing as a necessary part of the drive toward "excellence in education," although the union admits that testing can be overdone. Overall, the NEA takes a skeptical—some would say obstructionist—view of many recent educational reforms, while the AFT takes a hopeful—some would say opportunistic—view.

Relations with the larger labor movement, an issue we have discussed briefly, is important enough to deserve separate consideration as a fourth difference between the NEA and AFT. Since its founding in 1857 as the National Teachers' Association, the NEA has been quite status conscious, billing itself as "professional" in an attempt to distinguish teachers from mere "workers." Thus, until recently, the NEA steered clear of organized labor. The AFT, by contrast, has been affiliated with the American Federation of Labor since just after the AFT's founding in 1916. The AFT has always insisted that teachers are workers who aspire to be professionals. Joining a union and casting their lot with other workers does not make teachers less professional, according to the AFT. Teachers and other workers can find strength in numbers in their mutual quest for better salaries, benefits, and working conditions, and the labor movement can support teachers as they try to gain the control over their occupation that doctors and lawyers have over theirs.

Until the 1960s few teachers paid much attention to the AFT's calls to organize. The NEA effectively exploited antilabor sentiment, telling teachers they would be stooping to the level of blue collar workers if they joined the AFT, "that labor union." Even after the NEA itself began using the tactics of organized labor, the association was reluctant to sew the union label into its jacket. Frankly, many NEA members are still uncomfortable with the label, especially those who live where organized labor is unpopular. But the NEA *is* a union, recognized as such by the U.S. Department of Labor. The NEA is also a member of the Coalition of American Public Employees (CAPE), an organization whose major goal is winning collective bargaining rights for all public employees. Thus the NEA has, in a sense, joined the labor movement, but it refuses to join the AFL-CIO, arguing that doing so would compromise its independence. The AFT, for its part, refuses to leave the AFL-CIO, and this difference has frustrated efforts to merge the NEA and AFT.[6]

This list of differences was once much longer. One difference that has lost much of its significance is the NEA's willingness to admit school administrators as members. Throughout most of the NEA's history its administrative members, although only a small fraction of the association's total, aligned themselves with the even smaller group of college professors and effectively ran the show. The NEA's internal structure virtually duplicated the larger structure of public education: a few administrators, mostly males, held sway over a large number of teachers, mostly females. The men who ran the NEA were the same men who ran the public schools. Most teachers joined the association not because they wanted to but because their superintendents and principals said to. Until power began to shift away from administrators in the 1960s, the NEA was not really a *teacher* organization. Since then, classroom teachers have taken control of the NEA. As the organization has grown militant on "bread-and-butter" issues—another good union term encompassing salaries, benefits, and working conditions—many administrators have grown uneasy and left. Most of those who remain play minor roles.[7]

This changing of the guard has been a source of much amusement to the AFT, which classroom teachers have always controlled. Like other unions, the AFT draws a line between managers and workers, arguing that their outlook, interests, and work are fundamentally different. Teachers cannot be expected to stand up for their rights in an organization controlled by their bosses, the AFT reasons. Only recently has the NEA come around to this adversary point of view, and some members still find it hard to accept. In many rural and small-town systems, administrators still encourage teachers to join "our professional association, the NEA." In these systems administrators and teachers often have a comfortable if paternalistic relationship, and teacher militancy is something that takes place only in the newspapers. The point to remember is that although the days when administrators dominated the NEA and required teachers to join are gone, rural and small-town school systems are still a world apart from Chicago and New York.

Joining the NEA or AFT means different things in different systems. In some it is a statement of militant professionalism; in others, an expression of concern with bread-and-butter issues; in others, a means of self-protection; in still others, "just the thing to do." As a new teacher you should find out what the organizations stand for in your state and your school system. If both groups are viable and actively competing for members, find out what one can do for you that the other cannnot. You will probably discover that both are proud, and justly so, of what they have won for teachers through local, state, and national political activity. Ask questions about what they have done about salaries, class sizes, preparation periods, noninstructional duties, and other matters that will affect your life as a teacher every day.

As you listen to their recruitment pitches, you will discover that both organizations offer their members a wide range of services. The NEA publishes *Today's Education, NEA Today, NEA Research Bulletin,* and numerous other periodicals, while the AFT's publications include *American Educator* and *American Teacher.* Although the NEA is more involved in research and publication at the national level, members of both groups receive a variety of materials from their state and local organizations. State and local newsletters often contain information of immediate concern to teachers: job market news, recent court decisions, the status of education bills in the legislature, activities in the local schools, and so forth.

Both the AFT and NEA offer their members life and supplemental health insurance and, more importantly, liability insurance that provides protection in lawsuits arising from job-related activities. Often one of the first things a new teacher hears from NEA and AFT representatives is, "You'll wish you were a member if a student has an accident in your classroom and you get sued." As we will see in Chapter 5, that message is fair warning, but it sometimes puts off teachers who think such things happen only to other people. Both organizations will tell you that their local, state, and national dues, which usually total between $200 and $300 per year, are a sound investment. Ask for specific ways in which the investment has paid dividends. Something AFT and NEA representatives will certainly discuss with you in most school systems is collective bargaining, for both organizations would like to be your bargaining agent in negotiations with school boards.

COLLECTIVE BARGAINING

Seated on one side of a long, narrow table are representatives of the teachers in a school system. Facing them across the table are representatives of the board of education. At issue is the master contract for the system's teachers, a thick document of more than one-hundred pages, and today the discussion is focused on the starting salary for new teachers. Reminding the board of spreading teacher shortages and the importance of attracting bright people to teaching, the teacher representatives ask for a raise of $1,000. The board representatives reply that they are well aware of the supply-and-demand situation, but they are also aware of the tight budget. A thousand dollars? Extravagant. Out of the question. Two hundred would be more like it. The negotiations wear on into the evening and into the days and nights that follow. No one is completely satisfied with the compromise raise of $450, but both sides feel the pressure to work through the rest of the contract, which spells out teacher salaries, benefits, working conditions, and grievance procedures in great detail.

Most of America's public school teachers bargain with their school boards in sessions similar to this one. About one-third of the states have laws that mandate a collective bargaining process borrowed directly from labor-management relations. Teacher representatives and board representatives must hammer out an agreement on the terms of a contract, and if they are unable to do so there are provisions for resolving the impasse. Another one-third of the states specify a milder form of bargaining that requires school boards to "meet and confer" with teachers. Here board members must listen to teachers in a formal session, but the boards retain the decision-making power. The remaining states have no laws on collective bargaining in the public schools, but some local boards in these states negotiate with teachers on a limited basis. Only one state, North Carolina, prohibits collective bargaining for teachers.[8]

The AFT pioneered collective bargaining in public education. In fact, the AFT's success with the practice accounts for much of the organization's recent growth. In the late 1950s the AFT mounted an organizing campaign in the New York City schools in an effort to get the union moving again. At the time, New York's 50,000 teachers were splintered into a bewildering array of organizations according to their subjects and grade levels. The AFT's strategy, engineered by former high school teacher Albert Shanker and other experienced union leaders, was to hit hard on bread-and-butter issues common to all teachers, bring them together in a single unit, and win the right to bargain collectively with the board of education. After a bitter struggle punctuated by a one-day strike in November 1960, the board agreed to a collective bargaining election. In 1961 New York's teachers endorsed bargaining by a 3-to-1 margin and voted to be represented by AFT Local 2, the United Federation of Teachers, giving the local the right to bargain for the city's entire teaching force.[9]

The AFT's victory went into the record books as a turning point in the history of teacher organizations. Teacher militancy spread quickly, first to other big cities and then beyond. During the 1960s and 1970s the AFT grew four times as fast as the NEA. Albert Shanker went on to become president of the AFT, an office he still holds. The NEA had to take notice. After first trying to dismiss the AFT's militancy as "unprofessional," the NEA gradually followed suit. Today both organizations believe collective bargaining, combined with political action, offers the best hope for better salaries, benefits, and working conditions. Both groups also regard the combination of bargaining and politics as the best strategy for professionalizing public school teaching.[10]

The mechanics of collective bargaining are not difficult to understand. First, the teachers in a school system choose a union to represent them. Usually the teachers vote by secret ballot; in other cases they fill out authorization cards, or the locals competing for representation submit membership lists. The union that wins the support of the majority of teachers becomes the exclusive bargaining agent for all teachers in the system. (Some states allow the school board to negotiate with more than one local representing teachers, but this procedure is rare because it is time consuming and divisive.) The exclusive bargaining agent has the obligation to represent every teacher fairly—a tall order, since some teachers may be members of a rival union and some of no union. Most states have regulations to insure that the bargaining union takes the interests of both members and nonmembers into account.[11]

In some states with a strong union tradition, *agency shop* contracts may require teachers who are not members of the bargaining union to pay the local a fee, generally the same amount as union dues. This fee reimburses the local for its work as the teachers' bargaining agent. "Compulsory unionism!" some teachers charge, arguing that the regulations force them in effect to join the union whether they want to or not, running roughshod over their freedom of choice. Prounionists reply that since the local is obligated to negotiate on behalf of all teachers, and since nonmembers and members alike reap the benefits won through bargaining, all teachers should share the costs. Although the U.S. Supreme Court has ruled that agency shop regulations are constitutional, the National Right to Work Committee, through its branch the Concerned Educators against Forced Unionism, has mobilized to fight them.[12]

Once teachers have selected their bargaining agent, both the union and the school board choose negotiating teams. In small school systems a team of teachers (often the officers of the union) sits down at the table and talks directly with members of the board. In many systems administrators are part of the board's team. As unions and boards become more sophisticated with collective bargaining, both usually seek the advice of lawyers who specialize in labor-management relations. The larger the school system, the more likely that both sides call in even more outside help, with unions looking to their state and national offices, and boards to their state and national associations. Both sides may also employ professional negotiators.

What they negotiate—the scope of collective bargaining—varies considerably from system to system and state to state, but salaries, benefits, and working conditions are the bottom line. Some union leaders are content to negotiate bread and butter issues, for they know that many "rank-and-file" teachers (yet another union term) want their bargaining agent to deliver the economic goods, period. Other leaders with broader goals envision the day when collective bargaining will give teachers a voice in virtually every policy decision in the public schools, from the content of the curriculum to teacher evaluation plans. As we will see later in this chapter, the vision of these leaders is becoming a reality in some school systems. The eyes of teacher unionists throughout the nation are on the contracts recently negotiated in Rochester, New York, and Dade County, Florida, contracts that empower teachers with some of the rights and responsibilities that Carnegie and Holmes recommend. There is even talk of collective bargaining entering a new phase as teachers, administrators, and board members share power voluntarily, emphasizing cooperation rather than confrontation.[13]

To teachers in school systems that do not bargain at all, however, this vision seems remote indeed. Rochester, New York, and Raleigh, North Carolina, are two different worlds. Tough political battles lie ahead for teacher unionists who want to expand the scope of negotiations and extend bargaining rights to more teachers. The AFT and NEA support federal legislation that would allow every public school teacher in the nation to bargain. Opponents counter that such a law would violate states' rights and hand over control of public education to teacher unions.

But collective bargaining seems destined to stay, to expand, and eventually to involve teacher unions and school boards throughout the nation in the process of give and take. More often than not, the process is long and slow. Occasional flashes of insight and humor lighten up the tedious deliberations. Usually the process results in a new contract that all board members and all teachers have the right to examine and ratify. If the two sides reach an impasse at the table, however, most states have laws that outline steps for breaking the deadlock. The first step is typically mediation, in which a neutral third party makes suggestions in an attempt to promote a compromise. The mediator, whose recommendations are usually not made public, cannot mandate a solution. If mediation fails, fact finding is a second step. After both sides argue their case before a fact-finding panel, the panel usually goes public with a set of recommendations, putting pressure on the board and union to agree, but the fact finders cannot dictate an agreement. Under binding arbitration, a third step in some states, the two sides agree to give a third party, chosen by mutual consent, the power to investigate their dispute and impose a solution.[14]

TEACHER STRIKES

Unions, bargaining, and strikes go together in the public mind. When students return to school every fall, the news media run stories about teacher strikes, usually playing up those staged by AFT locals in big city systems. "Do Chicago teachers strike every year?" one of my students asked me recently (and quite seriously). As many people see the situation, unions strike when they cannot get their way at the bargaining table, causing employers and often the public to suffer. This analysis overlooks the fact that teachers who do not have collective bargaining rights also go on strike. A rash of teacher strikes broke out during the years of rapid inflation that followed World War II, well before the rise of collective bargaining in public education, and some strikes still occur in schools systems that do not bargain. In fact, teachers in such systems argue that requiring board members to sit down, listen, and negotiate might well prevent strikes. To be sure, the AFT made its breakthrough in the 1960s by bargaining, threatening to strike, and in some cases carrying out its threats, but bargaining is not the *cause* of strikes.[15]

Instead, teacher frustration with low salaries and poor working conditions, aggravated by a sense of powerlessness, made teachers turn to collective bargaining in the first place and to strikes as a last resort. The state of the economy has played a major role; teacher strikes peaked during the double-digit inflation of the late 1970s and early 1980s, when increases in the cost of living far outstripped increases in teacher salaries. In the year 1979–80 alone, affiliates of the AFT staged 34 strikes and NEA affiliates struck 208 times. Since then, with lower inflation and better raises, teacher strikes have decreased to fewer than 100 per year, with most called by the NEA. The conservative national mood of the 1980s, which spawned a get-tough-with-unions attitude, has also made teachers less wiling to strike. Given the more than 15,000 school systems in the United States, even 250 strikes per year can hardly be called a runaway problem. Teachers, like other public employees, are aware of how much is at stake when they strike.[16]

Strikes are risky under any circumstances. They are literally desperate measures. In most states teacher strikes are against the law, and the U.S. Supreme Court has ruled that school boards can fire teachers who engage in illegal strikes. Judges can levy fines against unions and individual teachers who strike illegally; in rare instances striking teachers find themselves in jail. Strikes can also alienate parents and the general public. Beyond these problems, teachers face an ethical question when they strike. Can they justify denying students the opportunity to learn?[17]

Rest assured that teachers who decide to strike do think seriously about these issues. Striking teachers gamble that the school board will not fire large numbers of teachers because of the difficulty of finding replacements. In some cases teachers are willing to take the risk because they have community support. Conditions are so bad in some school systems that parents and other citizens side with teachers against the board. Other unions sometimes lend their support, especially if an AFT local is on strike.

Ethically, some teachers believe the short-term losses for students are outweighed by long-term gains for the whole school system. As the AFT and NEA like to point out, better salaries and benefits attract better teachers, and improving teachers' working conditions also improves students' learning conditions. If school boards force teachers to strike to reach those goals, the unions reason, then so be it.[18]

POLITICAL ACTION

A less dangerous if nearly as controversial strategy for attaining the same goals is political action. Public schools in the United States have always been involved in politics. Tax revenues support the schools, and public officials govern the schools. When administrators controlled the NEA, the association engaged in "dignified" political activity, lobbying Congress for federal aid to education and other measures. The NEA's state affiliates worked quietly with legislatures and school boards to secure tenure laws, retirement benefits, and health and sick leave provisions. The AFT also lobbied Congress, and some of its locals were deeply involved in city and state politics. Leaders of the more powerful AFT locals—such as Chicago, New York, and Atlanta—mastered the political arts only to encounter opposition from both the public and their own members. Many citizens argued, and some teachers agreed, that it was undignified and unprofessional for teacher organizations to engage in politics, if that meant such things as supporting candidates for office and taking stands on political issues.[19]

But since the 1970s the NEA and AFT have done exactly that. Undignified behavior? Not unless the entire way we govern ourselves in the United States is undignified, teacher unionists reply. Politics is the name of the game, and during the 1970s teachers realized that the members of almost every organized occupational group were playing the game. Some groups—doctors, lawyers, farmers, manufacturers—had been playing it seriously and successfully for years. Unprofessional behavior? Quite the contrary, say the unionists, for teachers are using politics to win more control over their occupation, and control is the very essence of professionalism.

In 1976 the NEA made national headlines by supporting the Democratic ticket of Jimmy Carter and Walter Mondale, the NEA's first endorsement in a presidential race. After the election Carter kept his promise to push for a cabinet-level department of education and more federal funding for education. During the 1970s the NEA and AFT waded into Congressional politics as well, endorsing candidates for the U.S. Senate and House of Representatives. Both organizations stepped up their activity in state and local politics. Both formed national, state, and local political action committees—PACs—to raise money through members' voluntary contributions. Every year the teacher PACS collect several million dollars to support endorsed candidates. The NEA-PAC alone contributes more than $2,000,000 annually to candidates for federal office, ranking it third in the nation behind the National Association of Realtors PAC and the American Medical Association (AMA) PAC.[20]

It should come as no surprise that most of the candidates the NEA and AFT endorse are moderate-to-liberal and Democratic, for such politicians tend to be prounion and willing to "invest in public education," a nice way of saying they are willing to spend more money on the schools. During the 1980s the NEA and AFT stuck with Democratic presidential tickets despite losses to Republicans Ronald Reagan and George Bush. The unions fared better in Congressional elections: more than 70 percent of the candidates the NEA endorsed, for example, were elected. The NEA boasts that it has an average of 6,000 members in each Congressional district—a formidable political force.[21]

Does this mean that every teacher unionist is a moderate-to-liberal Democrat and votes accordingly? No. Teachers have diverse political views and party affiliations, and polls suggest that almost as many teachers voted for Reagan and Bush as for their Democratic opponents. But bread-and-butter issues are usually the decisive factors in political endorsements, just as they are in collective bargaining. Faced with one candidate committed to cutting taxes and reducing government spending for social programs and another candidate more willing to raise taxes and increase spending, the NEA and AFT have little difficulty choosing the latter.[22]

Today both organizations are digging in at the grassroots level, paying more attention than ever to local school board, state school board, state legislative, and gubernatorial races. AFT and NEA locals invite candidates to screening sessions in which teachers ask point-blank questions: How will you vote on teacher salary increases? On raising retirement benefits? Where do you stand on agency shop regulations? On raising state taxes? Based on the candidates' answers, teachers vote whether or not to make an endorsement in the various races and decide how much to contribute to each endorsed candidate.

After attending one such session I was impressed with how forceful the teachers were and how polite the candidates—would-be state legislators—were. After the candidates had gone, a frank discussion took place, the teachers voted, and the treasurer of the local association sat down to write out the checks. Weren't teachers simply buying politicians, I asked several members? They replied that the candidates were "making the rounds. Last night they went to the chamber of commerce; tomorrow night they'll be at the medical association; next week they'll visit the labor council and farm bureau. Why should teachers sit on the sidelines when everyone else is playing the game?"

Teacher organizations see political action and collective bargaining as complementary strategies—both are roads to power. Teachers exercise power indirectly by endorsing political candidates and lobbying in Congress and state legislatures. Teachers wield power directly when they bargain with school boards. Both strategies are controversial because they give power to a group that historically has had little.

Discussions of teacher power inevitably lead to questions about professionalism. What are the characteristics of a profession? To what degree does teaching have those characteristics? Will political action and collective bargaining make teaching more professional? The next section explores these questions.

A TEACHING PROFESSION?

Because *profession* has such a nice ring, people use the word in a variety of ways. The question "What is your profession?" may simply mean "What kind of work do you do?" Some people use "professional" in an attempt to add status and prestige to an occupation. Thus we hear of professional entertainers and professional secretaries. To other people, a professional is anyone who excels in a particular occupation—a highly professional mechanic or salesperson, for example. If we apply more stringent criteria, however, only a few occupations qualify as professions. Medicine, law, and theology are the oldest and most familiar; originally they were called the learned professions. Dentistry, architecture, and engineering are among the other occupations that have established themselves as professions.[23]

Developments in medicine and law over the last 150 years have set the modern standards for professionalism, but only in this century have doctors and lawyers become fully professional, organizing and controlling their occupations in ways that distinguish them from other types of work. Based on comparative studies of many occupations, sociologists have developed a set of characteristics to define the professions. They have paid particular attention to medicine, often referring to it as the "prototype" profession because medicine exhibits the characteristics to a greater degree than any other occupation. We can distill the discussion of professionalism in the sociological literature to a set of three major characteristics:.

1. A profession performs a unique, essential service for society.
2. A profession has a defined body of knowledge.
3. A profession has autonomy.[24]

You have probably noticed that throughout this textbook I avoid referring to teaching as a profession. I call it an occupation. My choice of words does not reflect a lack of respect for teaching—I respect it immensely—but rather the fact that teaching does not possess the characteristics of professionalism to the extent that medicine, law, and several other occupations do. Teaching does, however, exhibit the characteristics to a greater degree than most lines of work, prompting some to call teaching—along with nursing and social work—a *semi-profession* or, more optimistically, an *emerging profession*. Terminology is important. I am careful with my choice of words because I want them to remind you that teachers will have to make fundamental changes in their occupation if they want to make it more professional.

Our discussion of professionalism pulls together many of the main issues from the preceding chapters, touching on supply and demand, salaries, teacher competency, and teacher education. The key to professionalism, though, is the role that teachers themselves must play. Doctors and lawyers moved their occupations along the road to professionalism by taking collective action through the AMA and the American Bar Association (ABA). Many teachers believe they can professionalize their occupation by working together through the NEA, the AFT, or a merged organization.

A Unique, Essential Social Service

The first characteristic of a profession suggests that society regards some work as so vital—healing the sick is the best example—that it gives the members of one occupation exclusive rights to perform the work. Society allows the profession to "corner the market," in other words, to insure that the service is available at a high level of quality. Society must regard the service as essential, and it must be convinced that only the members of the profession can render the service to acceptable standards. Otherwise, society will not grant a monopoly for performing the service.[25]

Certainly Americans believe that teaching young people is an essential task, and society has given one occupational group, public school teachers, a monopoly of sorts in public education. As we saw in Chapter 3, standards for teacher education and certification vary considerably around the nation, but a person cannot teach in the public schools of any state without first obtaining a certificate from the state. The certificate may be issued on an emergency or provisional basis, but it is required nonetheless. Teaching in private schools is another matter. Most states do not require private school teachers, who make up about 15 percent of the nation's teaching force, to meet state education and certification standards. This situation opens a loophole without parallel in medicine, law, and most other professions. As we will see in Chapter 11, there are some good arguments against state regulation of private schools and their teachers. On the other hand, our society would not tolerate two classes of physicians—one licensed by the state, the other unlicensed, but both doing the same work—because we regard medicine as so important that we cannot entrust it to unlicensed practitioners.

But teaching? Many people believe that almost anyone can do it. Parents teach their children, after all, and most people have taught on the job, in church, or in a similar situation. Can teaching be so complex that only one occupational group, people with state certification based on an approved teacher education program, can perform the service? Many Americans answer no. Teacher education has a poor reputation, and state officials are quite willing to water down certification requirements when teacher shortages hit. Such factors make it difficult to argue that one group should have exclusive rights to teach in the public schools, much less that their rights should extend to private schools.

Although public school teachers and private school teachers will probably never become a unified professional group, promising developments that relate to the first characteristic of professionalism are underway. In the last chapter I expressed cautious optimism about teacher education and certification for public school teachers. Higher standards are sending the message that not just anyone can teach. The recommendations of the Holmes Group and Carnegie Forum for completely restructuring the occupation hold great promise. They deserve a fair trial. By allowing people with no formal teacher training to enter the occupation on its lowest rungs, however, are Holmes and Carnegie sending a mixed message? If bright people with just arts and sciences degrees can teach, the states may ignore the rest of the Holmes-Carnegie recommendations—especially the costly ones—and simply open New Jersey shortcuts (described in Chapter 3) into teaching. Why go to the extra trouble and expense? Citizens hear mixed signals. Not just anyone can teach, to be sure, but on the other hand the job requires little or no specialized training. Perhaps anyone who is intelligent and liberally educated can teach. And back we go to the nineteenth-century debates over teacher education.

A Defined Body of Knowledge

America's continuing uncertainty about these issues relates also to the second characteristic of a profession, a defined body of knowledge. Professionals have expertise not shared by the general public. People recognize that a body of knowledge called "the law" exists, for example, and they recognize attorneys as experts in the law. Professionals acquire their knowledge in specialized training programs, usually in graduate-level university programs. Bar examinations for lawyers, like similar examinations in other professions, assure the public that professionals are in command of their knowledge before they enter practice.[26]

Teaching does not fare well on this characteristic. The controversy over teacher education haunts the occupation here, too. Both inside and outside of universities, there is little agreement on the knowledge that teachers must master. One of the most damaging aspects of the controversy, as we have seen, is that teachers themselves belittle their training in education. Once they begin teaching they tend to ignore their training and to improvise, learning far more on the job, they say, than from their undergraduate and graduate education courses. The lawsuits over state certification examinations reflect the lack of consensus on what teachers need to know.

In this area of professionalism, just as in the first one, so much is riding on the outcome of the Carnegie and Holmes experiments. *If* they are successful, they may allow teaching to put some of its ghosts to rest. Every teacher will be able to claim expertise in a recognized academic discipline. Every teacher who moves up the career ladder will receive graduate-level training with a strong clinical emphasis. But is the body of knowledge about teaching strong enough to support such a program? And what, exactly, is the role of Carnegie's National Board for Professional Teaching Standards in defining the professional knowlege base? As I pointed out in the last chapter, medicine developed a knowledge base that actually worked *before* devising tests to measure it. In teaching, we are putting the cart before the horse if we expect a national board to devise tests before we have agreed on what works and what doesn't. The consensus on knowledge must come first, *then* the tests. It is encouraging, however, that teachers themselves have the strongest voice on the national board.

Autonomy

The words "teachers themselves," which I am using frequently in this discussion, hold the key to professionalism in teaching. Autonomy, the third characteristic of a profession, is the right of the members of an occupation to make their own decisions and use their own judgment. The members themselves are in charge. Professionals have two kinds of autonomy: individual and group. As individuals, professionals have the right to perform their work as they see fit, based on knowledge acquired through specialized training. Doctors, for example, enjoy a wide range of autonomy in their daily work. Society trusts them to make one decision after another as they diagnose their patients' illnesses and prescribe appropriate treatments. Doctors may turn to their colleagues for help and advice, but they do not have to check with a boss or supervisor before they act.[27]

As a group, doctors control their occupation through a network of state and national boards that set standards for medical education, licensing, and practice. Group autonomy is a relatively recent development in medicine. Although the AMA was founded in 1846, it took the organization three-quarters of a century to win doctors the right to regulate themselves. In the late 1800s medical education was notoriously poor. Licensing was a sham. "Quacks" were an embarrassment to competent physicians and a danger to people seeking medical care.[28]

Then a series of developments turned the occupation around. Over the course of several decades, scientific medicine gradually won acceptance among doctors. Because scientific medicine worked, doctors became willing to attend university medical schools to learn how to practice. This revolution in knowledge and training was already underway when the Carnegie Foundation for the Advancement of Teaching published *Medical Education in the United States and Canada* in 1910. Popularly known as the Flexner Report, this study was a call to continue upgrading the occupation. The Flexner Report capped—not caused—the trend toward scientific medicine. The report's greatest value was as a political document, for the AMA was able to use it to convince Congress and the state legislatures that doctors should control their occupation. Give doctors the right to regulate themselves, the AMA promised, and they will give the nation better medical care. The AMA fought and won its political battles, and medicine became a self-regulating profession with the AMA as its major professional association. Along the way the AMA also became one of the nation's most effective "unions," highly successful at safeguarding its members' interests.[29]

The lesson for teachers is that while there are good reasons to be optimistic about the prospects for professionalism, teachers have a long way to go in their quest for autonomy. Consider this old saying among teachers: "I may have to follow school board policies and take orders from the principal, but when I close the classroom door I'm in charge." To a degree, this statement is true—or rather was true. Until the late 1970s, teachers did indeed have a fair amount of individual autonomy, at least informally. They were able to use the teaching methods they thought appropriate, administer the tests they had designed, and grade students using their best judgment. Being able to work with relatively little direct supervision, escaping bureaucracy by closing the door, was one of the most attractive features of the occupation.

The back-to-basics movement and minimum competency testing changed the situation drastically, ushering in an era of standardized teaching, testing, and grading. Teachers now feel pressure from their bosses, school board members and administrators, to teach by the cookbook. As we will find in Chapter 10, the cookbook—often called an instructional pacing guide—tells them what to teach, how to teach it, when to teach it, and which tests to use to measure how much students have learned. One teacher recently joked with me that "the pacing guide tells us everything but when to go to the restroom, and that will probably be covered in next year's edition." The sad truth is that teachers have lost rather than gained individual autonomy. Backed into a corner, teachers in some school systems are fighting back with collective bargaining, trying to carve out areas in which they can use their judgment. Local unions now find themselves having to negotiate for a stronger teacher voice in student promotion, a decision that once rested entirely with teachers themselves.

Teachers have never had much group autonomy, which is another way of saying that teachers have never won the right to control their occupation. One reason is that most teachers are public employees, paid with public money, while most doctors and lawyers are in private practice, paid by their clients on a fee-for-service basis. (Predictably, as the public pays a larger share of the nation's medical bills, doctors rail against creeping government restrictions on their autonomy.) The public tries to regulate what it pays for, to be sure, but something more fundamental is involved in public education: a long tradition of state and local governance, grounded in the belief that citizens should control "their" schools. Given this tradition, we must face the fact that teachers will never have the group autonomy of doctors or lawyers.

PRESSING TOWARD PROFESSIONALISM

Victory for the NEA in Nevada

Teacher organizations are quick to point out, however, that the public regulates every profession to some degree. The task that lies ahead in teaching, as the NEA and AFT see it, is finding a way to balance public power and teacher power. In setting standards for teacher education and certification, teacher organizations want teachers to have more, but obviously not absolute, autonomy. In typical fashion, the NEA and AFT are pursuing the goal differently. The NEA is using its clout in state politics to push for *professional standards boards*, commissions with the authority to set standards for educating and certifying teachers. These boards include classroom teachers as voting members. Although state boards of education already consult with teachers on such matters—most boards, in fact, have teacher advisory councils—the NEA looks forward to the day when teachers themselves can actually vote on the standards rather than merely give advice. The NEA's ultimate goal is a professional standards board in every state, with teachers holding a majority of the votes on each one. Beginning in the late 1960s, California, Minnesota, Oregon, and a few other states established professional standards boards, but for years no state was willing to give teachers a controlling voice.[30]

The victory the NEA had been working for came in 1987, when the Nevada legislature created a nine-person board with teachers holding four of the seats, a school counselor or psychologist holding the fifth, and the remaining seats occupied by two administrators, a dean of education, and a state board of education member. Since teacher organizations represent school counselors and psychologists, the NEA proudly calls the Nevada board the nation's first "teacher-dominated" professional standards board. The bill creating the board passed overwhelmingly in the Nevada legislature, but the state board of education, state department of education, and local school boards lobbied hard against it. The executive secretary of the Nevada Association of School Boards stated bluntly that "these are not doctors, lawyers, accountants, and engineers. These are public employees, working in the public sector, and much public benefit is lost with them having total control."[31]

Teachers also have a majority of the seats on the Carnegie Forum's National Board for Professional Teaching Standards. Although this board does not have the power to set standards directly, it hopes that the certificates it issues will become prestigious enough to make the states want to follow its lead. The AFT has thrown its support behind this national board, on which the AFT has a better chance of holding its own with the NEA than on the state boards the NEA is almost certain to dominate. The different approaches of the two organizations are not mutually exclusive, however, for most professions have national *and* state standards boards.[32]

Opposition to group and individual autonomy for teachers is already mounting, as the Nevada situation demonstrates, but it comes less from the general public than from school administrators and school board members. They charge that teacher autonomy breaks the traditional chain of command within school systems and reduces the power of the state and local boards that represent the public. The charge is accurate. Instead of trying to deny it, teacher organizations will have to counter that changing the balance of power in public education is desirable. They must argue, as doctors did, that teachers can improve the quality of their services if they have more autonomy.[33]

In order to convince the public, teachers must begin to set standards of performance for their occupation. Unlike the NEA's existing "Code of Ethics for the Education Profession" and the AFT's "Bill of Rights," two documents that sit on the shelf and collect dust, the performance standards must be specific, and teachers themselves must enforce the standards. The Carnegie Forum argues that more accountability—some form of merit pay based on student achievement—must go hand in hand with more autonomy. Since teacher organizations have consistently opposed holding teachers accountable for student test scores—with good reason, as we have seen, accountability will be a bitter pill to swallow. But the AFT seems willing to try. Broadening the definition of accountability to include factors other than student test scores may make the pill more palatable. The new accountability may involve peer evaluation, for example. Teachers evaluating teachers, another recommendation of the Carnegie Forum, would be a major step toward professionalism, but peer evaluation is also controversial. Some teachers are as reluctant to take on the responsibility as some administrators and board members are to share it.[34]

Breakthrough for the AFT in Rochester and in Dade County

Notice how every change we consider leads to several others. We are talking about nothing less than a complete restructuring of teaching. The situation is not hopeless, though; a few union locals, mostly AFT, are negotiating experimental versions of the Carnegie proposals with their school boards, tying together salaries, evaluation, and autonomy. At the head of the pack is the Rochester, New York, school system, which has negotiated a path-breaking contract built on cooperation between the superintendent of schools and the president of the AFT local. With a Carnegie-inspired four-step career ladder in place, beginning teachers in Rochester earn $28,935 while average salaries of experienced teachers range from $32,651 to $45,774. Lead teachers, who can earn as much as $70,000, spend about half their time teaching and the rest serving as mentors in the peer assistance and review program.[35]

Teachers must be accountable, the Rochester superintendent insists. He expects student test scores to improve; he predicts that public support for the reforms will fall unless the scores rise. Teachers also work a longer school day and school year in Rochester, and they have given up seniority as the controlling factor in teacher transfers. Instead, school-based planning committees on which teachers have a strong voice decide on transfers. The most experienced teachers now get some of the toughest assignments, which is rarely the case in other school systems. Each school's planning committee makes decisions that were once the prerogative of the district's central office. The committees help each school develop a distinctive character, and the district has eliminated high school attendance zones to give students and parents a choice of schools. Clearly, Rochester is taking a risk. Teachers have new rights and new responsibilities. Will the risk pay off?[36]

People are asking the same question about the reforms in Dade County, Florida, the nation's fourth largest local system. As in Rochester, cooperation between a union president and school superintendent paved the way for reform. Dade County's teacher salaries are now the highest in Florida, and (like Rochester) the system is flooded with applicants for teaching positions. The experiment in Dade County involves "School-based Management/Shared Decision Making." Thirty-two schools are participating in a pilot program with two requirements: teachers and administrators in each school must share power, and student achievement must improve measurably. Each school has control of its own budget. Within limits, each school can vary such things as class size, the length of the school day, and perhaps most significantly, the mandated curriculum that tells teachers how, when, and what to teach. The results look promising.[37]

Rochester and Dade County are not the only school systems experimenting with teacher autonomy. The AFT locals in Cincinnati, Toledo, and Pittsburgh are also attracting national attention. The NEA is moving more cautiously, but several NEA locals in California have negotiated innovative contracts. So far, none of these attempts at reform has fallen flat on its face. But, of course, there is opposition.[38]

Undercurrents of Opposition

Running beneath the arguments against teacher autonomy are two strong undercurrents. One is antifeminism. Our discussion in the preceding chapters highlighted the perception of teaching as women's work. To the extent that some people still view women as second class and subordinate, teachers—along with nurses and social workers—will run into resistance in their bid for professional status. Today this kind of opposition is rarely expressed openly, but occasionally it slips out in such remarks as "After all, most teachers are only working for a second income" or "Women are naturals at teaching kids in a classroom, but most of them could care less about running a school system."[39]

The other undercurrent, antiunionism, comes to the surface more often. Critics charge that the NEA and AFT will use professionalism selfishly, to make life better for their members. Teachers will be the winners, with students, parents, and the general public the losers. Consider again the example of professional standards boards. There is little doubt that the unions will use their influence on the boards to set teacher education and certification standards high enough to reduce the supply of new teachers, a move that could drive up teacher salaries. Moreover, the unions give every indication that they will oppose relaxing the standards in response to teacher shortages. They will insist that if school boards want qualified teachers, better salaries, benefits, and working conditions are the only ways to attract them. "Self-serving," the critics say.[40]

The NEA and AFT reply that what is good for teachers is good for public education. The unions argue that while all professional associations try to take care of their own members, ultimately they have the interests of their clients at heart. Certainly doctors were thinking about doctors when they restricted access to their occupation. By making medicine a highly selective occupation, doctors insured that those who got in would live well. But they were also thinking about the public. When shortages of doctors develop today, state medical boards do not allow people with partial or no medical education to fill in, even on an emergency basis; instead, the profession maintains its standards, fees for medical care rise, medicine becomes even more attractive to young people, and a greater supply of licensed, fully trained physicians eventually meets the need. The AMA argues that what the public loses in short-term convenience it more than makes up in long-term quality. Don't Americans deserve the same quality in public education, the NEA and AFT ask?[41]

Yes, but . . . Trying to answer that question sends us back to others we have already considered. Can we justify giving one occupational group exclusive rights to teach in the public schools? Is the knowledge base for teaching strong enough to support an emerging profession? Is the public ready to trust teachers and their organizations with more autonomy? The questions are old, but some of the answers are new. Since the early 1980s people have been taking the questions seriously, for teacher organizations, respected study commissions, and some public officials are serious about making teaching a profession. Part of your job will be helping to find new answers if you take your place among America's teachers in the 1990s.

ACTIVITIES

1. Invite representatives of the NEA and AFT to speak to your class about their organizations' similarities and differences. Press them on what the differences really mean at the local level.
2. Talk with people who have a variety of different opinions about teacher organizations. Begin with classroom teachers, then expand your interviews to include such people as school administrators, school board members, parents, labor and business leaders, politicians, officials of the Democratic and Republican parties, and reporters.
3. Attend a collective bargaining session and a teacher organization's screening session for political candidates.
4. Discuss the concept of professionalism with representatives of the medical association and bar association in your community. Ask them to trace any parallels they see between the professionalization of their occupations and teaching.

SUGGESTED READINGS

Browsing through issues of the *American Teacher* and *NEA Today* is one of the best ways to learn more about teacher organizations. Local representatives of the NEA and AFT are usually happy to provide as many of their publications as you want to read. For an opposing point of view, locate some recent articles and books by Myron Lieberman (see note 40 below).

NOTES

1. The most complete historical studies of the NEA and AFT are Edgar B. Wesley's *NEA: The First Hundred Years* (New York: Harper & Row, 1957) and William Edward Eaton's *The American Federation of Teachers, 1916–1961* (Carbondale: Southern Illinois University Press, 1975). David Selden, *The Teacher Rebellion* (Washington: Howard University Press, 1985), carries the AFT's story through the mid-1980s, and Allan M. West discusses the modern NEA in *The National Education Association: The Power Base for Education* (New York: Free Press, 1980).

2. The *1988–89 NEA Handbook* (Washington: NEA, 1988) and *The 1984–86 Report of the Officers of the American Federation of Teachers* (Washington: AFT, 1986) provided much of the information for my discussion of the differences between the two organizations.

3. West, *The National Education Association*, pp. 22, 38. For the history of the state and local associations that provided the foundation for the NEA's rise to power, see Willard S. Elsbree, *The American Teacher: Evolution of a Profession in a Democracy* (New York: American Book Company, 1939). Elsbree's book, old but still useful, is the classic historical study of teachers and teaching.

4. The NEA's stands have provoked bitter attacks. See Sally D. Reed, *NEA: Propaganda Front of the Radical Left* (Washington: National Council for Better Education, 1984); Dan C. Alexander, Jr., *Who's Running Our Schools? The Case against the NEA Teacher Union* (Washington: Save Our Schools Research and Education Foundation, 1986); and Phyllis Schlafly, *Child Abuse in the Classroom* (Westchester, IL: Crossway, 1985).

5. Michael John Schultz, Jr., *The National Education Association and the Black Teacher: The Integration of a Professional Organization* (Coral Gables: University of Miami Press, 1970); Eaton, *The American Federation of Teachers*, pp. 159–60.

6. Marshall O. Donley, Jr., *Power to the Teacher: How America's Educators Became Militant* (Bloomington: Indiana University Press, 1976); Joel Spring, *American Education: An Introduction to Social and Political Aspects*, 4th ed. (White Plains, NY: Longman, 1989), pp. 232–246.

7. Wayne J. Urban, *Why Teachers Organized* (Detroit: Wayne State University Press, 1982), ch. 5; West, *The National Education Association*, p. 84.

8. Anthony M. Cresswell and Michael J. Murphy with Charles T. Kerchner, *Teachers, Unions, and Collective Bargaining in Public Education* (Berkeley, CA: McCutchan, 1980), pp. 153–157; Louis Fischer, David Schimmel, and Cynthia Kelly, *Teachers and the Law*, 2d ed. (White Plains, NY: Longman, 1987), pp. 38–40.

9. Eaton, *The American Federation of Teachers*, pp. 161–66; Stephen Cole, *The Unionization of Teachers: A Case Study of the UFT* (New York: Praeger, 1969).

10. Creswell and Murphy, *Teachers, Unions, and Collective Bargaining*, chs. 3–4.

11. Helpful sources of information on the mechanics of bargaining include Cresswell and Murphy, *Teachers, Unions, and Collective Bargaining;* Fischer, Schimmel, and Kelly, *Teachers and the Law*, ch. 3; and William G. Webster, Sr., *Effective Collective Bargaining in Public Education* (Ames: Iowa State University Press, 1985).

12. Fischer, Schimmel, and Kelly, *Teachers and the Law*, pp. 43–45. See the brochure *Compulsory Unionism in Education* (Springfield, VA: Concerned Educators against Forced Unionism, 1984).

13. Charles T. Kerchner, "A 'New Generation' of Teacher Unionism," *Education Week* (January 20, 1988), pp. 36, 30; Randall W. Eberts and Joe A. Stone, *Unions and Public Schools: The Effect of Collective Bargaining on American Education* (Lexington, MA: Heath, 1984), pp. 20–30; Cresswell and Murphy, *Teachers, Unions, and Collective Bargaining*, ch. 8; Webster, *Effective Collective Bargaining*, ch. 12.

14. On impasse procedures, see Cresswell and Murphy, *Teachers, Unions, and Collective Bargaining*, pp. 365–375; and Webster, *Effective Collective Bargaining*, ch. 14.

15. Cresswell and Murphy, *Teachers, Unions, and Collective Bargaining*, p. 81.

16. *Education Week*, September 24, 1984, p. 4.

17. Fischer, Schimmel, and Kelly, *Teachers and the Law*, pp. 50–51.
18. Cresswell and Murphy, *Teachers, Unions, and Collective Bargaining*, analyze strikes on pp. 341–364.
19. Urban, *Why Teachers Organized*, chs. 2–6, discusses the early political involvement of the NEA, AFT, and local teacher organizations in Chicago, New York, and Atlanta. For the ups and downs of teacher politics in these three cities, see Mary J. Herrick, *The Chicago Schools: A Social and Political History* (Beverly Hills: Sage, 1971); Celia Lewis Zitron, *The New York City Teachers Union, 1916–1964: A Story of Educational and Social Commitment* (New York: Humanities Press, 1968); and Joseph W. Newman, "A History of the Atlanta Public School Teachers Association, Local 89 of the American Federation of Teachers, 1919–1956" (Ph.D. dissertation, Georgia State University, 1978).
20. "Growing Up Politically," *NEA Today* (November 1987), p. 3.
21. *NEA Today*, the AFT's *American Teacher*, and other union publications are the best sources of current information on the political activity of the two organizations. Stanley M. Elam takes a critical look in "The National Education Association: Political Powerhouse or Paper Tiger?" *Phi Delta Kappan* 63 (November 1981): 169–174, and Chester E. Finn is more critical in "Teacher Politics," *Commentary* (February 1983): 29–41.
22. See note 21.
23. Amitai Etzioni, *The Semiprofessions and Their Organizations: Teachers, Nurses, and Social Workers* (New York: Free Press, 1969). Two other often-cited studies of teaching are Myron Lieberman, *Education as a Profession* (Englewood Cliffs, NJ: Prentice-Hall, 1956), and Robert B. Howsam, Dean C. Corrigan, George W. Denemark, and Robert J. Nash, *Educating a Profession* (Washington: American Association of Colleges of Teacher Education, 1985).
24. Ernest Greenwood, "Attributes of a Profession," and Dietrich Rueschemeyer, "Doctors and Lawyers: A Comment on the Theory of the Professions," in Ronald M. Pavalko, ed., *Sociological Perspectives on the Occupations* (Itasca, IL: F. E. Peacock Publishers, 1972), chs. 1 and 3; Eliot Freidsen, ed., *The Professions and Their Prospects* (Beverly Hills: Sage, 1973); Everett C. Hughes, *Men and Their Work* (Westport, CT: Greenwood, 1981).
25. Greenwood, "Attributes of a Profession," pp. 8–9.
26. Ibid., pp. 4–6.
27. Ibid., pp. 6–12.
28. Kenneth M. Ludmerer, *Learning to Heal: The Development of American Medical Education* (New York: Basic Books, 1988); Morris Fishbein, *A History of the American Medical Association, 1847–1947* (Philadelphia: Saunders, 1947).
29. Abraham Flexner, *Medical Education in the United States and Canada* (New York: Carnegie Foundation for the Advancement of Teaching, 1910). For an excellent discussion of these issues, see William R. Johnson, "Empowering Practitioners: Holmes, Carnegie, and the Lessons of History," *History of Education Quarterly* 27 (Summer 1987): 221–240.
30. Blake Rodman, "N.E.A. Pursues Its Plan To Establish State Boards Controlled by Teachers," *Education Week* (April 29, 1987), pp. 1, 20.
31. Blake Rodman, "Nevada Creates 'Teacher Dominated' Licensing Board," *Education Week* (August 4, 1987), p. 7.
32. Rodman, "N.E.A. Pursues Its Plan."

33. Lynn Olson, "Certification Panel Gets Cool Reception from Some Administrators," *Education Week* (May 27, 1987), pp. 1, 16–17.
34. Lynn Olson, "Carnegie Forum's Plan for Revamping Schools Is Seen as Tough Task," *Education Week* (May 27, 1987), pp. 1, 16–17.
35. Blake Rodman, "Friendship and Trust: Unusual Keys to Radical Pact," *Education Week* (September 30, 1987), pp. 1, 20–21.
36. Ibid.
37. Lynn Olson, " 'The Sky's the Limit': Dade Ventures Self-Governance," *Education Week* (December 2, 1987), pp. 1, 18–19.
38. Kerchner, "A 'New Generation' of Teacher Unionism"; Susan Moore Johnson, "Pursuing Professional Reform in Cincinnati," *Phi Delta Kappan* 69 (June 1988): 746–751. Two recent studies of the subject are Kerchner and Douglas Mitchell, *The Changing Idea of a Teachers' Union* (Philadephia: Falmer, 1988), and Susan Moore Johnson's chapter in *The Teacher: Ally in Educational Reform* (Scarsdale, NY: Work in America Institute, 1989).
39. Michael W. Apple, *Texts and Teachers: A Political Economy of Class and Gender Relations in Education* (Boston: Routledge & Kegan Paul, 1987) and "Work, Gender and Teaching," *Teachers College Record* 84 (Spring 1983): 612–628; Geoffrey Tabakin and Kathleen Densmore, "Teacher Professionalization and Gender Analysis," *Teachers College Record* 88 (Winter 1986): 257–279.
40. Rodman, "N.E.A. Pursues Its Plan." Myron Lieberman, whose book *Education as a Profession* (1956) set forth the classic arguments in favor of professionalizing teaching through collective bargaining and political action, has now reversed himself. In such later works as *Public Sector Bargaining: A Reappraisal* (Lexington, MA: Lexington Books, 1980), Lieberman insists that teachers' interests and the public interest are fundamentally different, and that teacher organizations consistently look after the former and neglect the latter.
41. Rodman, "N.E.A. Pursues Its Plan"; Arthur E. Wise, "A Case for Trusting Teachers to Regulate Their Profession," *Education Week* (October 8, 1986), p. 24.

CHAPTER 5

Exercising Your Rights and Fulfilling Your Responsibilities

Teachers need to know where they stand in relation to the law. Teachers who know their legal rights and responsibilities can put some of their doubts and fears to rest. No, the law is not so complex that it is impossible to understand. No, there is not a lawyer lurking around every corner, just waiting to file suit against you. Much of the legal paranoia that teachers share with other Americans is simply a fear of the unknown. When you reach the end of this chapter, I hope you feel a sense of relief from knowing more about your rights and responsibilities in three areas: *employment, liability,* and *expression.*

On the other hand, becoming more familiar with school law should also give you a greater sense of caution. When we discuss employment, for example, you will see that teacher tenure is not the ironclad guarantee to a lifetime job that it is reputed to be. In the area of liability, one of the issues we will examine is "The Teacher and AIDS," and you may be surprised to learn what your responsibilities are for students who have the disease. When we discuss expression, you will find that although academic freedom protects teachers, the protection it offers has limits. Throughout this chapter, you will see that the law is a two-edged sword. It gives teacher rights to exercise; it also gives them responsibilities to fulfill.

This chapter, which concludes Part 1 of the textbook, is not the only chapter that involves school law. Collective bargaining, teacher testing, merit pay—these are only three of the issues in the preceding chapters that illustrate the influence of law on teaching as an occupation. In Part 2 of this textbook, Schools and Society, the spotlight is on students more often than teachers, and the law helps illuminate such issues as school desegregation, bilingual education, and sex equity. The focus of Chapter 9 is the political arena in which the law originates. The debates we will examine in Part 2, "Issues for the 1990s," also involve legal questions. Who should control the curriculum? Should the government regulate private schools? Every chapter in *America's Teachers* bears the influence of school law.

EMPLOYMENT

Contracts

When you obtain your first teaching job, you will sign a *contract* with a local school board. A contract is a legally binding agreement, a statement of the rights and responsibilities of both parties, the teacher and the board. A contract typically specifies such things as salary, grade level or subject area, and the length of the school day and school year. A contract also obligates the teacher and the board to follow state school laws, state board of education policies, and local board regulations. In school districts with collective bargaining, the contract binds both parties to the master contract that the teacher organization and the board have negotiated. Most teachers sign annual contracts, although some work under continuing contracts that remain in effect until one party gives notice of intent to change the agreement. Read your contract carefully. You may want to discuss the contract with an official of the local teacher organization, since lawyers retained by the organization have almost certainly scrutinized the document, as have the school board's attorneys.[1]

Tenure

In most states, teachers have the protection of *tenure*, which is a status of protected employment granted to teachers after satisfactory service during a probationary period. While teachers are on probation (usually for three years), it is easy for school boards to dismiss them; after teachers receive tenure, dismissal is difficult. Tenure laws are controversial. Do they protect good teaching? Shield incompetence? It is impossible to understand the pros and cons of tenure without knowing its history.

Public school teachers campaigned for the passage of tenure laws in the early 1900s, stressing their need for protection from "petty political and social attacks." To say that teachers were vulnerable is an understatement. State school laws allowed local boards to fire teachers at will by simply not renewing their contracts. Teachers lost their jobs to administrative whim, political patronage, social prejudice, and religious intolerance. In most states, dismissed teachers received neither a statement of the charges against them nor an opportunity to defend themselves at a hearing. They were simply out of work and out of luck.[2]

Teacher organizations took the case for tenure to the public and the state legislatures. Flagrant miscarriages of justice often tipped the balance of opinion in the teachers' favor: teachers who were dismissed for having the "wrong" religion or belonging to the "wrong" political party; teachers fired for discussing a controversial issue from several points of view rather than just the "right" one; teachers who lost their jobs because they smoked or drank in public (or even in private). Citing examples like these to dramatize the case for tenure, teachers argued that they deserved the same kind of protection from arbitrary dismissal that civil service laws gave to other government employees.

After the District of Columbia passed a teacher tenure law in 1906 and New Jersey followed suit three years later, the quest for job security gradually spread across the nation. Supported by the NEA, AFT, and independent state teacher organizations, teachers in city school systems led the tenure campaigns. By 1937 seventeen states had passed some form of tenure legislation. Most of the early tenure laws applied just to urban teachers, but during the 1940s and 1950s state legislatures extended tenure to rural teachers as well.

Think of tenure laws as a bargain struck between teachers and local school boards. Tenure allows the boards to dismiss teachers for almost any reason during their probationary period, but after that the boards must have a very good reason. As part of the bargain, tenure laws leave teachers vulnerable while they are on probation. They are literally on trial. The future teachers in my classes often feel uneasy when they learn that school boards can dismiss an untenured teacher by simply not offering a new contract. In most states, the untenured teacher is entitled to no explanation and no hearing—and, of course, no further employment. I remind my students that this sense of insecurity is exactly what *all* teachers, 25-year veterans no less than beginners, felt without tenure. I hasten to add that even untenured teachers who can prove that their dismissal violates state or federal law—that they were fired because of their race or sex, for example—can win back their jobs if they are willing to go to court.

Dismissal

Obviously, tenure does not give absolute job security to any teacher. Tenure does, however, put the burden on the school board to prove that a tenured teacher is unfit for further employment. In most states, the local board must prove an tenured teacher guilty of one of the "3 i's": incompetence, insubordination, or immorality. Some states add the "u" of unprofessional conduct or even broader grounds, such as "good and just cause."

Incompetence is the inability to perform the job the contract calls for. To prove a teacher incompetent, school officials must show a pattern of behavior, a clear record of failure. In dismissal cases that reach the court system, charges of incompetence most often center on a teacher's inability to maintain classroom discipline. As we saw in Chapter 3, incompetence can also be the inability to speak or write grammatically, or it can be a lack of subject-matter knowledge. Incompetence can stem from a physical or mental condition—impaired hearing, for example, or mental illness—that renders the teacher incapable of effective work. The mere existence of a handicap is not proof of incompetence, however. The board must produce evidence that the teacher cannot perform adequately. In most dismissal cases, teachers face charges of not one but several kinds of incompetence—a "collapse of performance."[3]

Insubordination is the willful violation of reasonable rules or the deliberate defiance of school officials. A reasonable rule, according to the courts, is one that officials have the authority to issue, that is clear enough to be understood, and that does not violate a teacher's constitutional rights. In cases involving alleged defiance of school officials, the courts often look for a pattern of behavior rather than a single incident. When a tenured teacher consistently refuses to comply with reasonable requests from a principal or supervisor, for example, the courts are likely to rule in favor of dismissal.[4]

Although definitions of *immorality* vary from community to community and change from time to time, the courts have narrowed the range of immoral conduct that can deprive tenured teachers of their jobs. In general, the conduct must interfere with a teacher's effectiveness before it can become grounds for dismissal. In *Morrison v. State Board of Education* (1969), a landmark case involving homosexuality, the California Supreme Court ruled that "an individual can be removed from the teaching profession only upon a showing that his retention in the profession poses a significant danger of harm to either students, school employees, or others who might be affected by his actions as a teacher." The courts usually distinguish between public and private conduct, and they usually protect what adults do in private. But when a teacher's private conduct becomes a matter of public controversy, and when the controversy spills over into the classroom and impairs the teacher's effectiveness, the courts generally support dismissal. Moreover, immoral conduct involving teachers and their students—a sexual relationship, for example, or the use of alcohol or other drugs—is a sure ticket out of the occupation. We will return to the issues of life-style and other forms of personal expression in the last section of this chapter.[5]

The vagueness of the term *unprofessional conduct* is disturbing, but the courts have sometimes upheld the dismissal of tenured teachers on these and other broad grounds. The courts have reasoned that since society entrusts teachers with the important responsibility of working with young people, which calls into play numerous personal qualities ranging from "cleanliness" to "wisdom and propriety," school boards must have considerable discretion to determine who is fit for the task. In some cases the courts have interpreted unprofessional to mean immoral. In other cases unprofessional has been construed as unethical. The latter interpretation presents special problems, since teaching's two most prominent statements of ethics, the NEA's Code of Ethics and the AFT's Bill of Rights, have no legal standing. Even so, the courts have upheld the dismissal of teachers who use their classrooms for activities other than teaching, such as urging students to support a particular political candidate. The courts have also allowed the dismissal of "uncooperative" teachers. Unprofessional conduct and similar phrases are the catchalls of tenure law.[6]

In addition to the 3 i's and the u, tenured teachers can lose their jobs as a result of *reduction in force,* or "riffing." When enrollment in a school district falls sharply, when a district decides to reorganize its curriculum for economic reasons, or when a financial crisis makes severe budget cuts necessary, school boards can dismiss tenured as well as untenured teachers. Seniority usually dictates whose jobs go first. Such dismissals have been relatively rare, but they increased during the tax and budget-cutting era of the late 1970s and early 1980s.[7]

Due Process

Tenured teachers have the rights to *due process* that the Fourteenth Amendment guarantees to all citizens. Tenure gives teachers ownership of their jobs, for the courts have ruled that tenured teachers have a "property interest" in their positions. Because of the Fourteenth Amendment, no state can "deprive any person of life, liberty, or property, without due process of law." In *Goldberg v. Kelly* (1970) and other cases, the U.S. Supreme Court has ruled that due process rights include a statement of charges, sufficient time to prepare a defense, a hearing before a fair tribunal (usually the local school board), representation by legal counsel, the opportunity to present evidence and cross-examine witnesses, a transcript of the hearing, and appeal of adverse rulings.[8]

Trying to dismiss a tenured teacher is expensive and time-consuming. School boards can anticipate legal costs that run into the tens of thousands of dollars. The NEA and AFT usually pay the expenses of their tenured members whose jobs come under fire, although there are important exceptions. The organizations will not stand behind a confessed child molester, for example, or an admitted drug dealer. Without question, however, teacher organizations make it more difficult for school boards to dismiss tenured teachers, which leads some citizens to charge that tenure laws and union attorneys conspire to protect poor teaching. The NEA and AFT have a different point of view. They argue that teachers, like all citizens, are innocent until proven guilty.[9]

Even though local school boards win most of the dismissal cases that go to court, very few cases even reach the hearing stage before a local board. Unwilling to spend time and money on dismissal proceedings, some administrators and board members simply tolerate tenured teachers whom they know to be unfit for the classroom. Parents become incensed, and rightly so, when principals claim that their hands are tied because of tenure laws. Some principals transfer unfit teachers from school to school—a game called "pass the turkey" in the literature on tenure.[10]

Other principals take more constructive approaches. One is remediation— trying to help teachers improve. Assistance from other teachers often proves helpful, which makes the peer evaluation and peer assistance programs that we considered in Chapters 2 and 4 seem very promising. If remediation fails, the principal can try confrontation. After observing an inadequate teacher and compiling a "thick folder" of evidence, the principal can confront the teacher with stacks of evaluation forms, dated observations, complaints from parents, and so forth. The object is to convince the teacher that resignation is a better option than a dismissal hearing and a possible court battle. If confrontation fails, the principal can take the folder of evidence to a superior and argue for a dismissal hearing. The point is that administrators have options; they can do *something*. The laws outline grounds for dismissal, and it is the responsibility of administrators, admittedly an unpleasant and demanding one, to see that unfit teachers do not remain in the classroom.[11]

LIABILITY

A student falls in a classroom and breaks an arm. Several students come to school showing signs of child abuse. Parents confide in a teacher that their child has AIDS. Despite a teacher's best efforts, some students learn very little. What are the rights and responsibilities of teachers in each of these situations? Can teachers be sued and held liable for failing to fulfill their responsibilities? In the excellent book *Teachers and the Law,* Louis Fischer, David Schimmel, and Cynthia Kelly provide some answers.

Injuries to Students

According to Fischer, Schimmel, and Kelly, a student who is hurt while under a teacher's care must prove four things in order to hold the teacher liable for the injury:

1. The teacher owed a duty of care to the student.

. . .

2. The teacher was negligent.

. . .

3. The teacher's negligence was the cause of the student's injury.

. . .

4. The student was actually damaged by the teacher's negligence.[12]

In most injury cases that go to court, there is little question that the teacher had a duty to care for the student, and there is little question that the student sustained monetary damages. The dispute usually centers on the second and third requirements. Was the teacher negligent, and if so, did the negligence cause the injury?

The courts place great emphasis on the concept of *reasonable care*, "the degree of care a teacher of ordinary prudence" would exercise.[13] Take the example of a student who falls and breaks an arm in a teacher's classroom.

Court proceedings would probably revolve around several key questions. Was the teacher in the room at the time of the injury? Unless the teacher had an excellent reason not to be, the teacher's absence in itself could increase the chances of the teacher's being found liable. Could the teacher have foreseen the accident? Could the teacher have taken steps to prevent the accident? If the accident happened unpredictably—if the student simply lost balance and fell—the teacher would probably have little to worry about in court. But if the student slipped on water, for example, or tripped over a wire, there would be further questions about whether the teacher had made a reasonable effort to remove the hazards or keep the students away. Did the student fall while running? If so, did the teacher make a reasonable effort to stop the running? Questions like these help the court decide whether the teacher was negligent and whether the negligence resulted in the injury.

Teachers should know that they can be held liable for injuries that occur outside as well as inside the classroom. Teachers who provide transportation for students to field trips, athletic events, or debate tournaments are taking a risk, and the permission slips, waivers, and covenants not to sue that parents sign usually do not protect teachers from negligence suits. Regardless of what the piece of paper says, the courts usually allow an injured student to sue.[14]

Teachers can reduce their risk with liability insurance. Teachers should find out how much coverage (if any) they have through their school system's policy. Does the policy cover teachers in the classroom? Does it protect them while they are supervising extracurricular activities? Does it cover transporting students in a private automobile? A major benefit of membership in the AFT or NEA is being able to buy low-cost liability insurance designed especially for teachers. While it is possible to be overinsured, it is wise for a teacher to have personal liability insurance to supplement whatever protection the school district's policy provides.

Reporting Child Abuse and Neglect

The laws of every state require teachers to report suspected cases of child abuse and neglect. Every state grants teachers who make such reports immunity from civil and criminal suits. State laws vary in their requirements, but most call for an oral report to an administrator followed by a written statement. Let me stress that the law will protect teachers who act in good faith. Teachers should not hesitate to file a report if they believe that a student is a victim of abuse or neglect. In most states teachers can be fined or imprisoned if they do *not* make the report, and in some states they can be sued for negligence.[15]

The National Child Abuse Prevention and Treatment Act of 1974 defines child abuse and neglect as

> physical or mental injury, sexual abuse or exploitation, negligent treatment, or maltreatment of a child under the age of eighteen or the age specified under the child protection law of the state in question, by a person who is

responsible for the child's welfare, under circumstances which indicate that the child's health or welfare is harmed or threatened thereby.[16]

According to recent estimates, at least 2,000,000 children suffer abuse and neglect every year. Looking just at sexual abuse, one of four girls and one of ten boys will fall victim before their eighteenth birthday. Ninety percent of these cases will go unreported. These statistics suggest why it is important for teachers to pay close attention to the mental and physical conditions of their students. Statistics can only hint at the human dimensions of the problem, but they can put teachers on notice that they are *likely* to have abused and neglected children in their classes. Do not be blind to the problem.[17]

The Teacher and AIDS

How schools should respond to Acquired Immune Deficiency Syndrome (AIDS) is one of the most volatile issues in American education today. Almost every state mandates some form of AIDS education, and many teachers—certainly not just high school biology teachers—have a role in providing students information about the disease. Because of the highly charged controversies surrounding AIDS, some state and local school boards issue detailed teaching guides, telling teachers what to say, what not to say, and how to answer student questions. Should a teacher mention the word "condom" to a class of fifth graders, or should the teacher suggest only sexual abstinence? In how much detail should a teacher describe the sexual acts that can transmit the disease? The guidelines vary from state to state and district to district, and they raise academic freedom issues that we will consider in the last section of this chapter. Teachers should be familiar with the state and local AIDS policies that apply to them.[18]

Of greater emotional as well as legal concern for teachers is the issue of how to deal with students who have contracted the HTLV-III virus that causes AIDS. What should a teacher do after learning that a student has the virus? Many teachers are concerned that they could be sued for negligence for not reporting AIDS or, on the other hand, sued for invasion of privacy or infliction of emotional distress for making a report.

The medical facts about AIDS shape the court's attitude toward students with the disease. All teachers should know that AIDS has three stages. In the *carrier* stage, people test positive for the virus but show no symptoms; in the *AIDS-related complex* (ARC) stage, symptoms of an impaired immune system appear; and in the *full-blown* stage, the immune system breaks down and opportunistic infections develop. AIDS is progressive, incurable, and fatal. The disease advances through the three stages faster in some people than in others, however, and carriers may not realize that they have the virus for months or even years—until the first symptoms of ARC appear.[19]

Teachers should also know that people contract AIDS in a limited number of ways, primarily through sexual contact, hypodermic needles, transfusions of contaminated blood, and perinatal contact between mother and child. One of the few positive things about the disease is that it is hard to get. People do not catch AIDS through casual contact. It is most encouraging for teachers that there are no known cases in which a child has caught the disease from a classmate or playmate.[20]

Based on this medical evidence, the courts have ruled that students who have AIDS can come to school. The courts have applied Section 504 of the Rehabilitation Act of 1973 to AIDS victims:

> No otherwise handicapped individual in the United States . . . shall, solely by reason of his handicap, be excluded from participation in, be denied the benefits of, or be subjected to discrimination under any program or activity receiving Federal financial assistance.[21]

The courts allow school systems to isolate or exclude, on a case-by-case basis, AIDS victims whose condition or behavior—biting or drooling, for example—might endanger others.[22]

The word *might* is appropriate because, again, AIDS is difficult to catch. Even people in close physical contact with AIDS victims—caregivers who bathe AIDS victims and dress their skin lesions—have not contracted the disease. As for biting and drooling, the virus is detectable in the saliva of only 1 of 18 or 20 people who have AIDS. It bears repeating that there are no known cases in which a child has transmitted the virus to a classmate or playmate.[23]

Medical evidence does not always put fears to rest, however. AIDS strikes fear in the hearts of many students, parents, and teachers. The news media carry stories of irate crowds literally driving students with the disease out of school—in some cases running their families out of town. Thus the courts have had to weigh the student's right to privacy against the public's right to know. The verdict is clear. The student's right to privacy, which is protected by the Family Educational Rights and Privacy Act (1974) and the Education of All Handicapped Children Act (1975), prevails. These federal laws allow the release of medical information on a student to qualified persons—to a teacher, principal, or school nurse, for example—to protect health and safety. In the absence of a threat to health and safety, information on a student's medical condition is strictly confidential.[24]

Caught between public pressure and the legal obligation to educate students, many school districts form special teams to make case-by-case decisions about students with AIDS. Such teams often consist of a student's doctor, a public health officer, a doctor representing the school board, the school nurse, and the student's teacher(s). After reviewing information on the student's medical condition and behavior, the team makes a recommendation to the superintendent on whether the student should remain in school and whether anyone else needs to know that the student has AIDS.[25]

What school systems try to avoid is the public uproar that can occur if a student's condition becomes widely known. A teacher who breaches a parent's confidence and leaks information about a student with AIDS can start a chain of events that can force the student out of school—the law and the courts notwithstanding. In addition to inviting a lawsuit, the teacher's action can discourage other parents and students from coming forward with information about the illness.[26]

Many school systems have developed AIDS policies on how teachers should report cases of the disease. Find out whether your system has a policy and, if so, what it provides. In the absence of a clear policy, a confidential report to the principal is probably the teacher's safest course of action. AIDS policies in school systems, like court decisions on the disease, are relatively new and still evolving. If the number of cases reported in school systems continues to increase, however, teachers may soon become all too familiar with how to deal with the disease.

Educational Malpractice

Malpractice suits against physicians are common. The cost of malpractice insurance for doctors has soared, prompting some physicians to raise their fees, change their specialties, or even leave the profession. Teachers have faced the same kind of lawsuits, although far less frequently. Some parents have argued that just as teachers can be held liable for physical injuries to students under their care, they should also be liable for mental injuries—for educational malpractice. Although no educational malpractice suits have yet succeeded, two cases from the 1970s raise issues that teachers need to consider—issues that we have examined in a different light in other chapters of this textbook.

The most famous case, *Peter W. v. San Francisco Unified School District* (1976), involved a young man who sued the San Francisco public schools because he graduated from high school with only a fifth-grade reading level. Peter produced evidence in court that his IQ scores were at least average, and that teachers and administrators had informed his mother on numerous occasions that he was making adequate progress in school. Peter charged that the school system had acted negligently by giving him inadequate teachers, assigning him to inappropriate reading groups, and socially promoting him from one grade to the next. The system's negligence had damaged him, he claimed, by reducing his chances of finding a job.[27]

In weighing Peter's claim of negligence, the judge considered the lack of an agreed-upon knowledge base in education, an issue that we analyzed in Chapters 3 and 4. By what standard could he find the school system negligent, the judge wondered, when "the science of pedagogy itself is fraught with different and conflicting theories of how or what should be taught"? The judge ran into a further problem when he looked for a link between teacher behavior and student achievement. He concluded that student achievement is "influenced by a host of factors which affect the pupil subjectively, from outside the teaching process"— such factors as the home, the media, and an assortment of "physical, neurological, emotional, cultural, (and) environmental" forces. How could anyone isolate the influence of teachers—indeed, of schools—and hold them responsible for a student's reading ability? This, of course, is one of the questions that we asked about teacher evaluation in Chapter 2. The judge rejected Peter's claim, adding that a ruling in the student's favor would encourage countless other law suits of the the same kind, placing an impossible burden on the schools and the society. Peter W.'s lawsuit was an attempt to force accountability with a vengeance, and the judge turned it back.[28]

Another case, *Hoffman v. Board of Education of the City of New York* (1979), appeared to have a better chance of success. Danny Hoffman entered kindergarten with a severe speech defect. Scoring 74 on an intelligence test that emphasized verbal skills, Danny was placed in a class for mentally retarded students. Even though the school psychologist who administered the test recommended retesting within two years, stating that the child "obviously understands more than he is able to communicate," the school system never retested Danny. He graduated from high school after spending 11 years in classes for the retarded.[29]

At age 18 Danny took an intelligence test required by the Social Security Administration. He scored in the normal range, which caused him to lose both his Social Security benefits and his eligibility for rehabilitation training. At that point Danny sued the New York public schools for negligence. He charged that the school system had made a serious error, a mistake that had damaged him intellectually and psychologically. A lower court ruled in Danny's favor, awarding him $750,000 (later reduced to $500,000) in damages. The court argued that unlike the *Peter W.* case, *Hoffman* was a case of clearcut malpractice.[30]

The New York Court of Appeals reversed the decision. By a 4-3 margin, the justices ruled that the courts cannot second-guess the schools on academic matters. A court of law is not the appropriate place to question the "professional judgment of educators," the majority wrote.[31] Instead, students and parents who are unhappy with educational decisions can use the appeals procedures that state school laws provide. *Peter W.* and *Hoffman* established precedents that other courts followed in the educational malpractice suits of the 1980s. But will the precedents remain in place during the 1990s? The mounting pressure for accountability and the increasing willingness of courts to question the judgment of doctors, lawyers, and other professionals make it possible that educational malpractice suits may yet succeed.

EXPRESSION

Academic Freedom

Academic freedom for teachers is based on the First Amendment, which guarantees teachers along with all other citizens the right to free speech. Teachers argue that since their jobs involve working with knowledge and testing ideas, they need special protection as they experiment, question, and criticize. Democracy demands free teaching, they insist. The courts, however, have not always recognized the concept of academic freedom. Although the First Amendment went into effect in 1791 as part of the Bill of Rights, only in the twentieth century have elementary and secondary school teachers won a degree of protection for their academic work in the classroom. Even college professors, who work with older students and have the responsibility for generating new knowledge, have faced an uphill struggle for academic freedom. During this century teachers at all levels of education have won major victories, but the courts have made it clear that academic freedom is far from absolute.

Despite the protection of tenure laws, teachers still come under fire for discussing controversial issues and assigning controversial materials. Take the case of the Alabama teacher who had her eleventh-grade English class read Kurt Vonnegut, Jr.'s comic satire *Welcome to the Monkey House*. After several students and parents complained, the teacher's superiors told her to stop using the story, which they branded "literary garbage." The teacher refused. Defending the literary value of the work, she continued to discuss it in the classroom, whereupon the school system fired her for insubordination.[32]

The lawsuit she initiated to get her job back led to a precedent-setting court decision, *Parducci v. Rutland* (1970). The federal district judge who heard the case observed that academic freedom, while "fundamental to a democratic society," does have limits. Trying to define some of the limits, the judge considered two major questions. Had the school system shown that the assignment was inappropriate for the age group or grade level? Had the system shown that the assignment interfered with discipline or disrupted the educational process? On both counts, the judge weighed the evidence and answered no. Thus he ruled in favor of the teacher, stating that her dismissal had been "an unwarranted invasion of her First Amendment right to academic freedom."[33]

In other cases, the courts have had to determine the relevance of challenged assignments and teaching techniques to the curriculum. In general, the courts have ruled that teachers who deal with controversial topics that are a logical part of the subject at hand—a discussion of racism in an American history class, for example, or an assignment on human sexuality in a biology class—are operating within the limits of academic freedom. The limits stretch only so far, however. A teacher who constantly injects politics into a math class is probably out of bounds, for example, and anything a teacher does that substantially disrupts the class may not be protected by academic freedom.[34]

The courts generally protect teachers who use controversial teaching methods, *if* they can produce reasonable evidence that other members of the occupation consider the techniques valid. On the other hand, state and local school boards clearly have the right to dictate the content of the curriculum and to prescribe particular teaching techniques. The cookbook curriculum that I discuss as a threat to autonomy in several chapters of this textbook may be unwise, or so many teachers think, but it is also legal. Regarding the example of AIDS instruction that we discussed earlier, school systems apparently do have the right to control what teachers say about the disease. Teachers should check their instructional guides before they utter the words "safe sex."[35]

The courts have ruled that academic freedom is fundamental to a democratic society, then, but they have placed limits on the concept. In deciding where to draw the lines, the courts consider such factors as the age and grade level of students, effects on discipline and the educational process, relevance to the curriculum, the judgment of other educators, and state and local curriculum requirements.

The Teacher's Right of Public Dissent

With the rise of teacher unionism and the push for teacher power, teachers are more likely than ever to express their disagreement with administrators and school board members. Are teachers protected when they go public with their criticism? In *Pickering v. Board of Education* (1968), the U.S. Supreme Court considered a suit brought by Marvin Pickering, a tenured high school teacher who lost his job in Illinois because of a letter he published in a local newspaper. In a critical, sarcastic letter to the editor, Pickering took his superintendent and school board to task on the sensitive issue of school finance. He faulted his superiors for the way they raised and spent money, accusing them of shortchanging academics to enrich athletics. He also criticized the "totalitarianism" that stifled teacher dissent in the schools. The school board fired Pickering, claiming that he had damaged the reputations of his superiors and impeded the efficient operation of the schools system. Pickering filed suit to regain his job, arguing that the First Amendment protected his right to speak out.[36]

A state court upheld the dismissal, but the U.S. Supreme Court ordered Pickering reinstated. Several points in the decision deserve our attention. Most importantly, the Supreme Court upheld the teacher's right to make public statements on matters of public concern. Obviously, said the justices, school finance is a public concern. They argued that

> free and open debate is vital to informed decision making by the electorate. Teachers are, as a class, the members of a community most likely to have informed and definite opinions as to how funds allocated to the operation of the schools should be spent. Accordingly, it is essential that they be able to speak out freely on such questions without fear of retaliatory dismissal.[37]

Even though Pickering had made several erroneous statements in his letter, the court found no evidence that he had done so intentionally. Nor did the court find evidence that his letter had harmed anyone's reputation or interfered with the operation of the school system.

The court did place limits on the teacher's right of public dissent, however, implying that had his criticism disrupted his working relationship with an immediate superior—a principal or assistant principal, for example—the dismissal might have been justified. The court also observed that the need for confidentiality—the need to safeguard the privacy of a student's records, for instance—could override a teacher's right to speak out on a matter of public concern.[38]

The most important limitation on public dissent came in another Supreme Court decision, *Connick v. Meyers* (1983). The court held that "when a public employee speaks not as a citizen upon matters of public concern, but instead as an employee upon matters only of personal interest," the courts cannot interfere with personnel decisions.[39] According to this decision, not everything that goes on inside a school is a matter of public concern. In a later Florida case, a federal judge ruled that a teacher who had criticized teacher assignment policies—including the long-controversial practice of assigning coaches to social studies classes—had not raised a legitimate public concern. Instead, the teacher was simply disgruntled over "internal school policies." School finance is a public concern; job assignments, according to the judge, are not. He observed that "in the wake of *Connick*, the federal courts have substantially broadened the employer's rights to control employee speech activities that *relate to his employment.*"[40]

Teachers can publicly criticize their school systems, then, but only if their dissent involves a matter of public concern. Teachers can speak out within their systems on any educational issue, but even then they must be wary of causing disruptions and upsetting working relationships.

Other Forms of Expression

Here our focus expands to encompass broader forms of expression: such matters as personal appearance, political activities, and private life. As I pointed out in the discussion of tenure and dismissal, the courts have established the general principle that a teacher's behavior must reduce effectiveness in the classroom before the behavior can become grounds for dismissal.

Decisions are constantly changing, however, and a prime example of how they change with the times is the matter of personal appearance. When long hair, beards, and mustaches became popular in the late 1960s and early 1970s, the courts often came to the defense of male teachers who wore the hirsute styles. Arguing that grooming is a symbolic expression and therefore protected by the First Amendment, the courts tended to put the burden on the school system to prove that the hair disrupted the classroom. In more recent cases, however, the burden of proof has shifted to the teacher. Unless the teacher can prove that a school system's grooming regulations are irrational or unreasonable, judges are increasingly allowing the regulations to stand.[41]

The courts have given teachers even less leeway in dress. They have validated regulations requiring male teachers to wear coats and ties and female teachers to wear skirts longer than "minis," rejecting teachers' arguments that clothing is symbolic expression. Even so, the decisions suggest that the courts might protect articles of religious clothing—a Jewish teacher's yarmulke, for example, or clothing that is a mark of racial or ethnic pride—such as a black teacher's dashiki.[42]

The courts have also sent mixed signals on political activities. Reversing earlier decisions, the U.S. Supreme Court has made it clear that teachers cannot be dismissed because of their membership in radical organizations. Teachers can belong to the Communist Party or the Ku Klux Klan, for example, and still retain their jobs. If teachers show that they intend to further the illegal aims of an organization, however, they can be fired. Regarding participation in political activities, the courts have held that teachers, like all citizens, can vote, contribute to political candidates, express opinions on political issues, and display bumper stickers. But as public employees, how far can teachers go? Can teachers, like federal employees, be prohibited from managing political campaigns and playing other key roles? The NEA and AFT encourage their members to become involved in partisan politics. No court has yet curtailed such activity, but a test case could go to trial in the 1990s.[43]

Meanwhile, the courts have rendered conflicting decisons on whether teachers have to resign if they are elected to public office and, indeed, whether they can run for office without resigning. This issue has become quite controversial in some states. Is it a conflict of interest for teachers to serve in a state legislature, where they cast votes on education bills that directly affect their jobs? The answer may be yes in one state and no in the state next door. Look for more litigation on political activity as teacher power increases in the 1990s.[44]

Finally, there are the life-style issues that we discussed earlier in this chapter. The landmark decision in this area of expression is *Morrison*, which protected the rights of a homosexual teacher. Again, the critical issue is the degree to which teachers' private lives affect their work. Marc Morrison kept his job, but the courts have upheld the dismissal of other homosexual teachers when students, parents, and colleagues have protested their continued employment. Decisions affecting unmarried teachers who become pregnant or simply live with someone of the opposite sex are also mixed. The courts consider the circumstances of each case, sometimes affirming and sometimes rejecting the teacher's right to remain in the occupation.[45]

ACTIVITIES

1. Talk with several principals about the legal issues surrounding teacher tenure, especially the dismissal of unfit teachers. Interview several officers of a teacher organization and compare the responses.
2. Start a file of information on AIDS. Education journals are running more and more stories on the disease, often emphasizing legal issues. Write to state and local boards of education for policies that will apply to you as a teacher.

3. Where do you stand on the expression issues in this chapter? Stage a classroom debate on academic freedom, or public criticism of school system policies, or a teacher's right to have an unconventional life-style.

SUGGESTED READINGS

For a straightforward, plain-English discussion of teachers' rights and responsibilities, you can do no better than *Teachers and the Law* by Louis Fischer, David Schimmel, and Cynthia Kelly (see note 1, below). Another excellent source of information is *The Rights of Teachers*, an American Civil Liberties Union Handbook by David Rubin with Steven Greenhouse (see note 35).

NOTES

1. Louis Fischer, David Schimmel, and Cynthia Kelly, *Teachers and the Law*, 2d ed. (White Plains, NY: Longman, 1987), ch. 1.
2. For the history of teacher tenure see National Education Association, *The Problem of Teacher Tenure*, Research Bulletin, vol. II, no. 5 (Washington: NEA, 1924); Cecil Winfield Scott, *Indefinite Teacher Tenure: A Critical Study of the Historical, Legal, Operative, and Comparative Aspects* (New York: Bureau of Publications, Teachers College, Columbia University, 1934); and Commission on Educational Reconstruction of the American Federation of Teachers, *Organizing the Teaching Profession* (Glencoe, IL: Free Press, 1955), ch. 4.
3. Edwin M. Bridges, *The Management of Teacher Incompetence* (Stanford, CA: Institute for Research on Educational Finance and Governance, Stanford University, August 1983); Fischer, Schimmel, and Kelly, *Teachers and the Law*, pp. 28–29.
4. Fischer, Schimmel, and Kelly, *Teachers and the Law*, pp. 27–28.
5. Ibid., pp. 29–30.
6. Ibid., pp. 30–31.
7. Ibid., pp. 31–34.
8. *Goldberg v. Kelly*, 38 U.S.L.W. 4223 (March 24, 1970).
9. Bridges, *The Management of Teacher Incompetence*, pp. 19–20.
10. Ibid., pp. 23–25, 13–14.
11. Bridges, *The Management of Teacher Incompetence*, pp. 14–21. See also Bridges, *The Incompetent Teacher: The Challenge and the Response* (Philadelphia: Falmer Press, 1986), and Bridges and Patricia J. Gumport, *The Dismissal of Tenured Teachers for Incompetence* (Stanford, CA: Institute for Research on Educational Finance and Governance, February 1984).
12. Fischer, Schimmel, and Kelly, *Teachers and the Law*, p. 74.
13. Ibid., p. 59.
14. Ibid., pp. 65–66.
15. Bruce Beezer, "Reporting Child Abuse and Neglect: Your Responsibility and Your Protections," *Phi Delta Kappan* 66 (February 1985): 434–436.
16. National Child Abuse Prevention and Treatment Act of 1974 (P.L. 93–247), quoted in Fischer, Shimmel, and Kelly, *Teachers and the Law*, p. 66.

17. Marnell Holtgraves, "Help the Victims of Sexual Abuse Help Themselves," *Elementary School Guidance and Counseling* 21 (December 1986): 155–159.
18. See Debra Viadero, "C.D.C. Urges AIDS Instruction in Every Grade," *Education Week* (February 3, 1988), p. 4. A U.S. Education Department booklet on AIDS, *Schools without Drugs* (Washington: U.S. Department of Education, 1987), downplays the protective benefits of condoms.
19. Cathy Allen Broadwell and John L. Strope, Jr., "Students with AIDS," *West's Education Law Reporter* 49 (January 5, 1989): 1105–1114.
20. Debra Viadero and Peter Drotman, "Expert's Answers to Frequently Asked Questions about AIDS," *Education Week* (September 30, 1987), p. 6.
21. Rehabilitation Act of 1973, Section 504, quoted in Broadwell and Strope, "Students with AIDS," p. 1106.
22. Broadwell and Strope, "Students with AIDS," pp. 1106–1110.
23. Viadero and Drotman, "Expert's Answers," p. 6.
24. Viadero, "AIDS in Schools: Compassion vs. 'the Public's Right to Know,' " *Education Week* (January 20, 1988), pp. 1, 26; Broadwell and Strope, "Students with AIDS."
25. Viadero, "AIDS in Schools," p. 26.
26. Ibid.
27. *Peter W. v. San Francisco Unified School District*, 131 Cal. Rptr. 854 (Cal. App. 1976).
28. Ibid.
29. *Hoffman v. Board of Education of the City of New York*, 64 A.D.2d 369, 410 N.Y.S.2d 99 (1978).
30. Ibid.
31. *Hoffman v. Board of Education of the City of New York* 49 N.Y.2d 317, 424 N.Y.S.2d 376 (1979).
32. *Parducci v. Rutland*, 316 F. Supp. 352 (N.D. Ala. 1970).
33. Ibid.
34. Fischer, Schimmel, and Kelly, *Teachers and the Law*, pp. 120–125.
35. Ibid., pp. 125–127; David Rubin with Steven Greenhouse, *The Rights of Teachers: The Basic ACLU Guide to a Teacher's Constitutional Rights*, rev. ed. (New York: Bantam Books, 1984), pp. 130–131.
36. *Pickering v. Board of Education*, 225 N.E.2d 1 (1967), 391 U.S. 563 (1968).
37. *Pickering v. Board of Education*, 391 U.S. 563 (1968).
38. Ibid.
39. *Connick v. Myers*, 461 U.S. 138 (1983).
40. *Ferrara v. Mills*, 596 F. Supp. 1069 (S.D. Fla. 1984), 761 F.2d 1508 (11th Cir. 1986).
41. Fischer, Schimmel, and Kelly, *Teachers and the Law*, pp. 333–336.
42. Ibid., pp. 337–338, 346–347.
43. Rubin, *Rights of Teachers*, pp. 74–82; Fischer, Schimmel, and Kelly, *Teachers and the Law*, pp. 175–183.
44. See note 43.
45. Fischer, Schimmel, and Kelly, *Teachers and the Law*, pp. 220–224, 236–238; Rubin, *Rights of Teachers*, pp. 147–158.

PART II
Schools and Society

CHAPTER 6

History of American Education

DEBATES AND PATTERNS

This chapter uses debates and patterns to introduce the history of American education. The debates took place before the Civil War and at the turn of the twentieth century, yet they have a surprisingly contemporary ring. The patterns have appeared over the course of this century, and they are still shaping the schools. All historians try to avoid reading the present into the past—they call that the sin of "presentism"—but most historians believe that studying the past can help us live better in the present.

I have tried to capture the excitement of educational history by focusing on debates that occurred during two eras of educational reform. In both periods the future of the schools—and indeed, the future of the nation—hung in the balance as citizens debated fundamental questions about education: Whose children should go to school? What kinds of schools should they attend? What should they study? Who should control the schools?

Debates over these issues were especially heated before the Civil War and at the turn of the twentieth century. Looking back on the past, it is easy to understand why. Both eras were periods when the United States itself was changing rapidly, times when many people were convinced that they could improve the nation if only they could channel change in a constructive way. In both eras reformers who wanted to change the schools took their place alongside reformers with plans to remake other social institutions. And in both eras citizens spoke out freely for and against the proposals for reform.

After listening to the debates, we will turn our attention to twentieth-century patterns of education. We will examine four patterns: the competition for control of the schools; the local-state-federal balance of power; the quest for equal educational opportunities; and trends in the curriculum. Some historians argue that these patterns show more stability than change. They claim that the basic structure and basic purposes of American education have changed little during this century. Other historians disagree. They contend that the growing strength of teacher organizations and the development of the cookbook curriculum, to cite two examples we have discussed in earlier chapters, are fundamental changes—major breaks with the past.

HISTORICAL INTERPRETATION

In order to understand why historians disagree, you need to realize that history is not a literal record of the past. History is an *interpretation* of the past. History reflects the spirit of the times in which it is written; how historians view their own eras influences how they view the past. Historians select from the past those ideas and events that seem significant to them and then interpret what they have selected through the lens of their own experience. Although they do not deliberately distort the past, historians readily acknowledge that they "cannot jump out of [their] intellectual skin."[1]

You should be aware of several major varieties of historical interpetation. In the early 1900s, *celebrationist* historians dominated the history of American education. We call them celebrationists because they wrote glowing, inspirational accounts that were full of praise for both the nation and its schools. In their interpretation, the United States was a country of great virtue, and much of its virtue flowed from its wonderful schools. Concerned with preserving and extending public education, celebrationist historians saw the rise of public schools as a triumph of good over evil.[2]

By the 1920s and 1930s, *liberal* historians were criticizing the idealized picture the celebrationists had painted. In the liberal interpretation, the nation and its schools were basically good, but both had problems that cried out for attention. The liberals pointed out some of the biases in schools and society— biases against poor people and black people, for example. Liberal historians of the twenties and thirties stressed conflict, the clash of competing ideas and interests. The emphasis on conflict became especially pronounced during the Great Depression. As times changed, however, so did the liberal interpretation. During the 1940s and 1950s, liberal historians downplayed conflict and competition and emphasized consensus and cooperation. Liberal historians of this era seemed confident that the United States could solve its problems, and they called on public educators to play key roles in building a better nation.[3]

Revisionist historians displaced the liberals as the dominant interpretive force during the late 1960s and 1970s. Revisionist history portrayed the nation and its schools as flawed—fundamentally flawed, according to the harsher revisionists. In the revisionist interpretation, public schools were deliberately designed to protect the status of elite groups and keep the children of other groups in their place. Revisionist history written during the sixties and seventies had a pessimistic tone, for most revisionists believed that it was impossible to improve the schools without making fundamental changes in society, changes that people with wealth and power have successfully resisted.[4]

Since the late 1970s, historical interpretation has been in transition. Today no single point of view is dominant. The spirit of the times, however, continues to leave its stamp on history. Reflecting the more conservative national mood of the Reagan-Bush era, *neoconservative* historians—it would be unfair to call them celebrationists, but they do seem nostalgic for the good old days of American education—are offering their interpretation of such issues as changes in the curriculum, the effects of desegregation, and the place of traditional values in the schools. Revisionist and liberal historians, of course, are challenging the neoconservative point of view.[5]

As you read this chapter, remember that you are reading an interpretation of the past. I have included debates to expose you to different points of view, but you should be aware that as I wrote the chapter I constantly had to decide which debates to include and which to omit, how to present opposing positions on the issues, and so forth. In other words, this chapter is interpretive from beginning to end. Let me challenge you to judge the past for yourself as you read—be critical and think of different interpretations. I hope the chapter helps you catch the spirit of historical debate, the clash of opinions *in* the past as well as *about* the past.

COMMON SCHOOL REFORM
IN HISTORICAL CONTEXT

During the three decades before the Civil War, public education as we know it began to take shape. Americans built statewide public school systems—*common school* systems, they were originally called. Controlled to some degree by the state governments, common schools were different from the various kinds of locally controlled schools with which Americans were familiar. Common schools, according to the reformers who advocated them, would be common to all children; they would teach a common political creed; and they would instill a common morality based on nonsectarian religion.

Until the 1960s, most educational historians gave common school reform a favorable review. Celebrationists were hard pressed to criticize it at all. Liberals have generally viewed the common schools crusades as noble if imperfectly conducted. Revisionists, however, have charged that school reformers ran roughshod over the values and interests of certain groups—the poor, religious minorities, political dissenters—in the drive to bring schooling under state control. Neoconservative historians have come to the defense of the reformers, arguing that revisionists have exaggerated the drawbacks and downplayed the benefits of common schools. These contrasting historical interpretations recall the debates over schooling that occurred before the Civil War. In order to understand the debates, we need to be familiar with the locally controlled schools that common school reformers wanted to replace.

District Schools, Academies, and Other Schools

Had we been able to tour the new nation in the late 1700s and early 1800s, we would have seen a great deal of variation in education. In New England, where traditions of schooling were strongest, *district schools* had dotted the country-side well before the American Revolution. Massachusetts had led the way in 1642 with legislation requiring parents and guardians to make sure that their children could read, and that legislation was followed by an act of 1647 requiring every town of 50 or more families to appoint a reading and writing teacher. The religious and political influence of the Puritans on these developments was unmistakable. The Puritans believed that universal literacy would prevent the development of a pauper class, enable citizens to understand the law, and—most importantly—save souls. The 1647 school act was known as the "Old Deluder Satan Law," for it was intended to help people resist the wiles of the devil himself.[6]

The "New England model" of district schools grew out of this heritage. New England towns and townships were, on the average, six miles square. By the mid-1700s most of them contained several population centers or villages. As population growth continued, the towns gradually delegated control over the schools to the individual villages, which began to function as school districts. This decentralized model of schooling took local control of education to the extreme. The citizens of each village set their own school taxes and, through a committee of selectmen, hired the teacher (usually a man), established the length of the school year, and determined the course of study.[7]

The one-room district school took in boys and girls ranging in age from about 5 to about 15 years. Their attendance, limited by weather, distance, and farm work, was irregular. Literacy, morality, and religion were the heart of the curriculum, with memorization and recitation the dominant pedagogy. The teacher rarely stayed in one school for more than a session or two. For the children of the wealthiest New Englanders, tutors offered an alternative to the district school. The sons of the elite could then enroll in a *Latin grammar school*, a private school with a classical orientation.

District schools moved west after the Revolution with the passage of the Northwest Ordinances of 1785 and 1787. These laws, which governed the settlement of the territory west of the Allegheny Mountains, laid out land in townships that were six miles square, with each township divided into 36 sections one mile square. The sixteenth section, which fell close to the center of the township, was set aside for education—it often became the site of a district school. Other acts of Congress applied the sixteenth-section principle to the settlement of territory outside the Old Northwest. In this way the decentralized New England model came to many of the states admitted to the new nation. District schools were scattered throughout the Midwest by 1850 and across the Great Plains and Far West during and after the Civil War.

District schools were never as popular in the South, however, even in the newer southern states that came into the union with sixteenth-section lands earmarked for education. In the antebellum South a different model of education prevailed. The children of the wealthy had their tutors and private schools; "middling" whites attended academies (which we will discuss next), denominational schools, or the few district schools; poor whites received little or no formal education; and in most states black slaves were prohibited by law from learning to read and write.[8]

In the Middle Atlantic states—New York, New Jersey, Pennsylvania, and Delaware—yet another model of schooling developed. Here differences in ethnicity, language, and religion drew people into a variety of denominational schools, among them Dutch Reformed, Quaker, Jewish, and Roman Catholic. District schools and academies were more numerous in the Middle Atlantic region than in the South, but the pull of private religious education was strong.

Academies offered schooling to students who were at least middling in social status—or who had aspirations to be. Billing themselves as more practical than the Latin grammar schools, academies took in students whose ages usually ranged from about 14 to 25. The education that academies provided was supposed to be both "ornamental" and "useful," as Benjamin Franklin had explained in his 1749 proposal for an academy in Philadelphia. Franklin had outlined plans for a school that would place more emphasis on English grammar, composition, and public speaking than on Latin and Greek. History, mathematics, and science—subjects to which Latin grammar schools paid little attention—would be prominent in the curriculum. Carpentry, printing, farming, and other practical skills would also have a place. Such a course of study, Franklin argued, would prepare students to get ahead in life.[9]

But the academies that became increasingly popular throughout the nation in the first half of the nineteenth century rarely had so practical a slant. Ironically, Franklin's proposal led to the establishment of a school that evolved into the University of Pennsylvania, a classically oriented institution. Parents wanted their children to get ahead, to be sure, but most parents believed that an education in the classics was the key to social mobility. Thus the academies stressed practicality in moderation, careful not to steer too far away from the subjects that were the mark of middle- and upper-class culture.[10]

From our twentieth-century vantage point, academies were a curious blend of "public" and "private." Typically, academies held public charters and received public funds, but they also charged tuition and were governed by private boards of trustees. Academies also blurred the line that we draw between high schools and colleges. Most academies were more like the former; a few were more like the latter. Indeed, academies were sometimes called "people's colleges." Academies were usually coeducational, although some, like Emma Willard's Troy Female Seminary and Mary Lyon's Mount Holyoke Seminary, were exclusively for females. Such institutions made their reputations by offering women educational opportunities that were unavailable elsewhere. The popularity of academies grew rapidly between the Revolution and the Civil War.[11]

In the early years of the nation, then, Americans attended a variety of locally controlled schools. Such figures as Benjamin Franklin, Noah Webster, Benjamin Rush, George Washington, Thomas Jefferson, and James Madison spoke out in support of the "general diffusion of knowledge" among the populace. The republican spirit of the new nation included the belief that schooling had a crucial role to play in promoting nationalism, patriotism, and a balance between freedom and order. Most Americans were in agreement that schooling was a good thing and that the nation needed more of it.[12]

But this broad consensus concealed fundamental disagreements over the purposes and control of schooling. Jefferson and Rush, for example, differed over whether schools should impose order and virtue on students (Rush's position) or simply cultivate the inborn reason and moral sense that students bring to school (Jefferson's position). Clearly, Jefferson and Rush also disagreed over the nature of human beings. Interestingly enough, in the late 1700s Jefferson and Rush both proposed statewide school systems to put their educational ideas into practice—and their proposals fell on deaf ears. For more than half a century after the Revolution, in fact, Americans saw little need to involve the state governments in schooling.[13]

The Impact of Modernization

But the nation was changing. By the 1830s, three major trends were underway, exerting their strongest influence on New England and the Middle Atlantic states. Urbanization, industrialization, and immigration—historians call them the forces of *modernization*—were altering the way Americans felt about their nation and its schools. These trends were closely related. A worldwide movement of people from the farm to the city had begun, prompted by changes in agriculture and accelerated by the lure of factory jobs. Many of those who swelled the population of American cities like Boston, New York, and Philadelphia had been born in the rural areas of this nation, but many others were newly arrived from abroad. Immigration from Ireland and Germany was heavy in the three decades before the Civil War, bringing to the United States large numbers of people whose language was not English and whose religion was not Protestant. These immigrants seemed especially "foreign" to Americans of British descent.[14]

The entire process of modernization seemed threatening to many Americans, for the traditional community controls that worked well in small towns and rural areas seemed to break down in industrial cities. Agrarian communities were usually homogeneous, composed of people with similar backgrounds and beliefs. Out in the country, family, church, and neighbors kept people in line—everyone knew everyone else's business. In the heterogeneous cities, by contrast, people could and did go their own ways. The social and economic distance between rich and poor seemed to widen. The popular press constantly reminded the public of the consequences of urban poverty, playing up sensationalized accounts of crime and degradation: men turning to strong drink, women turning to prostitution, and children working in factories or roaming the streets at all hours. To some citizens it seemed that the cities were already out of control and that the entire nation would soon be in danger. Something had to be done.

Out of this ferment came an upsurge of reform, a remarkable variety of movements that had in common the urge to perfect and control the modernizing society. Urbanization, industrialization, and immigration held out the promise of great rewards, not the least of them economic development—thus the drive to perfect society—but they exacted a frightening toll that was painfully obvious on city streets—thus the quest for control. Temperance crusaders, prison reformers, advocates of women's rights, pacifists, abolitionists—these and many others worked to win popular support for their causes, sometimes competing and sometimes cooperating. Often an individual reformer worked for several causes simultaneously or moved from one to another over the course of a lifetime. School reformers mounted an educational crusade, often quoting scripture to prove that the changes they sought were the most fundamental: "Train up a child in the way he should go: and when he is old, he will not depart from it" (Proverbs 22: 6). Pay the schoolmaster today, they exhorted, or pay the jailer tomorrow. Thus the common school movements of the antebellum era were one piece in an elaborate mosaic of reform.[15]

Before the pace of modernization quickened in the 1830s, some Americans were already finding fault with the district schools. Even in Massachusetts, which prided itself as the nation's educational leader, decentralization yielded a patchwork of schools that varied tremendously from one district to the next. The lack of uniformity was evident in many ways, including the quality of teachers. It troubled James G. Carter, a Massachusetts educator and legislator, that his state had established no qualifications for teaching. The selectmen of each district, usually advised by local clergy, hired whomever they pleased. The result, as we saw in the introduction to Chapter 3, was often the employment of teachers "who know nothing, absolutely nothing, of the complicated and difficult duties assigned to them."[16] With an eye toward raising standards and eventually enforcing them statewide, James Carter in 1826 proposed a network of state colleges to train teachers.

But he had more on his mind, as the following warning on the perils of decentralization indicates.

> If the policy of the legislature, in regard to free schools, for the last twenty
> years be not changed, the institution, which has been the glory of New

England will, in twenty years more, be extinct. If the State continue to relieve themselves of the trouble of providing for the instruction of the whole people, and to shift the responsibility upon the towns, and the towns upon the districts, and the districts upon individuals, each will take care of himself and his own family as he is able, and as he appreciates the blessing of a good education. The rich will, as a class, have much better instruction than they now have, while the poor will have much worse or none at all. The academies and private schools will be carried to much greater perfection than they have been, while the public free schools will become stationary or retrograde.[17]

Carter's basic argument was that the state could no longer afford to entrust something as vital as schooling to the whims of local people. He envisioned schools that were less stratified by social class, accessible—at least at the lower levels—to rich and poor alike. Girls as well as boys would attend. Reaching this goal, he insisted, would require some degree of state control.

In time the Massachusetts legislature responded favorably to Carter's arguments. The first public *normal school* (teacher training institution) in the state as well as the nation opened in Lexington in 1839. But Carter had already won his greatest victory in 1837 with the creation of a state board of education, also the first in the nation, and the appointment of Horace Mann as its secretary. Mann, who would soon be called the father of public education in the United States, set out on a 12-year crusade to establish common schools throughout Massachusetts. Gradually other states followed suit. Connecticut established a state board of education with Henry Barnard as its secretary in 1838, and during the 1840s and 1850s common school movements appeared in most of the states outside the South. Even in that region there were common school crusaders, although before the Civil War the movement was not very successful outside a few cities.[18]

Common school reformers had ambitious goals. They wanted to provide at least three years of tax-supported schooling for every white child in the nation. In the cities they usually set their sights higher, proposing grammar schools and high schools for students who wished to go beyond the primary level. They wanted to upgrade teaching by setting standards for training and hiring teachers, who increasingly were young women (see Chapters 1 and 3). Centralizing some of the control of schooling at the state level was the key to reaching the other goals, they were convinced, for the reformers found how hard it was to rely on the power of persuasion alone. Even though Carter, Mann, Barnard, and other reformers were tireless promoters, collecting statistics, publishing reports and journals, and traveling from community to community to drum up interest in common schools, initially they obtained mixed results. But they were persistent, and they knew how to play the game of state politics. Some of them were lawyers, former holders of other political offices, or veterans of other reform crusades. Horace Mann was all of these: an attorney and former legislator who numbered temperance, prison and asylum reform, and abolition among his many causes. Battles over centralization would continue throughout the nineteenth century and even longer in the South, but state legislatures gradually gave state boards of education the ultimate political weapon: the power of the purse. With the passage of statewide school taxes, state boards could withhold funds from local districts to force compliance with state standards.[19]

DEBATES OVER COMMON SCHOOL REFORM

The common school crusades peaked in intensity during the 1840s and 1850s. Feelings ran high in legislative chambers, courthouses, town halls, and lyceums across the nation as citizens debated educational issues. When the reformers stood up to argue that district schools were not reaching many children, a typical reply was that local people could simply increase their financial support and improve the schools, making them more attractive to all students. To the argument that many teachers were unqualified, the reply came that better wages would attract better teachers—if the people really wanted them. As we saw in Chapter 3, the opponents often added that training in pedagogy was useless. The existing district schools had no inherent weaknesses, the opponents of common schooling suggested; it was the responsibility of local citizens to strengthen the schools as they saw fit. State-regulated common schools and normal schools were totally unnecessary.[20]

As the debates unfolded, it became clear that the reformers were using the word "common," not in the sense of "ordinary" or "only for the poor," but in three more inclusive ways. Common schools would be common to all children; they would teach a common political creed; and they would instill a common morality based on nonsectarian religion. Interestingly, outside of the South most of the opponents conceded the desirability of the first kind of commonality, although we know that few advocates on either side envisioned racially integrated schools. Still, conceding the importance of schooling for all children weakened the opponents' case when the discussion turned to "laggard" districts in which people seemed to care little about providing schools of any sort. In those instances, Horace Mann and other reformers argued, the best interest of both the children and the nation compelled the state to step in.[21]

The political, moral, and religious dimensions of commonality drew sharp attacks, even though the reformers tried to walk a tightrope in hopes of avoiding controversy. Orestes Brownson, editor of *The Boston Quarterly Review*, did his best to shake the tightrope in his critique of Horace Mann's *Second Annual Report of the [Massachusetts] Board of Education* in 1839. He wrote:

> Education, then, must be religious and . . . political. Neither religion nor politics can be excluded. Indeed, all education that is worth anything is either religious or political and fits us for discharging our duties either as simple human beings or as members of society.[22]

Building on this premise, Brownson posed the dilemma that public schools have always faced. If they excluded politics and religion, some people would regard the education they provided as worthless; if politics and religion were included, some people would take offense.

Politics

Orestes Brownson was a Democrat. Before the Civil War, his party supported schooling for all citizens but often opposed common schools. State governments should leave local schools in the hands of local people, said the Democrats. Common school reformers, by contrast, were more likely to be Whigs. Their party advocated an active role for the states as well as the federal government in securing internal improvements for the nation. In Massachusetts and in other states, the common school crusade was dividing people along traditional party lines. Turning his attention to the common political creed that Horace Mann, a prominent Whig, wanted to teach in the schools, Brownson dryly observed:

> Establish, then, your Whig board of education; place on it a single Democrat, to save appearances; enable this board to establish normal schools and through them to educate all the children of the commonwealth, authorize them to publish common-school libraries, to select all the books used in school, and thus to determine all the doctrines which our children shall imbibe, and what will be the result? We have then given to some half a dozen Whigs the responsible office of forming the political faith and conscience of the whole community.[23]

Mann and the common schoolers would admit nothing of the sort. They rejected the idea that teachers had to avoid discussing politics and government entirely or else offend students by taking sides on partisan issues. As Mann put it,

> Surely, between these extremes, there must be a medium not difficult to be found. And is not this the middle course, which all sensible and judicious men, all patriots, and all genuine republicans, must approve?—namely, that those articles in the creed of republicanism, which are accepted by all, believed in by all, and which form the common basis of our political faith, shall be taught to all. But when the teacher, in the course of his lessons or lectures on the fundamental law, arrives at a controverted text, he is either to read it without comment or remark; or, at most, he is only to say that the passage is the subject of disputation, and that the schoolroom is neither the tribunal to adjudicate, nor the forum to discuss it.[24]

The common schoolers were able to walk the tightrope in the arguments over the political aspects of commonality. Most Americans seemed content with the "middle course" Mann suggested—a course that involved *controlled* political discussion. To be sure, since Mann's day a variety of groups from across the political spectrum have objected that their views were not getting a fair hearing in the public schools, but the protests have never convinced large numbers of Americans to abandon the schools.

Morality and Religion

The common schoolers fell off the tightrope, however, in their quest for a common morality based on nonsectarian religion. For most nineteenth-century Americans, religion and morality were firmly linked; few even entertained the thought that the common schools could inculcate morality without also inculcating religion. In the context of the times, morality divorced from religion was no morality at all. But in an increasingly heterogeneous nation, where Catholics, Jews, people of other non-Protestant faiths, and people of no religious faith were becoming more numerous every year, how could the schools provide a common moral and religious education?

Mann naively believed that the answer lay in removing specific religious doctrine from the schools while retaining a common, nonsectarian creed as the basis for moral education. The nonsectarian creed he had in mind, however, was not a distillation of principles from religions around the world. Even though Mann was a Unitarian, he centered his faith on Christ, and he was well aware that most Americans thought of themselves as Christians. Thus "nonsectarian" came to mean "nondenominational Christian" in the language of Horace Mann and most other leaders of the common school movement.[25]

Once again Mann believed he had found a middle course, a compromise. How could anyone object to moral lessons based on nondenominational Christianity? Mann expressed it this way:

> In this age of the world, it seems to me that no student of history, or observer of mankind, can be hostile to the precepts and the doctrines of the Christian religion, or opposed to any institutions which expound and exemplify them.[26]

Orestes Brownson, however, found the compromise unacceptable. He spoke for many opponents of common schooling when he said:

> The board assure[s] us Christianity shall be insisted on so far, and only so far, as it is common to all sects. This, if it mean anything, means nothing at all. All who attempt to proceed on the principle here laid down will find their Christianity ending in nothingness. Much may be taught in general, but nothing in particular. No sect will be satisfied; all sects will be dissatisfied. For it is not enough that my children are not educated in a belief contrary to my own; I would have them educated to believe what I hold to be important truth.[27]

Brownson was a Roman Catholic. Like other members of his faith, he rejected moral instruction based on general Christian principles as watered-down and meaningless—some Catholics branded it "godless"—calling instead for moral instruction grounded explicitly in the doctrines of Catholicism. Would such instruction be possible in common schools regulated by the state? No, but it would be in district schools that left decisions on moral and religious education in the hands of local citizens. Many Catholics and a small number of Protestants took this position along with Brownson. In effect, the content of moral and religious education would be subject to majority rule in each district. In Catholic districts, Catholicism would prevail in the schools; in Methodist districts, Methodism would dominate; and so on. Those who were unhappy with the schools in their district could open parochial schools and receive public funds to support them, a practice that was widely accepted before the rise of common schools.

Brownson's vision of publicly funded sectarian schools clashed with Mann's vision of moral and religious commonality. Sectarian schools were divisive, Mann argued. He was relieved that most Protestants seemed content to teach their children specific religious principles at home and in church; Protestants generally accepted common schools that based moral instruction on what was called nonsectarian religion. Catholics, however, continued to protest, not only in Massachusetts but wherever they were a significant religious minority. Mann became alarmed as still other disputes over commonality broke out, making the possibility of compromise seem remote indeed.[28]

We have already seen that the common schoolers construed "nonsectarian religion" as "nondenominational Christianity." Catholics took the argument a step further, charging that "nondenominational Christianity," as put into practice in the common schools, was really "nondenominational Protestantism." Daily reading of the King James version of the Bible, "without note or comment," was standard practice in common schools—it was fast being written into law as state legislatures and state boards of education began to regulate the schools. Catholics objected that they used another translation of the Bible, the Douay version, and that it was dangerous to read the scriptures without commentary—students might interpret them incorrectly without guidance. The common schools were filled with Protestantism, they further complained. Many textbooks were replete with slurs against Catholics in general and Irish immigrants in particular. Protestant teachers and students often ridiculed Catholic students. How could Catholic parents send their children to such schools?

The most publicized battle over these issues occurred in New York City during the 1830s and 1840s. Trustees of the Public School Society were determined to increase Catholic enrollment, for they were convinced that Catholic children, especially those of recent immigrants, needed common schooling to fit into society. Otherwise, they might grow up as unsocialized outsiders. The trustees offered to edit some of the offensive passages from the textbooks, but they would not budge on reading the King James Bible without explication.

After Catholics rejected the offer and petitioned for public funds to support their parochial schools, a statewide political controversy erupted. In 1842 the legislature intervened to make New York City part of the state's common school system, at the same time banning the use of public funds to support sectarian religious instruction. Although similar battles would be fought in other places, the confrontation between Protestants and Catholics in New York City set two precedents. In state after state, legislatures withdrew financial support from sectarian education, and in city after city, Catholics withdrew into their own schools.[29]

THE TRIUMPH OF COMMON SCHOOLS

By the outbreak of the Civil War, common school reformers could sense that they had turned a corner. The failure to enlist Catholics in the school crusades had been a setback, to be sure, but there had been many victories. The idea of commonality had spread West and South as state legislatures committed themselves to the goals of tax-supported primary schooling for all white children, higher standards for training and hiring teachers, and a degree of centralized control vested in state boards of education. Even in the South common schools were a reality in some cities, and southern legislatures were trying to translate the commitment they had made on paper into actual schools for the rural South. Thus the framework to support statewide school systems was either in place or under construction throughout most of the nation.

For fifty years after the Civil War educators were busy building, reinforcing, and expanding the systems. Two trends illustrate their progress. The passage of compulsory school attendance laws, which appeared first in Massachusetts in 1852, quickened after the war, so that by 1900 the laws were on the books in 30 states, by 1910 in 40 states, and by 1918 in all states. Enforcement of the laws, haphazard at best before the turn of the century, became serious as state governments tightened their reins of control.[30]

A parallel development was the rise of public high schools. By now it should come as no surprise that Massachusetts led the way—Boston English High School opened in 1821—with other New England states, the Middle Atlantic states, and then the rest of the nation gradually following suit. Nineteenth-century public high schools present a paradox to educational historians. With regard to gender, the schools were surprisingly egalitarian. They gave girls a chance to compete on relatively equal footing with boys, and compete the girls did. Girls outnumbered and often outperformed boys in public high schools, a pattern that lasted into the early twentieth century. Regarding social class, the schools were highly exclusive. As late as 1890 only about 4 percent of all the young people in the eligible age group attended public high schools, while private high schools enrolled another 2 percent. Public secondary education had a limited appeal in the nineteenth century, primarily to middle class Americans who lived in cities. The wealthy, the poor, and the rural, in fact, sometimes challenged the right of governments to levy taxes for public high schools, arguing that the few who wanted secondary education for their children should pay for it themselves.[31]

A landmark decision of the Michigan Supreme Court in the *Kalamazoo* case (1874), however, gave public educators yet another victory, legally establishing a place for high schools as one rung on an educational ladder that extended from primary schools through colleges and universities. The *Kalamazoo* decision strengthened the framework of public school systems and readied them for unprecedented expansion in the early twentieth century. Public elementary schools soon bulged at the seams, and by 1920 almost one-third of the eligible age group was enrolled in secondary education, overwhelmingly in public high schools.[32]

PROGRESSIVE SCHOOL REFORM IN HISTORICAL CONTEXT

Once the students got to school, however, what were educators to do with them? This question goes to the heart of school reform during the progressive era, as historians call the period from the election of President William McKinley in 1896 through the entry of the United States into World War I in 1917. During these years public schools changed in several lasting ways. Arguing that the schools should meet the needs of an increasingly heterogeneous student body, educators diversified the curriculum and extended the work of the schools into new areas. Students began taking different courses and different programs depending on their abilities and "probable destinies" in life. The schools took on a host of new responsibilities: paying more attention to the health and home life of students, for example, and training students for specific vocations. Immigrant children and black children confronted the schools with special problems. How should the schools respond? The debates in the next section of this chapter, focused on the cultural theories of *assimilation, pluralism,* and *separation,* suggest some of the strategies that educators considered.

Historians differ in their interpretations of progressive school reform. To celebrationist historians, some of whom were reformers themselves, the diversified curriculum and the new social and economic responsibilities that the schools assumed were in the best interests of students as well as society. Liberal historians, regarding progressive reform as basically well intended, have nevertheless argued that certain reforms—vocational programs and low-ability classes, for example—often harmed the very students they were designed to help. Revisionist historians have suggested why: the thrust of progressive reform was *not* to help students, especially those on the lower rungs of the social ladder, but to serve the interests of corporate capitalism. Neoconservative historians have defended corporate capitalism, of course, but they too have been critical of public educators for fragmenting the curriculum and taking on too many social and economic responsibilities.

Keep these interpretations in mind as you read about progressive school reform. Our major concern here is with how the reforms affected immigrant and black children. At the end of this chapter and in Chapter 7, we will take a closer look at the curricular changes that began during the progressive era. Chapter 8 explores another legacy of progressive reform: the stratification of schools by social class.

Modernization Accelerates

Even though the reform movements that occurred during the progressive era were quite diverse, the popular belief that the nation could take charge of its affairs and move forward gave the era a degree of unity. The need for reform seemed great because the forces of modernization—urbanization, industrialization, and immigration—were once again in high gear, confronting the nation with problems and opportunities similar to those the pre-Civil War reformers had faced.

But now the stakes seemed even higher. In 1860 only 20 percent of Americans had lived in cities; by 1920 the figure had climbed to 51 percent, with more than 5,000,000 people crowded into New York City and more than 2,000,000 into Chicago. Industrialization continued to fuel the growth of urban America, but Horace Mann and his contemporaries, certainly no strangers to change, could hardly have anticipated the pace and scale of industrial development after the Civil War: the rapid growth of big business, the extreme concentration of wealth in the hands of the most successful capitalists, and the defensive flight of workers into labor unions.[33]

Many of the workers who took jobs in steel mills, meat-packing plants, garment factories, and other industrial settings were immigrants. The "new" immigration that occurred after 1870 made the "old" immigration seem mild by comparison. In the largest mass movement of people in history, approximately 28 million men, women, and children arrived in the United States from 1870 through 1920, so that by the twenties more than one-third of all the people in the nation were foreign-born or children of the foreign-born. Beyond their sheer numbers, more than half the newcomers were from Central, Eastern, and Southern Europe, bringing with them a host of differences in language, religion, food, work habits, and other cultural traits. To people who had already put down their roots in this country, these new immigrants seemed even more alien than the old Irish and German immigrants.

Just as in the decades before the Civil War, there were calls for change as Americans decided that something had to be done. The reforms that resulted show that "progressive" could mean different things in different contexts. Some reforms were designed to improve the lot of ordinary people: housing regulations to clean up the squalor of tenements, food and drug acts to insure stan-

dards of purity, and labor legislation to establish a reasonable work day and to
get children out of the labor force. Other "progressive" reforms betrayed a lack
of faith in ordinary people. Immigrants were greeted with laws designed to
minimize their influence on the nation, and black Americans lost rather than
gained rights during the period. Today, three-quarters of a century later, some of
these reforms appear quite liberal, others profoundly conservative, still others a
curious mixture.[34]

Liberal and Conservative School Reformers

School reform during the progessive era was just as complex. John Dewey
stands out as the major educational theorist of the era; the theory that he and his
followers developed, in fact, became known as *progressivism*. Social worker
Jane Addams and black sociologist W. E. B. DuBois were among the liberal
reformers who were concerned, like Dewey, with social justice and social service. In this chapter we will call Addams and DuBois to the podium to present
the case for liberal reform; in the next chapter we will pay closer attention to
Dewey. Conservative reformers, represented here by school administrator and
historian Ellwood P. Cubberley and black leader Booker T. Washington, had a
different set of priorities, an agenda centered on social order and business
efficiency. Conservatives outnumbered liberals and often held positions that gave
them more direct influence on the schools. Moreover, most of the teachers,
administrators, and school board members who were responsible for putting
educational reforms into practice on the front lines took an eclectic yet fundamentally conservative approach, paying lip service to the ideas of a Dewey,
perhaps, but acting more like a Cubberley in their day-to-day work.[35]

DEBATES OVER PROGRESSIVE
SCHOOL REFORM

Nowhere is the complexity of reform more clearly illustrated than in the debates
over the schooling of immigrant children and black children, debates strikingly
similar to those we can hear today. Two cultural theories dominated the debates.
According to the theory of *assimilation*, it was the duty of the schools to fit
children into society by washing out cultural differences and ironing in values
and behaviors that conformed to Anglo-American ways. Here was the idea of
the "melting pot," as most Americans understood it—a crucible that would melt
away the immigrants' cultural differences. According to the theory of *separation*, by contrast, certain cultural groups were so different that their children
were better off attending separate schools, preparing them to reside in separate
neighborhoods, hold separate jobs, and lead separate lives as adults. Members
of these groups were not candidates for the melting pot, for they were regarded
as too different to assimilate—that is, as incurably inferior. The schools, taking

their cues from the rest of the nation, used these theories to develop two distinct educational agendas: schools to promote assimilation for immigrant children, and schools to foster separation for black children. Also singled out for separation throughout the Southwest were Mexican-Americans and Indians, with California adding Oriental children to the list of those schooled separately.[36]

Assimilation for Immigrant Children

Ellwood Cubberley stated the case for the assimilation of immigrants in the textbooks that he wrote for teachers and administrators. Cubberley, an up-from-the-ranks school administrator who became dean of education at Stanford University, was one of the most prominent education professors of his day and a leading celebrationist historian. His textbooks went into numerous editions, influencing several generations of American educators. Had you decided to become a teacher 60 or 70 years ago, your introduction to education might well have been a course taught with one of Cubberley's books. In the well-thumbed volume from which I took the following quotation, the administrator who originally owned the book underlined and annotated Cubberley's views on the new immigrants:

> These Southern and Eastern Europeans were of a very different type from the North and West Europeans who preceded them. Largely illiterate, docile, often lacking in initiative, and almost wholly without the Anglo-Saxon conceptions of righteousness, liberty, law, order, public decency, and government, their coming has served to dilute tremendously our national stock and to weaken and corrupt our political life. . . . They have created serious problems in housing and living, moral and sanitary conditions, and honest and decent government, while popular education has everywhere been made more difficult by their presence. The result has been that in many sections of our country foreign manners, customs, observances, and language have tended to supplant native ways and the English speech, while the so-called "melting pot" has had more than it could handle. The new peoples, and especially those from the South and East of Europe, have come so fast that we have been unable to absorb and assimilate them, and our national life, for the past quarter of a century, has been afflicted with a serious case of racial indigestion.[37]

Nevertheless, Cubberley looked to the future with characteristically progressive optimism. If immmigrant children would only attend public schools rather than the "foreign-language parochial schools," Cubberley opined as he gestured toward the Catholic and Lutheran churches, they would begin to lay aside their Old World culture and pick up American ways. The diversified public school curriculum, he believed, offered vocational courses that would help many immigrant children make a contribution to society. The process of Americanization might take two or three generations to complete, but Cubberley felt sure that the public schools, "our greatest agency for unifying the diverse elements of our population," were up to the task.[38]

The Middle Course of Pluralism

Few public educators disagreed with Cubberley. A strong consensus supported the policies of assimilation he advocated. Two liberal reformers who did dissent were Jane Addams and John Dewey, both of whom tried to chart a middle course between assimilation and separation. Certainly it would be undesirable if each immigrant group went its own way, turning inward and never learning what it means to be American. Such separation would fragment the nation, they acknowledged. But total assimilation would also be unwise, they insisted, for already it was driving a wedge between immigrant parents and their children, depriving the immigrants as well as other Americans of a valuable cultural heritage.

The middle course that Addams and Dewey were seeking eventually became known as *pluralism*. According to this theory, every person is expected to learn the common culture—in this nation, the English language, American history, and the American political system, among many other things—but other cultures are not only tolerated but encouraged. As Addams told the National Education Association in 1908,

> the schools ought to do more to connect these children with the best things of the past, to make them realize something of the beauty and charm of the language, the history, and the traditions which their parents represent. . . .
> If the body of teachers in our great cities could take hold of the immigrant colonies, could bring out of them their handicrafts and occupations, their traditions, their folk songs and folk lore, the beautiful stories which every immigrant colony is ready to tell and translate; could get the children to bring these things into school as the material from which culture is made and the material upon which culture is based, they would discover by comparison that which they give them now is a poor meretricious and vulgar thing. Give these children a chance to utilize the historic and industrial material which they see about them and they will begin to have a sense of ease in America, a first consciousness of being at home. I believe if these people are welcomed upon the basis of the resources which they represent and the contributions which they bring, it may come to pass that these schools which deal with immigrants will find that they have a wealth of cultural and industrial material which will make the schools in other neighborhoods positively envious.[39]

Addams's commitment to pluralism was based on her experience as a social worker and leader of the settlement house movement. She founded Hull House in Chicago in 1889 to encourage contact between privileged women (like Addams herself) and poor people, believing that both could profit from the exchange. Mutual respect was the cornerstone of her philosophy. Addams envisioned settlement houses as community centers that offered educational, social, and recreational programs; she hoped that they would serve as models for public schools and other public agencies. To her disappointment, public educators found little that they wanted to emulate, for they saw little in the immigrant cultures that they regarded as worth saving. Addams was alarmed that the vocational courses into which many immigrant children were steered led to meaningless, repetitive jobs that, she predicted, would produce alienation and drug abuse.[40]

In Addams's day, as today, the issue of language was especially sensitive. Why should the public schools teach students in any language but English, critics wanted to know. Hadn't the schools always used English as the medium of instruction? Conveniently ignored in most of the debates was the history of bilingual public schools in such cities as Cincinnati, Cleveland, Indianapolis, St. Louis, New Orleans, and San Francisco, some of which were using languages other than English as a medium of instruction before the Civil War. Responding to parents who wished to preserve their ethnic culture, some public schools offered bilingual instruction, usually in German and English, as late as World War I, when antiforeign sentiment forced the programs to close. Although bilingual public schools were the exception, not the rule, they set an early precedent for a pluralistic approach to public education, an approach that would become popular in the 1960s and 1970s.[41]

Separation for Black Children

If immigrants were tossed into the melting pot and expected to emerge, completely assimilated, within a few generations, black Americans received no such treatment. Some immigrants were enthusiastic supporters of assimilationist public schools; others, as Cubberley pointed out, rejected them for parochial schools. Blacks, with few exceptions, did not have a choice. In parts of the nation, most notably the rural South, they were lucky if they could go to school at all. As the progressive era opened in 1896, the United States Supreme Court handed down its decision in the *Plessy v. Ferguson* case, which placed the stamp of judicial approval on the "separate but equal" doctrine. The decision gave a railroad company in Louisiana the right to segregate black passengers in train cars that were clearly separate and supposedly equal, and it quickly became the legal basis for segregation in other walks of life, including public education.

The result was a steady deterioration in the quality of black education as a bad situation became worse. In the South, where more than 90 percent of blacks lived, the gaps in financial and physical resources between white schools and black schools widened. At the end of Reconstruction in 1877 the South had spent $1.50 to $2.00 per white student for every dollar spent per black student, a ratio of almost 2 to 1; by the end of the progressive era the ratio had increased to perhaps 4 to 1. These figures estimate regional averages; we know the gap was wider, appallingly wider, in many rural systems, and some historians put the overall ratio of white to black expenditures as high as 15 to 1. Whatever the exact figures, it is obvious that "separate but equal" really meant "separate and unequal." The situation was worst in the South, but elsewhere racial attitudes hardened as lines were drawn to separate blacks and whites, either by law (as in the South) or by custom (as in most of the nation). Race riots and lynchings left ugly scars across the face of the country. In an era often remembered for social progress and uplift, black Americans found their educational rights eroding along with their voting rights, property rights, and other civil rights.[42]

This is the highly charged context in which we must listen to the debates over black education in the progressive era. Perhaps the most important was the long running debate between Booker T. Washington and W. E. B. DuBois, two black leaders whose social and educational views were as different as their backgrounds. Washington, born in Virginia just before the Civil War, literally worked his way *Up from Slavery*, as he explained in his aptly titled autobiography. The education he received at Hampton Institute, an industrial school for blacks in Virginia, convinced him that hard work, practical training, and cooperation with whites were the keys to success for blacks. He put his ideas into practice as head of Tuskegee Institute in Alabama, building the school from the ground up as a national model for the education of black teachers, farmers, and other workers. Washington soon became the best known and most influential black person of his day.[43]

DuBois, born in Massachusetts just after the Civil War, attended integrated public schools, graduated from all-black Fisk University in Nashville, studied abroad at the University of Berlin, and capped his education at Harvard University, where he became the first black in the nation to earn a Ph.D. As a professor at Atlanta University and later as a leader of the National Association for the Advancement of Colored People (NAACP), DuBois spoke out sharply against all forms of racial discrimination. He pushed for equal access to schools at every level, but his heart was in higher education, which he hoped would prepare "the talented tenth"—the most gifted 10 percent of young black people—to become the leaders of their race.[44]

DuBois was too radical and outspoken for the times, but Washington was so popular that he was often invited to address white audiences, a distinction that few other blacks could claim. By the 1890s Washington was already in demand on the lecture circuit, but his 1895 speech at the Cotton States and International Exposition in Atlanta cemented his reputation as "the spokesman for his race." On this occasion the audience consisted of whites and blacks, seated in separate sections. Washington's thesis was that the two races would have to cooperate in order to move the South forward economically. He carefully distinguished between economic and social progress, however. With words chosen to admonish blacks and reassure whites, Washington said:

> The wisest of my race understand that the agitation of questions of social equality is the extremest folly, and that progress in the enjoyment of all the privileges that will come to us must be the result of severe and constant

struggle, rather than of artificial forcing. . . . The opportunity to earn a dollar in a factory just now is worth infinitely more than the opportunity to spend a dollar in an opera house.[45]

Delivering the line that would prove to be the most quoted in the speech, Washington held his hand high: "In all things that are purely social we can be as separate as the fingers, yet one as the hand in all things essential to mutual progress."[46] Thus Washington struck the conservative chords of social order and business efficiency.

Despite his reference to factory work, the industrial education that Washington advocated for black people did not emphasize preparation for city jobs in plants and machine shops; instead, the accent was on rural life, for Washington believed that blacks could make their greatest contributions in farming and farm-related crafts. Moreover, he used the word "industrial" much as we use "industrious" today, stressing such values as efficiency, punctuality, thrift, obedience, and cleanliness more than specific job skills. Above all, he urged black people to adopt the proper attitudes toward work and their place in the economic order. As he cautioned in the Atlanta speech,

> Our greatest danger is, that in the great leap from slavery to freedom, we may overlook the fact that the masses of us are to live by the production of our hands, and fail to keep in mind that we shall prosper in proportion as we learn to dignify and glorify common labor and put brains and skill into the common occupations in life, shall prosper in proportion as we learn to draw the line between the superficial and the substantial, the ornamental gewgaws of life and the useful. No race can prosper till it learns that there is as much dignity in tilling a field as in writing a poem. It is at the bottom of life we must begin, and not at the top.[47]

Industrial education worked its way into black schools at every level. In some elementary schools it threatened to crowd academic studies into a corner, and as the small number of black students who were able to continue their formal education discovered, it was firmly entrenched in high schools and colleges as well.[48]

It angered DuBois that the ideas Washington articulated were so widely accepted. Few blacks and fewer whites paid attention as DuBois and other black activists outlined dissenting points of view. Ellwood P. Cubberley's teacher education textbooks, for example, contained words of praise for Washington and industrial education but no mention of the alternatives. As Cubberley explained matter of factly to future teachers and administrators, "[the Negro's] peculiar mental makeup and character have made his vocational and industrial education almost a necessity."[49] These words struck college-educated blacks like a slap in the face.

In the early 1900s DuBois established himself as Washington's most vocal critic. As a professor at Atlanta University, DuBois knew firsthand how difficult it was to raise money for black colleges and universities with a strong academic orientation. Northern philanthropists were sending money South, to be sure, but Washington's endorsement of industrial education carried so much weight that Tuskegee, Hampton, and other similar schools were receiving the lion's share. Atlanta, Fisk, and other black institutions with more traditional academic programs found it difficult to compete. Adding insult to injury, white philanthropists sometimes required them to develop industrial programs as a condition for receiving financial support. DuBois believed that "progress in human affairs is more often a pull than a push, a surging forward of the exceptional man, and the lifting of his duller brethren slowly and painfully to his vantage-ground."[50] How could the black race produce the professionals and leaders that it needed when the deck seemed to be stacked against academic programs?

In his book *The Souls of Black Folk* (1903), DuBois grappled with that question and went considerably further, offering a pointed critique of Booker T. Washington's overall approach to black-white relations. Calling Washington's 1895 speech the "Atlanta Compromise" and referring to him with more than a hint of sarcasm as "the most distinguished Southerner since Jefferson Davis," DuBois charged that Washington had asked blacks to trade their political power, civil rights, and higher education for "industrial education, the accumulation of wealth, and the conciliation of the South." Blacks had made the bargain, DuBois noted, and three things had occurred:

1. The disfranchisement of the Negro.
2. The legal creation of a distinct status of civil inferiority for the Negro.
3. The steady withdrawal of aid from institutions for the higher training of the Negro.

These movements are not, to be sure, direct results of Mr. Washington's teaching; but his propaganda has, without a shadow of a doubt, helped their speedier accomplishment. . . . And thus Mr. Washington faces the triple paradox of his career:

1. He is striving nobly to make Negro artisans business men and property owners; but it is utterly impossible, under modern competitive methods, for workingmen and property-owners to defend their rights and exist without the right of suffrage.
2. He insists on thrift and self-respect, but at the same time counsels a silent submission to civic inferiority such as is bound to sap the manhood of any race in the long run.
3. He advocates common-schooling and industrial training, and depreciates institutions of higher learning; but neither the Negro common schools, nor Tuskegee itself, could remain open a day were it not for teachers trained in Negro colleges, or trained by their graduates.[51]

Although DuBois' ideas may sound more acceptable than Washington's to our modern ears, we must remember to judge both men by the standards of their times rather than ours. By all accounts, both were sincere and well intended. Washington was not trying to sell black people short—he was trying to make the best of a miserable situation. Recently, in fact, historical evidence has come to light indicating that Washington worked behind the scenes to support civil rights litigation he could not afford to endorse in public. By the same token, DuBois was not the elitist his blunt statement on "the exceptional man" and "his duller brethren" might suggest. Most of the black college students he taught came from poverty backgrounds. DuBois saw what they could achieve when given the opportunity, and he refused to compromise their future. His work with the NAACP helped pave the way for the modern civil rights movement.[52]

PROGRESSIVE SCHOOL REFORM
IN PERSPECTIVE

When progressive reformers, liberal and conservative, stepped back to survey what they had accomplished, conservatives could see more reasons to be pleased. Assimilation and separation were well established in educational theory and practice; pluralism, by contrast, was so undeveloped and unrefined that it had yet to be named. To be sure, all school reformers could point with pride to shared victories: public schools were virtually everywhere, with centralized, statewide systems in place even in the South; the passage and enforcement of compulsory attendance laws was filling the schools with unprecedented numbers of students—the 1920 census found that over 90 percent of children aged seven to thirteen were in school; and more and more of them were continuing their formal education through high school. Reflecting the growing consensus that the schools had to assume new social and economic responsibilities to meet the needs of a diverse student body, the diversified curriculum was rapidly winning acceptance. Another victory that virtually all educational reformers could celebrate was the trend toward more specialized training for teachers. Colleges and universities were adding departments of pedagogy during the progressive era, state teachers colleges were emerging, and state normal schools and high school normal programs were in their heyday. In an era that fell in love with statistics, the facts and figures on the schools looked good.

Liberal reformers could take heart that a new theory of education, *progressivism,* was receiving a great deal of rhetorical support, especially among professors of education and school administrators. Since progressivism was so closely associated with John Dewey, the leading liberal reformer, liberals had high hopes that progressivism would eventually usher in a new era of social service and social justice in the schools. Imagine their disappointment when, in the years after World War I, the nation took a conservative turn and "returned to normalcy"—business as usual. The spirit of liberal reform was a dead letter, as far as the schools were concerned, but professors of education continued to preach, and adminstrators increasingly encouraged teachers to practice, "progressive" methods of classroom instruction. By the 1920s the methodology had been dubbed *progressive education*.[53]

Liberals were also disappointed that the academic discipline of psychology, to which many "progressive" educators were turning in their quest to make teaching and learning more scientific, was becoming another justification for the new status quo. As intelligence testing became widespread in the schools during the 1920s, educators gathered evidence that seemed to support what they were already doing: placing immigrant children, black children, and poor children generally in low-ability classes and vocational programs.[54]

Thus it was the form but not the substance of progressivism that influenced the schools after the war—the rhetoric but not the spirit. At the end of this chapter and throughout the next one, we will examine the controversy over how much the schools changed as a result of progressive influence, whether or not they improved, and who deserves the credit—or the blame.

TWENTIETH-CENTURY PATTERNS OF EDUCATION

We can now look back on nine-tenths of the twentieth century and identify major trends in the schools. Since many of the chapters in this book provide historical perspectives on the issues that they examine, the purpose of this section is to outline broad patterns to help structure the analysis presented elsewhere. Four patterns are especially important: competition among school board members, administrators, and teachers for control of the schools; the changing balance of educational power among the local, state, and federal levels of government; the quest for equal educational opportunities; and trends in the curriculum.

Competition for Control of the Schools

The first pattern, competition for control, has roots in the progressive era. "Let's get the schools out of politics" was the rallying cry of conservative reformers who charged that local school boards were inefficient and corrupt. The problem, they said, was that school boards in major cities had too many members with too many different points of view to do business efficiently. The boards were packed with "petty local politicos" elected from the various wards (political subdivisions) of the city. According to the reformers, such board members lacked a vision of what was good for the system as a whole—they were interested only in the schools in their own wards and, to make matters worse, some of them were on the take, soliciting bribes, kickbacks, and payoffs. The reformers' solution? Smaller school boards with members elected or appointed at-large, with each member representing the city as a whole rather than an individual ward.[55]

The trend toward smaller boards with at-large members swept the nation during the progressive era, spreading from major cities into other school systems. One result was the appearance on local boards of more people that the reformers liked to call "the better sort"—successful businesspeople and professionals, most of them upper-middle and upper class—and a sharp drop in the number of members with lower socioeconomic status. A closely related trend was the rise to power of "professional" school administrators. As enrollments increased and the management of school systems became more complex, local board members gladly turned over more responsibility to superintendents and their growing administrative staffs. "Let the experts manage the schools" was another popular slogan during the progressive era, signaling a shift of power away from board members and toward upper-level administrators. As the twentieth century wore on, local superintendents consolidated their power, claiming that only experienced educators with advanced degrees from university departments of educational administration had the expertise necessary to run the schools. A class of "professional" educators was emerging.[56]

Teachers felt lost in the shuffle. In many respects they had been more comfortable with the situation that had existed before progressive reform. Many teachers had known the board member who represented their ward—a shopkeeper from the neighborhood, perhaps. The smaller, at-large board seemed remote, aloof—a group of elites. The worst development from the teachers' point of view was the attempt to apply the "sound and cheap" principles of scientific management to the schools. Merit pay and promotions based on evaluations by administrators and supervisors posed the greatest threat, as we saw in Chapter 2.

In 1920, 86 percent of America's teachers were women. Just when the numerical dominance of women in the occupation was greater than at any time before or since, however, women were losing power in the school system hierarchy. Most elementary school principals had been women in the late nineteenth century; during the twentieth century women watched these administrative positions go increasingly to men. High school principalships had always belonged to men. Educational historian David Tyack aptly describes the situation:

> Hierarchical organization of the schools and the male chauvinism of the larger society fit as hand to glove. The system required subordination; women were generally subordinate to men; the employment of women as teachers thus augmented the authority of the largely male administrative leadership.[57]

In the early decades of the twentieth century, teachers organized to protect their interests and improve their economic security. Their early organizations were local groups that responded to local problems. Teacher organizations gave women the opportunity to lead, but these groups, too, were often male dominated. With the NEA in the hands of college professors and administrators, some local teacher organizations affiliated with the AFT, a small, struggling union.[58]

From the 1920s through the 1950s, teachers had to strain to make their voice heard in school system policy, even when they spoke through an AFT local. Over the last three decades, however, the situation has changed. The AFT led the way by showing how collective bargaining can amplify the teachers' voice. After scoring organizing victories in New York City and several other large systems, the AFT became a power to be reckoned with. In short order the NEA also became a teacher union, a national giant with strength in every state and in most local school systems. For the first time, teachers had a collective voice in educational policymaking at all three levels of government, and the voice of female teachers was stronger than ever. As we have seen, the new power of teacher organizations is highly controversial. Supporters say teachers are beginning at last to act like professionals rather than employees; detractors say just the opposite is true.

The Local-State-Federal Balance

The increasingly complex politics of teacher organizations add their own weight to the educational balance of power among the local, state, and federal levels of government, the second pattern of twentieth-century education we will consider. Recall the debates over the merits of local versus state control of public education—the tension between the idea that citizens should be able to run their local schools as they see fit and the idea that a degree of centralized control is necessary to insure minimum standards of education. Notwithstanding the state-wide standards promoted by school reformers, local school boards still enjoyed a great deal of autonomy at the turn of the century, for the regulations imposed by state legislatures and state boards of education left plenty of discretion at the local level.

As the century unfolded, the states gradually tightened their reins of control, often in response to controversies and shortcomings in local school systems. Several examples illustrate the trend. Complaints about the content of textbooks—often involving religion or politics, just as in Horace Mann's day— led to more power for state textbook committees, but local school officials usually were able to choose from several titles on the state-approved list or, in some states, simply to ignore the list. Arbitrary dismissals of teachers triggered the passage of state tenure laws, often after successful campaigns by teacher organizations, but local boards could still fire probationary teachers without stating a reason, and administrators could make life miserable for tenured teachers who violated local mores.

Financial problems also enhanced state control. During the Great Depression thousands of local school systems declared insolvency and closed. Faced with already wide gaps in spending between rich systems and poor systems within virtually every state, legislatures stepped in to provide relief, mandating minimum levels of local support as a condition for receiving state aid. Lawsuits from citizens and advocacy groups led to a still greater state role i.. _ finance beginning in the 1960s. Financial problems were also behind the trend toward consolidation of local school systems. In 1900 there were approximately 150,000 independent school districts in the United States; today there are about 15,000. State legislatures justified consolidation on the grounds of economic and academic efficiency—more programs could be offered to more students at lower cost—but local people complained that their control over the schools was slipping away.[59]

Such complaints are not new. Most of them would seem familiar to Horace Mann. What would strike him as novel, though, is the federal government's growing involvement in public education during the twentieth century. Even a Whig like Mann, an advocate of active government, never envisioned public education as a major item on the federal list of "internal improvements." But in 1917 the federal government made its first annual appropriations to secondary schools through the Smith-Hughes Act, which was designed to promote vocational education. For the next few decades the federal role was focused, with Congress trying hard not to step on state and local toes. A series of federal relief acts aided schools during the Depression, the G.I. Bill (1944) helped veterans further their education, and the National Defense Education Act (NDEA) of 1958 entered the schools in the space race.

The real breakthrough in federal involvement came during the 1960s and 1970s, when the federal government began targeting most of its assistance toward students whose education had been a low priority in state and local school systems: poor, minority, handicapped, and female students. Judicial activism in the federal courts complemented the high profile that Congress maintained in public education, and Lyndon Johnson said he wanted to go down in history as an "education president." We will take a closer look at federal involvement in other chapters, especially Chapter 9, but here it is important to note the mixed reviews that the new federal role received. Once again debates over centralized control, this time control at the federal level, broke out across the nation, and during the 1980s Ronald Reagan capitalized on a strong backlash as he cut federal involvement in education.

Part of the backlash reflected the general distrust that Americans have always had of central government, but part of it was based on the newer and more specific concern that the federal government was paying too much attention to certain groups of students—poor, minority, handicapped, and female— and promoting their advancement at the expense of the rest. This development was an ironic reversal of the situation during the first half of the twentieth century, when members of the same groups criticized the federal government for its lack of interest in their plight.[60]

The Quest for Equal Educational Opportunities

As we examine the third pattern of twentieth-century education, we will use black Americans as a case in point. Since the 1920s the NAACP and other organizations working on behalf of black people had brought legal pressure to bear on public schools and colleges, seeking better treatment for black students and teachers. At first the results were disappointing: Southern states continued to spend several times as much money on white as on black children, and in other regions of the nation, particularly in large industrial cities, schools became more segregated rather than less. In the late 1930s, however, the tide began to turn as blacks won court decisions that eventually led to equal salaries for black and white teachers. Other litigation started the long process of desegregating colleges and universities. The major victory came with the United States Supreme Court's landmark decision in *Brown v. Board of Education of Topeka* (1954). The court unanimously overturned *Plessy v. Ferguson* (1896) for elementary and secondary schools, declaring that "in the field of public education the doctrine of 'separate but equal' has no place." The struggle to translate the court's words into action continues today.[61]

The modern civil rights movement that gathered strength in the post-*Brown* era not only helped improve educational opportunities for black students; it also inspired other Americans to press for better education for their children. During the 1960s and 1970s, members of other racial and ethnic minority groups, women, the handicapped, and the poor mounted their own campaigns, and the schools responded in a variety of ways, often by developing special programs with federal funds. Renewed interest in bilingual instruction and the growth of multicultural education led to arguments reminiscent of earlier debates over assimilation, separation, and pluralism. Despite the backlash against federal involvement in education during the 1980s, educators continued to show concern—at least rhetorical concern—for students who became known as the "at risk." In Chapter 8 and other chapters, we will analyze the current status of the quest for equal educational opportunities.

Trends in the Curriculum

The final twentieth-century pattern is a fascinating study of the relationship between educational theory and educational practice. Historians enjoy investigating the evolution of the *formal* curriculum, the one discussed in teacher education courses and written down in school board policies. Usually the historical analysis focuses on major studies and reports that have influenced the curriculum. To show how the curriculum has changed during the twentieth century, historians often begin by describing the nineteenth-century curriculum as subject centered, revolving around a set of academic subjects that were said to strengthen the mind in the same way that physical exercise strengthens the muscles. The report most often cited to illustrate this "mental discipline" approach came from the NEA: the *Report of the Committee of Ten on Secondary School Studies* (1893).[62]

The NEA's study committee, dominated by college presidents, argued that the best way to prepare students for life was to discipline their minds with the academic subjects that would also prepare them for college—this at a time when only 6 percent of the eligible age group went to high school and only 2 percent went on to college. Although the committee recommended several alternatives to the then-fashionable concentration on Latin and Greek, it affirmed the idea that schools should challenge *all* high school students with a subject-centered curriculum, and it suggested that elementary schools take a similar approach. This point of view came under attack in the twentieth century, but two subject-centered theories of education, *essentialism* and *perennialism*, continued to influence the schools. I will argue in Chapters 7 and 10 that essentialism—its most recent incarnations are back to basics, the new basics, and excellence in education—has had more influence on educational practice than any other theory.

But at times during the twentieth century there has been a strong pull away from a curriculum centered on subjects and a push toward a curriculum that attempts to balance academic content, social needs, and student interests. The report that historians use most often to illustrate this trend also came from the NEA, but this one appeared at the end of the progressive era, 25 years after the Committee of Ten: the *Cardinal Principles of Secondary Education* (1918). The study group that produced the report, the Commission on the Reorganization of Secondary Education, was dominated by high school principals and professors of education who urged the development of a diversified, more flexible curriculum with different programs designed to prepare *all* students for *all* aspects of life. By 1918 almost one-third of the eligible age group was going to high school, and the NEA's commission envisioned a time when almost all students would. (By 1930 half the age group was in high school, and today the figure is near 95 percent.) To meet the needs of a heterogeneous student body, the NEA commission recommended that educators reorganize and supplement the traditional academic subjects in order to pay more attention to such areas as health, leisure, and vocation. The *Cardinal Principles* reflect *progressivism*, the modern theory of education developed primarily by John Dewey and his followers. As we will see in the next chapter, however, Dewey was often unhappy with what happened when progressivism was translated into practice in the schools.[63]

Describing twentieth-century changes in the curriculum as an ongoing battle between mental discipline and the Cardinal Principles or as a contest between traditional and modern theories of education allows historians to simplify an immensely complicated process and explain it in understandable terms. Now historians are beginning to investigate what teachers actually *did* with the formal curriculum. We know that progressivism was popular in teacher education programs by 1920, but how and when did the progressive methods teachers and administrators learned about in their education courses actually work their way into elementary and secondary classrooms? How much did teachers change the formal curriculum after they shut the classroom door? Our answers to such questions are tentative at best.

How Teachers Taught, a recent book by Larry Cuban, is forcing historians to rethink their standard explanations, for Cuban has discovered more constancy than change in twentieth-century classrooms. Using photographs, textbooks, tests, recollections of teachers and students, and other sources that historians have often neglected, Cuban argues that teacher-centered instruction—in which the teacher stands up front and spends most of the time talking to the whole class—has remained dominant throughout this century. Even though progressives have urged teachers to become more student centered by letting students exercise more responsibility and by teaching them individually or in groups, most teachers have not changed. Cuban estimates that since 1900, about two-thirds of America's teachers, including over 90 percent of high school teachers, have stuck firmly to teacher-centered instruction. About 25 percent of teachers have tried a few student-centered techniques, developing "hybrids" that blended with their routine, and only 5 to 10 percent have been true believers in student-centered instruction.[64]

Why so little change? According to Cuban, the organizational structure of schools and the occupational culture of teaching work against change. The structure of schools requires teachers to maintain order, cover a body of material, and show evidence that students have learned. Quite simply, teacher-centered instruction helps teachers get the job done. Student-centered instruction, on the other hand, is risky. It reduces the authority of teachers; it disrupts the quiet routine. From the teachers' point of view, students may or may not learn when they have more freedom. Most teachers prefer to settle for tried and true methods rather than invest their time and energy—scare commodities—in an experiment.

Have teaching methods really changed little since the days of the NEA's Committee of Ten? Before accepting or rejecting Larry Cuban's arguments, you need to become familiar with philosophies and theories of education, for they offer a way of thinking about teaching and learning that complements the historical analysis in this chapter.

ACTIVITIES

1. Now that you have read this chapter, think about your own interpretation of American educational history. Are you a celebrationist, a liberal, a revisionist, or a neoconservative?

2. Debate some of the issues in this chapter with friends whose interpretations of history differ from yours.

3. Conduct an oral history project. Interview older citizens with diverse social and educational backgrounds about their experiences in school.

4. Compile a history of an older elementary or secondary school to see the local effects of national educational trends. Oral history, microfilmed newspaper accounts, and school system records are some of the sources you may be able to use.

SUGGESTED READINGS

The books listed in notes 2 through 5 can help you see the history of American education from several perspectives. A recent book that compares interpretations and also sets forth the author's revisionist point of view is Joel Spring's *The American School, 1642–1985: Varieties of Historical Interpretation of the Foundations and Development of American Education* (see note 11).

NOTES

1. Robert Allen Skotheim, ed., *The Historian and the Climate of Opinion* (Reading, MA: Addison-Wesley, 1969), p. 2.
2. Ellwood P. Cubberley, one of the conservative reformers mentioned later in this chapter, was also a major celebrationist historian. His textbook *Public Education in the United States: A Study and Interpretation of American Educational History* (Cambridge, MA: Houghton Mifflin, 1919) remained a standard in teacher education courses as late as the 1950s.
3. See Merle Curti, *The Social Ideas of American Educators* (New York: Scribner, 1935), and Lawrence A. Cremin, *The Transformation of the School: Progressivism in American Education, 1876–1957* (New York: Knopf, 1961).
4. Examples of revisionist educational history include Michael B. Katz, *The Irony of Early School Reform: Educational Innovation in Mid-Nineteenth Century Massachusetts* (Boston: Beacon Press, 1968); Clarence J. Karier, Paul C. Violas, and Joel Spring, *Roots of Crisis: American Education in the Twentieth Century* (Chicago: Rand McNally, 1973); and Samuel Bowles and Herbert Gintis, *Schooling in Capitalist America: Educational Reform and the Contradictions of Economic Life* (New York: Basic Books, 1976).
5. Diane Ravitch is the most prominent of the new conservatives. She stirred up controversy among educational historians with the publication of *The Revisionists Revised: A Critique of the Radical Attack on the Schools* (New York: Basic Books, 1978) and *The Troubled Crusade: American Education, 1945–1980* (New York: Basic Books, 1983).
6. Two important studies of the colonial era are Bernard Bailyn, *Education in the Forming of American Society: Needs and Opportunities for Study* (Chapel Hill: University of North Carolina Press, 1960), which called attention to the importance of educational agencies other than schools, and Cremin, *American Education: The Colonial Experience, 1607–1783* (New York, Harper and Row, 1970).
7. One of the best accounts of district schools is Robert L. Church and Michael W. Sedlak, *Education in the United States: An Interpretive History* (New York: Free Press, 1976), ch. 1.
8. Gerald L. Gutek traces the colonial roots of these regional variations in *Education in the United States: An Historical Perspective* (Englewood Cliffs, NJ: Prentice-Hall, 1986), ch. 1.
9. Albert Henry Smith, ed., *The Writings of Benjamin Franklin*, vol. 3 (New York: Macmillan, 1904–1907), pp. 395–421.

10. Church and Sedlak, *Education in the United States: An Interpretive History*, ch. 2.
11. Joel Spring, *The American School, 1642–1985: Varieties of Historical Interpretation of the Foundations and Development of American Education* (White Plains, NY: Longman, 1986), pp. 19–22; H. Warren Button and Eugene F. Provenzo, Jr., *History of Education and Culture in America*, 2d ed. (Englewood Cliffs, NJ: Prentice-Hall, 1989), pp. 85–90.
12. Spring, *The American School*, ch. 2.
13. Ibid.
14. Two studies of modernization and its effects are Clinton Rossiter, *The American Quest, 1790–1860: An Emerging Nation in Search of Identity, Unity, and Modernity* (New York: Harcourt Brace Jovanovich, 1971), and Robert H. Wiebe, *The Segmented Society: An Introduction to the Meaning of America* (New York: Oxford University Press, 1975).
15. An old but still useful study emphasizing the "humanitarian" aspects of the various reform crusades is Alice Felt Tyler, *Freedom's Ferment: Phases of American Social History from the Colonial Period to the Outbreak of the Civil War* (Minneapolis: University of Minnesota Press, 1944).
16. James G. Carter, *Essays on Popular Education . . .* (1826), in David B. Tyack, ed., *Turning Points in American Educational History* (Waltham, MA: Blaisdell, 1967), p. 153.
17. Ibid., p. 155.
18. An excellent study of the movement is Carl F. Kaestle, *Pillars of the Republic: Common Schools and American Society, 1780–1860* (New York: Hill & Wang, 1983). One of the newer studies is Charles Leslie Glenn, Jr., *The Myth of the Common School* (Amherst: University of Massachusetts Press, 1988).
19. Church and Sedlak, *Education in the United States: An Interpretive History*, ch. 3.
20. A typical defense of district schools came from the Committee on Education of the Massachusetts House of Representatives in 1840, reprinted in Rush Welter, ed., *American Writings on Popular Education: The Nineteenth Century* (Indianapolis: Bobbs-Merrill, 1971), pp. 85–96.
21. Spring discusses various aspects of commonality in *The American School*, ch. 4.
22. Orestes Brownson, *The Boston Quarterly Review* (October 1839), in Michael B. Katz, ed., *School Reform: Past and Present* (Boston: Little, Brown, 1971), p. 280.
23. Ibid., p. 281.
24. Horace Mann, *Twelfth Annual Report of the [Massachusetts] Board of Education* (1848), in Cremin, ed., *The Republic and the School: Horace Mann on the Education of Free Men* (New York: Bureau of Publications, Teachers College, Columbia University, 1957), p. 97.
25. Joseph W. Newman, "Morality, Religion, and the Public Schools' Quest for Commonality," *Review Journal of Philosophy and Social Science* 4 (Winter 1980): 18–32.
26. Mann, *Twelfth Annual Report*, p. 102.
27. Brownson, *The Boston Quarterly Review* (1839), in Katz, ed., *School Reform*, pp. 280–281.
28. R. Freeman Butts, *Public Education in the United States: From Revolution to Reform* (New York: Holt, Rinehart and Winston, 1978), pp. 114–120.
29. Three studies of the confrontation in New York are Vincent P. Lannie, *Public Money and Parochial Education: Bishop Hughes, Governor Seward, and the New York*

School Controversy (Cleveland: Case Western Reserve University Press, 1968); Kaestle, *The Evolution of an Urban School System: New York City, 1750–1850* (Cambridge: Harvard University Press, 1973), pp. 145–158; and Ravitch, *The Great School Wars: New York City, 1805–1973* (New York: Basic Books, 1974), pp. 3–79.
30. Butts, *Public Education in the United States*, p. 181.
31. David Tyack and Elizabeth Hansot, "Historical Puzzles about Gender and Education," *Educational Researcher* 17 (April 1988): 33–41; U.S. Department of Education, Center for Education Statistics, *Digest of Education Statistics, 1985–86* (Washington: U.S. Government Printing Office, 1986), p. 40.
32. *Stuart et al. v. School District No. 1 of Kalamazoo* (1874). The classic histories of secondary education are Edward A. Krug's *The Shaping of the American High School, 1880–1920* (New York: Harper & Row, 1964) and *The Shaping of the American High School, 1920–1941* (Madison: University of Wisconsin Press, 1972).
33. Robert H. Wiebe, *The Search for Order, 1877–1920* (New York: Hill & Wang, 1967) provides an excellent historical context, emphasizing the impact of modernization.
34. John D. Buenker, *Urban Liberalism and Progressive Reform* (New York: Scribner, 1973); Gabriel Kolko, *The Triumph of Conservatism: A Re-Interpretation of American History, 1900–1916* (New York: Free Press of Glencoe, 1963).
35. Church and Sedlak, *Education in the United States: An Interpretive History*, discuss liberal and conservative reformers in ch. 9.
36. Raymond A. Mohl, "Cultural Assimilation versus Cultural Pluralism," *Educational Forum* 45 (March 1981): 323–332.
37. Cubberley, *Public Education in the United States*, pp. 485–486.
38. Ibid., p. 489.
39. Jane Addams, "The Public School and the Immigrant Child" (1908), in Daniel Calhoun, ed., *The Educating of Americans: A Documentary History* (Boston: Houghton Mifflin, 1969), pp. 421–423.
40. Ellen Condliffe Lagemann, ed., *Jane Addams on Education* (New York: Teachers College Press, 1985).
41. David B. Tyack, *The One Best System: A History of American Urban Education* (Cambridge: Harvard University Press, 1974), pp. 106–109.
42. Louis R. Harlan, *Separate and Unequal: Public School Campaigns and Racism in the Southern Seaboard States, 1901–1915* (Chapel Hill: University of North Carolina Press, 1958), pp. 255–256. See also Horace Mann Bond, *The Education of the Negro in the American Social Order* (Englewood Cliffs, NJ: Prentice-Hall, 1934), and Henry Allen Bullock, *A History of Negro Education in the South: From 1619 to the Present* (Cambridge: Harvard University Press, 1967).
43. Booker T. Washington, *Up from Slavery* (New York: Doubleday, 1901).
44. W. E. B. DuBois, *The Autobiography of W. E. B. DuBois: A Soliloquy on Viewing My Life from the Last Decade of Its First Century* (New York: International Publishers, 1968).
45. Washington, "Address . . . [on] September 18, 1895," in Calhoun, ed., *The Educating of Americans*, p. 351.
46. Ibid., p. 350.
47. Ibid.
48. Donald Spivey, *Schooling for the New Slavery: Black Industrial Education, 1868–1915* (Westport, CT: Greenwood Press, 1978).

49. Cubberley, *Public Education in the United States*, p. 744.
50. DuBois, *The Souls of Black Folk* (Chicago: A. C. McClurg, 1903), ch. 6.
51. Ibid., ch. 3.
52. See Louis R. Harlan, *Booker T. Washington: The Making of a Black Leader, 1856–1901* (New York: Oxford University Press, 1972), and *Booker T. Washington: The Wizard of Tuskegee, 1901–1915* (New York: Oxford University Press, 1983).
53. Cremin, *The Transformation of the School*.
54. Erwin V. Johanningmeier, *Americans and Their Schools* (Chicago: Rand McNally, 1980), ch. 13.
55. Joseph M. Cronin, *The Control of Urban Schools: Perspectives on the Power of Educational Reformers* (New York: Free Press, 1973).
56. Raymond E. Callahan, *Education and the Cult of Efficiency: A Study of the Social Forces That Have Shaped the Administration of the Public Schools* (Chicago: University of Chicago Press, 1962); Tyack and Hansot, *Managers of Virtue: Public School Leadership in America, 1820–1980* (New York: Basic Books, 1982).
57. Tyack, *The One Best System*, pp. 59–65. The quotation is from p. 60.
58. Wayne J. Urban, *Why Teachers Organized* (Detroit: Wayne State University Press, 1982).
59. Educational historians need to pay more attention to relations between the local and state levels. One study that does provide some historical perspective is Frederick M. Wirt and Michael W. Kirst, *Schools in Conflict: The Politics of Education* (Berkeley, CA: McCutchan, 1982).
60. Spring, *The Sorting Machine Revisited: National Educational Policy since 1945*, rev. ed. (White Plains, NY: Longman, 1989); Henry J. Perkinson, *The Imperfect Panacea: American Faith in Education, 1865–1976*, rev. 2d ed. (New York: Random House, 1977), ch. 5; Frank J. Munger and Richard F. Fenno, Jr., *National Politics and Federal Aid to Education* (Syracuse: Syracuse University Press, 1962); Hugh Davis Graham, *The Uncertain Triumph: Federal Education Policy in the Kennedy and Johnson Years* (Chapel Hill: University of North Carolina Press, 1974).
61. Richard Kluger, *Simple Justice: The History of Brown v. Board of Education and Black America's Struggle for Equality* (New York: Knopf, 1976); Meyer Weinberg, *A Chance to Learn: The History of Race and Education in the United States* (London: Cambridge University Press, 1977).
62. *Report of the Committee of Ten on Secondary School Studies* (Washington: National Education Association, 1893).
63. Commission on the Reorganization of Secondary Education, *Cardinal Principles of Secondary Education* (Washington: U.S. Government Printing Office, 1918); U.S. Department of Education, *Digest of Education Statistics, 1985–86*, p. 40.
64. Larry Cuban, *How Teachers Taught: Constancy and Change in American Classrooms, 1890–1980* (White Plains, NY: Longman, 1984), ch. 6.

CHAPTER 7

Philosophies and Theories of Education

"WHY" QUESTIONS

Every chapter in this textbook asks "why" questions, questions of rationale and purpose, but this chapter digs deepest into human experience for the answers. Here we will use the discipline of philosophy to study schools and society. Most introduction to education textbooks challenge prospective teachers to personalize educational philosophy by developing their own, a request that seems reasonable enough. As you read this chapter, try to relate each philosophy and each theory to your own experience. As we go about our careers and lives, there is all too little time to ask "why" questions, and thus we may never see the values and assumptions that underlie what we do and what we believe. One value of philosophy, then, is that it requires us to pause and reflect on deeply personal matters.

But as much as philosophy has helped me understand myself and my teaching, it has given me even more guidance as I have tried to make sense of the changes that I have seen in education during my lifetime. Studied in conjunction with history, philosophy has helped me analyze controversies that seem to reappear, albeit in slightly different guises, with surprising regularity. Why do Americans keep sending their schools back to basics every few years, for instance? What is back? What is basic? And what are the alternatives? Although I cannot guarantee that you will have all the answers after you have read this chapter, you will have some of them. Just understanding the questions is a step forward.

The chapter opens with an overview of four schools of philosophy: *idealism, realism, pragmatism,* and *existentialism*. These are philosophies of life, encompassing education as well as other aspects of living. After a brief look at each philosophy, we will turn to a more extensive discussion of three educational theories: *perennialism, essentialism,* and *progressivism.* These theories apply the philosophies directly to education.

FOUR PHILOSOPHIES

Each philosophy offers answers to three basic questions:

What is real?	Each philosophy has a *metaphysics,* a particular explanation of the nature of reality.
How do we know?	The answers each philosophy provides to this question constitute its *epistemology* or view of the nature of knowledge.
What is of value?	Each philosophy has an *axiology* or value system. Such questions as "What is right?" and "What is good?" are in the realm of *ethics.* "What is beautiful?" is a matter of *aesthetics.*

Idealism

The roots of idealism lie in the thinking of the Greek philosopher Plato. Idealists believe that reality is ultimately spiritual. The physical world we know through our senses is only a manifestation of the spiritual world. Idealists acknowledge a macromind—a universal force, a creator, a God—that is responsible for the whole of existence. We humans have souls and microminds. Our souls resided with the macromind in a transcendental realm before they united with our bodies, giving our microminds a spiritual character that can never be lost.

Idealists believe that our major responsibility on earth is getting our microminds as closely in touch as possible with the macromind. We can do so by looking inward rather than outward. Since our souls once lived in the spiritual realm, our minds are capable of recalling absolute and unchanging truth. Truth is already in our minds. We should not look for it outside of ourselves. We cannot rely on our five senses in the search for truth, for our senses give us distorted information on the physical world, and the physical world is itself an imperfect manifestation of the spiritual world. We must seek the truth within our minds, relying on contemplation and introspection.

We cannot go it alone, however. We need help on our quest. Idealists believe that we can recall the truth if we stimulate our minds with the best thoughts of the best human minds. Some human minds have grasped more truth than others, which is another way of saying that some microminds reflect the macromind far better than others. Most humans operate at the level of opinion, often incorrect opinion, and only a few have been very successful in the quest for truth. But how can we identify these enlightened thinkers, and how can we examine their thought?

We must concentrate on ideas that have stood the test of time, idealists answer. Throughout history educated people have cherished certain works of literature and art, for example. These works have endured because they are superior representations of the truth. The minds of the writers and artists who produced them were more closely in touch with the truth than were the minds of their contemporaries. Since our time on earth is limited, we should use it wisely, concentrating on the best literature and art and the best of our human heritage. This heritage, organized in the form of academic disciplines, is the curriculum that idealists want us to study in school.[1]

Realism

Realism is another old philosophy, with roots in the thinking of Plato's student Aristotle. All realists emphasize the physical world, and some believe that nothing else exists, although others say that a spiritual realm exists as well. In trying to explain the origins of the physical world, most realists admit the likelihood of a divine being or creator, although here again realism provides room for several points of view. Some realists believe that the physical world is a result of mere chance; others argue that a divine being set the world in motion and then sat back to watch; still others insist that the creator maintains active involvement with the world. Realists are also divided over whether humans have souls, but they agree that humans have minds capable of rational thought, a quality that distinguishes us from other creatures on earth.

Our major responsibility is getting to know the physical world. We can do so by using our senses and our rationality. In contrast to idealists, realists urge us to look outward rather than inward. Using our senses, we collect information on the physical world. Using our rational minds, we process the information by sorting, classifying, and abstracting it. And thus we acquire knowledge.

Like idealists, realists believe in absolute and unchanging truth, but to realists truth lies in the natural law that governs the universe—the law of gravity, for example, or the laws of reproduction and genetics. Humans know the truth to the degree that they understand natural law. Not all realists are scientists, of course, but realists argue that all people who seek reliable knowledge about the world must conduct their quest in the same way, relying on their senses and their rationality.

Experiencing the world is the best way to learn about it, realists say, but, given limited time, we cannot afford to learn randomly, taking life as it comes. We must structure learning based on the experiences of those who have preceded us. Over the years, educated people have sorted and classified what they have learned into academic disciplines, the organized bodies of knowledge that we know by such names as history, mathematics, literature, and science. These subject-matter disciplines provide the framework for formal education.[2]

Pragmatism

Compared with idealism and realism, pragmatism is a newcomer. As a formal philosophy, its roots lie in late nineteenth century America, in the work of mathematician Charles Sanders Pierce, psychologist William James, and philosopher John Dewey. All three were deeply influenced by Charles Darwin's theory of evolution with its emphasis on change and adaptation. Like realists, pragmatists urge us to concentrate on the physical world. Some pragmatists believe that there is nothing else; others refuse to speculate, whereas still others believe in a spiritual realm but say that it can be known only through faith, not reason. They agree, however, that change is the most important characteristic of physical reality and that the human mind, endowed with rationality, can understand reality by coming to grips with change.

John Dewey, whose work as a school reformer we examined briefly in the last chapter, believed that adapting to change is the major challenge we face in life. He urged us to take an experimental approach to life. Drawing on the work of Darwin, Dewey viewed human beings as organisms interacting with their environments. He called the process of interaction experience—a key concept in pragmatic philosophy. Experience brings us face to face with a series of problems, and we learn as we try to solve the problems. Dewey urged the use of the scientific method in problem solving, in schools and throughout society.

Wedded as they are to change and adaptation, pragmatists do not believe in absolute and unchanging truth. For pragmatists, truth is what works. Truth is relative, because what works for one person may not for another, just as what works at one time or in one place or in one society may not work in another. Pragmatists admit that the concept of relative truth, applied to morality, could lead to chaos. They insist, though, that morality is social rather than personal. Certainly a society cannot allow people to act just as they see fit, completely unrestrained, but pragmatists point out that a society inevitably changes its morality over time and that one society's morality may be another's immorality.

Like realists, pragmatists believe that we learn best through experience, but pragmatists are more willing to put that belief into practice. While realists are concerned with passing organized bodies of knowledge from one generation to the next, pragmatists stress applying knowledge—using ideas as instruments in problem solving. Realists and idealists call for a curriculum centered on the academic disciplines, but pragmatists prefer a curriculum centered on problems, a curriculum that draws the disciplines together to solve problems—an *inter*disciplinary approach.[3]

Existentialism

"Existence precedes essence," declared Jean-Paul Sartre, the French philosopher who popularized existentialism in the years after World War II. Unlike the other philosophies we have discussed, which seek to define the nature of human beings and then suggest how they should live, existentialism begins with the fact of existence. We have no choice about being born, but from that point on we face an infinite number of choices. Each of us must define his or her own essence. Each of us is an experiment of one. Each of us has the freedom—and the obligation—to choose how to live. No one else can make these decisions for us.

Although a few existentialists have tried to combine their philosophy with traditional religion, most are not interested in speculating about a creator and a spiritual realm. Rather, they urge us to get on with the task of defining our lives in the physical world, a world devoid of purpose and meaning according to most existentialists. They make much of the concept of *angst*, the feeling of pervasive dread that comes with the realization that each of us is alone in a meaningless world. But rather than being overwhelmed with desperation, we should go forward with hope, for we can create the lives we want. We can choose to be self-determined; we can give meaning to our lives.

As we saw in the discussion of pragmatism, leaving people free to determine their own morality runs the risk of anarchy. This risk is present to an even greater degree in existentialism. But unlike pragmatists, who try to deal with the problem by making morality social rather than personal, existentialists are unwilling to trust society, for they view society as often—some of them would say usually—oppressive. Instead they ask each of us to choose morals with the interests of all of us in mind. As Sartre said, "I am responsible for myself and for all."

With their concern for promoting choice and independence, existentialists prefer an education that offers students as many alternatives as possible. Certainly there is no set curriculum; students should have the freedom to explore as they see fit. Existentialists do believe that some subjects are better suited than others to promoting self-expression. Literature, the arts, and other subjects that raise questions rather than present answers are high on the existentialists' list.

Unlike idealism, realism, and pragmatism, existentialism has not yet produced a theory of education comparable to those we will examine in the next section. Existentialism has influenced the schools, however, and we will conclude this section by looking at its effects. Van Cleve Morris, one of the best-known advocates of existentialist education, points out how the rise of the counterculture in the late 1960s brought a kind of "street existentialism" into the schools. Humanistic psychology and values clarification became popular. Many students and some teachers vowed to "do their own thing." Caught up in the spirit of the times, school systems made graduation requirements more flexible so that students could choose relevant, meaningful courses. Some educators questioned the value of grades—what right did one human being have to impose a value judgment on another? These trends were beneficial in part; if nothing else, they forced an examination of educational rituals. "You'll act this way because I think it's good for you" was no longer an acceptable justification.

But unfortunately, says Morris, this "parody of existentialism . . . left out the most important thing that existentialism teaches: *personal responsibility*." Genuine existentialists resent the charge that their philosophy has ushered a "no-fault morality" into the schools, a value system no more complex than "If it feels good, do it." Yet some critics are saying just that, roping together existentialism and pragmatism and branding them as modern philosophies that have had disastrous effects on school and society. Today, as we will see in the next sections, theories of education based on the traditional philosophies of idealism and realism are basking in popularity, while educational theory based on modern philosophy is on the outside looking in.[4]

THEORIES OF EDUCATION: AN OVERVIEW

Educational theories are applications of philosophy to education. The two older philosphies, idealism and realism, have combined to produce two theories of education, perennialism and essentialism. These traditional theories went almost unchallenged in their dominance of education until the last 100 years. The modern philosophy of pragmatism applied to education has produced progressivism, a theory that has competed with the traditional theories throughout the twentieth century. Looking back on the century, we will see an especially competitive tug of war between essentialism and progressivism.

Out in the schools, it is difficult to find any of the three theories in pure form—when theory is put into practice, some things are lost in translation. Most teachers are eclectic, blending this theory with that and changing the mix from time to time. Thus we will examine educational theory alongside educational practice, pointing out discrepancies between what the theorists say and what actually goes on in the schools.

The questions with which educational theory is concerned may be less sweeping than "What is real?"; "How do we know?"; and "What is of value?" They are far reaching, nevertheless. Each theory tries to answer four basic questions:

- What is the purpose of education?
- What is the content of the school curriculum?
- What is the place of students?
- What is the role of teachers?

Now we will see how perennialism, essentialism, and pragmatism answer the questions.

PERENNIALISM

Perennial means everlasting. This theory of education, derived from the philosophies of idealism and realism, emphasizes knowledge that has endured. From idealism perennialists get their interest in spiritual knowledge, in ideas that seem so transcendent they must reflect a higher intelligence. From realism comes the perennialists' willingness to study the physical world using their senses and rationality. Perennialism itself has stood the test of time—it is an old educational theory that shaped the development of European universities, dominated higher education in the United States until the late nineteenth century, and exerts a continuing influence through the work of Robert M. Hutchins and Mortimer Adler. Indeed, a revival of interest in perennialism is now underway, led by Adler and his Paideia Group.

Hutchins, a president of the University of Chicago, presented a succinct rationale for perennialism in his book *The Higher Learning in America* (1936): "Education implies teaching. Teaching implies knowledge. Knowledge is truth. Truth is everywhere the same. Hence, education should be everywhere the same."[5] The education that perennialists advocate focuses on both intellect and character, on enlightenment as well as goodness. They believe that a careful study of our cultural heritage reveals more agreement than disagreement on such questions as What is beautiful? What is moral? Thus they look for continuities in human existence, intent on passing time-honored concepts from one generation to the next.

Perennialists stress the authority relationship in teaching and learning. If teachers are knowledgeable people of good character, as perennialists insist that they must be, then they should not hesitate to take command in the classroom. Students are incompletely formed human beings. They should not come to school expecting to dictate the terms of their education, for they have less knowledge and maturity than the adults with whom they will be working. The very idea of a "student voice" in a "democratic classroom"! Students may question ideas, of course—perennialists require them to think critically—but they must never challenge the teachers' authority.

The Great Books

Critics have joked that perennialists won't even read books written after 1900, much less use them in school. The joke exaggerates the point, but the charge is just accurate enough to irritate perennialists. In fact they do like modern works, but they are more comfortable with those that have stood the test of time. During the 1930s Robert Hutchins, Mortimer Adler, and other perennialists tried to revive the classical tradition in higher education with a curriculum based on the "great books of Western civilization." They assembled a set of books ranging from Plato's *Republic* to the Bible to the Constitution of the United

States to Einstein's *On the Electrodynamics of Moving Bodies*, books that in their judgment represent the best of western civilization.[6]

A great book, they argued, is one that accomplishes just what it sets out to do—it does not need to be rewritten; a great book is always contemporary—it does not need to be reinterpreted; a great book can be read by almost anyone; and a great book helps people develop standards of taste and judgment. Unfortunately, many of the debates over perennialism as an educational theory have been little more than arguments over the books on Hutchin's and Adler's shelf. Why did they choose this book but not that one? What about Oriental, African, and other non-western cultures? What about modern fiction? Can very young students understand the books? These arguments have settled nothing.

The Paideia Proposal

In 1982 Adler, who chairs the board of editors of *Encyclopaedia Brittanica*, breathed new life into perennialism with the publication of *The Paideia Proposal*. He and his associates in the Paideia Group are no longer arguing the merits of a particular set of books. Instead, they are promoting a particular kind of education for all students. Make no mistake about it—this is a far reaching proposal. What the Paideia Group advocates is schooling that is the same for everybody, with no tracking and virtually no electives. For 12 years all students would pursue the same curriculum, which Adler has organized into "three distinct modes of teaching and learning."[7]

He calls the first mode *acquisition of knowledge*. Using didactic methods, teachers acquaint students with fundamental knowledge in three subject-matter areas: language, literature, and fine arts; mathematics and natural sciences; and history, geography, and social sciences. The second mode of teaching and learning is *development of skill*. Here teachers act like "coaches" who help students learn to *do*; that is, they help students acquire the basic skills of reading, writing, speaking, listening, observing, measuring, estimating, and calculating. Students get their only elective in this area: their choice of a second language. *Enlargement of understanding*, the third mode, goes to the heart of perennialism by emphasizing ideas and values. Teachers use not didactics and coaching but the Socratic method of questioning and discussing; students study not textbooks but books and art forms that represent the best of human endeavor.

Very much alive in his eighties, Adler genuinely enjoys responding to criticisms of *The Paideia Proposal*. I once had the privilege of seeing him in action at an academic conference as he took on a roomful of friendly and not-so-friendly critics with obvious relish. "You are an elitist, just as perennialists have always been," one critic charged. "Your proposal sounds like the curriculum of an exclusive prep school 'back East.' " "You are the elitist," Adler replied. "I am trying to make education in the United States truly democratic by giving all students the high-quality schooling that has been reserved for a privileged few."[8]

"You are trying to educate all children as if they were all alike, when actually they are all different," another critic stated. "There is infinite variety in human beings. One child may be a rose, so to speak, while another may be a tulip and still another a violet. Just as roses, tulips, and violets require different amounts of light, water, and heat to thrive, so too do children need different kinds of education." "Your analogy is fundamentally flawed," Adler shot back, with more than a hint of irritation. "The plants you named are members of different species. All human beings are members of the same species. Children are inherently alike, and all deserve the same excellent education."

Somewhat more cautiously, another critic stood up and said, "But students do differ in their academic abilities. Let's face it—some are smarter than others. The curriculum you advocate may suit the academically gifted, but it is inappropriate for below-average or even average students." Smiling now, Adler replied, "Certainly some people have a greater capacity for learning than others. Some of us are large containers who can hold a great deal; some of us are medium-sized; some of us are small containers with small capacities. The mistake educators make is pouring different liquids into the different sizes. The large containers often get wine, the excellent education offered in the best public and private schools. The medium-sized containers get water, an education of lesser quality. Perhaps the greatest tragedy is that the small containers usually get dirty water—make-work courses, vocational training, a curriculum that is admittedly third-class. We in the Paideia Group want to pour the same wine into all containers, irrespective of size. We want to educate all students up to their capacity."

Adler seemed less confident fielding questions about teachers and teacher education. Given prevailing salaries and working conditions, can this nation attract the moral, intelligent people needed to make the Paideia Proposal work? Given the kind of education that students receive in the vast majority of public and private schools today, is it reasonable to expect those students to become the kind of teachers Adler wants? Even if all prospective teachers receive a liberal arts education in college, as Adler demands, will they be able to bring perennialism to life in the classroom? Adler admits that finding favorable answers to these questions will not be easy, but he insists that we try: "An ideal—even a difficult one—excites everyone's imagination. To say it cannot be done is to beg the question. We've got to try it."[9]

Adler and his associates are putting their ideals to the test in the real world of the public schools. They have taken over selected schools in Atlanta, Chicago, and Oakland, where they are educating—a better word might be reeducating—teachers and challenging students with a perennialist curriculum. The Paideians asked for "tough" schools full of the students who otherwise might be getting dirty water.

It is hard not to admire Adler for trying, but it is also hard to imagine perennialism succeeding on a large scale in the United States. Although Adler defends himself well at academic meetings, easily deflecting charges of elitism, he may find it impossible to counter the socioeconomic biases that run so deeply through the history of American education. Simply stated, public educators have consistently given up on certain children—poor and minority students in particular—and perennialists have tended to wall themselves off in private schools with carefully chosen students. Can Adler now persuade us to do otherwise?

Meanwhile, perennialism lives on in a very few schools in the United States, most of them elite independent schools. It also survives in a few religious schools. A small number of public school teachers also try to put perennialism into practice, but they are increasingly frustrated by the behavioral objectives and standardized tests that tend to skew the curriculum toward lower-level skills. These innovations have come to the schools as part of our nation's most recent back-to-basics movement, which we will examine in the following section.

ESSENTIALISM

Of all the theories of education, essentialism has had the greatest influence on elementary and secondary schools in the United States. Its popularity may wax and wane, but essentialism never fades away entirely. It is like a durable undercoat of paint. Educational reformers may cover it temporarily with other theories, but when times and fashions change, essentialism appears once again. Essentialists sometimes say their theory is what remains when we peel away the "fads and frills" of American education. To go back to basics is to go back to essentials, but it is becoming increasingly difficult to get a consensus on what is essential and what is not.

Essentialism, like its close relative perennialism, is grounded in the philosophies of idealism and realism. Idealism gives essentialism its emphasis on the human mind as a precious, some would say sacred, treasure that if properly educated can show the way to a full, rich life. Realism gives essentialism an emphasis on the physical world. Since people live in the world, they must acquire the knowledge and skills necessary not only to survive but to live well. Although the term "essentialism" was not coined until the 1930s, when traditional educators were organizing to do battle with progressive educators, the principles of essentialism dominated the district schools and common schools of nineteenth-century America. The twentieth century has witnessed a struggle between essentialists and progressives (whose ideas we will study next), with the former having more influence on daily practice in the schools and the latter having a stronger voice in colleges of education.

Essentialism and perennialism, grounded as they are in idealism and realism, have a great deal in common. In addition to the similarities that should already be obvious, both theories of education dismiss the criticism "But some students can't handle your curriculum" with a terse "Certainly they can—all but the very small percentage of students who have severe mental deficiencies." Advocates of both theories are comfortable with the image of students as receptacles or containers into which teachers pour knowledge. Both theories are conservative, not necessarily in a political sense—Adler, for instance, is left of center in his politics—but in a cultural sense, for both emphasize passing a cultural inheritance from one generation to the next.

There are also important differences between essentialism and perennialism. The essentialist curriculum is less wedded to the classics. It is likely to contain more modern literature, for example, and to feature more knowledge and skills of recent vintage—computer science and word processing. Notwithstanding Adler's attempts to avoid debates over the Great Books in promoting the Paideia Proposal, most perennialists do have a preference for older, tried-and-true works, and even though Adler says he has found a place for the manual arts in his curriculum, perennialist schools are not exactly rushing to add courses in cooking and auto repair. Essentialists, on the other hand, have long favored industrial arts courses in theory, although in practice they tend to look the other way when only the less academically talented students sign up for them.

During the twentieth century, essentialism has surged forward three times, in each case capitalizing on recurring public beliefs that the schools have gone soft and the schools are involved in social engineering. In the late 1930s William Bagley led the essentialist crusade. During the 1950s the "academic critics"—such professors of the arts and sciences as Arthur E. Bestor, James B. Conant, and Mortimer Smith—launched their attacks. In the late 1970s and throughout the 1980s, essentialist banners were flying again, as the conservative theory inspired a variety of educational reforms, ranging from the minimum competency movement to the Five New Basics outlined in the report *A Nation at Risk* (1983).

William C. Bagley and the 1930s

William C. Bagley, a professor of education at Teachers College, Columbia University, emerged during the 1930s as the most prominent and articulate spokesperson for essentialism. Faced with the social upheaval of the Great Depression, Bagley looked to the schools to provide stability in the midst of change. Above all, he argued, the schools should equip students with the basic academic skills they need to survive in society and to continue their education. He charged that many students were graduating from high school "essentially illiterate." Tracing their problems back to the elementary schools, he called for a renewed emphasis on reading, writing, and arithmetic. If essentialism stands for nothing else, it stands for mastery of the 3Rs.[10]

But it stands for much more, Bagley said. The schools must conserve and transmit our cultural heritage. "An effective democracy demands a community of culture," he maintained. "Educationally this means that each generation must share a common core of ideas, meanings, understandings, and ideals, representing the most precious elements of the human heritage."[11] Like many essentialists and perennialists, Bagley downplayed differences of opinion regarding the content of the curriculum. "There can be little question as to the essentials," he asserted, urging a program of history, geography, health, science, the fine arts, and the industrial arts, supported by continuing instruction in the 3Rs.[12]

Schools must also stress morality, Bagley maintained. Such cornerstone values as honesty and respect for other people's property are as essential in the orderly operation of schools as they are in the very existence of society. So are obedience, discipline, and hard work. Much learning is simply not fun, Bagley argued, nor should students come to school expecting to have a good time. More than the advocates of any other theory of education, essentialists call attention to the importance of work, sometimes appearing to believe in work for its own sake. Essentialist teachers wear the mantle of authority in the classroom, insisting on order and making no apologies for instilling traditional values in students.

The Academic Critics of the 1950s

The academic critics were articulate, colorful, and for the most part bitter in their attacks on American education. The titles of their books tell much of the story: Bestor's *Educational Wastelands: The Retreat from Learning in Our Public Schools* (1953) and *The Restoration of Learning* (1955) were the perfect complements to Smith's *And Madly Teach* (1949) and *The Diminished Mind: A Study of Planned Mediocrity in Our Public Schools* (1954). Conant offered less biting criticism in *Education and Liberty: The Role of Schools in a Modern Democracy* (1953) and *The American High School Today* (1959).[13]

Whether their tone was vicious or gentle, the academic critics agreed on the key points. The public schools, by embracing a progressive theory of education that made them responsible for meeting their students' every need—personal, social, and otherwise—had strayed from their central purpose: providing intellectual training in the basic skills and academic disciplines. This change hurt all students, the critics maintained, but gifted students suffered the most. The schools had abandoned their Jeffersonian mission of identifying bright students, whatever their backgrounds, and preparing them to lead the nation. The critics had no difficulty identifying the villains of the drama. John Dewey led the list, followed by professors of education who had infected teachers with progressivism. Teacher education was the biggest joke on college campuses, they charged, but state certification standards were written so that only people trained in colleges and departments of education could become teachers.

Bestor and Smith, as professors of history, leaned heavily on the liberal arts in their proposals for reform. In 1956 they helped organize the Council for Basic Education, which is still one of the most prominent voices of essentialism. Conant, trained in chemistry, appreciated the liberal arts but placed more emphasis on science and math. After the Soviet Union put Sputnik I into orbit in 1957, Conant's ideas became tremendously popular. Fed up with progressive pedagogy, Americans turned to the schools to help the nation win the space race. Congress passed the NDEA in 1958; math, science, and foreign language teachers suddenly found themselves in great demand; and students across the nation found out what it meant to build science projects. Essentialism was in the driver's seat.

Many Americans look back on those days with nostalgia, recalling them as a time of academic excellence. To be sure, the schools were excellent for some students in some schools. If you were fortunate enough to live in a financially secure suburban school district, and if you were in the college preparatory track, you probably did receive a rigorous, academically demanding education, particularly in the technologically-oriented subjects that were in vogue. Excellence was not uniformly distributed, however. Within those same suburban school districts it was business as usual for students in the lower ability groups, especially those in the vocational tracks. Essentialism probably did bring more academic rigor to the students caught in the middle—those in the general track—although their program continued to be less demanding than the college prep curriculum. Moreover, academic excellence was out of reach of the nation's poorest school systems, even with the federal government's financial assistance. It is also questionable that the new math, the new science, and the new social studies deserved the label of excellence. If we take the word of the students, teachers, and parents who struggled with them, they were academic disasters. Arts and sciences professors do not like to be reminded that they led the schools down the "new" paths, only to beat a hasty retreat when the innovations failed.

Back to Basics in the 1970s and 1980s

Since the mid-1970s, going back to basics has been all the rage. To people who have studied the history and philosophy of American education, much of the recent rhetoric of school reform has a familiar ring. There are echoes of William Bagley in the calls for good old-fashioned morality and discipline in the classroom. Charges that the schools became soft and affective in the mid-1960s as they tried to engineer a racially integrated society recall the academic critics of the 1950s. James Conant would surely approve the renewed emphasis on science and math, although this time we are racing not the Soviet Union but Japan, West Germany, and other friendly industrial powers. And once again it has become fashionable to poke fun at teacher education, much to the delight of the Council for Basic Education.

Public pressure on the schools to stress the 3Rs—"Teach our children reading, writing, and arithmetic if you teach them nothing else"—is also familiar. Although the pressure has varied in intensity over the years, it has always been a force to be reckoned with. More thoughtful essentialists have tried to remind the public that basic skills are just the beginning of formal education. When theory becomes practice, however, essentialism has consistently promoted such a fixation on basic skills that some students have received drill in the 3Rs and hardly anything else. It has always been easy for college professors to blame parents, teachers, and administrators for corrupting essentialism in this way, but the corruption has occurred nevertheless. It is widespread today.

What is different about the current back-to-basics movement is that behavioral psychology has influenced the schools to a far greater degree than ever before, as educators have combined behaviorism and essentialism in powerful new ways. We will return to this issue in Chapter 10, but here it is important to note behavioral psychology's emphasis on observable, measurable results. The marriage of essentialism and behaviorism has produced a variety of standardized tests designed to offer the public scientific proof that students are learning. In response to the public outcry for more basics, the curriculum for most students has narrowed. Educators have deemphasized music, art, health, physical education—and in some cases even science and social studies—because they are not basic enough, it seems, particularly for elementary school students. Given the difficulty of measuring higher-level academic skills with standardized tests, the curriculum has tilted, even in middle and secondary schools, toward lower-level skills. In math classes students spend far more time practicing computation than solving application problems; in social studies they memorize lists of battles and generals rather than analyze issues and trends. Test scores are rising, the public is impressed, but many teachers know better.

To their credit, some essentialists are crying foul. A Nation at Risk (1983), the report that shaped many of the educational debates of the eighties, was essentialist to the core. Prepared by the Reagan administration's National Commission on Excellence in Education, the report curtly rejected today's obsession with minimum competency testing and lower-level skills. It proposed instead a curriculum built on Five New Basics, all of them to be taught with a higher-level emphasis. Four years of English, three years of mathematics, three years of science, three years of social studies, and one-half year of computer science should be the *minimum* requirements for *all* high school students, the commission urged. Foreign language should be the sixth basic for college-bound students, and the report also gave a nod of approval to the fine and performing arts.[14]

With its references to "the essentials of a strong curriculum" and their role in preserving "the mind and spirit of our culture," A Nation at Risk tried to get essentialism out of the behavioral rut it has been stuck in since the late 1970s. Whether that is possible remains to be seen. For one thing, the report had its share of inconsistencies and contradictions. On the one hand it tried to be egalitarian by insisting on a higher-level curriculum for all students, but on the other it deliberately evoked nostalgia for the schools of the late 1950s and early 1960s, conveniently ignoring the grossly unequal educational opportunities that characterized that era. Along the same lines, the Cold War and Sputnik rhetoric was so strong in the report, which called on science and math to ride to the rescue of America once again, that teachers of other subjects wondered how they would fare under this Conant-like version of essentialism. Even the attack on minimum competency testing and the lower-level mediocrity it promotes struck some people as halfhearted, for the report turned right around and recommended the development of "a nationwide (but not federal) system of state and local standardized tests ."[15] Teachers who were already under pressure to tailor their teaching to the existing national, state, and local tests were not encouraged.

William Bennett, secretary of the U.S. Department of Education during most of Ronald Reagan's second term in office, continued the quest to move essentialism to a higher plane. In *James Madison High School* (1987) and *James Madison Elementary School* (1988), Bennett outlined his vision of essentialism as it might be. Rich in Western culture and steeped in the democratic ethic, the work ethic, and the Judeo-Christian ethic—Bennett regards these as the common elements of American culture—the James Madison curriculum goes well beyond the 3Rs. We will use this curriculum as a model of thoughtful essentialism in Chapter 10.[16]

Although Bennett is a critic of teacher education, a few voices from within colleges and departments of education have joined him in speaking out for essentialism. Columbia University's Teachers College, long identified with progressivism, was also the academic home of William Bagley and other essentialists during the 1930s, and today it is home to educational historian Diane Ravitch. The author of several books and numerous articles in such respected publications as the *Atlantic Monthly, New Republic,* and *New York Times,* Ravitch commands a national audience.

She likes to compare America's changing educational moods to the swings of a pendulum. Throughout this century the schools have swung back and forth, she says, embracing progressivism for a time only to return to traditionalism, a term that encompasses essentialism as well as perennialism. Ravitch makes it clear that her sympathies lie with the traditionalists, those educators who reject social engineering and soft pedagogy. Despite her Teachers College background, Ravitch is critical of teacher education, calling like most essentialists for reductions in the number of education courses required of prospective teachers. Ravitch's lucid writing and moderate-to-conservative politics, which reflect the nation's current mood, have helped win her a wide readership.[17]

In 1987 Diane Ravitch and Chester Finn, an essentialist professor of education then serving as assistant secretary in the U.S. Department of Education, captured national attention with *What Do Our 17-Year-Olds Know?* Based on the results of a history and literature test administered by the National Assessment of Educational Progress (NAEP), Ravitch's and Finn's answer was not much. E. D. Hirsch, Jr., an English professor at the University of Virginia, had already made the best-seller lists in 1987 with *Cultural Literacy: What Every American Needs to Know.* Perennialist Allan Bloom released *The Closing of the*

American Mind, a biting critique of higher education, that same year. These books stressed the importance of passing the nation's cultural heritage from one generation to the next, and they touched off a debate over the role of the schools in increasing cultural literacy. We will listen to this debate in Chapter 10.[18]

As the new decade begins, traditional theories of education are in command. Essentialism is setting the agenda for the curriculum debates of the 1990s. As Bennett, Ravitch, Finn, and Hirsch readily admit, however, there is a gap between essentialism as a theory and essentialism as practiced in the schools. After all, the schools have been going back to basics since the mid-seventies, and still there are problems. Of course there are, say the progressive critics, whose theory of education we will examine next.

PROGRESSIVISM

In the 1890s John Dewey, then a professor at the University of Chicago, went shopping for school furniture. He had just started a laboratory school at the university with a group of parents who were dissatisfied with the traditional education their children were receiving. Now the problem was finding suitable desks and chairs, and none of the school supply stores in Chicago had what Dewey was looking for. Finally one dealer made a remark that struck Dewey as so insightful that he included it in his book *The School and Society* (1899): "I am afraid we have not what you want. You want something at which the children may work; these are all for listening."[19]

For Dewey, that comment got to the essence of the traditional classroom, "with its rows of ugly desks placed in geometrical order, crowded together so that there shall be as little moving room as possible, desks almost all of the same size." Listening is the only educational activity that can take place in such a setting, Dewey claimed, "because simply studying lessons out of a book is only another kind of listening; it marks the dependency of one mind upon another. The attitude of listening means, comparatively speaking, passivity, absorption; . . . the child is to take in as much as possible in the least possible time."[20]

An old joke in colleges of education is that Dewey wanted the words "Here Lies the Man Who Convinced Americans to Unbolt School Desks from the Floor" chiseled on his tombstone. Funny or not, the joke does point out the symbolic importance of something as ordinary as school furniture. Dewey looked into traditional classrooms and saw passivity, rigidity, and uniformity locked into place. Teachers, the dispensers of knowledge, had their places at the front; students, the receivers of knowledge, had their places in the rear. Like many observers, Dewey saw similarities between classrooms and factories, but unlike many Dewey did not approve of what the similarities suggest. Schools should not be places where adult "supervisors" give orders while child "employees" grudgingly sit and listen, their minds often a thousand miles away. Instead, schools should be places where adults serve as guides and advisers to students who are actively involved in their education, doing things that are interesting to them as well as important to society.

Dewey was both philosopher and educator, and the principles of pragmatism, the philosophy that he helped develop, directly influenced his educational ideas. Given a world in which change is the central feature, education must help people adapt. Not for Dewey was the education preferred by idealists and realists, an education based on truths passed from one generation to the next, an education students absorb. Dewey called instead for an education based on what works for the present generation, an education students *experience* as they interact with the environment. Students are not receptacles or containers, Dewey argued. They are organisms. They need to be active. They learn best by doing.

The theory of education that Dewey advocated came to be known as progressivism, for it developed during what historians call the progressive era in American history. As we saw in the last chapter, at the beginning of the twentieth century a spirit of reform was in the air. Because John Dewey was a liberal reformer, progressivism in education has always been linked to liberalism. The linkage is less direct than it may seem, however, because most of the people who translated educational theory into practice—teachers, administrators, school board members—were moderates and conservatives. It took time for Dewey's progressivism to work its way into teachers colleges and from there into the schools, and when *progressive education* did appear in classrooms it was often difficult to recognize the original ideas. Beyond the social and political differences that separated theorists and practitioners, Dewey's writing was dense, ponderous, and easily misinterpreted. Few educators read his work carefully, and those who did disagreed over how to use his ideas in the classroom.[21]

Throughout his long life, which spanned the Civil War and the atomic age, Dewey kept claiming that his ideas had been misquoted, misunderstood, and misapplied in the schools. We should be sympathetic, but only to a point. After all, as a pragmatist Dewey insisted that the ultimate test of a theory is the difference the theory makes in practice. Just as we saw that perennialists, despite Hutchin's and Adler's egalitarian rhetoric, have reserved their brand of education for a few students in a few schools, and that educators have consistently corrupted essentialism, denying its full benefits to many students despite the good intentions of Bagley, Bestor, and Bennett, we must evaluate progressivism in the same way, judging not only theory but practice.

Dewey based his educational theory on his view of democracy. As he explained in his best-known book, *Democracy and Education* (1916), democracy is more than a form of government. It is a way of life. The essence of democracy is people working together cooperatively to find solutions to common problems. The schools in a democratic society bear a great responsibility, for they must help give people the problem-solving skills that they need to make democracy work. Dewey was very much the liberal progressive in his belief that ordinary people can contribute to society if the schools help them to do so, and he went even further. Unless America's schools equip all students to solve problems, democracy cannot survive.[22]

Children, Society, and Their Problems

But on which problems should the schools focus? According to Dewey there are two sources from which problems can be selected: children and society. Students can suggest problems that they are having, and society is full of problems that cry out for solutions. Unfortunately, Dewey continued, the traditional curriculum does justice to neither. A collection of facts and skills pigeonholed into academic subjects, the curriculum may make sense to college-educated adults, but it is remote from children's experience and out-of-touch with pressing social problems. Imagine how Dewey's ideas sounded at the turn of the century. They were nothing short of heresy to traditional educators. What? Ask the *children*? But they're too immature to make suggestions about their education. And why bring the problems of society into the classroom? Shouldn't schools keep a safe distance from society, striving to be above politics, beyond controversy, and apart from the unpleasant realities of life?

Dewey replied to the traditionalists in several ways. Hadn't they noticed the bored looks on children's faces? To the degree that the schools ignore problems that concern students, the schools are meaningless to students. Hadn't the traditionalists noticed how difficult it was to move the nation forward, even in a progressive era? To the degree that the schools ignore problems that beset society, the schools are useless to society. Moreover, in *The Child and the Curriculum* (1902) and later works, Dewey urged traditionalists to recognize that student problems and social problems are identical. The questions even the youngest children ask—Do others like me? Should I share my belongings? What makes automobiles run? Why are vegetables better for me than candy?—are scaled-down versions of questions society asks. Students do not come to school to get ready for life—they are already alive. Education is not preparation for life—it is life.[23]

Dewey wanted schools to be miniature societies, "embryonic communities" that simplify, purify, and integrate the cultural heritage. In his Laboratory School at the University of Chicago, students engaged in such "real life activities" as gardening, weaving, woodworking, and metalworking. Since everyone has to eat, for example, Dewey and his fellow teachers found it easy to build on the natural interest children have in food. As students worked in the school garden, they began to understand—many of them for the first time—where food comes from and how important it is to any society. With student interest presumably running high, resourceful teachers provided gentle guidance as students investigated how food production has changed over the years, why some nations have more food than others, how seeds germinate—the possibilities were endless. Science, geography, history, and other academic subjects were no longer the center of the curriculum. Instead, the curriculum was at once child-centered and society-centered, with subject matter brought into play as necessary to study particular problems or issues.

In 1904 Dewey moved from the University of Chicago to Columbia University in New York City, where his reputation grew steadily. Although he concentrated more on philosophy than education after the publication of *Democracy and Education* in 1916, Dewey soon became the nation's preeminent educational theorist. He developed a strong following among the faculty of Columbia's Teachers College, attracting a group of dedicated professors who spread his ideas—more precisely, their interpretation of his ideas—to numerous teachers and administrators. As Teachers College established itself as the top school of education in the country, Dewey and his followers were in an influential position indeed. During their heyday in the 1920s, 1930s, and 1940s, they were the pacesetters in educational theory.

Progressivism in the Classroom

How much educational practice changed is a hard question to answer, as Larry Cuban's book *How Teachers Taught* suggests (see Chapter 6). As early as World War I, however, there were signs of growing interest in progressivism. In 1918 the Commission on the Reorganization of Secondary Education, a committee of the National Education Association, issued what would prove to be one of the most significant educational reports of this century. Titled *Cardinal Principles of Secondary Education*, the report called on secondary educators to broaden their aims, to do more than offer a relatively small group of students a traditional academic curriculum. The report encouraged schools to prepare *all* students for *all* aspects of life. The cardinal principles were an ambitious statement of the schools' responsibilities for seven broad areas of life: health, command of fundamental processes (basic academic skills), worthy home membership, vocation, civic education, worthy use of leisure, and ethical character.[24]

Despite warnings that the schools were asking for more than they could handle, progressivism gained ground. Another breakthrough came in 1918 when William Heard Kilpatrick, a Teachers College professor who had studied under Dewey, published "The Project Method." This article was Kilpatrick's attempt to translate Dewey's ideas into a set of practical guidelines for teachers. *Foundations of Method* (1925), Kilpatrick's elaboration on the article, became *the* methods textbook in many teacher education programs. Education should revolve around "wholehearted purposeful activity in a social situation," said Kilpatrick. Using the problems and questions that students brought to school as a point of departure, teachers were to help students design projects that taught social lessons and conveyed academic content as well. If students were curious about buying and selling, for example, they could set up a store in the classroom. Using play money, they could learn to make change. The thoughtful teacher could stock the shelves with items that would stimulate further learning.

Buying a cotton shirt, for example, might get a student interested in where cotton is grown and how clothes are made. The student who spent money too quickly would have to face the realities of budgeting. If another student turned into a loan shark, the teacher could help the class decide how to handle the situation.[25]

Kilpatrick's project method seemed easy to understand and easy to use in the classroom—deceptively easy, as it turned out. Almost immediately distortions appeared, and the popular press had a field day with progressive education. By some accounts, a few teachers simply turned things over to the students. With "What do you want to do today, kids?" as their major question, these teachers provided little guidance. Other teachers were willing to be more directive but found it difficult to come up with a steady stream of projects that did justice to children, society, and subject matter. Teacher educators and curriculum specialists rushed in with preplanned projects that laid out almost everything in advance—stimulation, problems and questions, subject matter content, probable outcomes, and new interests—but spontaneity and student motivation suffered.

Journalists of the 1920s sniped away at child-centered private schools that seemed to lack structure of any kind, at least to the casual observer. Why, the children sang, danced, and made pottery all day! They read books and did arithmetic only when they wanted to. And so the caricatures went. Journalists who were aware of the Progressive Education Association, organized in 1919 with an accent on child-centered private education, could lampoon the first two principles on the association's charter, "freedom to develop naturally" and "interest the motive of all work." "Scientific study of pupil development," another principle, somehow received less attention in the press. To many citizens and some teachers, progressivism became little more than a set of slogans. Learning by doing. Educating the whole child. Teaching students, not subjects.[26]

Dewey, Kilpatrick, and other theorists spoke out against the distortions of progressivism in the schools and the distortions of the distortions in the press. The image of progressivism as totally permissive was especially irritating to Dewey. "The child does not know best," he reminded his supporters and detractors alike. Trusting students to make intelligent decisions with little or no adult guidance "is really stupid. For it attempts the impossible, which is always stupid; and it misconceives the conditions of independent thinking."[27] Nor did Dewey agree with his Teachers College followers on all matters. Tired of seeing progressivism reduced to playing store, Dewey cautioned against projects so trivial they miseducated students. Kilpatrick's method was only one alternative, he pointed out.

Whereas Kilpatrick seemed almost ready to discard the entire subject-matter curriculum and replace it with a series of projects, Dewey wanted to make academic subjects more responsive to the needs of students and society. If the curriculum began with the experiences of students, as the students gained maturity they could delve into subject matter in a rigorous way that might even please the traditionalists. Dewey's scientific method of problem solving was structured and systematic. He also believed that there was a time and place for didactic instruction—for a teacher to stand at the blackboard and show students how to work a math problem, for example—and a time and place for students to memorize and practice their multiplication tables. In other words, Dewey was no pedagogical libertine.[28]

It troubled Dewey that much of what passed as progressive education had only tenuous connections to social reform. Before World War I, progressivism in education had been part and parcel of the larger reform movements; after the war progressive education went its own way, enjoying its greatest popularity in private schools. During the 1930s, as the nation faced the Great Depression and the rise of totalitarian governments abroad, Dewey was encouraged as progressive education become more society centered. This version of progressivism made more headway in public schools. It was impossible for educators to ignore unemployment, bread lines, and fascism; progressive education offered a way to infuse social issues into the curriculum. The social studies, which progressive educators had developed during the 1920s as an interdisciplinary, problem-centered subject, enjoyed an upswing in popularity. Students took field trips and studied problems in their own communities. Kilpatrick's project method seemed ideally suited to this kind of progressivism, for students and teachers could design their projects around studies of city and county governments, housing conditions, New Deal public works programs, and the like.

Social Reconstructionism and Critical Theory

A politically focused form of society-centered progressivism called *social reconstructionism* also developed during the 1930s. Inspired in part by Dewey's reaction against the permissiveness and lack of social concern in child-centered progressivism, social reconstructionists went to another extreme with their desire to use the schools to engineer a new society. George S. Counts, a Teachers College professor, galvanized the annual meeting of the Progressive Education Association in 1932 with his speech "Dare Progressive Education Be Progressive?" Calling on teachers to become leaders of social change, Counts urged them to take stands on controversial social issues and prepare students for the emerging society. Teachers should increase their power by joining teacher unions and casting their lot with the labor movement and other forward-looking groups. Counts's book *Dare the School Build a New Social Order?* (1932) became the charter document of reconstructionism.[29]

Counts, Kilpatrick, and several of their colleagues at Teachers College, most notably Harold Rugg and John Childs, joined other professors of education and the arts and sciences to publish *The Social Frontier*, a journal that served as the voice of reconstructionism. John Dewey, a regular contributor to the journal, was at the center of all this activity, even though he occasionally chided his followers for their naive faith in the power of schools to change society.[30]

Social reconstructionism, a fusion of progressive pedagogy and left-of-center politics, had little direct influence on the schools. Even though the nation became more liberal during the 1930s, most educators and school board members simply did not share the reconstructionists' vision of an emerging society that, if not exactly socialist, was clearly collectivist. Predictably, reconstructionism drew the fire of people who were educationally conservative, politically conservative, or both. A series of social studies textbooks produced by Harold Rugg fell victim to a censorship campaign in the late 1930s and 1940s, and conservative critics have cited the social reconstructionists' writings as evidence of a left-wing conspiracy to control the schools.[31]

Social reconstructionism has stayed alive as a minority point of view in colleges of education, however, and during the 1980s it helped inspire *critical theory*, a pedagogy designed to "empower the powerless and transform existing social inequalities and injustices." Although some critical theorists are scornful of Dewey as a liberal who did not go far enough in his proposals for reform, others acknowledge the similarity between critical theory and social reconstructionism. After all, social reconstructionism reflected the politically acute side of Dewey's thought. Beginning with the premise that "men and women are essentially unfree and inhabit a world rife with contradictions and asymmetries of power and privilege," critical theorists work to help students and teachers escape oppression. They especially focus on how social class, race, and gender affect schooling.[32]

In many respects critical theorists *are* contemporary social reconstructionists. Two of the most prominent critical theorists are Henry Giroux and Peter McLaren of Miami University, Ohio, and one of the most accessible introductions to critical pedagogy is McLaren's *Life in Schools* (1989). Although the influence of critical theory is increasing inside colleges of education, it remains small outside.[33]

Life Adjustment

By the time the academic critics launched their attack in the 1950s, progressive education had undergone a name change. Now the dominant strain of progressivism was called *life adjustment* education. More than the name had changed—Dewey's ideas could hardly be recognized. On a rhetorical level, to be sure, life adjustment incorporated elements of both child-centered and society-centered pedagogy, but in theory and practice it departed from Dewey's progressivism at almost every turn. The rationale for life adjustment was that schools were not preparing large numbers of students for the realities of modern life—particularly the world of work. There were well-developed programs for the 20 percent who were college bound and the 20 percent who were in the vocational track, but what were the schools doing for the majority of students, the 60 percent in the middle? Surely they did not need a rigorous academic program, the life adjusters asserted, and just as surely they did not belong in wood shop or metal shop.[34]

What they did need was training in good habits that would pay off on almost any job; help with their immediate personal problems as well as the ones they would face as adults: advice on how to spend their leisure time, which was predicted to be more plentiful in the years after World War II; and preparation for good citizenship. Students in the general track soon found themselves in such courses as "Developing an Effective Personality," "Marriage and the Family," and "Metropolitan Living." Designed to focus and integrate the curriculum, core courses that revolved around class discussions and field trips were popular.

John Dewey turned 90 as life adjustment education hit its stride and the academic critics mounted their attack. He wrote little about education in his last years, but it is not difficult to imagine his disappointment with what was passing for progressivism in education. Perhaps he held his peace because he found himself agreeing with the critics on many points. Certainly the basic assumption of life adjustment education, that only students who were headed for college needed a curriculum with substantial academic content, made Dewey recoil. He knew that vocational educators were the theorists and strongest advocates of life adjustment, which surely made him suspicious. Dewey had parted company with vocational educators in the early 1900s when he realized that they wanted to give job skills to a few students—the academic castoffs, most of them poor and minority students—while he wanted to give all students the chance to work with their hands and to sample a variety of occupations. Now a vocational education mentality was limiting the education of another group of students, those in the large general track; essentialists were getting the credit for saving the schools; and Dewey was getting the blame.

Blaming Progressivism for the 1960s and 1970s

Dewey died in 1952, but today it is fashionable to blame progressivism for everything that went wrong in the schools from the mid-sixties through the mid-seventies. Historian Diane Ravitch, who likes to wear the mantle of the academic critics of the 1950s, is a leading spokesperson for the new essentialist criticism. One of her targets is *open education*, a vaguely defined movement that involved, if nothing else, knocking down walls between classrooms and giving students more freedom. Open education drew much of its inspiration from British infant schools with a strong child-centered orientation. Even though British open educators were careful to distinguish their approach from Dewey's, Ravitch implicates progressivism by association. Admittedly, few people have anything good to say about open education today—more often than not it was noisy and chaotic—but is it fair to point the finger at progressivism?[35]

When students demanded more relevant courses in the 1960s and 1970s, educators responded by making things easy and elective, encouraging students to pick and choose their way through a cafeteria-style curriculum that included science fiction English courses, values clarification social studies courses, consumer math courses, and the like. Even many of the brightest students steered clear of foreign languages, advanced math and science, and other demanding courses while teachers, parents, and other adults stood by and watched. No matter that this do-your-own-thing pedagogy resembled a distorted version of existentialism more than a distorted version of progressivism—Ravitch chalks it up as another failed experiment in progressive education. Compensatory education, school integration, and affirmative action are, of course, the social engineering legacy of progressivism.

Critics on the New Right go even further. As this nation underwent a moral revolution that brought sex, drugs, and rock and roll into the schools, to some people it seemed that the schools themselves were to blame. Didn't John Dewey say that values are relative? Hasn't he had a great deal of influence on education? Don't some teachers practice values clarification? Affirmative answers to such questions provide some citizens all the evidence they need to implicate progressivism (and sometimes existentialism too) in a secular humanist conspiracy.

Progressivism Today

Although progressivism is out of step with current educational theory and practice, it does have its advocates. Among the many reports that were released in the wake of *A Nation at Risk* (1983), three stand out because they present such a different vision of American education: Ernest Boyer's *High School* (1983), John Goodlad's *A Place Called School* (1984), and Theodore Sizer's *Horace's Compromise* (1984). These studies are progressive in their less authoritarian view of education. They are critical of the essentialist attempt to *make* students learn. Students and teachers should work cooperatively, the contemporary progressives urge, rather than at cross purposes. More learning would take place in classrooms if teachers would talk less and students would participate more. State attempts to legislate learning and monitor the results with standardized tests have hurt more than they have helped.[36]

Although Boyer, Goodlad, and Sizer make different recommendations for the curriculum, they all call for a common core of studies. All three criticize ability grouping and tracking, and they all underscore the importance of exposing every student to the cultural heritage. Boyer and Sizer, in fact, are members of the Paideia Group, and they acknowledge their debts to Mortimer Adler. They differ from the chief perennialist, however, in that they encourage students to tailor their own curriculum beyond the core, to go into more depth on subjects that especially interest them. All three authors stress the importance of independent study projects, and Boyer even calls for a service program in which students would do volunteer work in the school and the community.

To essentialist critics, these recommendations sound like John Dewey revisited—a noble vision, perhaps, but naive. Yet one thing that distinguishes Boyer, Goodlad, and Sizer from the contemporary essentialists we have discussed is that the three progressives base their reports on far more extensive observation in the schools. Boyer, Goodlad, and Sizer have personally visited numerous schools, and their research teams have logged thousands of hours of classroom observation. Their work reflects this approach—it puts their reports in touch with the conditions that students and teachers face every day. Boyer, Goodlad, and Sizer recognize that teachers are overburdened with students, paperwork, and outright baby-sitting chores. They are aware of the problems that students bring to school. In short, their reports are sensitive to the social context of education.

Thus the three progressives understand the process of informal bargaining that takes place between students and teachers in the classroom. In Boyer's words, the deal amounts to "Keep off my back, and I'll keep off yours."[37] Sizer calls the bargaining a "Conspiracy for the Least, the least hassle for anyone." Describing the bargaining he observed in one classroom, Sizer explains that the teacher

> saw some 150 students each day. He was on his feet in front of his classes four and a half hours every day, a performance that would have exhausted the hardiest actor. The students sat in classrooms . . . almost six hours per day, an arduous bit of immobility indeed, rugged on the rump. The requirements of the school were to be in attendance, to be quiet, orderly, and predictable, and to pass tests of multiple-choice questions of easily divined nature. So why not agree to minima, genially applied? To do otherwise was to upset the principal's public relations applecart. This was a happy school.[38]

In contrast to the essentialists we have discussed, Boyer, Goodlad, and Sizer recognize that major changes in the occupation of teaching, the organization of schools, and the relationship between teachers and students must occur in order to break the bargain. The noses-to-the-grindstone approach of essentialism will not work.

Sizer chairs the education department at Brown University and heads a grassroots coalition that is putting his ideas to the test in schools across the nation. Goodlad, a professor of education at UCLA, heads another grassroots network. Boyer is president of the Carnegie Foundation for the Advancement of Teaching. Despite their prominence, however, progressivism as a theory of education remains on the outside looking in. Powerful social and political forces help keep essentialism in command, as we will find in Chapters 9 and 10.

ACTIVITIES

1. Visit the central office of a local school system and ask for a copy of the system's philosophy of education (sometimes called a statement of goals and purposes). Compare it with the philosophies and theories in this chapter. Try to obtain an earlier statement of goals from the same system and analyze the changes.

2. Interview currently employed teachers who represent a variety of philosophies and theories.
3. Talk with retired teachers about swings of the educational pendulum—how one educational theory may have displaced another during their careers.
4. Observe in a public or private school that seems to be dominated by a theory of education different from yours.

SUGGESTED READINGS

A good way to continue learning about philososphies and theories of education is to read one or more general works and then focus your study according to your interests. Listed below are some of the best general books; see the notes for more specialized sources.

Gutek, Gerald L. *Philosophical Alternatives in Education* (Columbus, OH: Merrill, 1974).
Morris, Van Cleve, and Young Pai. *Philosophy and the American School,* 2d ed. (Boston: Houghton Mifflin, 1976).
Power, Edward J. *Philosophy of Education: Studies in Philosophies, Schooling, and Educational Policies* (Englewood Cliffs, NJ: Prentice-Hall, 1982).
Wirsing, Marie E. *Teaching and Philosophy: A Synthesis* (Boston: Houghton Mifflin, 1972).

NOTES

1. For further reading see J. Donald Butler, *Idealism in Education* (New York: Harper & Row, 1966).
2. William O. Martin, *Realism in Education* (New York: Harper & Row, 1968), and John Wild, *Introduction to Realist Philosophy* (New York: Harper & Row, 1948), provide further information.
3. See Ernest E. Bayles, *Pragmatism in Education* (New York: Harper & Row, 1966), and John Childs, *American Pragmatism and Education* (New York: Holt, Rinehart and Winston, 1956).
4. Three studies from the 1960s, when existential education enjoyed rising popularity, are Van Cleve Morris, *Existentialism in Education: What It Means* (New York: Harper & Row, 1966); Maxine Greene, *Existential Encounters for Teachers* (New York: Random House, 1967); and George F. Kneller, *Existentialism and Education* (New York: John Day, 1964). To go directly to the source, read Jean-Paul Sartre's *Being and Nothingness,* translated by Hazel E. Barnes (New York: Philosophical Library, 1958). The quotations from Morris are from his chapter "Establishing a Philosophical Point of View," in Donald E. Orlosky, ed., *Introduction to Education* (Columbus, OH: Merrill, 1982).
5. Robert M. Hutchins, *The Higher Learning in America* (New Haven: Yale University Press, 1936), p. 66.
6. Robert M. Hutchins, *Great Books: The Foundation of a Liberal Education* (New

York: Simon & Schuster, 1954). See also the excellent discussion in Christopher J. Lucas, *Foundations of Education: Schooling and the Social Order* (Englewood Cliffs, NJ: Prentice-Hall, 1984), ch. 3.

7. Mortimer J. Adler, *The Paideia Proposal: An Educational Manifesto* (New York: Macmillan, 1982), *Paideia Problems and Possibilities* (New York: Macmillan, 1983), and *The Paideia Program: An Educational Syllabus* (New York: Macmillan, 1984).

8. Based on my notes and recollections, I have reconstructed these exchanges, which took place at the annual meeting of the American Educational Studies Association, Milwaukee, November 4, 1983.

9. "Quality, Not Just Quantity," *Time* (September 6, 1982), p. 59.

10. Two key documents of the early essentialist movement are William C. Bagley's *Education and Emergent Man* (New York: Ronald Press, 1934) and "An Essentialist's Platform for the Advancement of American Education," *Educational Administration and Supervision* 24 (April 1938); 241–256. Lucas analyzes essentialism in *Foundations of Education*, ch. 2.

11. Bagley, "An Essentialist's Platform," p. 253.

12. William C. Bagley, "The Case for Essentialism in Education," *Journal of the National Education Association* 30 (October 1941), p. 202.

13. Arthur E. Bestor, *Educational Wastelands: The Retreat from Learning in Our Public Schools* (Urbana: University of Illinois Press, 1953) and *The Restoration of Learning* (New York: Knopf, 1955); Mortimer Smith, *And Madly Teach* (Chicago: Regnery, 1949) and *The Diminished Mind: A Study of Planned Mediocrity in Our Public Schools* (Chicago: Regnery, 1954); James B. Conant, *Education and Liberty: The Role of Schools in a Modern Democracy* (Cambridge: Harvard University Press, 1953) and *The American High School Today* (New York: McGraw-Hill, 1959).

14. National Commission on Excellence in Education, *A Nation at Risk: The Imperative for Educational Reform* (Washington: U.S. Government Printing Office, 1983).

15. Ibid.

16. William J. Bennett, *James Madison High School: A Curriculum for American Students* (Washington: U.S. Department of Education, 1987) and *James Madison Elementary School: A Curriculum for American Students* (Washington: U.S. Department of Education, 1988).

17. *The Schools We Deserve: Reflections on the Educational Crises of Our Times* (New York: Basic Books, 1985) is a collection of Diane Ravitch's essays on education. Also see her history *The Troubled Crusade: American Education, 1945–1980* (New York: Basic Books, 1983).

18. Diane Ravitch and Chester E. Finn, Jr., *What Do Our 17-Year-Olds Know?: A Report on the First National Assessment of History and Literature* (New York: Harper & Row, 1987); E. D. Hirsch, Jr., *Cultural Literacy: What Every American Needs to Know* (Boston: Houghton Mifflin, 1987); Allan Bloom, *The Closing of the American Mind* (New York: Simon & Schuster, 1987).

19. John Dewey, *The School and Society* (Chicago: University of Chicago Press, 1899 [1927]), p. 32.

20. Ibid.

21. The classic study of the movement is Lawrence A. Cremin's *The Transformation of the School: Progressivism in American Education, 1876–1957* (New York: Knopf, 1961). Also useful are Henry J. Perkinson, *The Imperfect Panacea: American Faith*

in Education, 1865–1976, 2d ed. (New York: Random House, 1977), chs. 2 and 5, and Lucas, *Foundations of Education*, ch. 6.

22. John Dewey, *Democracy and Education: An Introduction to the Philosophy of Education* (New York: Macmillan, 1916).
23. John Dewey, *The Child and the Curriculum* (Chicago: University of Chicago Press, 1920).
24. Commission on the Reorganization of Secondary Education, *Cardinal Principles of Secondary Education*, Bulletin No. 35 (Washington: U.S. Government Printing Office, 1918).
25. William H. Kilpatrick, "The Project Method," *Teachers College Record* 19 (September 1918): 319–335, and *Foundations of Method* (New York: Macmillan, 1925).
26. See Patricia A. Graham, *Progressive Education: From Arcady to Academe—A History of the Progressive Education Association, 1919–1955* (New York: Teachers College Press, 1967).
27. John Dewey, *Art and Experience* (New York: Capricorn Books, 1934), pp. 40, 32.
28. Dewey published many of his criticisms of progressive education in *Experience and Education* (New York: Macmillan, 1938).
29. George S. Counts, *Dare the School Build a New Social Order?* (New York: John Day, 1932).
30. A forthcoming book on *The Social Frontier* is James M. Giarelli, ed., *Education and Public Philosophy*.
31. C. A. Bowers, *The Progressive Educator and the Depression: The Radical Years* (New York: Random House, 1969). Theodore Brameld of Boston University became the major voice of social reconstructionism in the 1950s and 1960s. See his books *Toward a Reconstructed Philosophy of Education* (New York: Holt, Rinehart and Winston, 1956) and *Education for the Emerging Age* (New York: Harper & Row, 1965).
32. Peter McLaren, *Life in Schools: An Introduction to Critical Pedagogy in the Foundations of Education* (White Plains, NY: Longman, 1989), pp. 160, 166.
33. Ibid.
34. Lucas, *Foundations of Education*, pp. 183–85; Cremin, *Transformation of the School*, pp. 332–338.
35. Ravitch, *The Schools We Deserve* and *The Troubled Crusade;* Roland Barth, *Open Education and the American School* (New York: Agathon Press, 1972); Lillian S. Stephens, *The Teacher's Guide to Open Education* (New York: Holt, Rinehart and Winston, 1974).
36. Ernest L. Boyer, *High School: A Report on Secondary Education in America* (New York: Harper & Row, 1983); John I. Goodlad, *A Place Called School: Prospects for the Future* (New York: McGraw-Hill, 1984); Theodore R. Sizer, *Horace's Compromise: The Dilemma of the American High School* (Boston:. Houghton Mifflin, 1984).
37. Boyer, *High School*, p. 16.
38. Sizer, *Horace's Compromise*, p. 156.

CHAPTER 8

Sociology of Education

Sociologists study people in groups. The discipline of sociology is valuable to teachers and other educators because it enables us to see patterns in human behavior, patterns we might otherwise overlook since so many individuals demand our attention in school. Without demeaning the importance of individuals in the least, sociology helps us realize that people's behavior reflects the positions they occupy in society. In other words, we can better understand schooling if we think of it as more than just a steady stream of individuals pouring through an institution. We need to step back, consider the individuals as members of social groups, and sort out the patterns in their behavior.

As a teacher I quickly learned that *social class, race, ethnicity,* and *gender* have a powerful effect on the process of education. I found, to be blunt, that even in the schools of a nation that prides itself on equality of opportunity, some students are more equal than others. As pleasant as it would be to pretend that schools take in students from diverse social backgrounds and give them all the same opportunities to succeed, that simply does not happen. Students who are members of some social groups come to school with advantages, and schools are organized in ways that help them maintain their advantages. Other students arrive with two strikes against them, socially speaking, and schools often do little more than throw them the third strike.

With the nation's current interest in school reform, educators are increasingly turning to sociology for guidance on how to improve the schools. Sociologists view teaching and learning in a broader context than psychologists, whose advice educators have traditionally heeded. Now the attention is shifting away from individual motivation and time on task, for example, and toward the social structure of the nation and the organizational structure of the schools.[1]

In this chapter's opening section, we will examine social class differences in families and peer groups, differences that affect how well students do in school. One way schools respond to the differences is by separating students into ability groups and tracks, a process that brands many working-class students as second-class citizens. The next section surveys racial and ethnic groups and focuses on black and Hispanic students, highlighting the controversy over two strategies designed to improve their educational opportunities: desegregation and bilingual education. The section on gender focuses on both girls and boys, but the emphasis is on how females are the second sex in school, just as they are in society.

As you read this chapter, keep in mind the demographic trends we have discussed in earlier chapters. Remember that one in four students comes from a family living in poverty. Remember that by the turn of the century, as many as 40 percent of the nation's students will be black, Hispanic, or Asian. The public school students of one state, California, are already "minority majority." Consider, too, the fact that the "traditional" American family—a wage-earning father, a mother at home, and two or more school-aged children—is now a rarity. As we enter the 1990s, only 4 percent of American households fit that profile, while the percentage of students living with one parent is increasing. One in four students now comes from a one-parent family, and 40 percent of students will live in a one-parent family before reaching their eighteenth birthday.[2]

The trend toward one-parent homes illustrates how interwoven the factors of class, race, ethnicity, and gender are. Black and Hispanic students are far more likely than others to grow up in one-parent homes. Fifty-nine percent of black and 34 percent of Hispanic children are now living with one parent, as compared with 20 percent of white children. Furthermore, most one-parent households are headed by a woman, and female-headed households are twice as likely as male-headed households to be living in poverty. Although I have organized this chapter into separate sections on class, race and ethnicity, and gender, life is not so easily categorized. As you read this chapter, you should constantly look for connections and relationships, for you will see them often in the classroom.[3]

SOCIAL CLASS

Many Americans believe that the United States is relatively free of the rigid social stratification we often criticize in other nations, but our country also has social classes, a class structure that influences education more than we like to admit. While we can take pride in our efforts to educate children from all socioeconomic backgrounds, we should be concerned that once the students get to school, their backgrounds seem to play a powerful role in their success—or lack of it.

The American Social Structure

Based on studies conducted since the 1920s, sociologists have determined that the United States has a five-tiered class structure. In *Society and Education* (1989), Daniel U. Levine and Robert J. Havighurst describe the current social structure as follows:

upper class	2 percent of the population—people who have substantial wealth that is usually inherited
upper-middle class	16 percent of the population, including professionals, executives, managers, and more successful small business owners and farmers
lower-middle class	32 percent of the population, composed of white collar workers (such as clerks, salespeople, and teachers), small business owners and farmers, and better-paid skilled blue collar workers
upper-working class	32 percent of the population, composed of skilled and semiskilled blue collar workers (such as craftspeople and assembly line workers)
lower-working class	18 percent of the population, ranging from unskilled manual workers (the "working poor") to the chronically unemployed

Sociologists use such factors as income, occupation, education, and housing to place people on the social class hierarchy. The size of the classes and the rigidity of their boundaries vary considerably throughout the country; as a rule, the larger the community, the wider the extremes of poverty and wealth and the sharper the separation of classes.[4]

Sorting and Selecting in School

For as long as sociologists have studied social class, they have been intrigued with its effects on education. George Counts, whom we met in the last chapter as a social reconstructionist, was one of the first researchers to document how schools sort and select students by their social backgrounds. In *The Selective Character of American Secondary Education* (1922), Counts showed that children from more privileged backgrounds were not only more likely to attend high school, they were also more likely to take the school's most prestigious academic courses. In *Middletown* (1929), a detailed portrait of life in a medium-sized Midwestern city, Robert and Helen Lynd showed that while parents from all classes said they believed in the importance of formal education, students from higher-status families enjoyed school more and stayed in school longer.[5]

Research conducted throughout the nation added details to the picture. As we saw in Chapters 6 and 7, during the twentieth century educators have diversified the curriculum, developing different programs in their quest to "meet the needs" of students from different socioeconomic backgrounds. This trend, relatively new when Counts and the Lynds undertook their studies, soon swept the country. Other sociologists documented the results of the trend: the schools became stratified by social class. In the influential study *Who Shall Be Educated* (1944), which involved research in the South, the Midwest, and New England, W. Lloyd Warner and his associates used the metaphor of a sorting machine to depict educational stratification:

> The educational system may be thought of as an enormous, complicated machine for sorting and ticketing and routing children through life. Young children are fed in at one end to a moving belt which conveys them past all sorts of inspecting stations. One large group is almost immediately brushed off into a bin labeled "nonreaders," "first grade repeaters," or "opportunity class" where they stay for eight or ten years and are then released through a chute to the outside world to become "hewers of wood and drawers of water." The great body of children move ahead on the main belt, losing a few here and there who are "kept back" for repeated inspection.[6]

Warner concluded that although the machine provides upward mobility for a few working-class students, it "keep[s] down many people who try for higher places."[7]

A study that brought the picture into even clearer focus appeared in the post-World War II era. *Elmtown's Youth* by August B. Hollingshead became a classic because it highlighted a pattern that appeared again and again in later research. In a small-town Midwestern high school Hollingshead found a startling correspondence between the socioeconomic status of students and their academic program or track. As Table 8.1 shows, nearly two-thirds of the upper- and upper-middle-class students were enrolled in the college preparatory program, and the rest were in the general track. These higher-status students shunned the commerical (business-vocational) track. By contrast, more than a third of the working-class students were in the commercial program, and fewer than 10

TABLE 8.1. SOCIAL CLASS AND ACADEMIC PLACEMENT: ELMTOWN HIGH SCHOOL IN THE 1940s

Social Class	Percentage of Students in Track		
	College Preparatory	General	Commercial
Upper and upper-middle	64	36	0
Lower-middle	27	51	21
Upper-working	9	58	33
Lower-working	4	58	38

(*Source: Adapted from August B. Hollingshead*, Elmtown's Youth [*New York: Wiley*], p. 462. © 1949 by John Wiley. Reprinted by permission.)

SOCIOLOGY OF EDUCATION **189**

TABLE 8.2. SOCIAL CLASS AND ACADEMIC PLACEMENT: AMERICAN HIGH
SCHOOLS TODAY

	Percentage of Students in Track		
Social Class	College Preparatory	General	Commercial
Upper and upper-middle	80	20	0
Lower-middle	50	35	15
Upper-working	20	55	25
Lower-working	10	50	40

(*Source: Author's estimates based on Daniel U. Levine and Robert J. Havighurst,* Society and Education, *7th ed.* [Boston: Allyn & Bacon, 1989], pp. 45–50, and James S. Coleman, Public and Private High *Schools: The Impact of Communities* [New York: Basic Books, 1987], pp. 41–50.)

percent were in the college prep track. The placement of the lower-middle-class students fell between these two extremes.[8]

While it might be comforting to dismiss this phenomenon as a relic from the past, we cannot. The percentages have changed, but the pattern remains the same. Based on recent studies, my estimates of the current situation are in Table 8.2. As you compare it with Table 8.1, notice that although higher percentages of students from all social classes are in the college preparatory program—reflecting the increased popularity of higher education generally and the attempt to open college doors to students from lower socioeconomic backgrounds—the relationship between social class and academic placement is still strong. Upper- and middle-class students are still far more likely to be prepping for college, just as working-class students are more likely to be learning how to repair automobiles or rotate crops.

Other studies show that social class is correlated with almost every conceivable outcome of formal education, including grades, test scores, and participation in extracurricular activities. The higher your social class, the more likely you are to graduate from high school and attend college; the lower your social class, the more likely you are to drop out of school.[9]

But why? Now comes the hard part, for it is much easier to describe something than to explain it. At the outset we need to realize that although statistics allow us to make generalizations about group behavior, individuals within those groups may act quite differently. Some working-class students do well in school, just as some wealthy students do poorly. Furthermore, the fact that social class *correlates* with many outcomes of schooling does not necessarily mean that social class *causes* success or failure; other factors may be responsible. In a nation committed to equal opportunity, however, the strong statistical relationship between social class and so much of what goes on in school should prompt educators to take the "why" question seriously.

Families, Peer Groups, and Schools

Sociologists explain the influence of social class on education by analyzing the role of families, peer groups, and the schools themselves. We will consider each of these in turn. Beyond the obvious fact that more affluent parents can give their children more of the things that money can buy—books, magazines, toys, trips, and so forth—social class affects family life in several important ways. Linguistic studies show that working-class families often raise their children with a language system that differs significantly from the one used in school. Everyone speaks a dialect, as linguists point out, but some working-class dialects are very different from the "official" dialect of the school. Furthermore, working-class parents are less likely than middle- and upper-class parents to carry on extended conversations with their children and less likely to answer their children's questions as if they were talking with other adults. Beyond these differences, more and more working-class students whose primary language is not English are enrolling in America's schools, as we will see later in this chapter.[10]

Regarding disciplinary practices, working-class families tend to stress obedience based on respect for authority—"You'll clean up your room because I'm your mother and I told you to"—while middle- and upper-class parents are more likely to encourage obedience by cajoling and reasoning with their children—"Please straighten your room so you can find things more easily next time." Corporal punishment occurs more frequently in working-class homes, where many parents believe a certain amount of physical discipline is a good thing on principle; middle- and upper-class parents tend to use corporal punishment sparingly in exceptional situations.[11]

We would be wrong to conclude that working-class parents love their children less—fortunately, love does not recognize social class boundaries—just as we would be mistaken to apply the generalizations about any social class to all its members. But we would be blind to conclude that working-class children, as a group, come to school well prepared for what they will encounter. Such children often see school as an unfamiliar game with strange players and odd rules. Thus sociologists speak of the mismatch between the world that working-class children know at home and the world they discover at school. Some students adapt; many do not.

The working-class peer group may hinder the transition more than it helps. Here we must avoid stereotyping working-class students as rebels who hate school and all it represents and more privileged students as serious scholars with a deep respect for learning. Actually students from all social classes seem to care more about clothes, cars, sports, and friends than the academic subjects they are taking. Friends are especially important—by adolescence, they are the number one influence in students' lives. Still, there are differences among the social classes. Simply put, middle- and upper-class students are usually more willing to play the game. Typically they take the courses and make the grades necessary to keep their parents off their backs, participate in a few extracurricular activities, and qualify for admission to some sort of college. Over the last two decades more of these students have drifted into the general track in order to earn better grades with less effort. Among their friends, attitudes toward teachers and academic subjects may be quite cynical, but there is peer pressure to keep enough of the rules to stay in the game.[12]

One of the first lessons I learned as a new teacher was that working-class students often feel peer pressure *not* to play the game. Especially in schools that practice such extensive sorting and selecting that working-class students wear the label of losers, stepping out of character and doing well can be embarrassing—an open invitation for peer ridicule. I noticed that every time I gave one particular student a good grade, his friends gave him a hard time, so I tried to get around the situation by telling him his grades privately. This strategy worked reasonably well for him, but it failed with most of his peers. By the end of the year I was still trying to reach working-class students, but I had concluded that more than my classroom methods needed to change.

Ability Grouping and Tracking

Ability grouping and tracking, now so deeply entrenched that some educators cannot imagine schools without them, must bear some of the responsibility for what happens to working-class students. Ability grouping involves placing together students of similar ability for instruction in particular *subjects*—forming separate groups for fast, average, and slow readers, for example. Although research on the academic effectiveness of ability grouping is mixed, with as many studies unfavorable to the practice as favorable, many teachers believe that some grouping is necessary, especially in schools that enroll students whose academic skills vary considerably. How else, they ask, can a teacher do justice to 30 students reading on several different levels?[13]

One answer is that differences in academic ability are relatively small when children first enter school. The studies most favorable to ability grouping show that it offers only slight advantages to students in the top groups—their achievement tends to be as high in ungrouped classrooms. The studies least favorable to ability grouping show that it does significant harm to the achievement of the students in the bottom groups. Far from narrowing the academic differences children bring to kindergarten and the first grade, ability grouping appears to widen them.[14]

Jeannie Oakes, whose study *Keeping Track* (1985) has focused new attention on the inequities of ability grouping, has concluded that without ability grouping in the elementary grades, middle and high school teachers would have much easier jobs. As an alternative to ability grouping, Oakes and other sociologists suggest *cooperative learning*. Teachers form learning teams composed of students with different abilities, students work cooperatively rather than competitively, and teachers assign grades based on individual progress. Cooperative learning seems to be beneficial to students of all abilities, and it is especially helpful in keeping slower students from falling farther and farther behind.[15]

With ability grouping, by contrast, students grow apart academically as they grow older, and the conventional wisdom among educators is that by high school something more than ability grouping is not only desirable but essential. That something more is tracking, which involves placing students in different *programs*, often called college preparatory, general, and vocational. Some schools have developed *sub*programs to sort students out within the main three tracks: advanced-placement college prep, regular college prep; high general, low general; regular vocational, remedial vocational. As a result of tracking, some students take four years of math and science while others take only one or two. Some learn a foreign language while others pass the time in study hall. Some write essays while others fill in worksheets.[16]

Not surprisingly, students who take a less demanding curriculum perform less well on standardized tests. Research conducted by the ACT Assessment Program shows that students who do not complete a core curriculum in high school (four years of English and at least three years each of mathematics, social studies, and science) score significantly lower on the ACT's college entrance examinations than students who take the core. To put things positively, the data suggest that students from lower socioeconomic backgrounds have a great deal to gain from getting out of the lower tracks and into programs with higher standards and expectations. Put negatively, the best way for educators to insure that working-class students will never have a serious chance at jobs that require a college degree is to encourage or simply allow them to take the easy way out of high school.[17]

A walk through almost any tracked high school will reveal what research confirms: lower-track students receive an education that differs not just in the quantity and quality of academic courses but also in the *climate* of instruction. Lower-track students believe that their teachers are less concerned with academic skills than with their willingness to take orders and follow directions. Students in lower-track classes are less likely than others to have friends who want to go to college. Perhaps most seriously, tracking lowers the self-esteem of students in the least prestigious programs. Well aware they are the outcasts of the school, lower-track students band together in peer groups that guard their losers' image as if it were a badge of honor. Here is the *self-fulfilling prophecy* at its worst: lower-track students living down to expectations.[18]

Why do American schools continue to group and track? An international comparison may suggest some answers. In Japan, a nation whose educational practices many Americans seem eager to emulate, the state schools practice no ability grouping and much less tracking than our public schools, yet Japanese students regularly outperform ours on achievement tests. "But the Japanese are a homogeneous people, and we are not," comes the reply. That statement overlooks the fact that Japan has social classes too, but it does make a point: our nation's penchant for ability grouping and tracking seems to be more social than academic.[19]

Historically Americans have rarely questioned a set of basic assumptions about academic success, social class, and jobs. Throughout the twentieth century, as working-class children have come to school in larger numbers and stayed there longer, educators have voiced the assumptions in a variety of ways to justify ability grouping and tracking. Stated bluntly, the assumptions are:

1. Many children lack both the ability and the interest necessary to succeed in school.
2. These children come disproportionately from the lower social classes.
3. They are probably destined for jobs that involve working with the hands rather than the head.
4. Therefore, they need little or no academic training beyond the 3Rs.[20]

These assumptions have withstood challenges from educational theorists of all persuasions—perennialists, essentialists, and progressives. Most of today's educational reforms have the unmistakable ring of essentialism in their promise of more academic work for all students, but given the deeply ingrained assumption that many students are incapable of academic success, exactly what their work will consist of remains to be seen. Our challenge is to make schooling more than a reflection of children's social class backgrounds, more than an assumption about their future roles in the labor force.

RACE AND ETHNICITY: AN OVERVIEW

Although some people use the words interchangeably, race and ethnicity are not synonymous. Race is a *physical* concept, based on skin color and other physical characteristics; ethnicity is a *cultural* concept that involves such factors as language, religion, and nationality. Anthropologists generally speak of three races: Caucasoid (white), Mongoloid (yellow), and Negroid (black). Throughout the world, cultural differences have divided each race into numerous ethnic groups. Although many ethnic groups are subdivisions of a particular race, others are not. For example, people of the black race in the United States have developed a strong collective identity that has forged them into one ethnic group. Other ethnic groups, conversely, include more than one race. Hispanics, for example, can be of any race.[21]

Think of ethnicity as a "sense of peoplehood."[22] The members of an ethnic group have a shared identity based on a common history and a sense of common destiny. The members of the group often share a language, religion, and other cultural traditions, and they often have common geographical origins. In the United States, many ethnic groups identify themselves by the nation from which their ancestors came; thus we have German-Americans, Irish-Americans, Chinese-Americans, Swedish-Americans, Italian-Americans, Polish-Americans, Vietnamese-Americans, and a host of others. Native Americans, the people who inhabited North America before Europeans came to the continent, constitute an ethnic group with as many as 170 tribal subdivisions.

Other groups in the United States emphasize nongeographical factors as the basis of their ethnic identity. Jewish Americans stress the religion of Judaism, while Hispanic Americans are unified by the Spanish language. As these two groups illustrate, however, the members of a group may view their ethnicity in different ways. Many American Jews put less emphasis on religion than on shared historical experiences and a sense of common destiny. The word "Hispanic" is too general for some Americans, who may prefer the more specific ethnic identification of such names as Mexican-American, Puerto Rican, and Cuban-American.

The strength of ethnic ties also varies from group to group and person to person. The sense of peoplehood is usually stronger within groups of lower socioeconomic status. As people climb the ladder of success, they tend to think of themselves less as members of an ethnic group and more as members of a social class. Ethnic identity may also be weaker in large groups with a long period of residence in the United States. Americans whose roots lie primarily in England, for example, outnumber German-Americans (although barely so, according to census figures) to form the largest "ancestral group" in the nation. Yet English Americans—sometimes called white Anglo-Saxon Protestants or WASPs, a name that some of them do not appreciate—generally do not think of themselves as ethnic at all. Moreover, many Americans have such diverse ethnic backgrounds that they do not identify with any one group. They think of themselves as just Americans. Still, during the 1960s and 1970s the United States experienced an upsurge of ethnic consciousness, and schools developed programs in ethnic studies, multiethnic education, and multicultural education.[23]

The new wave of immigration to the United States since the late 1960s has accentuated the nation's ethnic and racial diversity. Coming primarily from Mexico, Asia, and Central and South America, the new immigrants have rekindled old debates over assimilation, pluralism, and separation. The number of Asian-Americans, for example, has doubled since 1970. About 3 percent of American students are now Asian-Americans, and as a whole their success in the schools has been remarkable. But the term "Asian-American" obscures ethnic differences among the recently arrived Vietnamese, Laotian, Thai, Cambodian, and Taiwanese-Americans and the better established Chinese, Filipino, Japanese, and Korean-Americans. The new arrivals are not as uniformly successful in schools and society as the popular stereotypes suggest. Language barriers and employment discrimination are still significant problems.[24]

Cultural differences and discrimination are also familiar to blacks and Hispanics, the two groups on whom we will focus in this section. These groups are still struggling to make it in the United States. Our analysis of social class shapes this discussion, for 37 percent of blacks and 30 percent of Hispanics are in families with incomes below the poverty level, as compared with 15 percent of all Americans.[25]

Turning our attention first to the education of black students, we will see that separation or segregation is still a major issue, but the debates over segregation have become more complex. Black Americans are now 12 percent of the total population, and 47 percent live outside the South. Surely it would astound both Booker T. Washington and W. E. B. DuBois that black students attend schools that are less segregated in Washington's native South than in DuBois's Northeast. As we will see, the nature of segregation itself has changed, complicating debates over how—or whether—to reduce it.[26]

We will also focus on the education of Hispanic children, who as a group have received relatively little attention until recently. Now 8 percent of the population, Hispanics may outnumber blacks early in the next century. Many Americans are surprised to learn that the segregation of Hispanic students, who are highly concentrated in a few states and a few cities, has increased while the segregation of black students has decreased. Another controversial issue for Hispanics is bilingual education, which puts the debates over pluralism in a contemporary light.[27]

BLACK STUDENTS

Desegregation in Historical Perspective

When the United States Supreme Court issued its decision in *Brown v. Board of Education of Topeka* (1954), the court raised a question that the nation is still struggling to answer. Can schools that are segregated ever be equal? Since 1954 Americans have discovered how complex the question is. In the wake of *Plessy v. Ferguson* (1896), black Americans had no more than the rhetorical equality suggested by the words "separate but equal." The rhetoric bore no resemblance to reality. Black schools were inferior to white schools, and it was impossible to pretend otherwise. There were obvious differences in such tangible factors as physical facilities, courses of study, pupil-teacher ratios, teacher salaries, and overall expenditures per student. These inequalities, although greatest in the South, existed throughout the nation. By the 1950s some school boards were narrowing—but by no means completely closing—the gaps between black and white schools, hoping to avoid or at least postpone a Supreme Court mandate for desegregation.[28]

When that mandate finally came on May 17, 1954, the court used language so clear and direct that even supporters of desegregation were startled. Can schools that are segregated ever be equal? The answer was a unanimous no. The justices cited social science evidence to support their conclusion that even when expenditures and other tangible factors are equal, segregated schools are psychologically damaging to black students. Thus the court declared that "separate educational facilities are inherently unequal"—an unequivocal answer.[29]

Brown represented such a direct confrontation with established educational practice that the court did not issue an enforcement decree for a full year. When it called for desegregation "with all deliberate speed" in 1955 and ordered the lower courts to supervise the process, opponents of desegregation seized on the word "deliberate" and proceeded to drag their feet. In the South, massive resistance blocked the way as governors vowed "segregation forever" and state legislatures stalled for time. Lengthy legal battles ensued. Battles were also fought out of court as riots and other acts of violence often made it necessary for federal troops to escort black children into newly desegregated schools. Taking massive resistance to the extreme, Prince Edward County, Virginia, simply closed its public schools from 1959 through 1964 to avoid desegregation. Confrontations of the same kind accompanied the desegregation of colleges and universities.[30]

But the quest for desegregated education drew strength from the Reverend Martin Luther King, Jr., and the larger civil rights movement, constant legal pressure from the NAACP, and after 1960, all three branches of the federal government. The major breakthrough came with the passage and enforcement of the Civil Rights Act of 1964. Title VI of the act gave federal officials the power to cut off federal funds to school systems that refused to desegregate. Other federal legislation passed in the mid-1960s made school systems throughout the nation, and especially in the South, increasingly dependent on federal funding. The Civil Rights Act, national in scope but admittedly aimed at the South, was a powerful weapon indeed.[31]

Federal pressure produced remarkable results—in some parts of the United States. Table 8.3 shows that public schools in the South, the *most* segregated in the nation as late as 1968, had become the nation's *least* segregated only four years later. They remain so today. Compare the trends in other regions—the

TABLE 8.3. SEGREGATION OF BLACK STUDENTS BY REGION, 1968–1984

Region	Percentage of Students in 90%–100% Minority Schools				
	1968	*1972*	*1976*	*1980*	*1984*
South	78	25	22	23	24
Border	60	55	43	37	37
Northeast	43	47	51	49	47
Midwest	58	57	51	44	44
West	51	43	36	34	29
U.S. average	64	39	36	33	33

(*Source: Gary Orfield*, Public School Desegregation in the United States, 1968–1980 [*Washington: Joint Center for Political Studies, 1983*], p. 4; Gary Orfield and Franklin Monfort, Are American Schools Resegregating in the Reagan Era?, *working paper no. 14* [Chicago: National School Desegregation Project, University of Chicago, 1987], pp. 313–314, 392.)

greatest contrast is between the South and the Northeast. Notice that northeastern public schools were the nation's *least* segregated in 1968, but they became *more* segregated while southern schools were moving rapidly in the opposite direction. Given the slow but steady progress of desegregation in western, midwestern, and border states, today the Northeast has the nation's *most* segregated public schools.[32]

De Facto versus De Jure

In order to understand these trends we must distinguish between two types of segregation: de jure and de facto. *De jure* means by law. De jure segregation is the result of legislation, policy, or official action: a state law or local school board policy requiring black students and white students to attend separate schools, for example, or a public official's statements supporting segregation. Because laws, policies, and officials had mandated segregation in every southern state, the eyes of the nation were on the South after the *Brown* decision. But de jure school segregation also existed in the border states and in school districts scattered throughout every region of the nation—the one in Topeka, Kansas, that the Brown family sued, for example. During the 1950s and 1960s, this kind of segregation was obvious and relatively easy to prove in court—a smoking gun.

Vestiges of de jure segregation remain today, but in guises that are more subtle and more difficult to document. De jure segregation may take the form of a principal who quietly discourages black students from requesting voluntary transfers to a predominantly white school, or a school board that opens new schools with attendance zones that increase segregation within the system. In a precedent-setting decision involving Yonkers, New York, a federal court of appeals ruled in 1987 that de jure segregation can even take the form of a city government that locates public housing projects in a way that promotes residential segregation.[33]

Most segregation in the United States today, however, is *de facto*, which means in fact. De facto school segregation is largely the result of segregated neighborhoods—the "fact" is that most Americans still choose to live among people of their own race. Such segregation is sometimes called voluntary, which is an accurate description only to the degree that people can choose housing without encountering racial discrimination—and can afford housing of their choice. Although the line between de facto and de jure segregation can be fine, as the examples in the preceding paragraph suggest, since *Brown* the Supreme Court and lower courts have tried to distinguish between the two. In two important decisions in the late 1980s, federal appeals courts reviewed the desegregation plans of Norfolk, Virginia, and Austin, Texas, two school systems that had been under court orders requiring busing as a remedy for de jure segregation. When the two systems convinced the courts that they were no longer practicing de jure segregation, the courts allowed them to reduce busing and return to neighborhood schools. These decisions had the effect of increasing segregation, for many of the schools are located in highly segregated neighbor-hoods.[34]

Urban School Desegregation

The distinction between de facto and de jure helps explain why public schools in the Northeast are more segregated today than they were in the 1950s. This change reflects demographic trends in the large urban areas of the Northeast, where whites have been leaving the central cities for the suburbs since the end of World War II. Many urban neighborhoods that were once white are now black or Hispanic. In addition, many of the whites who live in central cities today send their children to private schools. Thus the large public school systems in New York, Philadelphia, Boston, and Newark, once predominantly white, now have more black students than white; in New York and Newark, Hispanic students also outnumber whites.[35]

The same demographic trends that have affected city schools in the Northeast have changed the racial composition of urban school systems throughout the nation. The city systems in Baltimore, Atlanta, New Orleans, Memphis, St. Louis, Cleveland, Chicago, Detroit, Houston, Dallas, Denver, and Los Angeles—this list is representative but by no means exhaustive—have experienced racial and ethnic transition as city neighborhoods have changed. Minority students now outnumber white students in 23 of the 25 largest urban school systems.[36]

Can anything be done to desegregate large urban school systems? Advocates of desegregation have proposed metropolitan or cross-district desegregation plans involving the predominantly white suburban systems that usually surround big-city systems. These plans have met a great deal of resistance. Based on the Supreme Court's decision in *Milliken v. Bradley* (1974), a Detroit case, the courts have ordered cross-district desegregation only when they have found state or suburban school officials responsible for some of the segregation in the city—in other words, only when they have found the officials guilty of de jure segregation. Since the mid-1970s the courts have left urban school segregation largely untouched.[37]

Academic, Social, and Economic Effects of Desegregation

Turning our attention to the effects of school desegregation, we face a controversial question: Does desegregation improve the academic achievement of black students? How we answer the question depends on whose research we accept. One problem is that some researchers have approached the question with their minds already made up, obviously looking for evidence to support their ideological biases. Another problem is that researchers have studied the academic effects of desegregation using so many different methodologies and research designs that it is difficult to compare studies and draw conclusions. Despite these problems, answers are emerging from three decades of research on the question.

The basic answer is yes: the academic achievement of black students *usually* improves as a result of desegregation. Robert L. Crain, senior social scientist at the Rand Corporation and principal investigator at Johns Hopkins University's Center for the Social Organization of Schools, has narrowed the many studies on the question to 93, the best studies (in his judgment) in a large and very mixed body of research. Crain and his associates have drawn several explanations from these studies for why desegregation usually, but not always, improves achievement. Desegregation produces the greatest academic benefits when it begins early, with young children—the most rapid gains in achievement occur in the early primary grades. Moreover, the achievement of black students is highest in schools that are predominantly white and middle-class, but where blacks are at least 20 percent of the student body. Like other researchers, Crain attributes the gains for blacks less to the "whiteness" of desegregated schools than to the schools' middle-class standards. Middle-class schools usually have better teachers and more demanding programs, characteristics that benefit all students.[38]

Overall, Crain's research indicates that successful desegregation can

> raise a student's achievement in the first grade by a fraction of a year; if that student held on to this advantage throughout school, however, he or she would be approximately one grade level higher than if he or she had been in a segregated school.[39]

Since current estimates of the aggregate gap between black and white achievement put the difference at one-half year when children enter school, widening to two and one-half years by high school graduation, the academic benefits of desegregation can be significant. Along with other researchers, Crain notes that desegregation does not benefit blacks at the expense of whites—the achievement of white students rarely decreases and sometimes increases.[40]

Critics argue that desegregation does not always occur under the ideal conditions that Crain would like to see. In some systems it begins late: students attend segregated neighborhood schools in the elementary grades, and their first exposure to students of other races comes in middle and high schools that are desegregated because of their wider attendance zones. Another problem occurs in big-city systems, where what little desegregation there is often involves students of the same social class—working-class whites and working-class blacks. Tracking can also frustrate desegregation plans. As we have seen, tracking can result in vastly different programs and expectations for students within the same school. If black students go to a desegregated school only to end up in the lower tracks, their academic gains may be minimal. Unfortunately, this resegregation occurs frequently as a second-generation desegregation problem.

Enrollment statistics may show that a school is desegregated, but a walk through the halls may reveal that almost every classroom is highly segregated.[41]

Although academic achievement usually takes center stage in discussions of the effects of desegregation, its long-term social and economic benefits may be even more important. There is mounting evidence that desegregated schools are helping to desegregate society. Black students who graduate from desegregated schools are more likely to attend desegregated colleges and universities, live in desegregated neighborhoods, and hold jobs in desegregated work places. Employers prefer to hire blacks who graduate from desegregated schools. In addition, school desegregation seems to improve the racial attitudes of both whites and blacks toward their neighbors and co-workers. Robert Crain and his associates, who have conducted some of the research that supports these findings, believe that school desegregation can help reduce the economic distance between blacks and whites, a gap that may account for much racial prejudice.[42]

Busing

Public opinion polls on school desegregation show that Americans, black and white, are overwhelmingly for it. Mention the word "busing," however, and the races split, with far more blacks (66%) than whites (36%) in favor of busing for desegregation. But the most recent Harris Poll on busing, conducted in late 1986, reveals "one of the most dramatic turnarounds [of public opinion] in recent history." Forty-one percent of all the people polled supported busing for desegregation. Even more significant, according to pollster Louis Harris, is the fact that for the first time "a whole host of key segments of the American public now actually favor busing." Harris's survey found that people under 30, those most likely to have ridden buses to desegregated schools themselves, are also most likely to favor it. Sixty percent of those aged 18 to 24 and 51 percent of those aged 25 to 29 expressed support. Moving up the age brackets, support decreases, to a low of 26 percent among people 65 and older. But most significant, perhaps, is the finding that 71 percent of all families whose children have been bused for desegregation rate the experience as "very satisfactory," up from 54 percent in 1981.[43]

These findings may not erase the memories of the bitter controversies that erupted in the 1970s, when busing for desegregation became a volatile political issue. Academic researchers fanned the flames with studies that showed a connection between busing and "white flight" from public school systems. Other researchers countered that busing has generated the most resentment in central cities, which whites were leaving long before busing became a desegregation strategy. Conceding that busing may accelerate the loss of whites from central city schools, these researchers pointed out that some whites return to the schools once the controversy over a new desegregation program subsides, and that metropolitan plans involving city and suburban systems have produced less white flight than plans involving central city systems alone.[44]

What is the status of busing today? More than half of all students ride school buses every day, but only about 4 percent are bused solely for desegregation—most ride just to get to school. Nor is the emotionally charged image of "crosstown busing" accurate in most cases. The average school bus ride is about 15 minutes each way, with no difference in average length between all busing and busing for desegregation. While metropolitan (city-suburban) plans obviously increase time and distance on the bus, the longest school bus routes in the United States are not in metropolitan areas for desegregation but in rural areas for transportation. Many rural students ride the bus an hour or more each way, but the length of their rides rarely causes controversy.[45]

Magnet Schools

What bothers Americans most about busing for desegregation may be its involuntary nature—court orders from federal judges often trigger resentment. Americans also dislike riding school buses past their neighborhood schools, although the concept of neighborhood differs greatly from cities to suburbs to rural areas. Magnet schools are designed to overcome both objections. Sometimes referred to as schools so good that students volunteer to attend them, magnet schools offer special programs to attract students from throughout a school system. New York City's School of the Performing Arts and the Bronx High School of Science are two well-known examples, although they were established long before the term "magnet school" came into vogue. Magnet schools started in the 1970s and 1980s usually have *voluntary* desegregation—frankly, an alternative to court-ordered busing—as their major goal.

In addition to regular academic programs, magnet schools offer specializations not available elsewhere in a school system. One school may specialize in communications and mass media, another in health professions, another in foreign languages, still another in commercial art. For more traditional students, back-to-basics magnet schools featuring strict discipline and dress codes have proven popular in some systems.

The consensus is that magnet schools are a good supplementary desegregation strategy but that by themselves they probably cannot make a significant statistical dent in big-city segregation. They do offer the attractive prospect of positive, voluntary desegregation. Magnet schools are working especially well in the Houston Independent School District, where an expensive, extensive, aggressively promoted network of magnet schools has been the key factor in reducing the segregation of black and Hispanic students. Non-Hispanic white students are in the minority in Houston, yet the magnet programs have developed such a positive reputation that white students from suburban systems are now transferring to the city schools. Magnet schools have also led the way in the recent desegregation of the Milwaukee system. In other systems a lack of support from school board members, teachers and administrators, and especially parents and community leaders has yielded magnet programs with less impressive records.[46]

Debates over the education of black students continue. As the focus of the debates has shifted from equality to excellence, from access to ability, some educators have argued that it is time to pay less attention to the racial composition of schools and more to their academic quality. Highly segregated schools can be highly effective schools, they argue. In the next chapter we will examine effective schools research, which accepts segregation by race, ethnicity, and social class as a fact of life, especially in large cities.

Meanwhile the gaps between blacks and whites in achievement test scores are closing, a positive trend that deserves more publicity. Another positive trend is that the percentage of black students going to college appears to be leveling off at about 29 percent after declining for most of the 1980s. But many Americans are shocked to learn that about 25 percent of all 18- and 19-year-olds have not graduated from high school, and the figure for blacks is 35 percent. (Estimates of dropout rates vary greatly. According to some studies, the figures just cited, which come from the U.S. Department of Education, are too low. Some researchers have also found that dropout rates are increasing, with the rate for black and other minority students increasing even faster than the overall rate.) If it is true that our nation is at risk, as the National Commission on Excellence in Education contends, then black students are among those at greatest risk.[47]

HISPANIC STUDENTS

History and Demographics

Hispanics in the United States are a large, diverse, rapidly growing group. Actually Hispanics are several groups, unified culturally by the Spanish language and often the Roman Catholic faith but historically distinct. Mexican-Americans, 60 percent of all Hispanics in the United States, have a long history in the Southwest. By the early 1600s Spaniards and Mexicans had settled much of the land in the present states of California, New Mexico, Arizona, Colorado, and Texas. For 250 years the Spanish language and Catholic faith were dominant in this large territory, but the founding of the Texas Republic in 1836 and the victory of the United States in the Mexican-American War (1846–48) officially established a different culture, English speaking and Protestant.[48]

Despite assurances that the older culture would be protected and preserved, all but the most affluent Mexican-Americans became a colonized people. Public schools and Catholic schools stressed conformity to the English (now called Anglo) culture, but the goal was usually separation rather than assimilation. Heavy immigration from Mexico to the United States at the turn of the twentieth century, during World War II, and especially since the 1960s has produced a modern Mexican-American population that is concentrated in the Southwest, highly urbanized, largely working-class, and increasingly segregated.

Puerto Rico became a territory of the United States at the end of the Spanish-American War in 1898. A commonwealth since 1952, Puerto Rico has had a tense political relationship with the United States. Excluding the population of the island itself, 14 percent of Hispanics in the United States are Puerto Ricans. The poorest of American Hispanics, many Puerto Ricans travel back and forth between the island and the mainland, their circular migrations tied closely to the availability of jobs. Puerto Ricans are also the most segregated Hispanics in the United States, their children typically attending highly segregated schools in New York City and other central cites.

Cuban-Americans are the most prosperous Hispanics in the United States. Most have come to this nation since Fidel Castro's rise to power in the late 1950s. Many professionals and business people left the island during the 1960s and 1970s, to be joined by a group of much poorer refugees, the Marielitos, in 1980. Now 6 percent of American Hispanics, Cubans are heavily concentrated in the Miami-Dade County area. In general they are well educated and economically successful, but sharp class divisions separate the established residents and the newly arrived poor. Ethnicity, race, and class converge to make the Dade County Public Schools, where Cubans and other Hispanic students now outnumber non-Hispanic whites and blacks, one of the nation's most multicultural yet most segregated systems.

Most of the research on desegregation and academic achievement has focused on black students, but the few studies on Hispanics show similar patterns: their achievement is usually higher in desegregated schools. But while the segregation of black students in the nation as a whole decreased during the 1970s and changed little during the 1980s, the segregation of Hispanics increased throughout both decades. By the mid-1980s, 31 percent of Hispanic students were in schools whose enrollment was 90 percent to 100 percent minority. Although the U.S. Supreme Court ruled in *Keyes v. School District No. 1, Denver, Colorado* (1973) that desegregation plans should include Hispanic students, very few suits involving Hispanics have come to trial. For Hispanic parents and legal activists, school desegregation has not yet become a major issue, although recent evidence suggests that Hispanic support for busing as a desegregation strategy is increasing.[49]

The Controversy over Bilingual Education

Bilingual education has been a major issue for years. Based on opinion polls of Hispanics, bilingualism is not an artificial cause promoted by politicians and activists; it is the genuine desire of the vast majority of Hispanics. Seventy-four percent of Hispanics say their language goal is to be bilingual; 20 percent say their goal is fluency in Spanish only; 6 percent say English only. Thus the pressure Hispanics have brought to bear on educators for bilingual schooling reflects a strong preference for bilingual living. It also reflects the fact that as many as 40 percent of Hispanic students come to school with limited English proficiency (LEP) or no English proficiency (NEP).[50]

Some Americans react with alarm to the Hispanic call for pluralism in schools and society; to some, it seems that Hispanics are asking not for pluralism but for separation. Predictably, a backlash developed during the 1980s. California, where almost one-third of American Hispanics live and where more than half of all the public school students are minorities, became the first state to declare English its official language by a referendum of voters and the second state to amend its constitution accordingly. Other states have followed suit—more than 35 state legislatures have debated the issue, and almost 20 have passed an English-Only law. Former U.S. Senator S. I. Hayakawa of California, the honorary chair of an organization known as U.S. English, is leading a drive to make English the official language of the nation. This campaign is directed specifically against bilingual ballots and certain forms of bilingual education.[51]

As Chapter 6 indicates, bilingual education in the United States has a long but little-known history. In the late 1960s bilingualism became a hot issue once again when Congress passed the Bilingual Education Act of 1968. Responding to the complaints of Mexican-American parents in Texas, Congress resolved that students whose primary language is not English need some form of special assistance in school. The Supreme Court's decision in *Lau v. Nichols* (1974), which involved not Hispanics but Chinese in San Francisco, affirmed the principle: School systems must do *something* to help. The court prohibited the policy of submersion, which forces students with limited English proficiency to sink or swim with no special assistance in their native language. Standard practice in public schools for immigrants at the turn of the century, submersion remains the unofficial standard in some school systems today, *Lau* notwithstanding.[52]

Models of Bilingual Education

The Supreme Court left educators a great deal of leeway in deciding how to help LEP students, but during the Ford and Carter administrations the executive branch of the federal government tried to specify the kind of language assistance school systems had to provide. As some local school boards protested loudly against "federal forcing," attention focused on three competing models of bilingual education: *structured immersion, transitional bilingual*, and *bilingual/ bicultural maintenance*.[53]

All bilingual education involves instruction in two languages, but the three models differ in the amount of emphasis each language receives. In the structured immersion model, teachers who know both English and the students' native language provide instruction. Although students may ask questions in either language, teachers encourage them to use English, and teachers always speak in English. In the transitional bilingual model, teachers instruct students in their native language in some subjects—social studies or science, for example—to keep them from falling behind as they learn English. Designed to ease the transition from the native language into English, this model often features separate classes in English as a Second Language (ESL), in which students practice reading, writing, and speaking English. To complicate matters, some school systems claiming to use the transitional model actually use ESL alone, offering no instruction in the native language. Transitional bilingual education (or ESL alone) is especially popular with Asian-American students, whose parents usually stress mastery of English as the key to academic success. Although the structured immersion and transitional bilingual models employ different methods, they have the same goal: developing skills in English as quickly as possible, ideally during the early elementary grades. Under both models bilingual education ends when the students reach a specified level of English proficiency.

The third model, bilingual/bicultural maintenance, has a different goal: developing and increasing proficiency in both English *and* the other language. In every grade, students take some classes taught in their native language and some in English, often by teachers who are fluent in both. The curriculum highlights the students' ethnic culture in a multiethnic or multicultural program. It is this model of bilingual education that has drawn the most criticism from U.S. English and similar groups, even though the transitional model has been more widely used. The critics charge that bilingual/bicultural maintenance programs often produce students who speak two languages poorly, students who are unprepared to compete in an English-dominant culture. Defenders of bilingual/ bicultural maintenance reply that many programs do work well; they urge educators to acknowledge the bilingual or even Spanish-dominant subculture in which most American Hispanics live.

The controversy intensified in the early 1980s when the Reagan administration tried to change federal policy on bilingual education. Whereas the Ford and Carter administrations had encouraged school systems to use the transitional model, President Reagan resolved to give state and local officials more discretion, arguing that research did not favor one model over the others. Congress balked at the change, and most federal money remained earmarked for transitional instruction. The controversy entered a new phase in 1986, when the preliminary results of a study conducted ironically by Mr. Reagan's Department of Education rated the maintenance model most effective in developing language skills—in English as well as the native language. The more instructional time the students spent in their native language, the better their skills in that language *and* in English. When the study focused on proficiency in English alone, the transitional model still came in second and immersion last.[54]

The Hispanic commitment to bilingual schooling as a part of bilingual living remains strong. The growth of the Hispanic population is changing the political balance of power in several cities and states—Hispanics are winning seats on local school boards, as the next chapter points out. People who do not live where there is a large Hispanic population can easily underestimate the significance of current demographic trends. Early in the twenty-first century Hispanics may be able to command the attention of the nation and its schools as effectively as black people have in the last half of this century. Already it strikes many people as incongruous that within one school system, often within a single school, we can find teachers working hard to wash Spanish out of one group of students—often in classes stigmatized as remedial—and trying just as hard to iron Spanish into another group of students—usually in college prep classes.[55]

Meanwhile the statistical indicators on Hispanic students, like those on black students, are mixed. Relative to others, Hispanics students are closing the gap on achievement tests, but the Hispanic dropout rate is alarming: more than 55 percent of Hispanics have not received a high school diploma by age 18 or 19. Only about 17 percent of Hispanic 18- to 24-year-olds go on to college. Clearly, Hispanic students remain at risk.[56]

GENDER

Prospective teachers often seem less interested in discussing the influence of gender on the process of education than the influence of social class, race, and ethnicity. Younger female prospective teachers may react with amazement and even amusement to the suggestion that as the 1990s begin, male and female students receive different treatment in school. "No one ever put me down for being a girl—I took the courses I wanted to take and participated in whatever activities and sports I chose," one of my students said recently. Many male prospective teachers have the same attitude: "No, I don't think I had any advantages or disadvantages in school because of my sex." If an older student brings up the discrimination she (or occasionally he) faced in school, the rest of the class smiles and sighs with relief, grateful that things have changed so much. To many future teachers, unequal treatment based on sex is a thing of the past, a quaint relic from another age.

Have things really changed? When researchers asked students in grades three through twelve to respond to the question "If you woke up tomorrow and discovered that you were a (boy) (girl), how would your life be different?" the answers were surprisingly consistent. Students of both sexes readily admitted that boys have it better than girls. Boys do not have to worry much about their appearance, the students said, but girls must be concerned with attractiveness and neatness or risk rejection. Boys can participate in a wider range of activities and choose among more careers, the students continued. Girls have to watch their behavior more carefully—they have to be "nicer" than boys. The students were also aware that girls have to be more concerned with their safety. In short, students of both sexes saw few advantages to being female and few disadvantages to being male.[57]

Sex-Role Socialization

When confronted with such studies, prospective teachers tend to place the blame on the home: "Students must pick up those attitudes from their parents. Teachers would never favor one sex over the other." To be sure, there is abundant evidence that many parents still raise boys and girls differently. Males begin life as the preferred sex. By a ratio of more than 2 to 1, both future mothers and future fathers express their preference for boys. Some studies show that mothers tend to be physically and emotionally closer to their daughters, expecting them to need more attention and nurture. Fathers tend to be rougher and more physical with their sons, and boys receive more encourgement from both parents to be independent. While parents may tolerate girls who are tomboys, few will allow boys to be sissies. Fathers are especially harsh with sons who show traits and interests that society stereotypes as feminine.[58]

Sex-role socialization takes place outside as well as inside the family. Although it is now acceptable (and in some cases even fashionable) for girls to play with hammers and trucks, many stores continue to advertise and display boys' toys and girls' toys. Doctors' kits and tool boxes are for one sex; nurses' kits and kitchen sets are for the other. The games children play vary by sex, with girls' games more likely to take place indoors and more likely to emphasize cooperation over competition. Peer groups, churches, the media—all of these play major roles in teaching children proper behavior for males and females.[59]

Thus it is understandable that prospective teachers look outside the schools for the origins of sex-role socialization. But it is all too easy to overlook how schools reinforce stereotypes that students have learned elsewhere. Numerous studies conducted during the 1970s documented the masculine bias in textbooks, for example. One influential study of elementary school readers showed that the books featured two and one-half to three times as many males as females and portrayed males in almost six times as many occupational roles. In what some researchers have called "the cult of the apron," the books rarely showed women working outside the home; a few women were, of course, nurses, secretaries, or teachers. Studies of secondary school texbooks uncovered the same patterns. Social studies books rarely mentioned women; literature texts presented few selections by female authors; science texts downplayed the contributions of women; math books featured males more frequently than females in word problems; and so forth.[60]

After women's groups brought pressure to bear on publishers, the books began to change, but not as much as many educators think. A study of elementary school readers conducted in the 1980s found that while the overall ratio of males to females has narrowed, it is still nearly 2 to 1. Compared with the older textbooks, the books used today present more career options for both sexes, but males hold up to 80 percent of all the careers. Publishers have also modified secondary school texts, but often in cosmetic ways. Token females, like token racial and ethnic minorities, are now on prominent display, but males remain dominant.[61]

Such portrayals are unrealistic in a nation where females are 52 percent of the population and almost half of the labor force. More than half of married women are employed outside the home, and more than 90 percent of women work outside the home at some time during their lives. While women are moving rapidly into managerial positions and into the professions of law, medicine, and dentistry, men are not showing the same interest in fields women have traditionally dominated. Ninety-nine percent of secretaries and 97 percent of registered nurses are still women. In fact, most women who work outside the home remain in pink collar jobs that pay low salaries, which helps explain why the wages of fully employed women average only 65 percent those of men.[62]

Few textbooks reflect these realities, even though new stereotypes may be replacing old ones. The irony of the situation is that some conservative groups are now charging that textbooks have changed too much, to the point of promoting "nontraditional and antifamily life-styles." Often the evidence is a book's favorable portrayal of a female auto mechanic, a male nurse, or another stereotype-shattering character. Feminists, citing the continuing gap between the overall percentages of males and females in textbooks and the continuing masculine dominance of occupational roles in the books, counter that they have not changed enough.

Unequal Treatment in the Classroom

In the survey we examined at the beginning of this section, the students agreed that, in general, people treat boys better than girls. The students pointed out one major exception, however. Both sexes believed girls receive better treatment in school. The consensus was that teachers like girls more and pick on boys more. The students concluded, therefore, that girls have the advantage. Research suggests that the students' perceptions are right but that their conclusion is wrong. Girls *do* behave in ways that teachers like and reward. In the classroom girls tend to be quieter and more cooperative than boys. Girls depend more on their teachers and identify more closely with them—remember that 69 percent of all teachers and 86 percent of elementary school teachers are female. Some researchers describe the typical classroom as a feminized environment in which girls feel comfortable and at ease.[63]

Boys react to the classroom differently. Trained in the home to be more active and independent, boys often rebel against the routine of silence, seatwork, and conformity. Some rebel so strongly they refuse to learn; others channel their activity in ways that appear to give them the academic edge over girls. Empirical studies of classroom interaction show that boys quickly master the art of getting their teachers' attention. Boys are eight times as likely as girls to shout out answers in class, and teachers—male as well as female—usually play along and acknowledge the boys' participation. Strikingly, teachers are more likely to reprimand girls for calling out in class, often with a comment like "Please raise your hand if you want to answer." Overall, boys dominate classroom discussion by a ratio of 3 to 1 over girls.[64]

Thus teachers spend more of their time interacting with boys. The research also indicates that the quality of interaction differs, with boys more likely than girls to receive specific directions, praise, and criticism: "Draw the picture like this" as opposed to "Mm-hmm" or "Okay." Few teachers realize they teach this way, but videotapes of classes reveal the underlying patterns of interaction. Such behavior is slow to change precisely because it is unconscious and unintentional.[65]

Title IX

Some things have changed, however, and we can credit some of the progress that schools have made toward sex equity to Title IX of the Education Amendments of 1972. Title IX states:

> No person in the United States shall, on the basis of sex, be excluded from participation in, be denied the benefits of, or be subjected to discrimination under any educational program or activity receiving federal financial assistance.

Protecting both students and employees, Title IX has helped open up courses, activities, and jobs that were once officially or unofficially closed to one sex or the other. In part as a result of Title IX, boys now take homemaking and consumer courses and girls are enrolled in industrial arts and agriculture classes. Title IX has made a tremendous difference in athletic programs, putting the pressure on sometimes-reluctant schools to provide equal opportunities for female and male athletes. Title IX has helped female teachers move into administrative positions that were once controlled by the good old boy network.[66]

No legislation is a panacea, however. Although approximately one-third of the students in homemaking and consumer classes are now boys and one-fifth of the industrial arts and agriculture students are girls, boys still outnumber girls by about 9 to 1 in such technical subjects as electronics and auto repair. While more and more females are participating in school athletics, budgets are still tilted toward male sports. And despite the fact that more than half of the teachers taking school administration courses at some universities are women, 82 percent of elementary school principals, 93 percent of high school principals, and 98 percent of district superintendents are men. In the next chapter we will examine the controversy that erupted over the enforcement of Title IX during the 1980s.[67]

In some areas, however, females continue to make progress. Some of the most encouraging news is that girls are closing the gender gap in high school math and science courses. A few years ago it was unusual to find girls in upper-level classes; today it appears that girls are about equally represented in algebra, geometry, biology, and chemistry; and they are closing fast in trigonometry, calculus, and physics. The evidence on computer courses is less encouraging— some studies suggest that boys outnumber girls 2 to 1. Nor are all the gaps closed in higher education, where males continue to dominate the quantitative and scientific majors. In engineering, to cite the field with the greatest disparity, approximately 85 percent of the students are still men—but 99 percent were men in 1970.[68]

Cognitive Differences between Females and Males

Changing enrollment patterns are focusing new attention on the controversy over cognitive differences between females and males. For years psychologists and sociologists have debated whether girls as a group really have superior verbal skills and whether boys as a group are really better at mathematical and spatial tasks. As we summarize a complex body of research, the evidence suggests that:

1. Sex-related cognitive differences that standardized tests can measure generally do not appear until adolescence.
2. When differences do appear, they are small. Although females do slightly better on many tests of verbal ability and males slightly better on many tests of mathematical and spatial ability, differences *within* each sex are much greater than differences *between* the sexes. There are greater differences in math ability among boys, for example, than between boys as a group and girls as a group.
3. The proportion of the differences that seems to be due to biological as opposed to social factors is no more than 5 percent.[69]

Many researchers conclude that people make too much of the cognitive differences between males and females. Some students, parents, and even educators use sex as a convenient academic excuse: "Of course he doesn't like poetry—he's a boy." "I'm not very good at math and technical things—most girls aren't." The research literature simply does not support such sweeping statements. To be sure, there is disagreement over how much influence heredity has on sex-related cognitive differences. Some researchers point out that although girls are taking more math courses in high school, they are not closing the gap on standardized math tests. Even among students with similar backgrounds in math coursework, boys still have the edge on standardized tests. Genetics must be the explanation, these researchers conclude.[70]

Others counter that girls still experience subtle but powerful social pressure *not* to do well in math. Pointing to the divergence in boys' and girls' test scores during adolescence, they argue that girls who excel in math threaten boys on a traditionally masculine turf. Girls who want to be popular with the opposite sex had better not be too threatening. Peers, parents, teachers, counselors, textbooks, and other influences may also subtly—often unintentionally—discourage girls from being truly competitive with boys in math.[71]

Sex equity in education is not an issue that was resolved during the 1960s and 1970s. It remains alive and controversial. There are legitimate differences of opinion on how much progress the schools have made toward sex equity, just as people disagree over how well the schools have responded to the pressures exerted by social class, race, and ethnicity. The next chapter offers a look at the arena in which these differences of opinion meet head-on: the arena of politics. At the local, state, and federal levels, countless decisions, compromises, and tradeoffs not only chart the broad course of America's public schools but also steer them through their daily routine.

ACTIVITIES

1. Interview people who have been denied educational opportunities because of their social class, race, ethnicity, or sex.
2. Talk with public school officials about how their schools comply with Title VI of the Civil Rights Act of 1964, Title IX of the Education Amendments of 1972, and current federal guidelines on bilingual education.
3. Conduct your own research on bias in elementary and secondary textbooks. Locate examples of stereotypes based not only on sex but also on class, race, and ethnicity.
4. Stage a debate on some of the issues in this chapter. For additional evidence to support your arguments, see the suggested readings and notes.

SUGGESTED READINGS

One of the best textbooks on the sociology of education is *Society and Education* by Daniel U. Levine and Robert J. Havighurst, now in its seventh edition (see note 4, below). If you are interested in further reading and research, you may wish to begin with Levine and Havighurst. I have tried to make this chapter's documentation especially detailed; the notes below will lead you to more information and more analysis. Recent issues of the periodicals and government publications cited in the notes will help you keep abreast of the latest trends.

NOTES

1. Amy Stuart Wells, "Backers of School Change Turn to Sociologists," *New York Times* (January 4, 1989).
2. "Today's Numbers, Tomorrow's Nation," *Education Week* (May 14, 1986), pp. 14, 22; Patricia Albjerg Graham, "Black Teachers: A Drastically Scarce Resource," *Phi Delta Kappan* 68 (April 1987): 599; "In California, Nation's First Minority Majority," *Education Week* (September 21, 1988), p. 3.

3. "Percentage of Children Living with Both Parents, by Race and Hispanic Origin," *Education Week* (January 27, 1988), p. 2; Michael Harrington with Robert Greenstein and Eleanor Holmes Norton, *Who Are the Poor? A Profile of the Changing Faces of Poverty in the United States in 1987* (Washington: Justice for All, 1987).

4. Daniel U. Levine and Robert J. Havighurst, *Society and Education*, 7th ed. (Boston: Allyn & Bacon, 1989), pp. 6–16.

5. George S. Counts, *The Selective Character of American Secondary Education* (Chicago: University of Chicago Press 1922); Robert S. Lynd and Helen Merrell Lynd, *Middletown: A Study in American Culture* (New York: Harcourt, Brace & World, 1929), ch. 13.

6. W. Lloyd Warner, Robert J. Havighurst, and Martin B. Loeb, *Who Shall Be Educated: The Challenge of Unequal Opportunity* (New York: Harper & Row, 1944), p. 50.

7. Ibid., p. xi.

8. August B. Hollingshead, *Elmtown's Youth: The Impact of Social Classes on Adolescents* (New York: Wiley, 1949), pp. 168–192, 462.

9. Sarane S. Boocock, *Sociology of Education: An Introduction*, 2d ed. (Boston: Houghton Mifflin, 1980), ch. 3, and Jeanne H. Ballantine, *The Sociology of Education: A Systematic Analysis* (Englewood Cliffs, NJ: Prentice-Hall, 1983), ch. 3.

10. Sol Adler, *Poverty Children and Their Language: Implications for Teaching and Treating* (New York: Grune & Stratton, 1979); Catherine E. Snow, Clara Dubber, and Akke De Blauw, "Routines in Mother-Child Interaction," in Lynne Feagans and Dale Clark Farran, eds., *The Language of Children Reared in Poverty: Implications for Evaluation and Intervention* (New York: Academic Press, 1982).

11. Victor Gerkas, "The Influence of Social Class on Socialization," in Wesley R. Burr, Reuben Hill, F. Ivan Nye, and Ira L. Reiss, eds., *Contemporary Theories about the Family* (New York: Free Press, 1979).

12. Levine and Havighurst, *Society and Education*, chs. 5–6. The classic study of peer groups in the United States is James S. Coleman, *The Adolescent Society* (New York: Free Press, 1961). More recent studies include Philip A. Cusick, *Inside High School: The Student's World* (New York: Holt, Rinehart and Winston, 1971), and Christopher Johnson, "Subcultures in the High Schools," *Today's Education* 72 (April–May 1981): 30GS–32GS. Paul Willis, *Learning to Labour: How Working Class Kids Get Working Class Jobs* (Westmead, England: Saxon House, 1979), offers a British perspective.

13. James E. Rosenbaum, "Social Implications of Educational Grouping," in David C. Berliner, ed., *Review of Research in Education: 8* (Washington: American Educational Research Association, 1980), ch. 8; Penelope L. Peterson, Louise Cherry Wilkinson, and Maureen Hallinan, eds., *The Social Context of Instruction: Group Organization and Group Process* (Orlando, FL: Academic Press, 1984).

14. Jeannie Oakes, "Keeping Track, Part 1: The Policy and Practice of Curriculum Inequality," *Phi Delta Kappan* 68 (September 1986): 12–17, and "Keeping Track, Part 2: Curriculum Inequality and School Reform," *Phi Delta Kappan* 68 (October 1986): 148–154. In these articles Oakes extends the analysis in her book *Keeping Track: How Schools Structure Inequality* (New Haven: Yale University Press, 1985). See also Caroline J. Persell, *Education and Inequality: The Roots and Results of Social Stratification in America's Schools* (New York: The Free Press, 1977), p. 92.

15. Oakes, *Keeping Track;* Wells, "Backers of School Change Turn to Sociologists."

16. Arthur G. Powell, Eleanor Farrar, and David K. Cohen, *The Shopping Mall High School: Winners and Losers in the Educational Marketplace* (Boston: Houghton Mifflin, 1985); Rosenbaum, *Making Inequality: The Hidden Curriculum of High School Tracking* (New York: Wiley, 1976).
17. *ACT ISSUEgram* 6 (January 1986): 3–5.
18. Oakes, "Keeping Track, Part 1," pp. 16–17; Peterson, Wilkinson, and Hallinan, eds., *The Social Context of Instruction*, chs. 8–10.
19. See U.S. Department of Education, *Japanese Education Today* (Washington: U.S. Government Printing Office, 1987).
20. Among the recent studies analyzing these assumptions are Martin Carnoy and Henry M. Levin, *Schooling and Work in the Democratic State* (Stanford: Stanford University Press, 1985); Michael W. Sedlak, Christopher W. Wheeler, Diana C. Pullin, and Philip A. Cusick, *Selling Students Short: Classroom Bargains and Academic Reform in the American High School* (New York Teachers College Press, 1986); Ann Bastian, Norm Fruchter, Marilyn Gittell, Colin Greer, and Kenneth Haskins, *Choosing Equality: The Case for Democratic Schooling* (Philadelphia: Temple University Press, 1986).
21. Two comprehensive surveys of race and ethnicity are Stephan Thernstrom, ed., *Harvard Encyclopedia of American Ethnic Groups* (Cambridge: Harvard University Press, 1980), and Richard T. Shaefer, *Racial and Ethnic Groups*, 2d ed. (Boston: Little, Brown, 1984).
22. This definition is from Milton M. Gordon's classic study *Assimilation in American Life: The Role of Race, Religion, and National Origins* (New York: Oxford University Press, 1964).
23. James A. Banks, *Teaching Strategies for Ethnic Studies*, 3d ed. (Boston: Allyn & Bacon, 1983); Donna M. Gollnick and Philip C. Chinn, *Multicultural Education in a Pluralistic Society*, 2d ed. (Columbus, OH: Merrill, 1986). Banks served as guest editor of the April 1983 issue of *Phi Delta Kappan*, which featured eight articles on the past, present, and future of multiethnic education. According to the 1980 census, 26.34 percent of Americans say that all or some of their ancestors came from England, while 26.14 percent claim German ancestry.
24. Joel Spring, *American Education: An Introduction to Social and Political Aspects*, 4th ed. (White Plains, NY: Longman, 1989), pp. 150–153; U.S. Department of Education, Center for Education Statistics, *The Condition of Education, 1987 Edition* (Washington: U.S. Government Printing Office, 1987), p. 64; Levine and Havighurst, *Society and Education*, pp. 413–416.
25. U.S. Bureau of the Census, *Statistical Abstract of the United States: 1987, 107th Edition* (Washington: U.S. Government Printing Office, 1986), p. 442.
26. Ibid., pp. 35–36.
27. Census Bureau figures reported in "Hispanic Population Grows," *Mobile Press*, September 7, 1988.
28. Richard Kluger, *Simple Justice: The History of Brown v. Board of Education and Black America's Struggle for Equality* (New York: Knopf, 1976).
29. The complete text of the *Brown* decision is reprinted in Kluger, *Simple Justice*, pp. 779–785.
30. Kluger, *Simple Justice*, chs. 26–27; Laughlin McDonald, "The Legal Barriers Crumble," *Just Schools*, a special issue of *Southern Exposure* 7 (Summer 1979).
31. Gary Orfield, *The Reconstruction of Southern Education: The Schools and the 1964 Civil Rights Act* (New York: Wiley, 1969).

32. Gary Orfield, *Public School Desegregation in the United States, 1968–1980* (Washington: Joint Center for Political Studies, 1983), pp. 3–12; Gary Orfield and Franklin Monfort, *Are American Schools Resegregating in the Reagan Era?* working paper no. 14 (Chicago: National School Desegregation Project, University of Chicago, 1987), pp. 313–314, 392.

33. "Public Housing Policy Linked to School Segregation," *NOLPE Notes* 23 (August 1988): 1. Gary Orfield analyzes the relationship between housing segregation and school segregation in *Toward a Strategy for Urban Integration: Lessons in School and Housing Policy from Twelve Cities* (New York: Ford Foundation, 1981).

34. William Snider, "Courts Back Moves To End Busing Plans," *Education Week* (January 13, 1988), pp. 1, 23.

35. Orfield, *Public School Desegregation*, ch. 2.

36. Ibid. For a discussion of these demographic trends, see Kathryn M. Borman and Joel H. Spring, *Schools in Central Cities: Structure and Process* (White Plains, NY: Longman, 1984), ch. 1.

37. Using the criteria set forth in *Milliken*, in 1975 the courts did order metropolitan school desegregation in Wilmington, Delaware, and Louisville, Kentucky.

38. Rita E. Mahard and Robert L. Crain, "Research on Minority Achievement in Desegregated Schools," in Christine H. Rossell and Willis D. Hawley, eds., *The Consequences of School Desegregation* (Philadelphia: Temple University Press, 1983), pp. 103–125.

39. Ibid., p. 111.

40. See the discussion in Levine and Havighurst, *Society and Education*, ch. 9.

41. David J. Armor is one of the best-known critics of desegregation as a means of raising minority academic achievement. See *The Evidence on Desegregation and Black Achievement*, paper prepared for the National Institute of Education Panel on the Effects of School Desegregation (Washington: NIE, 1983). Harold B. Gerard and Norman Miller are also critical in *School Desegregation* (New York: Plenum, 1975), as is Ronald A. Krol in "A Meta Analysis of the Effects of Desegregation on Academic Achievement," *The Urban Review* 12 (December 1980): 211–224.

42. Jomills Henry Braddock II, Robert L. Crain, and James M. McPartland, "A Long-Term View of School Desegregation: Some Recent Studies of Graduates as Adults," *Phi Delta Kappan* 66 (December 1984): 259–264.

43. William Snider, "Opposition to Busing Declines, Poll Finds," *Education Week* (January 21, 1987), p. 6.

44. For arguments that busing is responsible for substantial white flight, see James S. Coleman, "Liberty and Equality in School Desegregation," *Social Policy* 6 (January–February 1976): 9–13, and David J. Armor, "White Flight and the Future of School Desegregation," in Walter G. Stephan and Joe R. Feagin, eds., *School Desegregation: Past, Present, and Future* (New York: Plenum, 1980), ch. 9. For counter arguments see Thomas F. Pettigrew and Robert L. Green, "School Desegregation in Large Cities: A Critique of the Coleman 'White Flight' Thesis," *Harvard Educational Review* 46 (February 1976): 1–53, and Rossell and Hawley, "Understanding White Flight and Doing Something about It," in Hawley, ed., *Effective School Desegregation* (Beverly Hills, CA: Sage, 1981), 157–184.

45. The statistics on percentages of students bused and the length of their rides have changed little since the publication of *Fulfilling the Letter and the Spirit of the Law* by the U.S. Commission on Civil Rights (Washington: U.S. Government Printing Office, 1976). Gary Orfield discusses the stability of metropolitan busing in "Public

School Desegregation" and in *Must We Bus? Segregated Schools and National Policy* (Washington: Brookings Institution, 1978).

46. Mary Haywood Metz, *Different by Design: The Context and Character of Three Magnet Schools* (New York: Methuen/Routledge and Kegan Paul, 1986); James Lowry Associates, *Survey of Magnet Schools* (Washington: National Institute of Education, 1984); Ronald G. McIntire, Larry W. Hughes, and Michael W. Say, "Houston's Successful Desegregation Plan," *Phi Delta Kappan* 63 (April 1982): 536–538; Borman and Spring, *Schools in Central Cities*, pp. 160–172.

47. U.S. Department of Education, National Center for Education Statistics, *The Condition of Education: Elementary and Secondary Education, 1988*, vol. 1 (Washington: U.S. Government Printing Office, 1988), p. 90, and *The Condition of Education: 1986 Edition* (Washington: U.S. Government Printing Office, 1986), pp. 30–31, 42–43, 118–119.

48. Historical and demographic information in this and the following paragraphs is from the Ford Foundation working paper *Hispanics: Challenges and Opportunities* (New York: Ford Foundation, 1984), pp. 5–16.

49. Mahard and Crain, *Research on Minority Achievement*, pp. 111, 113; Orfield, *Public School Desegregation*, pp. 12–20; Orfield and Monfort, *Are American Schools Resegregating?*; Snider, "Opposition to Busing Declines," p. 6.

50. "Hispanics Nurture Identity, Survey Shows," *Education Week* (September 19, 1984).

51. "In California, Nation's First Minority Majority," *Education Week* (September 21, 1988), p. 3; Susan M. Knight, " 'English Only' Push Opposed in Arizona," *Education Week* (October 21, 1987), p. 13; Chris Pipho, "Elections and Efficiency," *Phi Delta Kappan* 70 (Janaury 1989): 350.

52. Francesco Cordasco, "Bilingual Education: Overview and Inventory," *Educational Forum* 47 (Spring 1983): 320–334. Cordasco's multivolume *Bilingual-Bicultural Education in the United States* (New York: Arno Press, 1978) is a standard reference in this field.

53. *Hispanics: Challenges and Opportunities*, pp. 34–37, describes these models, as does Henry T. Trueba, *Bilingual Education: Models, Types, and Designs* (Rowley, MA: Newbury House, 1979).

54. James Crawford, "Immersion Method Is Faring Poorly in Bilingual Study," *Education Week* (April 23, 1986), pp. 1, 10. For reviews of other studies see Iris C. Rotberg, "Some Legal and Research Considerations in Establishing Federal Policy in Bilingual Education," *Harvard Educational Review* 52 (May 1982): 149–168, and Rudolph C. Troike, "Synthesis of Research on Bilingual Education," *Educational Leadership* 38 (March 1981): 498–504.

55. Charles R. Foster, "Defusing the Issues in Bilingualism and Bilingual Education," *Phi Delta Kappan* 63 (January 1982): 342–344.

56. U.S. Department of Education, *The Condition of Education: Elementary and Secondary Education, 1988*, vol. 1, p. 90, and *The Condition of Education: 1986 Edition*, pp. 30–31, 42–43, 118–119.

57. Carol Tavris with Alice R. Baumgartner, "How Would Your Life Be Different," *Redbook* (February 1983), pp. 92–95.

58. Levine and Havighurst, *Society and Education*, pp. 448–449. An excellent film that makes these points is *The Pinks and the Blues* (Paramus, NJ: Time-Life Video, n.d.)

59. Ballantine, *The Sociology of Education*, pp. 77–79, 81. See also Jean Stockard and M.M. Johnson, *Sex Roles: Sex Inequality and Sex Role Development* (Englewood

Cliffs, NJ: Prentice-Hall, 1980), and Constantina Safilos-Rothschild, *Sex Role Socialization and Sex Discrimination* (Washington: National Institute of Education, 1979).

60. Women on Words and Images, *Dick and Jane as Victims: Sex Stereotyping in Children's Readers* (Princeton, NJ: Women on Words and Images, 1975); U.S. Commission on Civil Rights, *Characters in Textbooks: A Review of the Literature* (Washington: Commission on Civil Rights, 1980).

61. Gwyneth Britton and Margaret Lumpkin, "Basal Readers: Paltry Progress Pervades," *Interracial Books for Children Bulletin* 14 (1983): 4–7; Donna M. Gollnick, Myra Sadker, and David Sadker, "Beyond the Dick and Jane Syndrome: Confronting Sex Bias in Instructional Materials," in Sadker and Sadker, eds., *Sex Equity Handbook for Schools* (White Plains, NY: Longman, 1982), ch. 3.

62. Levine and Havighurst, *Society and Education*, pp. 438–439; U.S. Department of Labor, *Time of Change: 1983 Handbook on Women Workers* (Washington: U.S. Government Printing Office, 1983), p. 55, 82.

63. Tavris and Baumgartner, "How Would Your Life Be Different?" pp. 94–95; Raphaela Best, *We've All Got Scars: What Boys and Girls Learn in Elementary Schools* (Bloomington: Indiana University Press, 1983); National Education Association, *Status of the American Public School Teacher, 1985–86* (Washington: NEA, 1987), p. 77.

64. Sadker and Sadker, "Sexism in the Schoolroom of the 1980s," *Psychology Today* (March 1985): 54–57.

65. Ibid.; Marlaine E. Lockheed with Susan S. Klein, "Sex Equity in Classroom Climate and Organization," in Klein, ed., *Handbook for Achieving Sex Equity through Education* (Baltimore: Johns Hopkins University Press, 1985), ch. 11.

66. Jeana Wirtenberg, Barbara Richardson, Susan Klein, and Veronica Thomas, "Sex Equity in American Education," *Educational Leadership* 38 (January 1981): 311–319.

67. Ibid.; Levine and Havighurst, *Society and Education*, pp. 448–451; Helen S. Farmer and Joan Seliger Sidney, "Sex Equity in Career and Vocational Education"; and Carolyn Shakeshaft, "Strategies for Overcoming the Barriers to Women in Educational Administration," in *Handbook for Achieving Sex Equity*, chs. 18, 8.

68. Sharon F. Rallis and Sharon A. Ahern, "Math and Science Education in High Schools: A Question of Sex Equity?" paper presented to the American Educational Research Association, San Francisco, April 1986; Patricia B. Campbell, "The Computer Revolution: Guess Who's Left Out?," *Interracial Books for Children Bulletin* 15 (1984): 3–6; Elizabeth K. Stage, Nancy Kreinberg, Jacquelynne Eccles (Parsons), and Joanne Rossi Becker, "Increasing the Participation and Achievement of Girls and Women in Mathematics, Science, and Engineering," in *Handbook for Achieving Sex Equity*, ch. 13.

69. One of the best analyses of these complex issues is Julia A. Sherman's "Sex-Related Cognitive Differences: A Summary of Theory and Practice," *Integrateducation* 16 (January–February 1978): 40–42. See also Levine and Havighurst, *Society and Education*, pp. 443–448.

70. Camilla P. Benbow and Julian C. Stanley, "Differential Course-taking Hypothesis Revisited," *American Educational Research Journal* 20 (Winter 1983): 469–473.

71. Karl L. Alexander and Aaron M. Pallas, "Reply to Benbow and Stanley," *American Educational Research Journal* 20 (Winter 1983): 475–477.

CHAPTER 9

Politics of Education

If politics is the pursuit of power and influence, then the politics of education is the quest to control the schools. Sometimes the quest generates so much controversy that the media play up a particular episode, and Americans who ordinarily take little interest in the schools stop and pay attention. When teachers go on strike or federal judges issue desegregation orders, average citizens follow the news and take sides. "Those teachers (or those judges) have gone too far this time," one citizen complains. "What do they want—to run the schools?" "No, they don't want complete control," another replies, "but they are willing to use the power at their disposal. Look at what the school board did to provoke the strike (or court order). Somebody had to call the board's hand."

Controversies can make the front page of the newspaper, but usually the quest for control of the schools goes on barely noticed by most Americans. The quest becomes part of the political routine. A local school board listens to a parent's concerns about standardized testing. A state legislature debates the education budget. The U.S. Senate's Education Committee holds hearings on the effectiveness of the Chapter I compensatory education program. The results of these deliberations may be even more far reaching than the effects of a strike or a court order, yet few citizens—including few teachers—pay close attention. This chapter shows what they are missing.

I will organize our discussion of politics around the three levels of government in the United States: *local, state*, and *federal*. At each level numerous groups compete for control. Major players in the politics of education include elected and appointed officials, ranging from school board members to legislators to judges; educational bureaucrats who work in local school systems, state departments of education, and the U.S. Department of Education; teachers and teacher organizations; other education groups, from university teacher educators to parent-teacher organizations; business groups; labor unions; foundations; testing companies; textbook publishers; religious groups; and individual citizens.

This list is long but incomplete. The reason is that so many hands work the controls of American public education. No single level of government and no single group of people are completely in charge. Instead, power is shared, and the balance of power among the levels and the groups is constantly shifting. In order to untangle a fascinating web of political influences, we will begin at the local level, move to the state and then the federal levels, and conclude the chapter with a discussion of educational finance.

LOCAL POLITICS OF EDUCATION

Most Americans want to run their schools from the grassroots up. The word "their" is significant. According to former President Ronald Reagan, a strong advocate of local control, citizens feel a pride of ownership in public education if they can speak out and be heard at the local level. After all, Mr. Reagan often said, local people know more about their schools than the politicians and bureaucrats in Washington and the state capital. He liked to remind the nation that the U.S. Constitution does not even mention education; it is a responsibility reserved to the states. He often added, however, that citizens can exercise the most direct control over education at the local level. A talk with a teacher, administrator, or school board member may be enough to get the job done. If not, local control makes it easier for citizens to clean house and make fundamental changes in the schools. By articulating these views so well, President Reagan touched feelings deep in the American psyche: pride in local involvement and distrust of centralized control.[1]

As we saw in Chapter 6, however, local control of public education has been slipping away since the last century. The effect of Mr. Reagan's education policies was to shift control downward from the federal level, which is what he intended, but in most cases only as far down as the state level. Had Horace Mann been able to hear Reagan's case for local control, he would have recognized the arguments, but Mann the state centralizer would have been pleased that the states, not the local school systems, picked up most of the control that the federal government gave away during the Reagan administration.[2]

Local Boards and Local Superintendents

Nevertheless, the American love affair with locally controlled schools continues. Opinion polls show that nearly two-thirds of Americans want their local governments to become more involved with education. In some of the nation's 15,000 local school systems, the voters do seem to be paying more attention to school board elections. Why, the candidates in some communities even run on the issues. I say this with tongue in cheek because local school board elections have traditionally been low-interest, no-issue events. Unless a controversy happened to be raging, candidates have often not even bothered to campaign. Given the public preference for local control, it is paradoxical that candidates in about half of all school board elections *still* do not take stands or campaign. In other communities, by contrast, the elections are issue oriented and hotly contested. Drive through a community just before a school board election and look for the candidates' signs. Read the local newspapers and see whether the candidates are addressing any issues.[3]

School board elections vary because communities vary. The power structure of a community has a strong influence on the way it selects people to oversee the public schools. Political researchers have developed a number of models to classify community power structures. Most of the models place communities on a continuum—from *monolithic* to *pluralistic*, for example—based on how widely political power is shared. Does a single group of community elites dominate local politics, or do several groups, elite as well as nonelite, compete for control?[4]

Monolithic communities in which one group calls the shots are often rural areas, small towns, or one-industry cities. In these communities, the group in control may appoint the school board; if the members are elected, incumbents usually run without opposition. At the other end of the continuum, *pluralistic communities* have competitive, sometimes bitter school board elections. In such communities, typically suburbs and diversified cities, the candidates stake out positions on key issues. Although they may state their positions as simply as "against new taxes" or "for traditional values," the candidates speak a language that the voters seem to understand.

Once elected to a local school board, the members are responsible for establishing policies for the school system. Local boards make policy within the limits set by the state legislature and state board of education. The state prescribes the minimum course of study required for high school graduation, for example, but the local board approves the courses that satisfy the requirements. The state sets the requirements for teacher certification, but the local board approves the hiring of teachers. The state sends down state and federal money, but the local board approves the local budget.

The concept of *policy approval* is important. Local board members tend to rely on the advice of the superintendent of schools, whom they appoint as the school system's chief administrator. The superintendent, along with other administrators in the central office and in the schools, is responsible for managing the system on a day-to-day basis. The superintendent recommends policies for the board's approval.[5]

Since the early 1900s, as I pointed out in Chapter 6, superintendents and their staffs have done far more than just manage and recommend. In effect, they have run the show. Superintendents enjoyed the peak of their influence from the 1920s through the 1950s. Board members held the votes, to be sure, but more often than not they rubber-stamped the superintendent's recommendations. Superintendents presented themselves as educational experts, the *real* professionals in the school system. Their graduate degrees in school administration and experience in the schools set them apart from everyone else—board members, teachers, parents, other citizens—or so they were able to claim.[6]

During the heyday of superintendents and their staffs, school board meetings were typically open-and-shut affairs. The superintendent set the agenda, coached the board through the meeting, and answered questions. At the end, the superintendent thanked the board for approving every recommendation intact. Local school board meetings were usually dull, respectable, and poorly attended.

There have always been exceptions to this idealized portrait, of course, and in some school systems the exceptions have become the rule since the 1960s. The AFT has long advocated teacher power, and superintendents and school boards have had to handle the larger AFT locals with care. The NEA, once little more than a punch-and-cookies society at the local level, has now become a formidable union with impressive strength at the grassroots level. Teacher power is a reality, a fact of political life. Another exception that has become a rule in some school systems is parent power. There have always been a few parents who refused to take "no" for an answer, parents who were determined to challenge a textbook, test, or discipline policy. Since the 1960s such parents have become more numerous and more insistent, or so it seems to teachers, administrators, and board members. These parents act as if the schools belong to *them*.[7]

Assertive school board members have also become the rule in some local systems. Superintendents and their staffs have lost a great deal of control, with board members chipping away at their power from above and teachers from below. In fact, board members occasionally align themselves with teacher organizations against school administrators, joining teachers in attacking the central office crowd.[8]

More often, though, assertive members come to the board with their own agenda. Fed up with high taxes and wasteful spending, they may try to bring sound business principles to the school system. They may poke into detailed financial records that other board members never knew existed; they may cross the line into management and invade the superintendent's turf. Assertive board members may try to reform the curriculum, in which case they will almost certainly lock horns with parents, teachers, administrators, and state officials. Or assertive members may be the only representatives of their race or ethnic group on the board, which may lead them to challenge such policies as minimum competency testing and ability grouping. Assertive local board members often grow frustrated when they find that other players in the politics of education, whether in the same community, the state capital, or Washington, can make it so difficult to change the schools.[9]

Local Board Members:
Demographics and Representation

What kind of people serve on local school boards? Since Americans cling so strongly to their belief in local control, it seems reasonable to find out more about the board members who represent the people. In the nation as a whole, the average board member is a white male, aged 41 to 50, college educated, with an annual income of $40,000 to $49,000. He is most likely to be a professional, manager, or business owner, in that order. Of course, people with other demographic characteristics also serve on local school boards. Almost 40 percent of local school board members are women—a dramatic increase over 1978, when only 26 percent were women. Minorities, however, hold fewer than 6 percent of the seats on local school boards. In 1987, 3.6 percent of the members were black and 1.5 percent were Hispanic. Minority representation has in fact declined slightly since the early 1980s.[10]

Discussing this profile, the students in my introduction to education classes often say that local school board members "look just like average politicians." Local school board members *are* politicians. Under the broad definition of politics as the pursuit of power and influence, local board members are directly involved in the quest for control of the schools—but so are numerous other people, including teachers and parents, whom we usually do not think of as politicians. Perhaps we should, because some of them are as involved as board members in the quest for control. What my students have in mind, however, is the more traditional view of a politician as an office seeker or office holder. Ninety-two percent of local school board members are elected to office, and almost all of them run in nonpartisan contests in which they do not declare their affiliation with a political party. The remaining 8 percent are appointed by a mayor, city council, county commission, or another governmental body.[11]

How well local school board members represent their constituents is a controversial issue. Demographically, they do not reflect the American population. Females, who make up 52 percent of the population, are still underrepresented on local school boards. Blacks and Hispanics, who together are about 20 percent of all Americans and 25 percent of all public school students, are *seriously* underrepresented. And unlike most local school board members, most Americans are not college educated, nor are most Americans professionals, managers, or business owners. The elite makeup of local school boards has been a sensitive issue since the rise of common schools, with underrepresented groups complaining that board members neglect their children's educational needs. Blacks and Hispanics, other racial and ethnic groups, the poor—their complaints are well documented if not well heeded.[12]

"Do you have to be one to represent one?" This blunt, provocative question, recently directed to the local school board in my community, goes to the heart of the matter. From one point of view, the answer to the question is a definite yes. If a group has been the victim of long-standing discrimination, members of that group have developed insights into critical issues that other people, however sympathetic and well intended, simply lack. Black Americans understand segregation, for example, as white Americans never can. The very idea of an all-white school board drawing up a desegregation plan for a school system that is one-half black! In a school system with a substantial percentage of black students, black representation on the school board is not just desirable. From this point of view, it is essential. The same reasoning is often applied to Hispanic representation, and less frequently to the representation of women, the poor, and other groups.

From another point of view, this kind of reasoning is dangerous. It smacks of quotas. If the courts can order changes in election procedures that virtually insure the election of blacks to local school boards—as indeed the courts have—what will be next? A decision that, depending on a school system's demographic makeup, a certain percentage of board members must be women, or working class people, or people with no more than a high school education? Granted that school board members and their constituents often come from different backgrounds, the representatives can make an extra effort to stand in other people's shoes. There is no single black, Hispanic, female, or working-class perspective; there are many. Besides, two-thirds of local board members say they regard themselves as trustees who can act as their own judgment dictates rather than delegates who are obligated to do what their constituents want. Thus the idea of demographic representation seems wrongheaded to some Americans.[13]

Local School Board Elections: At Large or by Districts?

Although it is doubtful that court decisions will ever go as far as the paragraph above suggests, legal challenges to election procedures may well increase the percentage of blacks and Hispanics on local school boards. We saw in Chapter 6 that many communities elect their school board members *at large*: every voter can cast a ballot for every position on the board. Candidates campaign throughout the school system, for they are supposed to represent the whole community rather than particular neighborhoods or districts. Many school systems that once elected school board members from districts switched to at-large elections in the early 1900s. Turn-of-the century reformers argued that people with the reputation and resources necessary to mount a system-wide campaign had broader vision than people elected to represent individual districts. Reformers referred to the board members that at-large elections produced, successful professionals and business people by and large, as persons of "the better sort."[14]

At-large elections not only introduce a social class bias into school board politics; in systems where whites compete with blacks and/or Hispanics for control of the schools, they also introduce a racial and ethnic bias. I am not exaggerating when I describe the elections as competitions for control. In most at-large elections, the voters polarize by race and ethnicity, with whites voting for whites, blacks for blacks, and Hispanics for Hispanics. Apparently many Americans believe you *do* have to be one to represent one. Except in communities where blacks or Hispanics are in the majority, at-large elections virtually insure that whites sweep every seat on the local school board.[15]

The balance of political power is shifting, however, and the changes now underway are a fascinating case study in the politics of education. In *Bolden v. City of Mobile* (1980), a voting-rights case that originated in my Alabama community, the U.S. Supreme Court ruled against a group of black voters who were challenging Mobile's at-large elections. According to the court, the plaintiffs failed to prove that the city had adopted and maintained at-large elections with a discriminatory *intent*. Two years later, in an amendment to the Voting Rights Act of 1965, Congress overrode the decision by stipulating that plaintiffs need only show the discriminatory *effect* of election procedures.[16]

Encouraged by this change, black and Hispanic voters have filed a series of lawsuits against at-large elections. Beginning in the Southeast, spreading to the Southwest, and now reaching the rest of the nation, the legal challenges may reverse the decline in minority representation on school boards. In Mobile, the change from at-large to by-district procedures led to the election of two blacks to a five-person board, mirroring almost exactly the racial composition of the community. With the end of at-large elections in several Illinois cities, blacks are serving on local school boards for the first time in the twentieth century. Hispanics have won similar court battles in the Southwest, and the potential for further change is great. In Texas, where Hispanics are aggressively filing election suits, about 80 percent of the local school systems still elect their board members at-large. Native Americans, the nation's oldest and poorest ethnic group, have recently won a decision ending at-large elections in Big Horn County, Montana.[17]

Even though the courts have allowed the scope of at-large election suits to broaden, from discrimination against blacks to discrimination against Hispanics and now Native Americans, the courts have acted cautiously. In every case the burden has been on the racial or ethnic group to prove that at-large elections have kept members of the group out of office. The courts have not allowed the scope to broaden to social class—to discrimination against poor people as a group—even though the evidence is clear that school systems switched to at-large elections in order to insure the dominance of high-status board members. Could poor people argue that at-large elections continue to deny them seats on school boards? An intriguing question, certainly, but the courts have consistently refused to consider social class as a factor comparable to race and ethnicity in discrimination suits.

The most striking demographic trend on local school boards is toward more female members. The percentage of minorities may start to rise again in the 1990s, but given the current level it has quite a distance to climb. The trend is certainly not toward poorer board members. About 40 percent of public school families have incomes below $20,000, as compared with 5 percent of local school board members. Although the demographics of local school boards have changed in recent years, the conclusion that George S. Counts reached in his pioneering study *The Social Composition of Boards of Education: A Study in the Social Control of Public Education* (1927) still rings true:

> The [typical] board shows a tendency to be narrowly selective. It is com-
> posed, for the most part, of college and university men who occupy favored
> positions in society. The dominant classes of our society dominate the board
> of education.[18]

STATE POLITICS OF EDUCATION

A varied cast of characters takes the stage as our discussion turns to the state level. Although I will put the spotlight on elected and appointed officials— governors, legislators, state school superintendents, and state school board members—you should be aware that many other actors have important roles. Lobbyists for groups ranging from teacher organizations to the chamber of commerce compete for control of the schools. Insiders know that restaurants in the state capital are where the real political business takes place. Lobbyists invite legislators to dinner, remind them of campaign contributions, and ask them to take particular stands on key educational issues. The governor and his staff receive the same treatment, and so, to a lesser degree, do the state superintendent of schools, top officials in the state department of education, and members of the state board of education.

Meetings of the state board, once sleepy affairs, have become lively and controversial. Parents, teachers, and other citizens ask for time on the agenda to state their views on issues ranging from secular humanism in textbooks to certification tests for teachers. The courts also play a role in the politics of education, for various actors ask them to referee disputes with other actors. These examples suggest the large number of players and the wide range of issues involved in the state politics of education.[19]

Legislatures, Governors, Superintendents, Boards, and Departments

The ultimate responsibility for public education in each state rests with the state legislature. Much of the responsibility is financial, for the legislature has the authority to levy taxes and appropriate money to the schools. In many states, the state government is the major source of funding for the public schools. While the legislature is in session, much attention naturally focuses on the education budget, which is often one-third to one-half of all the money the state government spends. Legislators who serve on the education committee, the finance committee, and other committees with direct influence on the schools play leading roles in the state politics of education.

During the 1980s, state legislatures stepped up their involvement in educational policy making. Pressing well beyond financial matters, legislators tackled issues ranging from high school graduation requirements to teacher education standards. Along with governors, they reasserted their control over the schools. Later in this section we will focus on the emergence of governors and legislators as school reformers.

State legislatures cannot run the schools alone, however, and historically they have delegated some of their authority to other groups. In every state but Wisconsin, the legislature has created a state board of education to oversee the state school system. Within the limits established by the legislature, state school boards carry out three major responsibilities: setting standards for elementary and secondary schools; setting standards for teacher education and certification; and distributing state and federal funds to local school systems. Although these duties may look dry on paper, they are anything but. Just ask board members who have voted on a "No Pass, No Play" policy for high school athletes how strongly people feel about that issue, or ask them how many people tried to sway their votes on teacher certification testing.

Demographically, state board members are an exaggerated version of local board members. To an even greater degree than their local counterparts, state board members are white, male, college educated, middle aged, and professional or managerial. In about two-thirds of the states, the governor appoints the members of the state board of education; in two states, the board members serve *ex officio*—by virtue of their holding another state office. In the rest of the states, voters elect the board. The issues of representation that we analyzed at the local level also apply to the state level, and minority voters are now challenging at-large elections to state boards of education.[20]

State board members turn over the management and operation of the state school system to a superintendent and an administrative staff. The state superintendent is typically an up-from-the-ranks educator with experience as a teacher, an administrator, and often a local superintendent. Many state superintendents still come up through the "good old boy" education network. About 90 percent of them are white males—middle-aged fellows who have learned how to get along. In about half the states, the state board appoints the state superintendent. In five states, the state superintendent serves ex officio, and in the rest, voters elect the state superintendent.[21]

Historically, state superintendents have played *the* leading roles in the state-level politics of education. Horace Mann's official title in Massachusetts was Secretary of the State Board of Education, but in fact he was America's first activist state superintendent. Following in Mann's footsteps, state superintendents have tended to overshadow state board members. Billing themselves, like local superintendents, as educational experts, they have used their influence to shape policy. With the emergence of reform-minded governors and legislators during the 1980s, however, state superintendents have lost some of their power.

If the state board's chief administrator is the state superintendent, the board's administrative staff is the state department of education. Ranging from secretaries and clerks to experienced educators with doctoral degrees, state department personnel are the bureaucrats who conduct the daily business of the state school system. State departments have grown in size and importance— some of the larger ones employ more than 1,000 people. State department employees do such things as conduct research, issue teaching certificates, draw up curriculum guides, supervise testing programs, and make accreditation studies of local schools. During the 1980s, the responsibilities of state departments for curriculum and testing increased tremendously.[22]

Excellence in Education: The States Discover School Reform

With the release of *A Nation at Risk* (1983) and the flood of education reports that followed, the states found a political issue they could run with. Who could be opposed to a slogan as positive as "excellence in education"? Governors, legislators, state school superintendents, and state board of education members scrambled to be first in line to make the schools excellent. In other chapters we have discussed some of the results of state reform. Teacher salaries have increased, most dramatically in states that have lagged behind the national average. Standards in teacher education and certification have risen in almost every state. Higher standards for students, which we will examine closely in the next chapter, have also resulted from state reform. Understandably, higher salaries and higher standards have required higher levels of state spending.[23]

Excellence, as defined by state reformers, has come to mean *more* of something: higher salaries, higher standards, higher spending. In one sense this approach is exactly what the times call for. Consider the example of higher teacher salaries, which are long overdue. If salaries have increased in the school system where you plan to teach, you should probably thank the state government first. In the states that boast the most impressive gains in teacher salaries, governors and state legislators can rightfully take the lion's share of the credit. (And they have.) But before you write a letter or make a phone call to the state capital, realize that higher salaries are a two-edged sword.

Responding to pressure from business leaders, governors and legislators are insisting that teachers prove themselves worthy of better pay. The titles of two recent reports from the Committee for Economic Development (CED) accurately describe the orientation of business leaders: *Investing in Our Children: Business and the Public Schools* (1985) and *Children in Need: Investment Strategies for the Educationally Disadvantaged* (1987). The CED sees education as an investment, and a sound investment pays dividends. Believing that better schools are the key to economic growth, such groups as the CED and the Carnegie Forum on Education and the Economy are pressing for accountability. They want the states to show the payoff from education dollars—that higher teacher salaries, for instance, produce higher student achievement.[24]

Teachers, as we have seen, have legitimate concerns about accountability. They are wary of merit pay plans that base teacher salaries on student test scores. Teachers are also doubtful that career ladders will help their occupation as much as they help state politicians. Tennessee teachers joke that their state's ladder has done more for former Governor Lamar Alexander's career than it will for any teacher's. When teachers express such reservations publicly, as they often do through state affiliates of the NEA, the same governors and legislators who raise salaries accuse teachers of being irresponsible and ungrateful. This political pattern, played out frequently during the 1980s, seems likely to continue into the 1990s.

The state drive to set higher standards for teachers and students is also a mixed blessing. On the one hand, higher standards—like higher salaries—are long overdue. As a teacher educator, I am embarrassed that the states have had to force colleges and universities to turn out teachers who are at least literate. But I confess that my colleagues and I did little to raise standards before the states stepped in. As a former high school teacher, I resent the state-mandated, measurement-driven curriculum. But I remember too many students sliding through school, bored and unchallenged, taking the easiest courses in an easy curriculum. In short I acknowledge the problems. Most Americans do. Now we need to take a critical look at the state reforms intended to solve the problems.

In the era just before *A Nation at Risk,* the major state response to educational problems was jumping on the back-to-basics bandwagon that was already rolling through local school sytems. Minimum competency tests for students were the most visible result of this first wave of state reform—by 1979, 37 states had mandated them. Some states also raised grade point averages and college entrance exam scores required for admission to teacher education programs. Although the states often copied one another, especially in adopting minimum competency tests, there was little coordination of state efforts.[25]

Within the states, much of the leadership came from state boards and departments of education. State board of education members, traditionally among the least important state politicians, were finally beginning to stretch their muscles, as if waking up from a long nap. State departments of education, led by state superintendents, were putting new board policies into effect. In most states, however, educational reform had still not attracted the sustained attention of governors and state legislators.

The release of *A Nation at Risk* in 1983, followed by report after report on the schools, changed the situation. Suddenly almost every state politician wanted to be a school reformer. The result was a second wave of reform, a wave that moved across the states in a surprisingly uniform way. Almost every state raised high school graduation requirements, expanded minimum competency testing into an array of "student performance indicators," and developed new tests for teacher education and certification.

Governors provided much of the leadership for these second-wave reforms. Since 1983, the mark of a politically astute governor has been a task force on education and a series of reports with excellence as their theme. Such "education governors" as Lamar Alexander of Tennessee, Thomas Kean of New Jersey, Rudy Perpich of Minnesota, Richard Lamm of Colorado, and Bill Clinton of Arkansas have gone even further, making school reform the central theme of their administrations. Alexander, Clinton, and other southern governors have been especially visible leaders, obviously relishing the national exposure that school reform has given them.[26]

Now state school reformers are coordinating their efforts. Governors exchange ideas in meetings of the National Governors' Association and the Education Commission of the States. The National Association of State Boards of Education provides a similar forum for state board members, and state school superintendents work together through the Council of Chief State School Officers. State legislators have their own caucuses on education. Across the nation, the result of all this activity has been an emphasis on higher standards—of a sort.[27]

The Politics of More of the Same

Operating at a distance from the local schools—above the action, we might say—state reformers have a peculiar perspective on public education. They have a wealth of information at their disposal, and staff members can generate more at a moment's notice. In meeting after meeting, state officials pour over seemingly endless statistics: population, per capita income, school expenditures, dropout rates, test scores. These quantitative data give the officials a quantitative view of schools; they think in terms of measurable inputs and measurable outputs. Thus the higher standards that the states mandate are almost always quantitative rather than qualitative. They call for *more of the same* rather than something different. If one math course is good for high school students, then two courses are better, and three or four courses are best. If a literacy test for prospective teachers is good, then a literacy test and a teaching field test are better, and . . . State officials are less concerned with the content of math courses than the number of courses. They worry less about the content of teacher tests than the number of tests.[28]

It is not surprising, then, that classroom teachers, the people closest to the action, are not very enthusiastic about school reform. In a recent national survey, *Report Card on School Reform: The Teachers Speak* (1988), nearly half the teachers reported that their morale has worsened since the release of *A Nation at Risk*. Teachers object to the regulations and paperwork that have accompanied state reform. Teachers feel bypassed—understandably so, since state reformers have rarely consulted them. There is a more positive side, however: about two-thirds of the teachers report higher student achievement in reading, writing, and arithmetic.[29]

Yet the statistics on student achievement—the performance indicators that state officials swear by—are curiously mixed. On minimum competency tests and national achievement tests that states have mandated as quality control measures, the scores are indeed up. Many teachers explain, however, that the scores are up because they are teaching the tests—not because students are learning more. On the NAEP, a battery of tests for which teachers do not rehearse their students, the trends are either flat or declining. Scores on the SAT and ACT college entrance examinations, which former U.S. Secretary of Education William Bennett put on a "wall chart" to compare one state to another, have also stagnated.[30]

One hopeful sign is that some state officials recognize that "real excellence cannot be imposed from a distance. Governors don't create excellent schools; communities—local school leaders, teachers, parents, and citizens—do."[31] The words come from Lamar Alexander, who as chair of the National Governors' Association spoke for the education governors who produced *Time for Results: The Governors' 1991 Report on Education*.[32] Acknowledging the complaints of teachers, the governors admit that state reform has spawned regulation after regulation. They propose "some old-fashioned horse trading. We'll regulate less, if schools and school districts will produce better results . . . [and] be accountable for the results."[33] Putting aside the connotations of the word "accountable" for the moment, we can hope that a third wave of reform, this one beginning at the grassroots level, may correct some of the excesses of the first and second waves.

Since the governors' report appeared, however, there have been few signs that the states are loosening the reigns of control. If anything, some of the education governors are tightening the reigns. Spurred into action by Governor Thomas Kean and State School Superintendent Saul Cooperman, the New Jersey legislature has passed a law that allows the state to take control of local school systems that the state declares to be "academically bankrupt." Few people would argue that the schools in Jersey City, the first system hauled into academic bankruptcy court, are models of excellence. But it will be interesting to see whether state officials are any more successful than local people at solving deeply entrenched local problems. The nation's education governors seem to be insisting that local systems follow the lead of the states in trying to make schools excellent by mandating more of the same.[34]

FEDERAL POLITICS OF EDUCATION

President Ronald Reagan put his mark on the politics of education during the 1980s. Mr. Reagan's New Federalism realigned the roles of all three levels of government. The control of public education shifted downward, as we have seen, with state governments gaining most from the transfer. The responsibility for paying for the schools also changed, as federal funding for education fell dramatically during Mr. Reagan's first term in office. He predicted that the New Federalism would encourage state and local governments to become more involved in education. They would fill in the gaps left by federal withdrawal.

While Mr. Reagan was reducing federal funding and control, however, he was enhancing the role of the executive branch as an education advocate. The U.S. Department of Education, which Mr. Reagan came into office promising to close down, became instead a national platform for the advancement of a conservative educational agenda—a "bully pulpit," Secretary of Education William Bennett liked to call it, conjuring memories of Teddy Roosevelt. With the media providing plentiful exposure, it was difficult for anyone who kept up with the news to miss the goals that President Reagan, his three secretaries of education, and other department officials were urging for the nation's schools. More than any other president since Lyndon Johnson, Ronald Reagan shaped the way that Americans think and talk about education.

How long Mr. Reagan's mark will remain on the politics of education is another matter. On the one hand, few people expect the return of a Lyndon Johnson-Great Society approach. After all, Reagan turned the educational conversation around, changing the emphasis from *equity* to *excellence*, from *access* to *ability,* from *needs* to *standards of performance*. William Bennett, Chester Finn, Diane Ravitch, and other conservative educators who came into the spotlight during the 1980s will continue to command attention as the nation moves into the 1990s. To many Americans, their rhetoric will remain persuasive.[35]

On the other hand, the New Federalism was unraveling before Mr. Reagan left office. During his second term, members of Congress from both political parties recognized that federal budget cuts had put local school systems with large numbers of at-risk students into dire straits. Many big city and rural systems with poor tax bases were simply unable to make up for lost federal funds. Congress reasserted its role in educational policy making, and federal education budgets began to grow again. The last budget that Mr. Reagan himself submitted looked like the work of a moderate Democrat rather than a conservative Republican. During the 1988 presidential campaign, it was hard to tell George Bush from Michael Dukakis on the education issues. Both candidates said they wanted to be "education presidents," and both advocated a stronger role for the federal government. Secretary of Education Lauro Cavazos, whom President Bush reappointed after Cavazos served as President Reagan's third education secretary, is less conservative than his predecessor, William Bennett. Although the Great Society may not come back, more federal funding and more federal control of education almost certainly will.[36]

Even so, the educational politics of the 1980s broke with the politics of the preceding decades. In order to understand why the Reagan administration worked so hard to engineer the break, we need to examine the federal role in education as it has evolved since the 1950s. The analysis in this section highlights the roles of presidents, Congress, and the federal courts, but you should remember that many other actors are involved, just as at the state and local levels.

Federal Money and Federal Influence

When Dwight Eisenhower watched John Kennedy take the presidential oath of office in 1961, the federal government was providing about 4 percent of the money for the nation's public schools. By the time Lyndon Johnson turned over the executive branch to Richard Nixon in 1969, the federal share had risen to 8 percent. When Ronald Reagan took over from Jimmy Carter in 1981, the federal contribution to the public school budget stood at an all-time high of 9 percent. Leaving office in 1989, Mr. Reagan was pleased that he had been able to trim the federal share back to the mid-1960s level of 6 percent.[37]

These figures provide a very rough sketch of the federal government's involvement in education. Seeing such figures for the first time, many prospective teachers express surprise—not that the percentages show a long increase followed by an abrupt decrease, but that *all* the percentages are so small. Compared with state and local funding, federal funding for education has never been great. Yet the federal government has managed to wring a relatively large degree of control out of a relatively small amount of money.

We can explain this phenomenon in two ways. First, federal courts have exercised much of the control. Consider the example of school desegregation. Many legal scholars regard the U.S. Supreme Court's ruling in *Brown v. Board of Education* (1954) as the most far-reaching court decision of the twentieth century. It is true that the federal government has spent a great deal of money carrying out the mandates of *Brown* and subsequent school desegregation decisions, but state and local governments, businesses, and individual citizens have spent even more. One reason the federal government's control exceeds its funding, then, is that federal courts can order sweeping changes and pass most of the costs of compliance on to other governments and other people.

Second, the federal government has increased the impact of its education dollars by earmarking them for particular purposes and insisting that state and local school systems spend them according to federal guidelines. *Categorical aid* to education—money provided with strings attached—enables federal officials to maintain control over federal dollars, even after the money has passed through state boards and departments of education and into the hands of local school officials. During the 1960s and 1970s, Congress justified categorical aid as an essential political safeguard. State and local school officials had consistently neglected the needs of poor, minority, handicapped, and female students, the argument went, so how could these same officials be trusted to spend *general aid*—money provided with fewer restrictions—wisely and equitably? While there was more than a little Congressional self-righteousness in the argument, there was also an abundance of factual support, as Chapters 6 and 8 of this textbook indicate.

Ronald Reagan tried to change the terms of the argument. Even if categorical aid had been necessary during the 1960s and 1970s, he stated, it had outlived its usefulness. The people closest to the schools deserve more control over federal aid, Mr. Reagan insisted. As the nation has matured, state and local officials have changed—they have become more sensitive to the needs of all students. Besides, he added, the courts are there to protect students who encounter discrimination. Congress was not convinced. Despite Mr. Reagan's efforts, the categorical approach remains the key to federal aid to education. It offers the federal government a way to focus and magnify the effects of its spending.

The Cold War, the Poverty War, and Other Battles

Historians say that America's elementary and secondary school students have marched off to war several times as the federal government has drafted them to fight a variety of enemies. Mixing school children into military metaphors may seem startling, but in this case the imagery is appropriate. After the Soviet Union orbited the satellite Sputnik I in 1957 and added a threatening new dimension to the Cold War, Congress responded by passing the National Defense Education Act (NDEA) of 1958. Believing that America's students could help win the war, Congress provided categorical aid to improve math, science, and foreign language instruction in the schools. Through the NDEA, the federal government hoped to gain a scientific, technological, and military advantage over the USSR.[38]

During the 1960s, President Johnson declared a War on Poverty, and Congress sent students into action all along the front lines. The Economic Opportunity Act (EOA) of 1964 gave the nation Project Head Start, a program designed to help preschool children compensate for what was then called "cultural deprivation"—in plain English, the negative effects of being poor. Compensatory education became a key weapon in the poverty war, and it remains so today. When Congress passed the Elementary and Secondary Education Act (ESEA) of 1965, the federal government launched its major educational offensive in the poverty war. Congress aimed the act at students who were "disadvantaged," another euphemism for poor. Title I reading and math programs brought compensatory education into the elementary grades. Other titles (sections) of the original ESEA provided money for libraries and instructional materials, for example, and educational research. Initially funded at $1 billion, by 1981 ESEA had provided more than $30 billion in categorical aid to state and local school systems.[39]

The Civil Rights Act of 1964 became a major federal weapon against racial and ethnic discrimination, which Congress regarded as a major cause of poverty. As the federal government channeled more money into public education, it gained powerful leverage over state and local school systems, especially in the South, the nation's poorest region. Making federal dollars contingent on desegregation brought southern school systems into line, and the many victories along this front of the poverty war encouraged Congress.[40]

Poverty, however, proved to be an elusive enemy. Congress broadened its attack by expanding the ESEA, adding the Education of Handicapped Children Act (Title VI) in 1966 and the Bilingual Education Act (Title VII) in 1968. By 1972, when Congress was ready to mount a new educational offensive, a president with a different set of priorities sat in the White House. Richard Nixon had less enthusiasm than Lyndon Johnson for fighting a domestic war on poverty, and Mr. Nixon was preoccupied with the hot war in Vietnam. Although Congress shared his preoccupation, it found time to pass the Education Amendments of 1972, which included funds for a variety of categorical programs: desegregation assistance under the Emergency School Aid Act, ethnic studies under the Ethnic Heritage Act, and improved education for Native Americans under the Indian Education Act. The best-known of the 1972 amendments is Title IX, which prohibits sex discrimination in all educational institutions—preschool, elementary, secondary, and postsecondary—that receive federal funds.[41]

By the 1970s, poverty was not the only or even the major enemy that the federal government was fighting with education. Although the Vietnam War had made military metaphors unpopular, it was obvious that the legislative and judicial branches of the federal government were still home to many "happy warriors" (with due respect to Hubert Humphrey). The mood of the public, however, was changing. The media played up the backlash against federal activism. The controversy over school desegregation moved outside the South as federal judges tried to untie the knot of de facto and de jure segregation. Although desegregation proceeded uneventfully in many school systems, the media paired the words "busing" and "Boston" in the public consciousness. The association was not a pleasant one.[42]

Congress charged into battle on behalf of the handicapped with Public Law 94-142 (1975), which affirmed the right of all children to receive an appropriate education at public expense. The media played up the exceptions rather than the rule: teacher complaints about having to draw up IEPs (Individualized Educational Programs) rather than new opportunities for handicapped students, and the high cost of educating the most severely handicapped rather than the ease with which schools accommodated the majority of exceptional children.[43]

The backlash intensified. Many citizens believed that the federal government had gone too far. In the late 1970s, President Jimmy Carter became the symbol of all that was wrong. The first presidential candidate endorsed by the NEA, Mr. Carter stuck to the federal educational agenda of the 1960s and early 1970s—just when the word "liberal" was becoming a pejorative in American politics. Federal spending on education reached new heights during the Carter administration, and at the president's insistence, Congress voted narrowly to establish a cabinet-level Department of Education. To head the new department, Carter chose Shirley Hufstedler, a federal judge, judicial activist, and feminist. As Ronald Reagan pointed out on the campaign trail, the symbolism could not have been more appropriate.

Mr. Reagan Comes to Washington

Ronald Reagan made short work of Jimmy Carter in 1980 and shorter work of Walter Mondale four years later. Education was not the main issue in either campaign, but the differences between Reagan and his Democratic opponents on the federal role in education mirrored their basic differences. Reagan promised to get the federal government off people's backs; Carter and Mondale promised to use the federal government to solve people's problems. Americans went to the polls and made two clear choices.

The educational goals that emerged during Mr. Reagan's first term came to be known as the "Five Ds": diminution of the federal education budget, deregulation of federal programs, deemphasis on education as a federal priority, disestablishment of the Department of Education, and decentralization of control to state and local school systems. During his first term, Mr. Reagan was generally successful in advancing these priorities. Although Congress refused to shut down "ED," as the department is often called, the president certainly had his way with the education budget. By 1984, in inflation-adjusted dollars, the federal government was spending 21 percent less on elementary and secondary schools than it had in 1980.[44]

Political observers were astonished at the change that had come over Washington. Even among liberal Democrats in Congress, there seemed to be a consensus that state and local school systems needed to rely less on Washington and more on themselves. A symbol of the new consensus was the Education Consolidation and Improvement Act (ECIA) of 1981. Under the umbrella of the ECIA, the administration redesigned and renamed the Title I compensatory education program, the pride of the happy warriors of the sixties and seventies. Title I became Chapter I of the ECIA, and much more than the name changed. Simplified eligibility requirements and fewer regulations from the Department of Education gave state and local school officials more control, and several years of budget cuts reduced the number of children that the program served by nearly 800,000. As classroom teachers saw it, the change from Title I to Chapter I meant three things: fewer federal regulations, fewer federal dollars, and fewer students in the program. Mr. Reagan also advocated *block grants*—a new name for general aid—to consolidiate categorical programs. When Congress passed Chapter II of the ECIA, folding 28 categories into one grant program with few strings attached, the president predicted that block grants would become the wave of the future.[45]

As impressive as these victories were, by the end of Mr. Reagan's first term the federal politics of education were in stalemate. Mr. Reagan had held spending in check, reduced the regulations in some programs, and halted the addition of new categorical programs. Congress, however, had held the line against block grants. The turning point came when lobbyists for special, vocational, and bilingual education, fearful that the categorical programs they had spent years developing would be lost in the shuffle, mounted a successful campaign to keep their areas out of the block. Chapter II, Mr. Reagan's temporary victory, started small and stayed small. Most federal aid to education remained categorical. The principle that federal money comes with strings attached remained intact.[46]

Then, during Mr. Reagan's second term, the political stalemate broke. With both houses of Congress controlled by the Democrats, federal spending on education increased. The budget for the Department of Education rose from $15.4 billion in 1984 to more than $21 billion in 1989, although in constant dollars federal spending on elementary and secondary education remained more than 20 percent below the 1980 level. Congress flexed its muscle by adding new categorical programs. In education, as in other areas, the president and the new majority in Congress were engaged in a test of strength.[47]

One of the best examples of the confrontation was the running battle over the enforcement of federal civil rights laws. Throughout his presidency, Mr. Reagan's critics in Congress charged that he was soft on segregation and sex discrimination. By 1988 the Reagan administration had sought the dismissal of several hundred desegregation cases in school systems that judges had either declared desegregated or determined to be in compliance with court-approved settlements. If the systems had proved their good faith for at least three years, the administration argued, then court supervision and busing for desegregation could end. According to President Reagan, it was time to restore local control, "as both the Constitution and common sense command." Congressional critics and civil rights groups replied that ending court supervision and busing would be tantamount to resegregation. Both sides claimed victory in this battle. On the one hand, courts allowed the Norfolk, Virginia, and Austin, Texas, systems to end their busing programs. On the other, local school boards in Georgia and several other states voted to remain under court supervision rather than risk new court battles with civil rights organizations.[48]

Congress was the clear victor in the showdown over the U.S. Supreme Court's 1984 decision in the *Grove City College v. Bell* case, which involved the Title IX ban against sex discrimination. The court had ruled that in enforcing Title IX, the government could cut off federal funds only to specific programs, not to entire institutions. For example, if the athletic program of a high school discriminated against women, the federal government could withhold funds from that program only, not the entire school. If the discrimination occurred in a program that received no federal funds, the federal government could not enforce Title IX at all—even if the institution or its students accepted federal money for other purposes. The *Grove City* decision severely restricted the enforcement of civil rights laws, not only Title IX but also the Civil Rights

Act of 1964, the Rehabilitation Act of 1973, and the Age Discrimination Act of 1975. In the wake of the decision, the Department of Education closed or limited more than 800 discrimination cases.[49]

The battle lines were drawn. The Reagan administration had supported the Supreme Court decision; its attorneys had filed briefs urging the court to limit the enforcement of civil rights laws. A bipartisan majority in the Senate and the House, however, argued that Congress had originally intended to give the federal government the broadest possible powers of enforcement. Thus the Civil Rights Restoration Act, which was designed to restore pre-*Grove City* policy, came to the floor of Congress in 1988. Both houses passed the act overwhelmingly, clarifying the federal government's right to cut off funds to entire institutions if any of their programs practiced discrimination. Overriding a presidential veto to make its point, Congress reasserted federal control of education in the area of civil rights—the focus of federal concern since the 1950s.[50]

The Economic War, the Moral War, and Educational Advocacy

Looking back on the Reagan years, educators in the 1990s and beyond will probably attach less significance to reductions in federal spending and federal control—the priorities that dominated Mr. Reagan's first term but weakened during his second—than to the advocacy role that emerged almost accidentally with the success of *A Nation at Risk*. No one in the administration expected the report to become an overnight sensation, but it did. No one expected the report to do more than the New Federalism to galvanize the states into action, but it did. *A Nation at Risk* became the educational document of the decade. The president who had been highly critical of federal involvement in education became an avid practitioner of a certain kind of involvement: advocacy. Talk may be cheap, but it can also be effective. Without spending much money and without exercising much control, the Reagan administration used exhortation and persuasion to advance its educational goals.[51]

Advocacy became a call to arms, as once again the federal government sent America's students into battle. *A Nation at Risk* drafted them to fight an international economic war against such friendly enemies as Japan, Korea, and West Germany. Educational historian Joel Spring has called this competition the "Sony War,"[52] for *A Nation at Risk* calls up images of a full-scale invasion of Sonys, Hyundais, and Telefunkens:

> Our nation is at risk. Our once unchallenged preeminence in commerce, industry, science, and technological innovation is being overtaken by competitors throughout the world. . . . If an unfriendly foreign power had attempted to impose on America the mediocre educational performance that exists today, we might well have viewed it as an act of war. As it stands, we have allowed this to happen to ourselves. We have even squandered the gains in student achievement made in the wake of the Sputnik challenge.

. . . We have, in effect, been committing an act of unthinking, unilateral educational disarmament.[53]

"History is not kind to idlers," the report warned. "We live among determined, well-educated, and strongly motivated competitors."[54] The result of this kind of advocacy, as we saw earlier in this chapter, was a new wave of school reform. Almost every state produced a report that echoed the call to arms of *A Nation at Risk*—make the schools excellent, or suffer the economic consequences. Then the states went into action, and some local school systems are still wondering what hit them. Although the Reagan administration was not completely satisfied with the way state school reform proceeded—it trampled local control in its path—the energy that *A Nation at Risk* unleashed was stunning. Gearing students up for economic competition became the educational mission of the decade.

Could advocacy of another cause unleash another tidal wave of reform? Mr. Reagan pondered this question in 1985 when William Bennett succeeded Terrel Bell as secretary of education. Bell deserved much of the credit for *A Nation at Risk,* but he lost favor within the administration because "movement conservatives" considered him too liberal. As he explained in his memoirs, he came under constant pressure from "White House ideologues" who were determined to lower the federal government's profile in education and civil rights. Bell also lost points because he was not a strong advocate of school prayer and other moral issues that were high on the agenda of the president's New Right constituents. The appointment of William Bennett, however, delighted conservatives. Heading the Department of Education during most of Reagan's second term, Bennett used the Department of Education's bully pulpit for moral advocacy.[55]

With the "Five Ds" of the first term weakening under Congressional assault, William Bennett tried to forge his own agenda: the "Three Cs" of content, choice, and character. Content, the first C, was not new; it merely elaborated and extended the message of *A Nation at Risk.* Choice, the second C, was not new either; Mr. Reagan was already on record as a supporter of tuition tax credits and educational vouchers, which we will discuss in Chapter 11. What really distinguished the administration of "Mr. ED," as Washington insiders called Bennett, was the third C of character. The quest for character became a new crusade for the schools—a moral war.[56]

To the delight of social and religious conservatives, Bennett became the point man for the administration's entire moral agenda. Using the Judeo-Christian tradition as his theme, Bennett brought together Mr. Reagan's calls for organized school prayer and good old-fashioned discipline and Mrs. Reagan's "Just Say No" antidrug campaign. (Bennett would later agree to lead President Bush's crusade against drugs.) Opposition to abortion fit easily into the theme, and so did sexual abstinence as the best defense against AIDS. For Bennett, morality touched every aspect of education. What works? His main answer was hard work. The work ethic is not uniquely Protestant, he told Americans, but it is essential for success in education and every other endeavor. Bennett took on the NEA and other "vested interests" in education with moral fervor, casting them as the villains in the drama of school reform. What made him so attractive to some Americans and so irritating to others was his right-versus-wrong, friends-versus-enemies approach to the politics of education.[57]

As effective an advocate as William Bennett was, the moral war he tried to start never caught on at the state and local levels to the degree that the economic war had. Perhaps the thrust of *A Nation at Risk* toward people's pocketbooks was more powerful than Bennett's appeal to their morality. Perhaps the eyes of the nation were still on the bottom line: dollars and cents. Whatever the case, *A Nation at Risk* became the Reagan administration's most durable educational legacy. The report had the unintended effect of putting politicians at all three levels of government in the mood to invest more money in the schools. President Reagan himself left office having submitted his largest-ever budget for education; President Bush and Secretary Cavazos have promised to maintain or increase federal funding for the schools. The most important trend since *A Nation at Risk*, however, has been the growth of state spending on education, as we will see in the concluding section of this chapter.

EDUCATIONAL FINANCE

Where children live has a powerful effect on the quality of the public schools they attend. Real estate agents are well acquainted with the question "How good are the public schools?" for parents who have the resources to do so shop for homes with the quality of education in mind. Although public schools differ in many ways, one of the most important variables is *per-pupil expenditure*—the amount of money spent per student. Think of per-pupil expenditure as a financial package put together by local school boards with money received from the local, state, and federal levels.[58]

Table 9.1 ranks the states by their average per-pupil expenditures. As you can see, the annual cost of educating the nation's "average" public school student is over $4,000. Variations among the states are wide. One state's average per-pupil expenditure is less than $2,500, while nine states spend more than twice that amount. Viewed another way, the differences are even more glaring. In every classroom of 25 students, the states of Alaska, New Jersey, New York, and Connecticut spend about $100,000 more every year than Alabama, Mississippi, Utah, and Arkansas. Per-pupil expenditures tend to be highest in the Northeast, followed by the Midwest, the West, and the Southeast, but notice the exceptions to this rule.

In the nation as a whole, average per-pupil expenditures have risen by about 28 percent, adjusted for inflation, from the late 1970s through the late 1980s, with most of the increase coming in the post-*Nation at Risk* era of state school reform. To set the record straight, most of the new money has not gone

TABLE 9.1. AVERAGE PER-PUPIL EXPENDITURES ACROSS THE NATION, 1987–88

State	Per-Pupil Expenditure	State	Per-Pupil Expenditure
1. Alaska	$7,038	27. W. Virginia	3,895
2. New Jersey	6,910	28. Hawaii	3,894
3. New York	6,849	29. California	3,892
4. Connecticut	6,217	30. N. Carolina	3,892
5. D. Columbia	5,643	31. New Mexico	3,880
6. Rhode Island	5,456	32. Iowa	3,846
7. Wyoming	5,453	33. Nevada	3,829
8. Massachusetts	5,396	34. Arizona	3,694
9. Pennsylvania	5,063	35. Texas	3,685
10. Wisconsin	4,997	36. Nebraska	3,641
11. Delaware	4,994	37. Indiana	3,616
12. Vermont	4,949	38. Missouri	3,566
13. Maryland	4,890	39. Kentucky	3,355
14. Oregon	4,574	40. N. Dakota	3,353
15. Minnesota	4,503	41. S. Carolina	3,333
16. Florida	4,389	42. Tennessee	3,189
17. Colorado	4,378	43. S. Dakota	3,159
18. Maine	4,276	44. Louisiana	3,078
19. Kansas	4,262	45. Oklahoma	3,051
20. Virginia	4,226	46. Georgia	2,939
21. Illinois	4,217	47. Idaho	2,814
22. New Hampshire	4,132	48. Alabama	2,752
23. Michigan	4,122	49. Mississippi	2,692
24. Washington	4,081	50. Utah	2,657
25. Montana	4,061	51. Arkansas	2,410
26. Ohio	3,907	U.S. average	4,216

(*Source: National Education Association,* Rankings of the States, 1988 [*Washington: NEA, 1988*], p. 55. *Figures show expenditures per pupil in average daily attendance. Reprinted by permission of the publisher.*)

into teachers' pockets. Their salaries, as you may recall from Chapter 2, have risen by only 7 percent since the late 1970s. Most of the 28 percent increase has gone to pay for other state reforms.[59]

Local Property Taxes: Some Districts Are More Equal Than Others

Keep in mind that average state per-pupil expenditures, while useful in making comparisons among the states, conceal variations *within* the states. Per-pupil expenditures tend to be highest in suburban school districts, followed by urban, small town, and rural systems. Travel around the country, and you will almost always find the highest per-pupil expenditures in the suburbs of major cities. Why do the students who live in suburban Shawnee Mission, Kansas, for example, have more money spent on their public education than students who live in nearby Kansas City, in small-town Mullinville, or on a farm out on the plains? The main reason is that suburban residents are able to raise more money for the schools though local property taxes.

But suburbs are not all alike. Some are more affluent that others, and local property taxes work to the advantage of wealthier communities and to the disadvantage of poorer communities. In some cases, suburbs with high *property values* can set their *tax rates* low and still rank at the top of the state in per-pupil spending. Consider the example of two school districts of about the same size, located in the same state. One district serves an upper middle class suburb where the homes have an average market value of $200,000. The other district is in a working class suburb (it could just as well be a small town or a central city that has fallen on hard times) where the market value of property averages $50,000.

To keep things straightforward, let us assume that property is taxed at full market value in this state. The residents of the upper middle class suburb have set their school tax rate at $1 per $100 of property value. The average home in this suburb, therefore, brings in $2,000 for the local schools. With the average family paying school taxes of $2,000 each year, these citizens can truthfully say they are trying hard to support public education. The residents of the working class suburb, however, have set their tax rate twice as high—at $2 per $100 of assessed value—yet the average home in their community generates only $1,000 for the schools. These residents can say they are trying twice as hard, but their

TABLE 9.2. PERCENTAGE OF PUBLIC SCHOOL REVENUE CONTRIBUTED BY FEDERAL, STATE, AND LOCAL GOVERNMENTS

School Year	Percentage of Revenue		
	Federal	*State*	*Local*
1919–20	0.3	16.5	83.2
1929–30	0.4	16.9	82.7
1939–40	1.8	30.3	68.0
1949–50	2.9	39.8	57.3
1959–60	4.4	39.1	56.5
1969–70	8.0	39.9	52.1
1979–80	9.2	49.1	41.7
1981–82	7.4	47.9	44.7
1983–84	6.9	47.8	45.3
1985–86	6.6	49.4	44.0
1987–88	6.2	50.2	43.6

(*Source: Figures for years 1919–20 through 1969–70 are from U.S. Department of Education, Center for Education Statistics,* Digest of Education Statistics, 1987 [*Washington: U.S. Government Printing Office, 1987*], p. 107. Figures for 1979–80 through 1985–86 are from National Education Association, Estimates of School Statistics, 1987–88 [*Washington: NEA, 1988*], p. 21 Figures for 1987–88 are from National Education Association, Rankings of the States, 1988 [*Washington: NEA: 1988*], pp. 42–44.)

effort—a technical term in school finance that means exactly what it says—
yields them only half as much.[60]

You can appreciate the significance of this example if you think again of
school finance as a package. In the nation as a whole, local governments
contribute 44 percent of the money that goes into the package, and almost all
the local money comes from property taxes. As Table 9.2 indicates, local
governments have historically shouldered most of the burden of paying for
public education. Table 9.2 also shows, however, that state governments have
assumed a progressively larger share of the burden throughout this century,
motivated in part by the desire to make the quality of education more uniform
within each state.

In 1920, when local goverments were responsible for raising more than 80
percent of school revenue, the differences in per-pupil expenditures within the
states were staggering. The amount of wealth in a local community virtually
dictated the amount of money spent on the local schools. As we saw in Chapter
6, race and ethnicity also influenced expenditures, for it was standard practice to
spend less on black and Hispanic students. In the early twentieth century, then,
it was not at all unusual for some districts to spend 5, 10, or 15 times more per
student than other systems within the same state.

State Funds: Reducing the Inequalities

Such gaps have narrowed but have not completely closed as the states have
increased their educational spending. Most states have developed *equalization
plans* that base the amount of state funding that each district receives on such
factors as local wealth, effort, and student characteristics (the percentage of
poor, minority, and handicapped students, for example). In our example of the
upper-middle-class suburb and the working-class suburb, a state equalization
plan would bring per-pupil expenditures in the two districts closer together. The
state department of education would send more state money to the poorer
district, and that district would probably receive more federal aid as well, since
it would be likely to have more students who qualify for categorical federal
programs.[61] (See Table 9.3.)

Two major court decisions of the 1970s shaped the trend toward more state
funding. In *Serrano v. Priest* (1971), the California Supreme Court considered
the complaint of John Serrano, who would surely identify with our two-suburb
example. Serrano and his family lived in Baldwin Park, a blue-collar suburb of
Los Angeles. Baldwin Park's property tax rates were twice as high as those in
wealthy Beverly Hills, but because of vastly different property values, the
Baldwin Park school district was able to spend only half as much per student.
With class sizes increasing and textbooks in short supply, Serrano was unhappy
with the public schools his two children attended.[62]

The California Supreme Court ruled that the state's school finance system,
heavily dependent on local property taxes, "invidiously discriminates against the

TABLE 9.3. PERCENTAGE OF SCHOOL REVENUE CONTRIBUTED BY FEDERAL, STATE, AND LOCAL GOVERNMENTS, STATE BY STATE, 1987–88

Percentage of Revenue					
Federal		**State**		**Local**	
1. Mississippi	15.73	Hawaii	91.21	D. Columbia	89.78
2. Alabama	12.37	New Mexico	76.32	New Hampshire	89.56
3. West Virginia	12.12	Washington	73.58	Nebraska	68.19
4. New Mexico	11.89	Alabama	69.95	Oregon	66.99
5. Louisiana	11.51	Kentucky	69.49	South Dakota	63.28
6. D. Columbia	10.22	California	69.23	Michigan	61.19
7. Kentucky	10.10	Delaware	68.65	Virginia	60.25
8. Tennessee	9.63	Alaska	67.31	Vermont	56.94
9. Arkansas	9.36	Oklahoma	64.86	Colorado	56.34
10. South Dakota	8.99	North Carolina	64.52	Nevada	55.78
11. Hawaii	8.67	Arkansas	61.30	Wisconsin	55.19
12. South Carolina	8.26	Idaho	61.17	Maryland	54.86
13. Montana	7.92	West Virginia	61.05	Illinois	54.64
14. Georgia	7.58	Indiana	59.99	Connecticut	53.76
15. Delaware	7.55	Utah	57.25	Missouri	53.70
16. North Dakota	7.44	Minnesota	56.86	New Jersey	53.10
17. California	7.38	Georgia	56.16	Wyoming	52.76
18. Illinois	7.38	South Carolina	55.60	Rhode Island	52.49
19. Idaho	7.36	Louisiana	54.76	New York	51.61
20. Alaska	7.34	Mississippi	54.52	Kansas	51.48
21. Texas	7.00	Maine	54.24	Iowa	51.27
22. Florida	6.64	Arizona	53.46	Pennsylvania	49.61
23. North Carolina	6.36	Florida	52.53	Massachusetts	47.60
24. Oregon	6.29	North Dakota	51.16	Texas	47.19
25. Vermont	6.04	Tennessee	50.40	Ohio	44.64
26. Washington	5.79	Ohio	49.66	Arizona	43.00
27. Missouri	5.77	Montana	49.25	Montana	42.83
28. Utah	5.71	Massachusetts	46.70	North Dakota	41.40
29. Ohio	5.70	Pennsylvania	46.12	Florida	40.83
30. Massachusetts	5.70	Texas	45.81	Maine	40.24
31. Oklahoma	5.66	Kansas	43.83	Tennessee	39.97
32. Iowa	5.56	New York	43.41	Minnesota	38.53
33. Maine	5.52	Rhode Island	43.25	Utah	37.04
34. Maryland	5.30	Iowa	43.17	Georgia	36.26
35. Nebraska	5.25	New Jersey	42.74	South Carolina	36.14
36. New York	4.98	Wyoming	42.52	Indiana	36.00
37. Colorado	4.83	Connecticut	42.15	Louisiana	33.74
38. Virginia	4.78	Missouri	40.53	Idaho	31.46
39. Wyoming	4.72	Wisconsin	40.24	Mississippi	29.75
40. Kansas	4.70	Nevada	40.06	Oklahoma	29.48
41. Minnesota	4.61	Maryland	39.84	Arkansas	29.35
42. Wisconsin	4.57	Colorado	38.82	North Carolina	29.12
43. Pennsylvania	4.27	Illinois	37.98	West Virginia	26.83
44. Rhode Island	4.26	Vermont	37.01	Alaska	25.35

(Continued)

TABLE 9.3. (CONTINUED)

Percentage of Revenue					
Federal		*State*		*Local*	
45. Nevada	4.16	Michigan	35.16	Delaware	23.80
46. New Jersey	4.16	Virginia	34.97	California	23.39
47. Connecticut	4.09	South Dakota	27.73	Washington	20.62
48. Indiana	4.01	Oregon	26.73	Kentucky	20.41
49. Michigan	3.65	Nebraska	26.55	Alabama	17.68
50. Arizona	3.54	New Hampshire	7.29	New Mexico	11.79
51. New Hampshire	3.15	D. Columbia	NA	Hawaii	0.12
U.S. average	6.22		50.19		43.59

NA = not applicable. (*Source: National Education Association,* Rankings of the States, 1988 [*Washington: NEA, 1988*], pp. 42–44. *Reprinted by permission of the publisher.*)

poor because it makes the quality of a child's education a function of the wealth of his parents and his neighbors." The court ruled that the California system violated the right to equal protection of the laws guaranteed by both the state constitution and the Fourteenth Amendment to the U.S. Constitution. Obviously, said the court, the school laws of California were not protecting rich and poor citizens equally; the laws were making public schools as unequal as the wealth of the communities in which they were located.[63]

The *Serrano* case created a sensation in school finance, precipitating a flood of similar lawsuits in other states. When a case from Texas, *San Antonio Independent School District v. Rodriguez,* reached the U.S. Supreme Court in 1973, many observers predicted a ruling similar to *Serrano*—a national mandate to reform school finance. The cases were virtually identical: unequal per-pupil expenditures, reliance on local property taxes, even a lead plaintiff who was poor and Hispanic. But the court issued no such mandate. Instead, it left the matter up to the states. In a 5-4 decision, the majority pointed out that the U.S. Constitution does not guarantee the right to an education. The Fourteenth Amendment, therefore, cannot protect citizens from state school finance laws that make per-pupil expenditures vary from one district to another. The court suggested, however, that inequitable state laws might well violate state constitutions.[64]

Rodriguez shifted the action back to the state level, and in the years since the decision about half of the nation's state legislatures have overhauled their school finance systems to make them less dependent on local revenue. After the California Supreme Court reaffirmed its earlier decision and reissued its call for reform in *Serrano II* (1976), for example, the state share of the school budget went from less than 40 percent to almost 70 percent. In the late 1970s, for the first time in American history, the state share of the nation's total spending on education was greater than the local share.[65]

The battles over school finance are still raging, even if no clear pattern is emerging in state court decisions. During the 1980s, state judges in West Virginia, Montana, and Texas ordered their legislatures to make per-pupil expenditures more uniform from system to system, while judges in Oklahoma and Florida let their states off the hook. Thus local differences persist. In some states, per-pupil expenditures in the wealthiest local districts still exceed those in the poorest districts by more than 4 to 1.[66]

Table 9.3 can give you an idea of which states have the greatest differences. Per-pupil expenditures tend to vary most from district to district in the states that rank high in the third column, local funding. School districts in these states, as a rule, are the most dependent on local property taxes. Per-pupil expenditures tend to be more uniform in the states that rank high in the second column, state funding. School districts in these states, as a rule, receive more equalization aid from state sales and income taxes. Notice, too, which states receive the most federal assistance. The southeastern states, with their large numbers of poor and minority students, are clustered at the top of the first column.

Educational Finance in the 1990s

The trend toward more state funding and more state control seems likely to continue into the 1990s. If it does, public schools will rely more on sales taxes and income taxes, the two major sources of state revenue. Tax increases are rarely popular, but the strong antitax sentiment symbolized by Proposition 13 during the late 1970s and early 1980s has subsided—at least for now. Polls conducted in the late 1980s show that between two-thirds and three-fourths of both the general public and business leaders say they are willing to pay higher taxes for the schools. In some states, governors and state legislators are pushing through sales and income tax increases to pay for school reform.[67]

Sales and income taxes are sensitive to a state's economic health, and the prognosis varies from state to state. Texas, Louisiana, Alaska, and other states that boomed when oil prices were high are now practicing the politics of retrenchment. Several of the northeastern and midwestern industrial states that appeared to be down for the count several years ago are staging an economic revival. Farm states throughout the nation, especially in the West and Midwest, continue to struggle with economic problems. Although the future of the Sunbelt still looks bright, its economic growth has slowed.

Recall the vast differences in average per-pupil expenditures from state to state (Table 9.1). The principle of financial effort applies here, too. Poorer states often try harder than wealthier states to raise money for public education—that is, poorer states often spend a greater portion of their total resources on the schools. But their effort yields lower per-pupil expenditures. If Congress does increase federal spending on education during the 1990s, talk of massive federal assistance to poorer states may revive. For years the NEA has argued that the three levels of government should split the total bill for public education evenly—each level should pay one-third. By varying the exact mix of local, state, and federal funding from district to district and state to state, one-third funding could make per-pupil expenditures relatively equal throughout the nation.[68]

Before the Reagan administration, the talk of one-third funding was serious; during the 1980s, the possibility seemed remote. Given the looming federal deficit, the Gramm–Rudman–Hollings mandate for reducing the deficit, and the strong tradition of state and local control, what are the odds that the federal government will increase its share of the public school budget from 6 percent to 33 percent? In the short run, there is no chance at all. In the long run, the odds are still not good, but the NEA is already talking with Congress about making one-third funding a target for the twenty-first century.

As America enters the 1990s, some states are desperately seeking relief from their economic ailments. State lotteries are becoming popular as a way to fund public education—"painlessly," their backers say. About 30 states now have lotteries, although most of the lotteries are not earmarked for public education. Apart from the moral and religious objections that some people have to lotteries, they are simply not producing the educational windfall that their advocates have promised. Lotteries create high public expectations of plentiful money for the schools, but in most cases they generate 2 percent or less of a state's school revenue.[69]

In Florida, for example, citizens believe that the state lottery has made the schools financially secure, yet it pays for the equivalent of only seven days of school a year—3 to 4 percent of the total school budget. The Illinois lottery pays an exceptionally high 20 percent of the bills, but it has given state legislators an excuse to divert sales and income tax money from public education into other areas. Since the schools have their lottery, tax revenue can go elsewhere. The Illinois schools lose from one source what they gain from another. Educationally speaking, state lotteries are not turning out to be a good bet.[70]

In Chapter 10 we will encounter a variety of quick fixes, sure cures, and panaceas as we examine trends in the school curriculum. You are preparing to teach at a time when, according to some Americans, public education is recovering from a long illness. Back to basics and excellence in education have put public schools back on their feet, some believe. Not so, other Americans argue. The recovery is an illusion created by standardized tests. Still other Americans broaden the scope of the argument to include private schools, whose vital signs, they insist, are getting stronger every day. We will examine the growing rivalry between public schools and private schools in Chapter 11. And thus we begin the last part of this textbook, "Issues for the 1990s."

ACTIVITIES

1. Attend a local school board meeting. Ask to interview several board members and the superintendent about local control, representation, and other issues discussed in this chapter.
2. Find out how state school reform has affected the schools in your state since the release of *A Nation at Risk*. Compare the views of teachers, administrators, elected or appointed school officials, and state legislators. Is "more of the same" a fair description of state reform?
3. Talk with two members of Congress, one Democrat and one Republican, about how the federal politics of education have changed since the new administration has been in Washington.
4. Contact the department of education in your state for information on how widely per-pupil expenditures vary from district to district. If your state has an equalization program, find out how it operates.

SUGGESTED READINGS

Joel Spring's *Conflict of Interests: The Politics of American Education* (see note 7) is an up-to-date blend of political theory and practice. Spring's analysis of changes in the federal, state, and local politics of education during the 1980s is especially valuable. Michael W. Kirst gained firsthand knowledge of the politics of education as president of the California State Board of Education. Two of Kirst's books are *Who Controls Our Schools? American Values in Conflict* (note 60) and, with Frederick M. Wirt, *Schools in Conflict: The Politics of Education* (note 7).

NOTES

1. See Ronald Reagan, "Excellence and Opportunity: A Program of Support for American Education," *Phi Delta Kappan* 66 (September 1984): 13–15.
2. David L. Clark and Terry A. Astuto, "The Significance and Permanence of Changes in Federal Education Policy," *Educational Researcher* 15 (October 1986): 4–13.
3. Alec M. Gallup, "The 18th Annual Gallup Poll of the Public's Attitudes toward the Public Schools," *Phi Delta Kappan* 68 (September 1986): 43–59; Beatrice H. Cameron, Kenneth E. Underwood, and Jim C. Fortune, "Politics and Power: How You're Selected and Elected to Lead This Nation's Schools," *American School Board Journal* 175 (January 1988): 17–19.
4. Willis D. Hawley and Frederick M. Wirt, eds., *The Search for Community Power* (Englewood Cliffs, NJ: Prentice-Hall, 1968); Michael Y. Nunnery and Ralph B. Kimbrough, *Politics, Power, Polls, and School Elections* (Berkeley, CA: McCutchan, 1971); Donald McCarty and Charles Ramsey, *The School Managers: Power and Conflict in American Public Education* (Westport, CT: Greenwood Press, 1971).
5. A classic study of local school board members and superintendents is L. Harmon

Zeigler and M. Kent Jennings, *Governing American Schools: Political Interaction in Local School Districts* (North Scituate, MA: Duxbury, 1974).

6. Ibid; Raymond E. Callahan, *Education and the Cult of Efficiency: A Study of the Social Forces That Have Shaped the Administration of the Public Schools* (Chicago: University of Chicago Press, 1962); David B. Tyack and Elisabeth Hansot, *Managers of Virtue: Public School Leadership in America, 1820–1980* (New York: Basic Books, 1982).

7. Joel Spring, *Conflict of Interests: The Politics of American Education* (White Plains, NY: Longman, 1988), ch. 5; Frederick M. Wirt and Michael W. Kirst, *Schools in Conflict: The Politics of Education* (Berkeley, CA: McCutchan, 1982), ch. 6.

8. Arthur Blumberg with Phyllis Blumberg, *The School Superintendent: Living with Conflict* (New York: Teachers College Press, 1985), chs. 5–6.

9. Ibid.

10. Beatrice H. Cameron, Kenneth E. Underwood, and Jim C. Fortune, "It's Ten Years Later, and You've Hardly Changed at All," *American School Board Journal* 175 (January 1988): 20.

11. Ibid; Cameron, Underwood, and Fortune, "Politics and Power," p. 18.

12. See note 11.

13. Cameron, Underwood, and Fortune, "Politics and Power," p. 19.

14. David B. Tyack, *The One Best System: A History of American Urban Education* (Cambridge, MA: Harvard University Press, 1974), part IV.

15. William Montague, "A Vote for Power," *Education Week* (December 9, 1987), pp. 1, 16–17.

16. Ibid., p. 16.

17. Ibid., p. 17.

18. George S. Counts, *The Social Composition of Boards of Education: A Study in the Social Control of Public Education* (Chicago: University of Chicago Press, 1927), p. 81.

19. For overviews of state school politics, see Spring, *Conflict of Interests*, ch. 4, and Wirt and Kirst, *Schools in Conflict*, chs. 8–9.

20. Dinah Wiley, *State Boards of Education* (Arlington, VA: National Associations of State Boards of Education, 1983), pp. 15–16; *Educational Governance in the States: A Report Prepared by the Council of Chief State School Officers* (Washington: U.S. Department of Education, 1983).

21. U.S. Department of Education, *Educational Governance in the States*; "Chief State School Officers," *Education Week* (May 14, 1986), p. 41.

22. Wiley, *State Boards of Education*.

23. Denis P. Doyle and Terry W. Hartle, *Excellence in Education: The States Take Charge* (Washington: American Enterprise Institute, 1985).

24. Committee for Economic Development, *Investing in Our Children: Business and the Public Schools* (Washington: CED, 1985), and *Children in Need: Investment Strategies for the Educationally Disadvantaged* (Washington: CED, 1987).

25. Denis P. Doyle and Terry W. Hartle, "Leadership in Education: Governors, Legislators, and Teachers," *Phi Delta Kappan* 67 (September 1985): 22–24.

26. Ibid.

27. Spring, *Conflict of Interests*, pp. 79–83.

28. See Arthur E. Wise, *Legislated Learning: The Bureaucratization of the American*

Classroom (Berkeley: University of California Press, 1979), and "The Two Conflicting Trends in School Reform: Legislated Learning Revisited," *Phi Delta Kappan* 69 (January 1988): 328–333. Michael W. Kirst discusses the quantitative mindset in "Sustaining the Momentum of State Education Reform: The Link between Assessment and Financial Support," *Phi Delta Kappan* 67 (January 1986): 341–345.

29. Carnegie Foundation for the Advancement of Teaching, *Report Card on School Reform: The Teachers Speak* (New York: Carnegie Foundation, 1988).

30. Reagan Walker, "Bennett: Test Gains at 'Dead Stall,' " *Education Week* (March 2, 1988), p. 6.

31. Lamar Alexander, *"Time for Results*: An Overview," *Phi Delta Kappan* 68 (November 1986): 203.

32. *Time for Results: The Governors' 1991 Report on Education* (Washington: National Governors' Association, 1986). Also see *Results in Education: 1987* (Washington: National Governors' Association, 1987).

33. Alexander, "Time for Results," pp. 202–203.

34. Lisa Jennings, "Jersey City Officials Seek to Block State's Attempted School Takeover," *Education Week* (June 8, 1988), pp. 1, 10.

35. Clark and Astuto, "The Significance and Permanence," argue that the shifts in federal educational policy that took place during the Reagan years will be long lasting.

36. For arguments that the 1990s will usher in educational policies different from those of the Reagan years, see Terry W. Hartle, "The Federal Role in the Post-Reagan Era," *Basic Education* 32 (November 1987): 2–5, and John F. Jennings, "The Sputnik of the Eighties," *Phi Delta Kappan* 69 (October 1987): 104–109.

37. See Table 9.2.

38. For contrasting accounts of the federal role since World War II, see Joel Spring, *The Sorting Machine Revisited: National Educational Policy since 1945*, rev. ed. (White Plains, NY: Longman, 1989), and Diane Ravitch, *The Troubled Crusade: American Education, 1945–1980* (New York: Basic Books, 1983).

39. Lynn Olson, "Title I Turns 20: A Commemoration and Debate," *Education Week* (May 1, 1985), pp. 1, 12–13; U.S. Department of Education, Center for Education Statistics, *Digest of Education Statistics, 1982* (Washington: U.S. Government Printing Office, 1982), p. 171.

40. Gary Orfield, *The Reconstruction of Southern Education: The Schools and the 1964 Civil Rights Act* (New York: Wiley, 1969).

41. Joel Spring, *American Education: An Introduction to Social and Political Aspects*, 4th ed. (White Plains, NY: Longman, 1989), ch. 8.

42. J. Anthony Lukas, *Common Ground: A Turbulent Decade in the Lives of Three American Families* (New York: Knopf, 1985).

43. Steven Carlson, " 'Appropriate' School Programs: Legal vs. Educational Approaches," *Exceptional Parent* 15 (September 1985): 23, 25–26, 28–30.

44. Clark and Astuto, p. 5; Denis P. Doyle and Terry W. Hartle, "Ideology, Pragmatic Politics, and the Education Budget," in John C. Weicher, ed., *Maintaining the Safety Net: Income Redistribution Programs in the Reagan Administration* (Washington: American Enterprise Institute for Public Policy Research, 1984), ch. 6.

45. Clark and Astuto, "The Significance and Permanence," pp. 5–6; Olson, "Title I Turns 20," p. 12.

46. Hartle, "The Federal Role," pp. 2–3.

47. Ibid.; Julie A. Miller, "21.2-Billion Budget Boosts Major Programs," *Education Week* (February 24, 1988), pp. 1, 17–19; Deborah A. Verstegen and David L. Clark, "The Diminution of Federal Expenditures for Education during the Reagan Administration," *Phi Delta Kappan* 70 (October 1988): 134–138.

48. William Snider, "Courts Back Moves to End Busing Plans," *Education Week* (January 13, 1988), pp. 1, 23 (the quotation is from p. 23); Snider, "Justice Officials Seek to End Many U.S. Integration Suits," *Education Week* (March 16, 1988), pp. 1, 15; Snider, "Justice's Desegregation Plan Hits Snag," *Education Week* (May 4, 1988), p. 9.

49. James Crawford, "Grove City Bill Nears First Senate Hurdle," *Education Week* (May 20, 1987), pp. 11–12; Julie A. Miller, "Senate Panel Clears Grove City Measure," *Education Week* (May 27, 1987), p. 14.

50. See note 49.

51. Lynn Olson, "Inside 'A Nation at Risk,' " *Education Week* (April 27, 1988), pp. 1, 22, 23.

52. Joel Spring, "Education and the Sony War," *Phi Delta Kappan* 65 (April 1984): 534–537.

53. National Commission on Excellence in Education, *A Nation at Risk: The Imperative for Educational Reform* (Washington: U.S. Department of Education, 1983), p. 5.

54. Ibid., p. 7.

55. Terrel H. Bell, *The Thirteenth Man: A Reagan Cabinet Memoir* (New York: Free Press, 1988).

56. Clark and Astuto, "The Significance and Permanence," pp. 10–11.

57. Ibid.

58. The standard textbook on school finance is Roe L. Johns, Edgar L. Morphet, and Kern Alexander, *The Economics and Financing of Education*, 4th ed. (Englewood Cliffs, NJ: Prentice-Hall, 1983).

59. National Education Association, *Estimates of School Statistics, 1987–88* (Washington: NEA, 1988), pp. 24–25, and *Rankings of the States, 1988* (Washington: NEA, 1988), p. 21.

60. In some states, local property taxes are based on an assessed value that is only a percentage of market value—often as low as 10 or 20 percent. These states usually have higher tax rates. For a discussion of these issues, see Michael W. Kirst, *Who Controls Our Schools? American Values in Conflict* (New York: Freeman, 1984), ch. 6.

61. Johns, Morphet, and Alexander, *The Economics and Financing of Education*, pp. 242–243.

62. Charles A. Tesconi, Jr., and Emanuel Hurwitz, Jr., *Education for Whom? The Question of Equal Educational Opportunity* (New York: Dodd, Mead, 1974), pp. 50–65; Spring, *American Education*, ch. 10.

63. Ibid.

64. Ibid.

65. David L. Kirp and Donald N. Jensen, "The New Federalism Goes to Court," *Phi Delta Kappan* 65 (November 1983): 206–210; William Montague, "Education-Finance Forumula Is Biased, Texas Court Rules," *Education Week* (May 6, 1987), pp. 1, 19.

66. William Montague, "West Virginia Finance Battle Enters Critical Phase," *Education Week* (September 30, 1987), p. 11; Montague, "Education-Finance Formula Is Bi-

ased"; Montague, "Judge Orders Montana To Revise Finance Formula by October 1989," *Education Week* (January 27, 1988), pp. 9–10; Tom Mirga, "Courts Back Finance Systems in Okla., Fla.," *Education Week* (December 9, 1987), p. 11.

67. Alec M. Gallup and Stanley M. Elam, "The 20th Annual Gallup Poll of the Public's Attitudes toward the Public Schools," *Phi Delta Kappan* 70 (September 1988): 38; "Business Leaders and Public Willing to Raise Taxes for Education," *Education Week* (May 20, 1987), p. 15.

68. National Education Association, *Rankings of the States, 1988,* pp. 52–54.

69. *Providing Incentives in the Allocation of State Aid for Schools* (Denver: Augenblick, Van de Water and Associates, 1984).

70. Chris Pipho, "The Lottery Luster," *Phi Delta Kappan* 69 (December 1987): 254–255.

PART III

Issues for the 1990s

CHAPTER 10

Teachers and the Curriculum

Autonomy: the right of the members of an occupation to make their own decisions and use their own judgment. Nearing the end of this book, I want to call attention again to teacher autonomy—the hallmark of professionalism. As autonomy relates to teachers and the curriculum, it is the freedom that teachers have to decide what and how to teach. Unfortunately, the curriculum trends that prevail as we enter the 1990s are reducing teacher autonomy, and this chapter explains how teaching and learning are changing as a result.

Trying to put this chapter in touch with the real world of the schools, I have applied our earlier discussion of philosophies and theories of education directly to the classroom. In Chapter 7 we examined a wide range of alternatives in search of what ought to be. Here we are more concerned with what is, and with what seems to lie ahead as we look into the new decade. Thus our focus is on *essentialism,* the theory that has dominated American education since the mid-1970s. Call it what you will—back to basics, the new basics, excellence in education—essentialism is in command. Its advocates have set the agenda for the curriculum debates of the early 1990s, and its critics are busy responding.

The chapter opens with a discussion of *back to basics* and *testing, testing, testing.* The repetition is intentional; it reflects the nature of the test-driven curriculum that has developed over the last decade and a half. We will pay special attention to the conflict between standardized testing and teacher autonomy. Next we will examine the status of essentialism as it moves into the 1990s. Essentialism's most thoughtful advocates—such people as E. D. Hirsch, Jr., Diane Ravitch, Chester Finn, and William Bennett—are not completely happy with what has happened under the banners of basics and excellence. We will use the curriculum of Bennett's James Madison Elementary School and High School as a model of essentialism as it might be—in contrast to essentialism as it is. The chapter concludes with a look at *literacy*, a complex concept that underlies much of the controversy over the curriculum. The debate over different kinds of literacy, especially *cultural* literacy, raises fundamental questions about what Americans need to know and what the content of the curriculum should be. Essentialists may have set the agenda for these debates, but throughout this chapter their critics will have ample opportunity to speak. Listen carefully to all sides.

BACK TO BASICS AND TESTING, TESTING, TESTING

In the mid-1970s Americans were convinced that public education was in deep trouble. The media gave the nation regular reports on problems in the schools: lax discipline, drug abuse, low standards, incompetent teachers. As proof positive that the schools were in bad shape, many citizens pointed to declining scores on standardized tests, most often to the decline on the Scholastic Aptitude Test (SAT). Although it may be difficult to see from our perspective in the 1990s, an era in which standardized testing permeates schools at every level, a significant change occurred when the American public accepted standardized test scores as an important indicator of educational quality.

The president of the College Entrance Examination Board (CEEB) traces the use of the SAT as a quality indicator back to 1974, when "an alert education reporter noticed that the scores had dropped from the previous year. He asked for the figures for earlier years, and was thus able to take public note of the fact that since 1963 there had been a gradual, steady decline."[1] Americans were fascinated. Right there in the numbers was scientific-looking documentation of a nationwide decline in the quality of education. And there, I contend, was a sign that back to basics and testing, testing, testing were just around the corner.

Outputs and Inputs

The alert reporter had picked up the nation's growing interest in judging schools by their outputs rather than inputs. Since the release of *Equality of Educational Opportunity* (1966), popularly known as the Coleman Report, the factory model of schooling that we discussed in Chapter 2 had been making a comeback. Average citizens were starting to evaluate schools not by the resources that go in but by the products that come out. According to the Coleman Report, there is little or no correlation between school inputs—facilities, programs, and teachers, the things that money can buy—and school outputs, *if* the scores of students on standardized achievement tests are used as the outputs. But should test scores be used that way? Ordinary citizens who had never thought much about standardized testing were puzzled at first. Most parents had never even seen their children's test scores. What could a set of scores tell you that a graded homework assignment, a report card, or a talk with a teacher couldn't?[2]

People who went to elementary and secondary school during the last two decades may find it hard to believe, but in the not-too-distant past, Americans were just not curious about standardized test scores. In the first place, students took very few standardized tests. The complete package typically consisted of one or two IQ tests, several batteries of a nationally normed achievement test, and (for some students) a college-entrance examination. That, in most school systems, was the extent of standardized testing. In the second place, after teachers, counselors, and administrators reviewed the test scores, into the files they went. Case closed. Educators rarely released information on scores to students or parents, nor did the news media publish school-by-school, system-by-system, and state-by-state comparisons.[3]

Before the 1970s, the question "How good are the local schools?" was usually a request for information on facilities, programs, and teachers. As the seventies wore on, however, the question became an invitation to discuss standardized test scores. Local school board members and administrators responded to *Equality of Educational Opportunity* as if James Coleman had insulted them to their faces. A frantic scramble to prove Coleman wrong ensued. Trying to argue with Coleman on his own terms, dollars against test scores, local officials adopted the factory model as their own. Hoisting the banner of accountability, they set out to prove that the schools could deliver scores for bucks. Citizens who had never paid attention to standardized testing had a bewildering array of nationally normed tests paraded before them: Stanford Achievement, Metropolitian Achievement, California Achievement, Comprehensive Basic Skills, Iowa Basic Skills. Without fully grasping the magnitude of the change, Americans were learning to think of the schools in a different way. Standardized test scores were becoming *the* measure of educational quality.[4]

By the mid-1970s, with the economy turning sour and a tax revolt brewing, it was obvious that the factory model was not providing the evidence that school officials needed to make public education look good. In most systems, scores on the national achievement tests were stagnant or declining. Then the media aggravated the situation by playing up the drop in scores. By the time the CEEB and the ETS issued a report on the causes of the SAT decline, the average composite score had fallen from 980 in 1963 to 899 in 1977. The composite would fall 9 more points before bottoming out at 890 in 1980 and 1981. "Why are SAT scores dropping?" people asked. But what they really wanted to know was "What's wrong with the schools?" By the late 1970s the two questions had become virtually synonymous.

What's Wrong with the Schools?

The CEEB report *On Further Examination: Report of the Advisory Panel on the Scholastic Aptitude Test Score Decline* (1977) contained several major conclusions, only one of which Americans wanted to hear. According to the report, there were actually *two* declines, one before 1970 and one after. Moreover, the declines had different causes. The major cause of the initial decline was a change in the pool of test takers. From 1963 to 1970, more students began taking the SAT—in particular, more poor and minority students who in earlier years would have been unable to attend college. Higher education opened its doors to these students, and the federal government showed the way by providing financial assistance. Thus the initial decline was not a sign that the schools were in trouble. Americans paid little attention to this conclusion, however. People still cite the "unbroken seventeen-year decline in SAT scores" as evidence that something went wrong in the schools in the sixties, something that did not go right again until the eighties.[5]

Americans have also ignored repeated warnings from CEEB and ETS that college entrance exams are not valid indicators of the nation's "Gross Educational Product." More than a third of all graduating seniors take neither the SAT nor its rival, the ACT. College entrance exam scores tell us nothing about this forgotten third, nor do they provide information on the one-fourth of all 18-year-olds who drop out of school before graduation. In addition, CEEB and ETS say that the SAT is an *aptitude test* that measures the potential for further academic work, not an *achievement test* that measures how much students have learned. Finally, CEEB and ETS caution against using college entrance exam scores to compare the states—as the U.S. Department of Education does with its wall chart—since the number and the socioeconomic background of the test takers vary so widely from state to state.[6]

What people do remember about *On Further Examination* is the conclusion that fit the conventional wisdom: one cause of the decline after 1970 was a "lowering of educational standards" in the schools. According to the report, teachers and administrators had responded to changing times and changing students by making concessions. Teachers and administrators were condoning high rates of student absenteeism. They were practicing grade inflation and social promotion. They were demanding less homework. They were allowing students to take the easy way out, and many students were doing just that: choosing the easiest courses and avoiding critical reading and careful writing. To be sure, the report also pointed the finger of blame at society—at one-parent homes, television, social and political turmoil, and poorly motivated students—but what the media played up in the report, and what Americans remember, is that the schools had lowered their standards.[7]

On Further Examination carefully avoided making teachers the lone villains of the drama. The media and the general public were not so careful. In the late

1970s and early 1980s, the nation declared open season on teachers, engaging in round after round of what the British call "teacher bashing." The assorted charges leveled against teachers were not so much false as misleading. For example, the charge that teachers are to blame for poor student writing skills is accurate enough to graze the target, but it is nevertheless a cheap shot. It is devoid of context; it ignores the social, political, and institutional influences on teaching and learning. How much writing do students do on their own, outside of school? Have the school board and the central office given teachers a decent writing curriculum to work with? And what about teaching load? As Theodore Sizer would later ask in *Horace's Compromise* (1984), how often can a high school teacher take home a stack of 120 to 175 compositions and do them justice? Factors like these limit what teachers can accomplish. In the era before Sizer, John Goodlad, Ernest Boyer, and others came to the defense of teachers, however, teacher bashers rarely pointed out such constraints. Quite the contrary, the message the public heard was that teachers had too few constraints. Given their weak intellectual ability, teachers had more autonomy than they deserved.[8]

Thus a major goal of the back-to-basics movement of the late 1970s and early 1980s was telling teachers what and how to teach, then testing their students repeatedly to insure that teachers had followed orders. In Chapter 7 I described the basics movement as a potent combination of essentialism and behaviorism. The desire to cut education down to the essentials led to an emphasis on reading, writing, and arithmetic at the elementary level and on English, social studies, science, and math at the secondary level. Using the tools of behavioral psychology, curriculum specialists reduced each of the 3Rs to a set of skills, and the other subjects to a collection of skills and facts. Because back to basics originated as a grass roots movement, it varied somewhat from one district to another, but within each district the goal was standardization: getting a uniform curriculum into place. Supervisors distributed curriculum guides that told teachers, in far more detail than ever before, what to teach and how to teach it. Standardized tests held teachers and students to the prescribed curriculum. The result, according to curriculum theorist Michael Apple, was the "deskilling" of the teaching force.[9]

To appreciate the significance of this change, consider the example of arithmetic. There are many skills involved in arithmetic and many methods of teaching children to add, subtract, multiply, and divide. Before the back-to-basics movement, teachers in most school systems had considerable freedom to decide which skills to emphasize and which methods to use. Teachers were able to vary their approach, in other words, based on their judgment and expertise. Anarchy? Not at all. Autonomy. Within certain limits, teachers had individual autonomy; they could help students as they thought best. Their individual autonomy within the classroom enabled teachers to stake their tenuous claim to professionalism—or more accurately, semiprofessionalism.

The Measurement-driven Curriculum

Central offices have distributed curriculum guides for years, of course, and teachers have generally ignored them. Remember the old saying among teachers: "When I close the classroom door, I'm in charge." Since the back-to-basics era, however, teachers have had to pay more attention to curriculum guides because standardized tests can now check up on teachers by checking on their students. To the degree that a local system's curriculum reflects the content of standardized tests, teachers feel pressure to teach by the cookbook. The *measurement-driven curriculum*—a curriculum in which tests shape teaching rather than the other way around—enables people outside the classroom to reach in and control instruction. I am not trying to make the process sound sinister. The advocates of measurement-driven instruction claim that external control can be quite positive, a "catalyst to improve instruction." The evidence they cite is higher scores on standardized tests—on the tests for which teachers directly rehearse their students, that is.[10]

Teachers have become especially adept at rehearsing students for minimum competency tests, a new breed of standardized tests developed during the back-to-basics era. These tests give school officials a way to monitor the work of teachers in every academic subject. Some minimum competency tests are system-wide final exams administered at the end of a semester or year; they determine a certain percentage of a student's grade in a course. Other minimum competency tests are checkpoint exams used to help decide whether a student should be promoted from one grade to the next. Still others are high school graduation exams covering a variety of basic skills that students will presumably need to survive in society. Developed first at the local level, minimum competency tests became a popular state reform in the years just before *A Nation at Risk*. Before the states took command of the excellence movement, they increased the momentum of back-to-basics by jumping on the minimum competency testing bandwagon.[11]

As we enter the 1990s, more than 40 states require some form of minimum competency testing, and many local systems have developed their own tests. For all their popularity with school officials, however, minimum competency tests have come under sharp attack since they first appeared. Even the essentialist *A Nation at Risk* brushed them aside with the comment that they "fall short of what is needed, as the 'minimum' tends to become the 'maximum,' thus lowering educational standards for all."[12] As we saw in Chapter 7, minimum competency tests stress lower-level rather than higher-level skills, which encourages teachers to emphasize rote learning rather than critical thinking. Yet minimum competency testing has weathered the storm. It is now more popular than ever.

Beyond its value to school officials as a classroom monitor, minimum competency testing is a powerful political tool. When school officials were desperately seeking test scores—any test scores—that were rising rather than falling, they hit on minimum competency tests. Soon a newsworthy pattern appeared in system after system and state after state. As students and teachers got the knack of the tests, scores rose steadily and impressively. Within two or three years, passing rates climbed well above 90 percent and stayed there. Minimum competency tests are still with us because they bring the public good news. The schools are doing a better job, they announce. Almost everyone's child is minimally competent.[13]

The other side of the coin is that some children do not pass the tests. An analysis of minimum competency tests used as high school graduation examinations shows that the students who fail are disproportionately poor, minority, and handicapped—the "at-risk." Almost without exception, teachers and administrators can identify these students before the tests are ever given. So why have the tests? Because they reassure the public that the schools have standards. They symbolize a get-tough mentality. They provide an educational box score that looks better than SAT scores.[14]

Today people can pick and choose from a variety of box scores, some of which make the schools look good and some bad. SAT scores, the old standard, rose to 906 in the mid-1980s but then stalled. ACT scores traced a similar pattern. The National Assessment of Educational Progress (NAEP), a battery of tests administered to a sample of 9- , 13- , and 17-year-olds at regular intervals since 1969, may be the box score to watch in the 1990s. The NAEP is expanding to cover more students and more subject areas, and for the first time, scores will be reported on a state-by-state basis. The new, improved NAEP may well become "the nation's report card ," or so a blue-ribbon panel headed by former Governor Lamar Alexander of Tennessee recommends. The most favorable NAEP trend of the past two decades is that poor and minority students have improved their scores, as they have on the SAT and ACT. For other students, scores on the NAEP have generally held steady or declined. The achievement trends among older students and brighter students are especially disappointing.[15]

The Children of Lake Wobegon

People who want to play up the good news, however, can brag about trends in the nationally normed achievement tests we discussed earlier. Or can they? John Cannell, a West Virginia physician, thought the news sounded a little too good when he heard that, in almost every local school system in his state, the scores of elementary students on the Comprehensive Test of Basic Skills were above the national norm. Since West Virginia, one of the nation's poorest states, ranks low on most other educational indicators, the doctor was surprised. Checking several neighboring states, he found that their students, too, were above average. With surprise turning to suspicion, in 1987 Cannell conducted a survey of achievement testing across the nation. He discovered that state superintendents in every state boast that their students are above average. In other words, scoring above the norm *is* the norm. In all 32 of the states with statewide testing programs, elementary students scored above average. In the 18 states with locally selected tests, elementary students in "the vast majority" of the districts scored above average. Across the nation, Cannell estimates that about 90 percent of the school districts and 70 percent of the elementary students are above the national norm.[16]

These happy results suggest that most Americans have moved to Lake Wobegon, Minnesota, Garrison Keillor's radio community where "the women are strong, the men are handsome, and all the children are above average." Statistically, of course, the results don't add up. It is impossible for 70 percent of the students and 90 percent of the districts to be above average. Friends for Education, a group started by Dr. Cannell, has filed consumer fraud complaints against the four major publishers of nationally normed achievement tests. The Lake Wobegon effect confirms what many teachers have been saying since the late 1970s: If the public wants higher scores, school officials will find a way to deliver them. "The main purpose of the tests is looking good," Cannell says.[17]

Curriculum Alignment

How does the Lake Wobegon effect work? Since national achievement tests are renormed only once every few years, school systems have a chance to align their curriculum with the tests. What "align" means is that central office personnel change the curriculum to conform to the content of the tests, and teachers put emphasis on material they know the tests will cover. While the norms stay fixed for several years, the scores rise. More and more students become above average. The news about the schools gets better and better.[18]

One of the most important curriculum debates of the 1990s will be over teaching the test. Are there ethical and unethical ways to teach a test? Most people agree that teaching specific items lifted right off the test is dishonest— "That's a form of cheating," one testing company representative flatly states— but some teachers do just that under pressure to raise scores. Is it ethical, though, to slant the entire curriculum toward the test to get better scores? Is it educationally sound? Students often take 10, 15, or more standardized tests every year, and teachers spend weeks prepping their classes to look good. "Skill-'n'-drill," teachers call it.[19]

It is helpful to look back on similar debates in the early days of the back-to-basics movement. Critics warned that standardized tests would soon dictate the content of the curriculum. No, defenders of the movement replied. Educators design the curriculum, and testing companies can devise tests to measure whatever educators want. Score one point for the critics. The critics also argued that there is more to any subject than any test can measure, but that given the pressure to raise scores, teachers would narrow their instruction to just the items on the test. Not to worry, said back-to-basics advocates. Good teachers already cover what the test covers, and bad teachers need to start somewhere. Score a point for both sides.[20]

As curriculum alignment increases, even excellent teachers are feeling the pressure to teach the test. Chris Pipho of the Education Commission of the States looks into the future of curriculum alignment:

> The advent of new, more powerful microcomputers now may be moving schools into yet another new era of accountability. . . . The selling point is higher test scores by aligning the instructional objectives with the goals and objectives of the state testing programs and other national normed tests. Test-item analyses and class, grade and school building status reports can be easily printed and instruction targeted to the weak areas. By cross-referencing objectives, teachers can locate the page in the textbook that can be used to help increase student test scores. . . . Principals and superintendents under the gun to look good on state test comparisons have in turn put teachers under the same kind of pressure.[21]

One superintendent whose system has aligned its curriculum to the tests says he is sold on the approach. His goal, cited by Chris Pipho, is to "be able to track every student on a day-to-day basis, objective-by-objective." The superintendent will be also able to track every teacher, in just the same way.

And so the discussion returns to teacher autonomy. In the late 1980s, teachers in St. Louis went to court to block an accountability plan that uses student scores on the California Achievement Test as part of a teacher evaluation plan. Holding teachers accountable for student test scores is unfair, the St. Louis Teachers Union objected, because the local curriculum is not adequately aligned with the national test. The school system responded by bringing student scores on local minimum competency tests into the evaluation plan. The entire curriculum is supposed to be aligned with these tests. If so, can the teachers still object to accountability? By asking for better alignment, St. Louis teachers may have cut their own throats on individual autonomy.[22]

Teachers in Philadelphia took a different approach. They could see the threat to their autonomy when the central office developed a standardized curriculum and a detailed pacing schedule for every subject and every grade, uniform standards for grading and promotion, and a complete set of well-aligned, standardized tests. The teachers protested. Pointing to the teacher empowerment goals of Holmes and Carnegie and citing the breakthrough union contracts in Rochester, New York, and Dade County, Florida, teachers called the Philadelphia plan a giant step backward.[23]

"There are teachers who don't operate professionally," one Philadelphia elementary teacher admitted. "But how do you improve the school system? From the very top on down, or is the best way to change to include the people responsible for delivering service—the teachers?"[24] The *Philadelphia Inquirer* reported that high school teachers were even more resentful; many of them were simply ignoring the plan. It remains to be seen, however, how much longer it will be possible for teachers to close their doors and teach as they see fit.

Although Philadelphia school officials have modified parts of the plan in response to teacher protests, many teachers are still unhappy. Curriculum alignment may end up in court in Philadelphia, too. The issues raised in Philadelphia and St. Louis will be debated in school systems around the nation as curriculum alignment—an enduring legacy of back to basics and testing, testing, testing—meets teacher autonomy head-on during the 1990s.[25]

ESSENTIALISM FOR THE 1990s

After the release of *A Nation at Risk* in 1983 talking about back to basics was out, but talking about the Five New Basics was very in. Four years of English, three years of mathematics, three years of science, three years of social studies, one-half year of computer science—the National Commission on Excellence in Education told Americans that these New Basics are essential for all high school students. The arts are also important, the commission stated, and college-bound students need at least one more basic, foreign languages.

A Nation at Risk gave essentialism a badly needed sense of direction. Back to basics was floundering. A grassroots movement by nature, it had lacked coherence from the start. The recommendations of the National Commission, however, handed the states a map they could use to chart the direction of school reform. Looking back on curriculum trends since 1983, essentialists are pleased with much of what they see. Most satisfying, perhaps, is the perception that virtually every state has moved its schools toward the New Basics. But when thoughtful essentialists look more carefully at what passes for excellence in education, they grow uneasy.

Getting the New Basics into Place

In *James Madison High School* (1987) and *James Madison Elementary School* (1988), William Bennett looked back on the 1980s and forward to the 1990s. Bennett personally wrote the reports, which we will examine as a well-conceived vision of essentialism. Obviously proud that state reformers have given a great deal of rhetorical support to the New Basics, he nevertheless cautioned fellow essentialists that "it is too soon to declare victory." Bennett said that despite the rush in the nation's statehouses to require more academic courses for high school graduation, as of 1987 only three states—Florida, Louisiana, and Pennsylvania—had mandated the complete set of New Basics for all students.[26]

English and social studies are not the problem. Most states now require four years of English and three years of social studies for high school graduation. The problem is raising requirements in science and math. Trying to prepare students for international economic competition, state reformers have focused much of their attention on these two subjects. Yet Bennett reports that the average public high school graduation requirement in science is 1.8 courses, only slightly more than the 1982 average of 1.5 and far short of the 3 courses recommended by *A Nation at Risk*. The trends in math are similar: an increase in the average graduation requirement from 1.6 to 1.9 courses, well below the recommend 3 courses. The average requirement in computer science barely registers on the scale: 0.1 courses. The states have moved toward the New Basics, to be sure, but as Bennett puts it, "much ground remains to be covered."[27]

Bennett is even more concerned that state school reformers have emphasized quantity over quality. As we saw in Chapter 9, excellence in education has often meant more of the same, especially for the least able students. One more year of worksheet science, another required course in skill-'n'-drill math—this is excellence? Mortimer Adler would say that the weakest students are still getting the dirty water. Bennett frankly acknowledges this problem and, as we will see in a moment, proposes some solutions.

Going to School with James Madison

The two James Madison reports provide a model essentialist curriculum. Every student at Madison High takes a four-year sequence in English: Introduction to Literature, American Literature, British Literature, and Introduction to World Literature. In social studies, all the students take Western Civilization, American History, and American Democracy. For their three years of math, students can select from Algebra I, Plane and Solid Geometry, Algebra II and Trigonometry, Statistics and Precalculus, and Calculus. The science curriculum requires students to choose three courses from Astronomy/Geology, Biology, Chemistry, and Physics, or Principles of Technology. James Madison puts less emphasis than the National Commission on Excellence in Education on computer science, subsuming it in the rest of the curriculum. This change reflects the trend toward making microcomputers a "transparent" part of the curriculum, just as textbooks and blackboards are transparent to students.[28] Madison puts more emphasis than the National Commission, however, on foreign languages. All students—not just the college bound—spend two years studying a foreign language. All students must also take two years of Physical Education/Health and one year of fine arts.

In each area of the curriculum, *James Madison High School* offers examples of challenging content. The recommendations for English and the social studies are especially rigorous. In British literature the selections include Chaucer, Shakespeare, Milton, Keats, Conrad, and Shaw. The world literature course for seniors features "a careful selection of European and non-Western" works, with the accent on Europe. In the American democracy course, the curriculum for the first semester involves democratic principles, spanning "the intellectual roots of the American Revolution and Declaration of Independence" and Martin Luther King, Jr.'s, "Letter from Birmingham Jail." During the second semester, students compare "American democracy and its rivals in the 20th century."[29] The curriculum for math, science, foreign language, and other subjects is just as demanding.

As we might expect, the curriculum at James Madison Elementary School is a downward extension of the high school curriculum. Consider the recommendations for English. Children should learn to read with literary classics, not the "Dick and Jane"-type stories that fill basal readers. Kindergartners at Madison Elementary start with fables, fairy tales, and nursery rhymes. As students move through the grades, they meet such authors as Hans Christian Andersen, Rudyard Kipling, and C. S. Lewis. By the eighth grade, they are reading William Shakespeare, Stephen Crane, and John Steinbeck. In many of today's elementary schools, by contrast, students learn to read from textbooks and workbooks that isolate skills from content—and the content itself is vapid. No wonder reading becomes a chore! In every subject and every grade, the curriculum at James Madison Elementary is designed to be academically challenging.

The Madison Curriculum and Its Critics

To the essentialist charge that the states have been slow to require more courses in science and math, the critics respond "of course." Of course the progress has been slow. There is a severe teacher shortage in science and math, they point out, and the federal government has done little to alleviate it beyond encouraging the school systems to hire almost anybody who has a bachelor's degree in science or math. Where is the kind of financial help that the federal government provided through the NDEA of 1958? Education officials in the Reagan and Bush administrations have replied that state and local school systems must solve such problems for themselves.

Critics also attack the James Madison curriculum as too Anglo-European. It does not give sufficient attention to non-Western cultures, they contend. Essentialists rise to defend the West, of course, but they also claim that other cultures receive more attention in the James Madison curriculum than they do in the curriculum of most schools.

Thoughtful essentialists seem to take the greatest pleasure in responding to the complaint that academic rigor just isn't for everybody. William Bennett paraphrases this criticism as "Some kids can't. Their color, class, or background will get in the way."[30] Yes they can, he fires back. He refers to another U.S. Department of Education report, *Schools That Work: Educating Disadvantaged Children* (1987), which concludes that the adults who run the schools—not the students—bear most of the responsibility for poor achievement. This conclusion reflects the position, long popular with essentialists, that kids will achieve if adults insist on achievement. If adults don't, kids won't.

To support this position, essentialists often cite the *effective schools re-*

search that came into vogue during the late 1970s and early 1980s. Defining effective schools as those in which poor and minority students make high scores on standardized tests, researchers found that such schools tend to have the following characteristics: teachers with high standards; a principal with effective skills in instructional leadership; an orderly but not oppressive climate; a clear set of goals; strong emphasis on basic skills; a high percentage of time on task; frequent evaluation of student progress; and close ties between home and school. Effective schools research informed many of the Department of Education's publications during the Reagan years, and the research remains popular with education officials in the Bush administration.[31]

Most of the findings of effective schools research are common sense, and essentialists tout them as such. Teachers and parents can safely ignore the "dopey" educational ideas of the 1960s and 1970s, Bennett says. They should rely instead on common sense—on what works.[32] Critics find it hard to argue against orderly classrooms and high standards, but they do fault the heavy emphasis on standardized testing. They charge that defining educational success as high test scores is modern essentialism's fatal flaw. Thoughtful essentialists want elementary students to cut their teeth on the classics, but the classics receive scant attention on the California, Stanford, Iowa, Metropolitan, and other nationally normed achievement tests that essentialists advocate as quality control devices. These tests focus instead on the skills in basal readers and workbooks.

Bennett speaks out against skill-'n'-drill, but teachers have learned how to deliver test scores. The poor and minority students whom Bennett admirably defends are the very students most likely to be skilled and drilled. As we enter the 1990s, measurement-driven instruction is pushing the curriculum away from the James Madison model, not toward it. The Madison curriculum with its rich content is out of alignment with existing standardized tests. When thoughtful essentialists look at today's schools, they are quite properly concerned with the gap between essentialism as it is and essentialism as it might be.

THE GREAT LITERACY DEBATE

Several books and reports that appeared in the late 1980s have stepped up the debate over what Americans need to know, why they don't know enough of it, and how to reform the school curriculum to help improve the situation. At the heart of this debate is the concept of literacy. Unfortunately, people often toss the concept around without bothering to define it. *Basic literacy* is the ability to read and write a simple message. By that standard, between 85 and 99.5 percent of adult Americans are literate. Estimates of about 95 percent appear to be the most accurate. Then there is *functional literacy*, the ability to read and write well enough to perform adequately in daily life. Because functional literacy is a highly subjective concept, estimates of the functional literacy of adult Americans vary widely, from a high of about 85 percent to an astonishing low of less than 50 percent. The media have focused a great deal of attention on Jonathan Kozol's *Illiterate America* (1985) and other alarmist studies that depict a nation hobbled by a massive, increasing illiteracy problem. According to Kozol, more than half the adult population will be functionally illiterate during the 1990s.[33]

Toward a More Sophisticated View of Literacy

When we consider that 25 percent of the nation's students drop out of school before high school graduation, perhaps even the gloomiest estimates of literacy should not shock us. Still, it is hard to believe that one out of every two adults lacks the literacy skills necessary to cope with life. *Literacy: Profiles of America's Young Adults*, a 1986 study conducted for the NAEP, dismisses alarmist estimates of rampant functional illiteracy as "scare figures." They may make good copy for the evening news, but they mislead the nation about the nature and extent of the problem. No, "people are not walking around bumping into walls because they can't read," the director of the NAEP study reassures us.[34]

The study suggests that Americans have an oversimplified view of literacy. It is not a single skill, something that people either have or lack. Literacy is a continuum of many skills. The ETS researchers who conducted the NAEP study identified three different kinds of literacy, each involving a number of skills: the *prose literacy* necessary for understanding and using information in narrative texts; the *document literacy* needed to understand and use graphic and tabular information; and *quantitative literacy,* the ability to do the arithmetic involved in balancing a checkbook, for example, or figuring a tip. For each kind of literacy, the researchers measured the performance of young adults on everyday tasks of varying difficulty.

The results are not surprising: the more complex the task, the poorer the performance. While almost 96 percent of young adults can locate a single item of information in a moderately long newspaper article, fewer than 9 percent can state the theme of a poem that uses an unfamiliar metaphor. More than 98 percent can find the expiration date on a driver's license, but only 10 to 30 percent can perform various tasks involving arrival and departure times on a bus schedule. While about 90 percent can add two figures on a bank deposit slip, fewer than 10 percent can use unit pricing to determine the best value at a grocery store.[35] America is not on the verge of collapse, to be sure, but "the question is whether people with only moderate literacy skills have the flexibility to shift into new environments." Faced with the changing demands of a technological society, the schools must stop "shooting for the bottom line," the president of ETS concludes. "We need to work for higher levels of performance than typically is accounted for in state minimum-competency standards."[36]

The Subtle Danger

The ETS president's little jab at one of the legacies of the back-to-basics movement foreshadowed more vicious sparring over the implications of the

NAEP study. *The Subtle Danger: Reflections on the Literacy Abilities of America's Young Adults* threw the first real punch. In *The Subtle Danger*, reading specialist Richard Venezky, educational historian Carl Kaestle, and labor economist Andrew Sum analyze the NAEP data and elaborate on the threat that minimum-competency literacy poses to the nation. Like the NAEP study, *The Subtle Danger* calls special attention to the lagging literacy skills of blacks, Hispanics, and poor people generally. Noting the strong relationship between the literacy of young adults and the educational backgrounds of their parents, the authors contend that the nation cannot afford to let illiteracy run in families. As minorities and the poor become a larger part of the school population and the labor force during the 1990s, "the costs to the economy, to the national defense, and to the attainment of economic and social-justice goals for our nation's race/ethnic groups could be high."[37]

The authors of *The Subtle Danger* contend that the schools take too narrow a view of literacy. They argue that "what is taught currently does not transfer well to everyday literacy demands." The reading curriculum, for example, focuses mainly on prose literacy, and within that area on stories and poems. The prose skills appropriate for literature are important, but they are by no means the only reading skills that people use outside of school. Thus the authors recommend that "in addition to the skills for understanding and enjoying fiction and poetry, [the schools] should emphasize those skills and strategies that underlie the processing of expository prose and non-continuous documents like bureaucratic forms."[38] Teachers should give students direct instruction in how to summarize technical articles and use tax tables, for example.

Families, schools, workplaces, and the media all have a role to play in improving literacy, the authors conclude, and in their recommendations for the schools they throw down the gauntlet to "cultural tradition" essentialists:

> Our emphasis on literacy skills for the K-12 curriculum is in contrast with those who have recently reasserted the importance of a cultural tradition in the teaching of literacy skills. Some believe that the schools lost their commitment to the traditional Western literacy core in the 1960s, in favor of content-free, value-neutral training. We are not sure to what extent this, in fact, occurred. In any case, our view is that the literacy skills students sorely lack—skills of logic, inference, and synthesis—have never been stressed in the schools and yet are imperative for autonomous, effective adult life.[39]

Chester Finn, assistant secretary of education in the Reagan administration, came out of the essentialist corner to take up the gauntlet. Finn, whom we met in Chapter 7, launched his attack in words that capture the spirit of the long-standing debate between essentialists and progressives. In a letter published in *Education Week*, Finn accused the authors of *A Subtle Danger* of grinding an axe against literature. Do they think literature is elitist, he asked rhetorically? They must, because they want students—at least certain students—to study "tables, graphs, and labels" instead of *My Antonia, 1984,* and *Wuthering ights.* Do the authors support tracking? They must, or perhaps they want to go even further and, "in a fit of totally misguided egalitarianism, . . . purge *everybody's* curriculum of literature." Finn concluded that the report reflects the thinking of "about two decades ago," when "a similar push for 'relevance' in the curriculum . . . helped shove American education down the slippery slope of mediocrity."[40]

Great literature is not the issue, Venezky, Kaestle, and Sum wrote back. Literacy is. The fallacy in Finn's argument is assuming that the reading curriculum must consist of *either* great literature *or* expository prose and documents, they stated, when actually it should consist of both. Rejecting tracking, the three authors reaffirmed their commitment to exposing all students to great literature. But great literature is not enough. "For the millions who read below the 4th-grade level, assignments on the relentless malice of Poseidon or the disinheriting of Cornelia will provide neither increased ability nor, unfortunately, any meaningful appreciation of our cultural heritage."[41]

Cultural Literacy

This exchange of sharply worded letters in *Education Week,* a newspaper with a specialized readership, set the stage for a debate on literacy before a much wider audience, a debate that continues as we enter the 1990s. A well-matched pair of essentialist treatises published in 1987 set the tone of the debate: *Cultural Literacy: What Every American Needs to Know* by E. D. Hirsch, Jr., and *What Do Our 17-Year-Olds Know? A Report on the First National Assessment of History and Literature* by Diane Ravitch and Chester Finn. The year 1987 also marked the appearance of Allan Bloom's *The Closing of the American Mind,* a perennialist critique of higher education. William Bennett drew heavily on these three books in his curriculum for the James Madison schools, and the books by Hirsch and Bloom were on the best-seller lists for weeks—a testimony to the continuing popularity of traditional theories of education.[42]

Taken together, these works advance the position that some knowledge is so valuable that all Americans should possess it. There is indeed a common culture, and the schools are obligated to transmit it. The spotlight in the literacy debate is now on *cultural literacy,* which its advocates define as familiarity with the knowledge that educated people share. The newsworthy part of the debate, of course, is the essentialist and perennialist claim that the schools are doing a woefully poor job of exposing students to the common culture. When Hirsch, Ravitch, Finn, and Bloom say that the schools are graduating one class after another of cultural illiterates, journalists stop to listen. Conservative newspaper columnists have had a field day criticizing the curriculum. James J. Kilpatrick has observed with characteristic bluntness that "The typical 11th-grader, culturally speaking, is an ignoramus." William F. Buckley, perhaps with tongue in cheek, has proposed to solve the problem by requiring students to pass "a common information IQ test" in order to get a driver's license.[43]

Such a test, says Buckley, could be based on the list of nearly 5,000 items that "every American needs to know" in the back of Hirsch's book *Cultural Literacy*. Drawn up by Hirsch and his associates, the now-famous list is an attempt to define a cultural knowledge base for the nation and its schools. As a prospective teacher, you should read the list—and the entire book—for yourself. There are many obvious choices on the list: Shakespeare, nuclear energy, California. There are also some curious choices: Fanny Farmer, eminence grise, Marianas Trench. Trying to validate the list, Hirsch sent a multiple-choice test based on some of the items to 600 lawyers, "on the assumption that lawyers are literate." Those who returned the test correctly identified an average of 92 out of 100 items. Since cultural literacy is, by definition, familiarity with the knowledge that educated people share, Hirsch pronounced his list valid. Then, presumably, he awarded a framed certificate of commendation to every lawyer who scored 92 or above.[44]

My last sentence reflects the more lighthearted criticism directed toward *Cultural Literacy*. Including the list in the book was a brilliant stroke of marketing—it made large numbers of people buy the book—but it may have been an intellectual blunder. The list makes for great cocktail party conversation, and that is part of the problem. The message of the book gets lost in the critics' jokes about the list. Veteran teacher Susan Ohanian, a frequent contributor to the popular education press, has called it a "loony list." Why does it include Babe Ruth and Ty Cobb but not Lou Gehrig or Hank Aaron, she wants to know? Why Gilbert and Sullivan but not Rogers and Hammerstein? Why the "Rime of the Ancient Mariner" but not *Moby Dick*? Why the trombone but not the tuba?[45]

The list is arbitrary, not in the sense of capricious or whimsical (check your dictionary), but in the sense of discretionary and perhaps even dictatorial. Although Hirsch regards the list as "provisional" and not "definitive," he titles the list "What Literate Americans Know." These 5,000 items are among the things that my educated colleagues and I know, he says, and look—some lawyers agree with us. Trying hard not to sound smug, Hirsch includes with every book a card that readers can return to suggest items for addition or deletion. By his very tone, however, Hirsch sets the list up for a fall. And by its very nature, the list turns cultural literacy into a game of Trivial Pursuit.[46]

Hirsch makes a stronger case for cultural literacy in the body of the book. "Facts and skills are inseparable," he says. Unless children become familiar with the traditional background information of literate culture, they will never be able to move from lower-level to higher-level academic skills. Content is not neutral. Only a curriculum that teaches reading skills in the context of literate culture can prepare young children to make sense of ever more complex reading. According to Hirsch, the content of worthwhile, significant reading *is* literate culture. The significant reading materials with which Americans can whet their minds are not stories about Dick and Jane and their successors; they are about Ulysses and the Cyclops, George Washington and Abraham Lincoln—

and approximately 4,996 other subjects. Unless students acquire this stock of factual information, all the "decoding skills" in the world can take them only so far.[47]

Until the 1940s, Hirsch argues, the schools supplied literate culture to students from all socioeconomic backgrounds. Then, under the influence of John Dewey, Wiliam Heard Kilpatrick, and other progressive educators, teachers and administrators overthrew the traditional, fact-based curriculum for a curriculum based on broad understandings and general skills. The new curriculum, harmful to all students, has been disastrous to students from "illiterate homes." Acquiring cultural literacy neither at home nor at school, these students have suffered most from the curriculum revolution. Children from "literate homes" suffered less in the early stages of the revolution, but as these more fortunate students grew up and *their* children went to school and studied the new curriculum, the decline in literacy from one generation to the next became noticeable. By the 1960s and 1970s the decline had become so obvious that the nation could no longer ignore it.[48]

Diane Ravitch and Chester Finn tell much the same story in *What Do Our 17-Year-Olds Know?* The schools got off the track when they shirked their responsibility for transmitting a common culture, and now the nation is suffering the consequences. To find out what 17-year-olds do know, Ravitch and Finn analyzed the first NAEP assessment of history and literature, a set of tests that high school juniors took in 1986. In both history and literature, the students answered only a few more than half of the multiple-choice questions correctly. The media were fascinated. Reporters told the nation that one-third of the students could not place Columbus's discovery of America or the signing of the Declaration of Independence within the correct half century. Two-thirds could not do the same for the Civil War. Half the students were unable to identify the theme of "Julius Caesar" or "Macbeth." Two-thirds could not say what *1984* is about—even though the test was administered in 1986. And so the results went.[49]

Like Hirsch, Ravitch and Finn recommend returning to a curriculum that gives every student in every grade a heavy dose of literate culture. "What is needed?" Ravitch and Finn ask. "In a word, more. More knowledge, more teaching, more study, more learning—more history, more geography, and more literature at all grade levels."[50]

As the 1990s begin, essentialists are staking out the high ground, presenting themselves as socially concerned advocates who want students from all backgrounds to have the very best curriculum the schools can offer. "Conservative curricular content is socially progressive," Hirsch claims.[51] Ravitch and Finn second the point, arguing that cultural literacy is essential for all students, not just those in honors classes. "We cannot settle for an education system that imparts 'passable' amounts of important knowledge to its more fortunate students while the majority learn less than the minimum required for successful participation in the society they are about to enter."[52]

The Critics Respond

As the debate over cultural literacy unfolds, critics of essentialism are trying to be careful about how they make their rebuttals. Most critics begin by saying that they too are against tracking, that they too want the best curriculum for all. Then they argue that the essentialists have misread both the past and the present. There never was a Golden Age of cultural literacy, the critics state; there never was an era when the schools pushed all students to high levels of achievement.[53]

There *was* an era when only a small group of students entered high school and an even smaller group exited with a diploma. In 1900, just 10 percent of the eligible age group went to high school and only 6 percent graduated. In 1920, 31 percent started and 17 percent finished, and in 1940 the percentages were 73 and 51. These statistics are for all 14- to 17-year-olds—the attendance and graduation rates of poor and minority students were much lower. Throughout these years, moreover, complaints abounded that even those students fortunate enough to get through high school were not acquiring literate culture.[54] Does this sound like the Golden Age Hirsch pines for, an age in which literacy was "effectively taught to disadvantaged children under a largely traditional curriculum"?[55] Surely this is not the era that essentialists want to recreate in the 1990s.

The critics, whether they style themselves progressives or not, also say it is time to stop flogging the ghost of John Dewey. Essentialism dominated American education from the mid-fifties through the mid-sixties, and since the mid-seventies it has been dominant again. Where *are* all the disciples of Dewey and Kilpatrick in today's schools, anyway? The critics' point is that essentialists must now accept the blame as well as the credit for a complete "generation" of students, the ones who entered kindergarten in the late 1970s and early 1980s and are graduating from high school today.

These students are not the children of general skills, broad understandings, and learning by doing; they are the progeny of back to basics, excellence, and testing, testing, testing. These are the students whose knowledge of history and literature is shocking; these are the ones whose SAT scores are stagnant as we enter the 1990s. Don't blame Dewey, the critics say. Blame, most charitably, the gap between essentialism as it is and essentialism as it might be. If the essentialists want to hold Dewey and his disciples responsible for the distortions of progressivism in the schools, then the essentialists must accept the responsibility for the distortions of their theory.

Ravitch, Finn, and Hirsch are no fans of multiple-choice testing, but they must realize that their fact-based curriculum is a perfect match for measurement-driven instruction. When they call for "more," what the students get is more of the same. Officers of the National Council of Teachers of English and the National Council for the Social Studies fear that the recommendations of Ravitch, Finn, and Hirsch—despite their good intentions—will only produce more emphasis on standardized testing and more pressure to teach the test. With the NAEP on its way to becoming the nation's report card, a new era of curriculum alignment may lie ahead. It does not reassure teachers when Finn responds to their concerns about teaching the test with "That's a problem I'd like to see us encounter before we dismiss it."[56]

And thus this chapter on the curriculum comes full circle. It ends as it began, on a note of concern for teacher autonomy. The conflict between the mandated, monitored curriculum and the freedom to teach is one of the most pressing educational issues for the 1990s.

ACTIVITIES

1. Interview teachers who have been teaching for at least 20 years on how the curriculum has changed while they have been in the classroom. Ask for their views on standardized testing, teacher autonomy, literacy, and other issues discussed in this chapter.
2. Talk with a public school system's curriculum specialist about the James Madison curriculum. Find out whether or not any students in the system already have such a curriculum, then ask how—and why—the curriculum for other students differs.
3. Invite professors who hold opposing views on literacy, especially cultural literacy, to have a debate or panel discussion in your class.

SUGGESTED READINGS

Cultural Literacy, the best seller by E. D. Hirsch, Jr., (see note 42) is an important, enjoyable book. Less well known but just as important and enjoyable is *The Subtle Danger* by Venezky, Kaestle, and Sum (see note 37). These two works offer sharply different visions of the curriculum. For still other points of view on the curriculum, select from the books we discussed in the sections on perennialism and progressivism in Chapter 7, or see *Critical Issues in Curriculum* and *Cultural Literacy and the Idea of General Education,* parts I and II of *The Eighty-Seventh Yearbook of the National Society for the Study of Education* (note 53).

NOTES

1. George H. Hanford, "Some Caveats on Comparing S.A.T. Scores," *Education Week* (October 8, 1986), p. 20.
2. James S. Coleman, Ernest Q. Campbell, Carol J. Hobson, James McPartland, Alexander M. Mood, Frederic D. Weinfeld, and Robert L. York, *Equality of Educational Opportunity* (Washington: U.S. Government Printing Office, 1966).
3. For a history of educational testing, see Clinton I. Chase, "How We Got Where We Are," ch. 2 of *Measurement for Educational Evaluation* (Reading, MA: Addison-Wesley, 1978).

4. See George F. Madaus, "Test Scores as Administrative Mechanisms in Educational Policy," *Phi Delta Kappan* 66 (May 1985): 611–617.

5. *On Further Examination: Report of the Advisory Panel on the Scholastic Aptitude Test Score Decline* (New York: College Entrance Examination Board, 1977), part 3. For more analysis of changes in the pool of test takers, see Harold Howe II, "Let's Have Another SAT Score Decline," *Phi Delta Kappan* 66 (May 1985): 599–602.

6. See note 5 and Hanford, "Some Caveats," p. 20.

7. College Entrance Examination Boards, *On Further Examination*, part 4. The quotation is from p. 31. For a critical discussion of the report, see Ira Shor, *Culture Wars: School and Society in the Conservative Restoration, 1969–1984* (Boston: Routledge & Kegan Paul, 1986), ch. 3.

8. Theodore R. Sizer, *Horace's Compromise: The Dilemma of the American High School* (Boston: Houghton Mifflin, 1984), prologue. I discuss teacher bashing in Chapter 3 of this text, in the section titled "Rediscovering Teacher Incompetency."

9. Michael W. Apple, *Education and Power* (Boston: Routledge and Kegan Paul, 1982).

10. W. James Popham, Keith L. Cruse, Stuart C. Rankin, Paul D. Sandifer, and Paul L. Williams, "Measurement-Driven Instruction: It's on the Road," *Phi Delta Kappan* 66 (May 1985): 628–634. For a pointed debate on these issues, see Popham, "The Merits of Measurement-Driven Instruction," and Gerald W. Bracey, "Measurement-Driven Instruction: Catchy Phrase, Dangerous Practice," *Phi Delta Kappan* 68 (May 1987): 679–682 and 683–686, respectively.

11. Richard M. Jaeger and Carol K. Tittle, eds., *Minimum Competency Achievement Testing: Motives, Models, Measures, and Consequences* (Berkeley, CA: McCutchan, 1980).

12. National Commission on Excellence in Education, *A Nation at Risk: The Imperative for Educational Reform* (Washington: U.S. Department of Education, 1983), p. 20.

13. Peter W. Airasian, "The Consequences of High School Graduation Testing Programs," *NASSP Bulletin* 71 (February 1987): 54–67; Madaus, "Test Scores as Administrative Mechanisms," 614–617; Laura Hersch Salganik, "Why Testing Reforms Are So Popular and How They Are Changing Education," *Phi Delta Kappan* 66 (May 1985): 607–610.

14. Airasian, "Consequences of High School Graduation Testing Programs," pp. 60–62.

15. Reagan Walker, "Bennett: Test Gains at 'Dead Stall,' " *Education Week* (March 2, 1988), p. 6; Lynn Olson, "Bennett Panel Urges Major Expansion of NAEP," *Education Week* (March 25, 1987), pp. 1, 8; Gregory R. Anrig, "Educational Standards, Testing, and Equity," *Phi Delta Kappan* 66 (May 1985): 623–628.

16. Robert Rothman, "Normed Tests Skewed to Find Most Pupils 'Above Average,' a Disputed Study Finds," *Education Week* (December 9, 1987), pp. 1, 14–15.

17. Ibid., p. 1.

18. Lynn Olson, "Districts Turn to Nonprofit Group for Help in 'Realigning' Curricula to Parallel Tests," *Education Week* (October 28, 1987), pp. 1, 19.

19. Robert Rothman, "E.D. Will Prepare 'Consumer Guide' on Standardized Tests," *Education Week* (February 17, 1988), p. 16.

20. For early debates on these and other issues, see Jaeger and Tittle, eds., *Minimum Competency Achievement Testing*.

21. Chris Pipho, "Curriculum Alignment—The Latest Accountability Model," *Education Week* (October 28, 1987), p. 26.

22. Blake Rodman, "Rating Teachers on Students' Test Scores Sparks Furor, Legal Action in St. Louis," *Education Week* (September 17, 1986), pp. 1, 18; Robert Rothman, "Using Pupil Scores to Assess Teachers Criticized as Unfair," *Education Week* (June 3, 1987), pp. 1, 18.

23. Robert Rothman, "Teachers v. Curriculum in Philadelphia?" *Education Week* (March 23, 1988), pp. 1, 20–22.

24. Ibid., p. 20.

25. For an excellent analysis of this clash, see Arthur E. Wise, "The Two Conflicting Trends in School Reform: Legislated Learning Revisited," *Phi Delta Kappan* 69 (January 1988): 328-333.

26. William J. Bennett, *James Madison High School: A Curriculum for American Students* (Washington: U.S. Department of Education, 1987), p. 2, and *James Madison Elementary School: A Curriculum for American Students* (Washington: U.S. Department of Education, 1988).

27. Bennett, *James Madison High School*, p. 2; U.S. Department of Education, National Center for Education Statistics, *The Condition of Education: Elementary and Secondary Education, 1988*, vol. 1 (Washington: U.S. Government Printing Office, 1988), pp. 66–67, 124.

28. For more information on trends in the use of microcomputers, see Thomas Plati, "Integrating Macintoshes throughout the Curriculum at Shrewsbury High School," *T.H.E. Journal* (Macintosh Special Issue, 1988): 46–48; Stanley Pogrow, "How to Use Computers to Truly Enhance Learning," *Electronic Learning* 7 (May/June 1988): 6, 8.

29. Bennett, *James Madison High School*, pp. 13, 19–20.

30. Bennett, *James Madison High School*, p. 6, and *Schools That Work: Educating Disadvantaged Children* (Washington: U.S. Department of Education, 1987).

31. See Michael Rutter, Barbara Maughan, Peter Mortimore, and Janet Ouston, *Fifteen Thousand Hours: Secondary Schools and Their Effects on Children* (Cambridge, MA: Harvard University Press, 1979); Wilbur B. Brookover, *Effective Secondary Schools* (Philadelphia: Research for Better Schools, 1981); Ronald R. Edmonds, "Programs of School Improvement: An Overview," *Educational Leadership* 40 (December 1982): 4–11.

32. James Hertling, "E.D. Report Stresses 'Common Sense,' " *Education Week* (March 12, 1986), pp. 10, 12; Leon Botstein, "Why 'What Works' Doesn't Work," *Education Week* (May 28, 1986) p. 21; August Franza, "Reagan's School Book: Does It Work?," *English Journal* 75 (September 1986): 20–22.

33. Robb Deigh, "Curse It, Count It, Cure It: The Arithmetic of Illiteracy," *Insight* (September 29, 1986): 10–14; Laurence D. Brown, "Four Books for Those Who Wish to Learn about Literacy," *Phi Delta Kappan* 67 (October 1985): 161–164; Jonathan Kozol, *Illiterate America* (Garden City, NY: Doubleday, 1985).

34. Irwin Kirsch and Ann Jungeblut, *Literacy: Profiles of America's Young Adults* (Princeton, NJ: National Assessment of Educational Progress, 1986). The quotations are from Lynn Olson's article "New Study Raises Concerns about Adult Literacy," *Education Week* (October 1, 1986), pp. 1, 16.

35. Kirsch and Jungeblut, *Literacy*, pp. 14–22.

36. Lynn Olson, "New Study Raises Concerns," pp. 1, 16.

37. Richard L. Venezky, Carl F. Kaestle, and Andrew M. Sum, *The Subtle Danger:*

Reflections on the Literacy Abilities of America's Young Adults (Princeton, NJ: Educational Testing Service, 1987), p. 33.
38. Ibid., pp. 7–8, 43.
39. Ibid, p. 43.
40. " 'None-Too-Subtle Danger' Lurking within New Report," *Education Week* (March 11, 1987), p. 23.
41. "No 'Veiled Attempt' to Reject Literature, Say Authors," *Education Week* (March 11, 1987), p. 24.
42. E. D. Hirsch, Jr., *Cultural Literacy: What Every American Needs to Know* (Boston: Houghton Mifflin, 1987); Diane Ravitch and Chester E. Finn, Jr., *What Do Our 17-Year-Olds Know? A Report on the First National Assessment of History and Literature* (New York: Harper & Row, 1987); Allan Bloom, *The Closing of the American Mind* (New York: Simon & Schuster, 1987).
43. James J. Kilpatrick, "11th-grade Ignoramuses," *Mobile Press-Register* (September 20, 1987); William F. Buckley, Jr., "A Real Driver's Test?" *Mobile Press* (June 10, 1987).
44. "Hirsch Defends Cultural Literacy List," *Education Week* (April 15, 1987), p. 9.
45. Susan Ohanian, "Finding a 'Loony List' While Searching for Literacy," *Education Week* (May 6, 1987), pp. 21–22.
46. Hirsch, *Cultural Literacy*, p. 146.
47. Ibid., ch. 5. The quotation is on p. 133.
48. Ibid., ch. 5. Hirsch elaborates on these views in "Restoring Cultural Literacy in the Early Grades," *Educational Leadership* 45 (December 1987/January 1988): 63–70.
49. Ravitch and Finn, *What Do Our 17-Year-Olds Know?* ch. 3.
50. Chester Finn and Diane Ravitch, "Survey Results: U.S. 17-Year-Olds Know Shockingly Little about History and Literature," *American School Board Journal* 174 (October 1987): 33.
51. E. D. Hirsch, "The Paradox of Traditional Literacy: Response to Tchudi," *Educational Leadership* 45 (December 1987/January 1988): 75.
52. Ravitch and Finn, *What Do Our 17-Year-Olds Know?* p. 252.
53. See, for example, William Ayers, " 'What Do Our 17-Year-Olds Know?': A Critique," *Education Week* (November 25, 1987), pp. 24, 18, and Stephen Tchudi, "Slogans Indeed: A Reply to Hirsch," *Educational Leadership* 45 (December 1987/January 1988): 72–74. A recent book that airs arguments on all sides of the debate is *Cultural Literacy and the Idea of a General Education*, part II of *The Eighty-Seventh Yearbook of the National Society for the Study of Education* (Chicago: NSSE, 1988).
54. U.S. Department of Education, Center for Education Statistics, *Digest of Education Statistics, 1985–86* (Washington: U.S. Government Printing Office, 1986), pp. 40, 69; Tchudi, "Slogans Indeed," pp. 72–73.
55. Hirsch, "Restoring Cultural Literacy in the Early Grades," p. 66.
56. Robert Rothman, "Teachers Dispute Studies' Counsel on Humanities," *Education Week* (September 16, 1987), p. 23.

CHAPTER 11

Private Schools versus Public Schools

One of the liveliest educational issues for the 1990s is the intensifying competition between private schools and public schools. Competition seems just the right word. Historically the advocates of both kinds of schools have been quick to argue the superiority of their particular brand of education. This chapter concludes *America's Teachers* with a look at the ongoing debate. First we will survey the three sectors of private elementary and secondary education—Roman Catholic schools, other religious schools, and independent schools—and examine a demographic profile of private schools and their students. Then we will focus on Catholic schools, the largest network of private schools in the United States, and fundamentalist Christian schools, the nation's second largest and fastest growing private schools. Catholic schools and fundamentalist schools, as different from each other as they are from public schools, illustrate the diversity of American private education. This chapter closes with a discussion of *tuition tax credits, vouchers,* and *government regulation* of private schools, highly controversial issues that are shaping the future of both private and public education.

Private schools offer alternatives to people dissatisfied with public schools. Although the distinction between public and private education was hazy until the middle of the nineteenth century—many church schools, for example, received public funds and were open to children of all faiths—the common school crusade drew a sharp line between *public* schools controlled by state and local school boards and *private* schools controlled by churches and individuals. Since then Americans have engaged in a running debate on the merits of private schools and public schools, with the arguments always spirited and at times bitter. Over the past few decades, as public education has struggled with more

276

than its share of problems, the debate has picked up enough momentum to sustain it well into the 1990s.[1]

THE THREE SECTORS OF PRIVATE ELEMENTARY AND SECONDARY EDUCATION

As we saw in Chapter 6, Roman Catholics built this nation's largest system of private schools on their religious objections to common schools. The religious emphasis in Catholic education continues, but Catholics are now calling more attention than ever to the intellectual quality of their schools, touting them as academic alternatives to public schools. Despite losses in enrollment since the mid-1960s, Catholic schools remain by far the largest sector of private education.

Other religious schools constitute the second largest sector of private education. Throughout American history people of many faiths have felt the need to give their children an education grounded in specific religious doctrine. Fundamentalist Protestants, the most prominent recent example, opened the fastest growing private schools of the 1970s and 1980s, complaining that the values they stress at home and in church clash with the values that dominate public education. Schools sponsored by Lutherans, Jews, and other religious groups offer still other alternatives to public education.

Independent schools with no religious affiliation, the third and smallest sector of private education, meet the needs of Americans seeking academic and social alternatives to public education—people ranging from those who feel that their children are languishing academically in public schools to those who want their children to be educated with other students from a similar socioeconomic background. Independent schools are also growing as we enter the 1990s.

Roman Catholic schools, other religious schools, and independent schools keep the public-versus-private-school debate alive. Zealous debaters often get carried away with their arguments and appeal more to the emotions than the intellect, for it is difficult to compare public schools and private schools objectively. Both kinds of schools are so diverse that we should be wary of such sweeping statements as "Private schools are academically superior" or "Public schools offer better socialization." Beyond the value judgments imbedded in these claims (What constitutes academic quality? What kinds of socialization are desirable?) we must realize that a Catholic school in central city Chicago, for example, may be quite different from a Catholic school in the suburbs of Atlanta. Social class, race, ethnicity, and sex—the sociological factors whose influence on public education we examined in Chapter 8—also affect private education, although Catholics argue that their schools minimize the negative effects of these factors better than public schools. We would discover even more diversity if we compared almost any Catholic school with almost any fundamentalist Christian school, and including independent schools would heighten the contrast even more.

Public schools, of course, vary at least as much. A suburban school in the Silicon Valley of California, a county school in rural Mississippi, and a magnet school in New York City would probably strike us as more different than similar, and these are only three of several hundred thousand public schools. In some communities virtually all students attend public schools, while in other communities public schools have become just what the common school reformers of the nineteenth century feared: schools that serve only the children of the poor. Thus we must take into account an incredible variety of schools when we generalize about public and private education.

A PROFILE OF PRIVATE SCHOOLS
AND THEIR STUDENTS

With these words of caution in mind, we can learn a great deal from a demographic profile of private education. Throughout the twentieth century, private schools have enrolled between 7 percent and 14 percent of the nation's elementary and secondary school students. As the 1990s begin, 11 percent of all students attend private schools, almost exactly the same percentage as in 1970. Private school enrollment fell to just under 10 percent in the early 1970s, then inched upward again toward 11 percent during the 1980s. Public school advocates who talk about large numbers of students returning from private schools need to recheck their arithmetic, but so do private school supporters who speak of a mass exodus from public education. Still, during the 1980s the trend in enrollment was toward private schools, a trend that private schoolers hope will continue.[2]

The diversity we discussed above helps explain why people have such different perceptions of whether private school enrollment is increasing or decreasing. During the 1980s private schools lost students in central cities, where private education has traditionally been strongest, but gained students in suburbs and nonmetropolitan areas. These patterns reflected major changes in the makeup of the private school population. Roman Catholic schools, which could claim almost 90 percent of private school enrollment in the mid-1960s and about two-thirds as late as 1980, now enroll 56 percent of private school students. The closing of Catholic schools that had served their urban parishes for long years is a highly visible reminder of the declining popularity of Catholic education. Many of the Irish, German, Italian, Polish, and other white ethnic families who have historically been the backbone of Catholic schools have moved to the suburbs, and they no longer seem as committed to Catholic education.[3]

Other religious schools, by contrast, now enroll 25 percent of all private school students, up from 21 percent in 1980. The growth of these schools has been most dramatic in suburbs, small towns, and rural areas, with newly

founded fundamentalist Christian schools growing most rapidly. Reliable enrollment figures on Christian schools are hard to come by, for many of them resist
regulation and even inspection by outsiders. Moreover, they are under the control of different faiths—Baptist, Methodist, Church of Christ, Assembly of God,
and many others. Christian schools do not constitute a distict system, as Catholic schools do, but together the fundamentalist schools account for as many as
half of the students in non-Catholic religious schools, or about 13 percent of all
private school students. Lutheran, Jewish, Seventh-Day Adventist, Episcopal,
Calvinist, and other religious schools, generally older than the fundamentalist
schools, also grew during the 1980s, but at a more modest rate.[4]

Independent private education encompasses a variety of institutions, including elite boarding and day schools, military schools, "segregation academies,"
experimental and alternative schools, and schools for handicapped children. As a
group they enroll 19 percent of private school students, an increase over the 15
percent they accounted for in 1980, but their growth has not been uniform.
Enrollment in elite independent schools, most of which are members of the
National Association of Independent Schools, went up in the early 1980s, then
briefly down, then up again in the latter part of the decade. Only a small
number of military schools have managed to survive the downward spiral of
interest in military education that began in the 1960s. A few independent
schools whose openly avowed purpose is maintaining racial segregation still
exist, but even in the Black Belt counties of the rural South their popularity is
waning. The fastest growing independent schools are those offering special
curricula and teaching methods. Ranging from Montessori schools to special
education schools, they boast that they tailor academic programs precisely to
their students' needs.[5]

Who are the students who attend private schools? Many private educators
are eager to shatter the stereotype that they cater almost exclusively to wealthy
white children. They point out that more than 55 percent of all private school
students—including more than 40 percent of those in independent schools—
come from families with incomes below $35,000. One of every seven private
school students has a family income of less than $15,000. The largest sector of
private education, Roman Catholic, can claim the greatest socioeconomic diversity. Historically Catholic educators have welcomed children from all social
classes, adjusting tuition to match family income. The fastest growing sector of
private education, fundamentalist Christian, appeals primarily to lower-middle
and upper-working class families. To be sure, the median income of all public
school families is only about 70 percent of the median income of all private
school families, but "havens for the rich" is a label that fits only a few private
schools.[6]

Racially and ethnically, however, private schools are much less diverse than
public schools. White students are three times as likely as black students to
attend private schools. In fact, the percentage of private school students who are
black *decreased* during the 1980s from 8 percent to 6 percent. For private

schools overall, incomplete data suggest that enrollment rates are rising among Asian students and falling among Hispanics.[7]

Looking just at Catholic schools, however, we can see a clearer pattern; students from the ethnic groups that have traditionally dominated Catholic education are being replaced by Hispanic, black, and Asian students. These students, sometimes called the new urban poor, are now more than 20 percent of the enrollment in Catholic schools. More than half of the black students are non-Catholics whose families are looking for an academic alternative to public education. Yet consistent with the larger trends, black enrollment in Catholic schools showed a slight decrease during the 1980s, a phenomenon attributed by some observers to improving public schools and by others to hard economic times for black Americans. The changing racial and ethnic balance of Catholic schools is a major topic of discussion among Catholic educators, and it promises to add fuel to the private-versus-public-school debates of the 1990s.[8]

ROMAN CATHOLIC SCHOOLS

The Issue of Academic Achievement

The academic quality of Catholic schools versus public schools is certain to be another key issue in the debates. James Coleman, a sociologist of education at the University of Chicago, has focused national attention on the issue with his widely discussed studies of student achievement in public and private schools. In *Public and Private Schools* (1981) and *High School Achievement: Public, Catholic, and Private Schools Compared* (1982), Coleman and his research associates argued that the best high schools—those whose students have the highest levels of academic achievement—share a set of characteristics. Their students attend school more regularly, take more academic (as opposed to general and vocational) courses, and do more homework. High performance schools have a more disciplined and orderly climate. These findings, which should hardly seem startling by now, are consistent with the research on effective schools that we reviewed in the last chapter. What made Coleman's research so controversial was his insistence that private schools are more likely to have these characteristics than public schools and that, as a result, private schools are academically superior.[9]

This is just the kind of generalization that is sure to draw the fire of critics. Public school defenders charged that Coleman's conclusions went well beyond his data. Since few of the private schools in his study were non-Catholic religious schools or independent schools, the critics claimed that Coleman's findings were valid, at best, for comparing Catholic schools and public schools. But furthermore, the critics continued, Coleman had failed to control adequately for student socioeconomic background. They pointed out that private school parents tend to have higher incomes as well as higher levels of education, suggesting that such factors—which sociologists have found to correlate with student achievement—account for the higher achievement that Coleman had attributed to private schools. The critics called attention to other studies that showed no significant differences in achievement between private school students and public school students from the same socioeconomic background.[10]

During the 1980s these arguments seesawed back and forth. Coleman admitted that his conclusions about non-Catholic private schools were tentative, but he stuck to his guns on Catholic schools. Reanalysis of Coleman's data has highlighted the difficulties of generalizing about private and public schools. If a consensus is forming at all, it is around the position that while Catholic schools do not offer academic advantages to *every* student, they do to *some* students: in particular, blacks, Hispanics, and other students whose parents are likely to have lower incomes and less education.[11]

Because these are the very students who often receive what philosopher Mortimer Adler calls "dirty water" in public schools, they have the most to gain from attending a Catholic school. On the other hand, affluent white students—those who fit the private school stereotype—are the students most likely to receive "wine" (or at least "clean water") in public schools. These students have the least to gain from attending a Catholic school. The ongoing debate over Coleman's research is standing much of the conventional wisdom about public and private schools on its head.

His latest study, *Public and Private High Schools: The Impact of Communities* (1987), should provide more than enough grist for the debates of the 1990s. Reasserting most of his original claims, Coleman tries to reinforce them in several ways. He pays more attention to differences between Catholic schools and other private schools and includes more data on student socioeconomic background. He also examines *gains* in student achievement over a two-year period instead of measuring achievement at only one point, as he did in his earlier studies.[12]

Catholic educators are welcoming Coleman's new research, but other private schoolers are likely to find a mixture of good and bad news. Looking at verbal and mathematical skills, Coleman contends that students in Catholic high schools show higher gains in achievement than students of comparable socioeconomic status in public schools *and* most other private schools. The evidence on achievement gains in Catholic schools strengthens his earlier conclusion that the schools themselves, not just the socioeconomic background the students bring to the schools, play a major role in academic success. As before, Coleman claims that the academic benefits of a Catholic education are greatest for black, Hispanic, and poor students. He also points out that dropout rates in Catholic schools are much lower than in public schools and most other private schools.[13]

The qualifying "most other" is necessary because the elite independent schools in Coleman's study, such as Phillips Andover Academy, have exceptionally high academic achievement and very low dropout rates. Other non-Catholic private schools, however, are comparable to public schools in many respects, and in some cases the other non-Catholic private schools fare worse by comparison. Students in such schools have higher dropout rates and lower achievement gains in both science and math than comparable students in public schools.[14]

Functional Communities and Value Communities

In *Public and Private High Schools*, Coleman injects several new elements into the ongoing debate. He argues that a *functional community* surrounds most Catholic and other religious schools. Although the students in these schools may not live in the same neighborhood, their "families attend the same religious services and know one another."[15] The support of this community helps families pass their values from one generation to the next. Independent private schools and a few public schools are surrounded by a different kind of community, a *value community* composed of "people who share similar values about education and childrearing but who are not a functional community."[16] As the name suggests, this kind of community also aids in the intergenerational transmission of values. Most public schools, by contrast, are grounded in *no* community. Public schools once drew students from rural areas, small towns, and ethnic neighborhoods that constituted functional communities, but no longer. Today's public school attendance zones rarely correspond to either functional or value communities. Thus, according to Coleman, most public schools have lost their base of community support.

Human Capital and Social Capital

Coleman argues that of all schools, Catholic schools are the most effective at increasing *human capital*, which economists define as the skills and capabilities that make people productive. Some students come from families in which human capital is lacking—their parents may be poorly educated and unemployed. Yet some families that lack human capital may have an abundance of *social capital*, which "exists in the *relations* between persons."[17] Families with social capital are close; parents and children share warmth, trust, and support. Some families, of course, lack both human capital and social capital, while other families have both. Still other families have human capital but lack social capital. The parents may be well educated, for example, but spend no time with their children.

Coleman points out that social capital exists in communities as well as families. People who attend the same church and share the same religious values can sustain one another. Thus he argues that the functional community surrounding Catholic schools can supply social capital to students who lack it at home. Coleman points to the remarkable success of Catholic schools with students from single-parent families, families in which both parents work outside the home, and families who rarely talk about school. To a greater degree than any other kind of school, Catholic schools offer the support that can help such students succeed.

Coleman puts his case for Catholic education into the larger context of "two orientations to schooling." Public educators try to keep parents at arm's length, he says, while private educators try to keep parents inside a community. Public schools are agents of the larger society and the state, trying to help children transcend the limitations of their family background. Private schools are agents and extensions of families, trying to help one generation transmit its values to the next.

"These two orientations are not in fundamental conflict," Coleman writes, as long as the values of the family and the society are similar.[18] When they clash, however, the families who feel the greatest sense of conflict turn to private schools, hoping to find the values they miss in public schools. Coleman uses this analysis to explain the rise of several different types of private schools. He contends that the search for homogeneous values led Catholics to start parochial schools before the Civil War, some whites to establish segregation academies after the *Brown* decision, and fundamentalist Protestants to open Christian schools during the 1970s and 1980s.

FUNDAMENTALIST CHRISTIAN SCHOOLS

Coleman's concept of community is an appropriate point of departure for our discussion of fundamentalist Christian schools. Most parents who send their children to Christian schools are products of the public schools. But public education has changed, the fundamentalists insist. They believe that today's public schools promote secular values that conflict with Christian values. Roman Catholics left the public schools because they were too Protestant; fundamentalist Christians are leaving the public schools because they are not Protestant enough. The fundamentalists are opening their own schools, incorporating them into a functional community that also includes the home and the church.[19]

Critics initially dismissed fundamentalist schools as just another variation on the segregation academy theme, and to be sure, the early stirrings of the Christian school movement did coincide with the desegregation of public schools in the South. Without question the desire to maintain racial homogeneity played a role in the founding of some fundamentalist schools. During the 1970s, however, critics began to notice that many Christian schools were enrolling both blacks and whites and that the schools were growing in parts of the nation where desegregation was simply not an issue. The schools are separatist by their very nature, but it now seems clear that the separation most fundamentalists have in mind is not racial.[20]

Inside Fundamentalist Schools

Paraphrasing the New Testament, fundamentalists say they are "in the world but not of the world." With their attention focused on obtaining salvation and preparing for life in the next world, virtually every subject in their schools is informed by a fundamentalist view of Christianity. Young children learn to read from textbooks that highlight morality and are strongly reminiscent of the *McGuffey's Readers* that were a staple of nineteenth-century public schools. In some Christian schools, students use the *McGuffey's Readers* themselves. The fundamentalist approach to science stresses God's role as creator, based on a literal interpretation of the book of Genesis. History is the story of God's relationship with people on earth. Modern literature to which fundamentalists often object in public schools—*The Chocolate War, Catcher in the Rye, Of Mice and Men*—is simply excluded from Christian schools. Such literary classics as "Romeo and Juliet" and "Macbeth" may be included but in expurgated editions.

Some Christian schools use a packaged, programmed curriculum that draws a great deal of criticism from nonfundamentalist educators. Produced by such companies as Accelerated Christian Education (ACE) and A Beka Book Publications, the curriculum features workbooks and other materials designed to let students proceed at their own pace with little or no assistance. A student might take a year-long course in algebra, for example, working independently in a room—sometimes in an individual cubicle—surrounded by other students taking different courses. The developers of these materials downplay the importance of interaction among teachers and students. Nor do the developers deem critical thinking important. Instead, according to the publishers of the ACE package, the curriculum is intended for "programming the mind to enable the child to see life from God's point of view."[21] Such materials allow churches with limited budgets to start their own schools inexpensively. They are also attractive to the small but growing number of *home schoolers,* parents who teach their children at home. Home schoolers often affillate with Christian schools in an attempt to satisfy state compulsory education laws.[22]

Critics of fundamentalist education often generalize the use of ACE and A Beka materials to all Christian schools. Certainly, from the perspective of any of the theories of education that we examined in Chapter 7, the programmed, memory-oriented, all-but-teacherless curriculum is an easy target. Many of the better-established Christian schools, however, have never used programmed materials, and some of the newer ones are discarding them. Fundamentalist schools, like fundamentalist Christians themselves, are not all alike.[23]

A visitor to some of the schools, in fact, might be surprised at how traditional—that is, essentialist—their approach to education is. Well-disciplined students, enthusiastic teachers, and a familiar core of basic subjects can evoke, on the surface, the atmosphere of suburban public schools of the late 1950s. But hearing an English teacher open discussion of a short story by asking "How would Jesus react in that situation?" or seeing a science teacher present evolution as a discredited theory may startle the visitor. If the visitor examines an application for a teaching position, such questions as "Do you sense that God has called you to be a Christian school teacher?" or "How much time do you spend alone with God, reading the Bible and praying?" make it impossible to miss the fundamentalist orientation.

The Struggle against Secular Humanism

That orientation, fundamentalists insist, offers the best hope for helping their children escape from secularism. Fundamentalists want their particular brand of Christianity to permeate every aspect of their schools, for they are firmly convinced that secular humanism, which they regard as another religion, permeates public education and every other aspect of public life. To fundamentalists, secular humanism is the belief that people are capable of charting their own course through life without divine assistance. In other words, human beings can set moral standards and make their own determination of right and wrong. So defined, secular humanism flies in the face of fundamentalist Christianity, which requires that people look to God for guidance and take their moral standards from the Bible. Fundamentalists argue that because secular humanism deals with ultimate concerns about life and reality, it is indeed a religion. Just as some people seek answers to ultimate questions in Christianity or Judaism, which are *theistic* religions centered on a deity, other people look to secular humanism, a *nontheistic* religion centered on human beings.[24]

Fundamentalists charge that since the 1960s, when the U.S. Supreme Court ruled group prayer in public schools unconstitutional in the *Engel v. Vitale* (1962) and *Abington v. Schempp* (1963) decisions, public education has been drifting away from its Judeo-Christian moorings. The moral and social revolutions of the 1960s and 1970s brought "sex, drugs, and rock and roll" into the schools, forcing students to make moral decisions at earlier ages. Just when students needed guidance more than ever, public education abandoned the yes-and-no answers found in a fundamentalist reading of the Bible for a situational morality that encourages students to weigh the consequences of their actions and make their own decisions.

Fundamentalist Christians also find the content of many public school textbooks objectionable. They claim that some social studies texts, for example, say too little about the role of the Judeo-Christian tradition in American history. Some literature books contain nonjudgmental portrayals of immoral behavior. Textbooks used in a variety of subjects, they say, convey the message "Think for yourself" rather than "Trust in God."

The cumulative effect of public education on students is subtle but powerful, fundamentalists conclude. By persuading students that they are in charge of their own destiny, public schools are promoting the religion of secular humanism. From the fundamentalist point of view, Christian schools that teach submission to God's will offer a clear alternative.

In order to understand the kind of education that fundamentalists want to foster in Christian schools, we must understand the changes they are trying to make in the public schools. Increasingly they are turning to the judicial system in their quest to reform public education, and recently they have won major battles in the lower courts only to encounter setbacks on appeal. The well-publicized case *Smith v. Board of School Commissioners of Mobile County* (1987) put secular humanism in the national spotlight. The case originated in Alabama, where a federal district court judge, siding with more than 600 fundamentalist plaintiffs, not only declared secular humanism a religion but banned 44 public school textbooks for promoting the religion. If the First Amendment means that public schools cannot advance the theistic religions of Judaism and Christianity, the judge reasoned, then neither can the schools advance the nontheistic religion of humanism.[25]

A federal circuit court of appeals rejected most of the district judge's arguments. The appeals court found that while certain passages in the textbooks are consistent with the set of beliefs that fundamentalists call secular humanism, other passages in the textbooks are consistent with the doctrines of Christianity, Judaism, and other theistic religions. "Mere consistency with religious tenets," the court of appeals wrote, "is insufficient to constitute unconstitutional advancement of religion." The court pointed out that the textbooks expose students to a variety of viewpoints and beliefs, some religious and some nonreligious. The overall "message" that the textbooks convey is neither the endorsement nor rejection of any religion; instead, the books represent "a governmental attempt to instill . . . such values as independent thought, tolerance of diverse views, self-respect, maturity, self-reliance and logical decision-making."[26]

In *Mozert v. Hawkins County Public Schools* (1987), a case that originated in Tennessee, another federal circuit court of appeals considered different issues but reached essentially the same conclusion. In this case, which like *Smith* made national headlines, a group of fundamentalist Christians complained that the content of their children's public school readers offended their religious beliefs. A federal district court judge ordered the school board to allow the students to "opt out" of their reading classes and learn to read apart from other students— in the library, in the study hall, and at home.[27]

The circuit court of appeals overturned the district judge's decision, concluding that requiring students to read a particular set of books is not the same thing as forcing them to accept a particular set of religious beliefs. "Instead, the record in this case discloses an effort by the school board to offer a reading curriculum designed to acquaint students with a multitude of ideas and concepts, though not in proportions the plaintiffs would like."[28]

The issue is, in part, one of balance and emphasis, but some fundamentalist Christians take a far more adamant stand. On certain matters they simply do not want their children to exercise independent thought. Certain questions, answered by the Bible, are not open to debate. Believing that their main responsibility as parents is instilling in their children the *one* correct outlook on the world, helping them "see life from God's point of view," some fundamentalists find the clash of ideas in the public schools unacceptable. Because the federal courts of appeal in both the *Smith* and the *Mozert* cases declined to decide what constitutes a religion for purposes of the First Amendment and whether secular humanism is in fact a religion, fundamentalists are likely to take the issues to court again during the 1990s.

Meanwhile the growth of fundamentalist schools continues, slower than a decade ago but still faster than any other private schools. During the 1840s and 1850s Roman Catholics became the first major defectors from the common school movement. By the year 2000 it may be clear whether fundamentalist Christians wil become the second.

PRIVATE SCHOOLS AND THE GOVERNMENT

State Regulation

Americans who strongly disapprove of the efforts of any religious group to reshape the public schools in its own image may feel just as strongly that churches and individuals should have the right to control their own private schools. But do they have the right? This question, answered inconsistently by courts and state legislatures for the last two decades, wil certainly be part of the private-versus-public school debates of the 1990s. The larger issue is state regulation of private education, which involves striking a delicate balance between the right of a state to insure that all children receive an education that meets minimum standards and the right of parents to educate their children as they see fit.

Although school laws vary considerably from state to state, we can divide the states into two groups in their approach to regulating private schools. In group one is the small and decreasing number of states—fewer than ten—that try to make all private schools meet the same standards as public schools. Catholic schools, other religious schools, independent schools, and public schools alike must comply with regulations covering everything from the school cafeteria to teacher education and certification to the curriculum. Most states, however, are in group two. They require all private schools to meet health and safety standards, submit attendance reports, and (in some cases) present student standardized test scores, but these states exempt religious schools from academic regulations governing teachers and the curriculum. The states in group two want some degree of control over private schools, but they try to avoid church-state entanglement over academic issues.[29]

Private schools react to government regulation in a variety of ways. Catholic schools willingly meet the standards of the states in which they are located. Even in group two states, Catholic educators voluntarily comply with academic regulations, boasting that their schools not only meet but exceed public school standards. Most independent schools and many other religious schools also comply with the regulations of the states in both groups.[30]

The controversy over regulation centers on fundamentalist schools and home schooling families, both of whom cite religious reasons for rejecting state standards, especially those that apply to academic matters. Bitter disputes and legal battles have broken out in group one states, for fundamentalists regard their schools as ministries of the church. They argue that just as churches are free to select preachers with whatever educational credentials the churches prefer, the choice of teachers should also be free from government interference. Churches should also have the freedom to determine the curriculum for their schools, since sensitive issues ranging from sexual morality to the origins of the universe are involved. Many home schoolers reject government regulation using variations of these same arguments.[31]

Educational officials in group one states respond that requiring private schools to meet minimum academic standards is not only reasonable but essential. Officials often raise the issues of professionalism that we examined in Chapter 4. Just as all states regulate the training and licensing of doctors to protect society from quacks and insure quality medical care, the states must also set standards for teacher education and certification. State officials point out that some teachers in fundamentalist schools do not even have college degrees, much less state teaching certificates. As many as half of home schooling parents are not high school graduates. Would society tolerate such a situation in medicine— or in dentistry, law, or any of the established professions? Certainly not.[32]

State school officials also claim that their curriculum regulations are broad enough to accommodate religious diversity. State standards often require only that schools teach certain subjects, leaving private schools a great deal of control over specific content. A course in biology, for example, could stress creationism and reject evolution but still satisfy state standards. Thus state officials argue that religious schools—as well as parents who teach their children at home—should have no objections to meeting minimum curriculum standards.

Naturally the debate does not end there. Fundamentalist educators and home schooling families challenge state officials to prove that graduates of state-approved teacher education and certification programs are measurably better than other teachers. As we have seen, state officials are hard pressed to do that. Ultimately, fundamentalists and home schoolers rest their case on their belief that education is a religious endeavor that government has no right to regulate.

State legislatures have taken a variety of stands in these disputes, and the courts have also sent mixed signals. In *Kentucky State Board for Elementary and Secondary Education v. Rudasill* (1979), a lower court rejected the state's attempt to make religious schools comply with academic regulations. The U.S. Supreme Court allowed the decision to stand. In *State [of Nebraska] v. Faith Baptist Church* (1981), a lower court took the opposite position and approved the academic regulation of religious schools. The U.S. Supreme Court allowed this decision, too, to stand. In both cases the Supreme Court said it found no justification in the U.S. Consitition for hearing arguments on the educational and religious issues involved, leaving states and private schools with no clear guidelines. The trend in state legislatures, however, is now toward loosening rather than tightening the academic reins on religious schools. Home schoolers are also finding an increasingly tolerant political climate as the 1990s begin.[33]

Tuition Tax Credits

Government financial support of private schools, like government regulation, is an old controversy that has run alternately hot and cold since before the common school era. During the 1980s the Reagan administration turned up the heat by advocating *tuition tax credits*—tax breaks for parents who send their children to private elementary and secondary schools. Ronald Reagan, the first president to support tuition tax credits, proposed a plan that would have allowed a private school family to reduce its federal income tax obligation by up to $500 ($300 in the Senate's version of the plan). The full credit would have been available only to families whose annual incomes are below $40,000, and families with incomes above $50,000 would have been ineligible for any credit.[34]

The national discussion of President Reagan's proposal and similar plans has made Americans more aware of arguments for and against tuition tax credits. Supporters of the credits usually argue that parents whose children attend private schools pay for education twice: once in the form of tuition payments to private schools and again in the form of tax payments for public schools. Since private school families receive no direct benefits from public education, they are entitled to relief from their double burden. Supporters also argue that tuition tax credits would be especially helpful to poor families by making it easier for their children to attend private schools. More affluent parents have the financial resources to choose private schools if they find public schools unsatisfactory; society should give poor parents, whose children often attend the worst public schools, the same option. Tuition tax credits would force public education to improve in the long run, supporters conclude, because public schools would have to compete head-to-head with private schools to attract students.

Opponents of tuition tax credits respond to the double-payment argument by pointing out that no family *has* to pay for education twice—private school attendance is a matter of choice. Since every state provides public schools for all children, society has no obligation to subsidize the choice of other schools. Besides, the opponents continue, sounding much like Horace Mann, all citizens receive indirect benefits from public education. Public schools prepare students to vote, work, and make other contributions to society as a whole. As for the argument that tuition tax credits would give poor families more educational options, opponents point out that $500, the maximum credit in President Reagan's proposal, would hardly make a dent in most private school tuition bills; the credit would simply be a bonus for those middle class families who already send their children to private schools. Far from improving public schools, opponents conclude, tuition tax credits would slap public schools in the face. By reducing government revenues, tuition tax credits would make it more difficult to give public education the financial support it needs to improve.[35]

Congress stood firm against tuition tax credits during the 1980s, effectively stalling the movement at the federal level. The debate continues, however, with a new twist. Opponents have traditionally used a constitutional argument against the tax credits, charging that since the vast majority of private school students attend religious schools, tuition tax credits would violate the First Amendment by giving government support to religion. Not true, supporters have replied—the financial benefits would go to parents rather than churches. The U.S. Supreme Court has never ruled on these exact arguments, but the court's decision in *Mueller v. Allen* (1983) may make them irrelevant.[36]

Mueller has given tax credits a new lease on life. The Supreme Court ruled that Minnesota's income tax deduction for educational expenses is constitutional, since the deduction is available to parents of private *and* public school students. Obviously the Minnesota legislature did not provide the tax break to aid religion, the court stated; the legislature wanted to help all parents meet the rising costs of education. Most of the plan's benefits do go to private school families, however, for they can deduct not only tuition but other educational expenses such as textbooks, supplies, and transportation. Public school families pay no tuition, of course, and their other school-related expenses are much lower. The *Mueller* decision, a legal breakthrough for tuition tax credits, has prompted several state legislatures to consider what supporters are now billing as "educational tax credits for public and private school families." The debate over their desirability will continue into the 1990s.[37]

Educational Vouchers

So will the debate over *educational vouchers,* for vouchers take the idea that the government should support both private and public schools several steps further. Vouchers are "tickets" that the government issues to parents to cover all or part of their children's educational expenses. Parents would be able to redeem the tickets at any public school or any approved, participating private school. Government approval would be based on the private school's willingness to admit students from all socioeconomic backgrounds, among other considerations, and the school's participation would be voluntary. Vouchers, like tax credits, are intended to give families more educational options.[38]

Voucher proposals involve far-reaching legal, financial, and administrative questions. Would vouchers violate the First Amendment? How much would they cost? Would the paperwork be manageable? Other questions strike sensitive socioeconomic nerves. What effect would vouchers have on segregation by class, race, and ethnicity? To put the question more bluntly, how many private schools would welcome an influx of poor and minority children? Moreover, there are strong differences of opinion over whether the nation's poorest families would have the information to make wise choices in an open educational marketplace and whether vouchers would be the entering wedge of unprecedented government regulation of private schools. The federal government, after all, has a record of trying to control what it pays for.[39]

This record makes many private schoolers understandably wary of vouchers, even though President Reagan, a popular conservative, proposed a voucher plan for the Chapter I compensatory education program. (See Chapter 9 of this book for more information on compensatory education.) Mr. Reagan suggested giving Chapter I assistance directly to poor families in the form of vouchers that they could redeem at either public or private schools. Congress refused to go along after debating the issues outlined in the above paragraph. Because vouchers represent a break with the nation's educational traditions, they are a political longshot as the 1990s begin.

As the debate over private schools and public schools continues, it seems appropriate to reflect on America's educational traditions. I hope my feelings about public education have come through in this book. I am critical of the public schools, but for what it is worth, they have my support. At the same time, I understand why some people support private schools. The activities I have suggested below are intended to help you see the contrast between the traditions of public education and private education. Think about the different principles that underlie the two traditions. How do you, as a prospective teacher, feel about the principles of public or *common* schooling? Have the principles worked well enough in practice to merit your support? Now ask the same kinds of questions about the three sectors of private schooling.

The more experience I have with American education, the longer and more complex my answers to such questions become—now they have filled the pages of this textbook. I hope this book helps you find your own answers. The ongoing debate over public schools and private schools brings *America's Teachers* to a fitting conclusion.

ACTIVITIES

1. Visit one school in each of the three sectors of private education—Roman Catholic, other religious, and independent. Talk with the teachers and principal in each school about some of the issues discussed in this chapter: the demographics of the student body, the qualifications and credentials of the teachers, the content and academic standards of the curriculum, and state regulations that affect the school. Also ask the teachers and principal why (or if) they prefer to work in a private setting, touching on such things as working conditions, salaries, and intangible rewards.

2. During your visit to each school request permission to talk with a group of students. Ask them, too, about some of the issues in this chapter, especially their reasons for attending a private rather than a public school.

3. Stage a debate in your college class on tuition tax credits, vouchers, and state regulation of private schools.

SUGGESTED READINGS

Since more than 80 percent of private school students attend schools with a religious orientation, reading *Religious Schooling in America,* edited by James C. Carper and Thomas C. Hunt (see note 19), is an excellent way to deepen your understanding of private education. The book contains sympathetic, well-documented chapters on Catholic, fundamentalist Christian, Lutheran, Jewish, and a variety of other religious schools. The most provocative and influential recent contribution to the public-versus-private school debate is *Public and Private High Schools: The Impact of Communities* by James S. Coleman and Thomas Hoffer (note 12). For an insightful look at a Christian high school, read Alan Peshkin's *God's Choice: The Total World of a Fundamentalist Christian School* (note 19).

NOTES

1. For an account of how the line between public and private schools was drawn, see Robert L. Church and Michael W. Sedlak, *Education in the United States: An Interpretive History* (New York: Free Press, 1976), chs. 2, 3, 6.
2. U.S. Department of Education, Center for Education Statistics, *Digest of Education Statistics, 1987* (Washington: U.S. Government Printing Office, 1987), p. 8, and *The Condition of Education: Elementary and Secondary Education, 1988,* vol. 1 (Washington: U.S. Government Printing Office, 1988), pp. 50–51, 106.
3. U.S. Department of Education, Center for Education Statistics, *The Condition of Education, 1986 Edition* (Washington: U.S. Government Printing Office 1986), pp. 189–190; Donald A. Erickson, "Choice and Private Schools: Dynamics of Supply and Demand," in Daniel C. Levy, ed., *Private Education: Studies in Choice and Public Policy* (New York: Oxford University Press, 1986), ch. 3; Bruce S. Cooper, "The Changing Demography of Private Schools: Trends and Implications," *Education and Urban Society* 16 (August 1984): 429–442; Cooper, Donald L. McLaughlin, and Bruno V. Manno, "The Latest Word on Private School Growth," *Teachers College Record* 85 (Fall 1983): 88–98.
4. See note 3.
5. See note 3 and Blake Rodman, "Independent-School Enrollments Slip," *Education Week* (May 14, 1986), pp. 1, 39; "Private Schools," *Education Week* (September 16, 1987), p. 9.
6. U.S. Department of Education, *The Condition of Education, 1986 Edition,* pp. 191–193, 201.
7. Ibid., pp. 193–195.
8. Ibid.; James G. Cibulka, Timothy J. O'Brien, and Donald Zewe, *Inner-City Private Elementary Schools: A Study* (Milwaukee: Marquette University Press, 1982); Bruno V. Manno, "Stereotypes, Statistics, and Catholic Schools," *Education Week* (November 13, 1985), p. 22; Anne Pavuk, "Catholic Schools Continue Enrollment Slide," *Education Week* (April 22, 1987), p. 9.
9. James S. Coleman, Thomas Hoffer, and Sally Kilgore, *Public and Private Schools* (Washington: National Center for Educational Statistics, 1981), and *High School*

Achievement: Public, Catholic, and Private Schools Compared (New York: Basic Books, 1982).

10. Several journals invited Coleman, his critics, and his defenders to take up these arguments at length in their pages: *Educational Researcher* 10 (August–September 1981), *Harvard Educational Review* 51 (November 1981), *Phi Delta Kappan* 63 (November 1981), and *Sociology of Education* 55 (April–July 1982).

11. See William Snider, "Poor, Wealthier Catholic High Schoolers Found Gaining at Same Rate in Studies," *Education Week* (March 5, 1986), pp. 1–11; Andrew M. Greeley, *Catholic High Schools and Minority Students* (New Brunswick, NJ: Transaction Books, 1982).

12. James S. Coleman and Thomas Hoffer, *Public and Private High Schools: The Impact of Communities* (New York: Basic Books, 1987).

13. Ibid., chs. 3–5. Coleman's studies of private schools led him to conclusions different from those he reached in *Equality of Educational Opportunity* (Washington: U.S. Government Printing Office, 1966), often called "The Coleman Report," in which he stated that achievement is more influenced by the socioeconomic background of students than by the characteristics of the schools they attend.

14. Coleman and Hoffer, *Public and Private High Schools,* chs. 3–5.

15. Ibid. p. 9.

16. Ibid., p. 10.

17. Ibid., p. 221, emphasis in the original.

18. Ibid., p. 4.

19. For an excellent case study of Christian education, see Alan Peshkin, *God's Choice: The Total World of a Fundamentalist Christian School* (Chicago: University of Chicago Press, 1986). Another fine account, sympathetic but evenhanded, is James C. Carper's "The Christian Day School," in Carper and Thomas C. Hunt, eds., *Religious Schooling in America* (Birmingham, AL: Religious Education Press, 1984), ch. 5.

20. David Nevin and Robert E. Bills, *The Schools That Fear Built: Segregationist Academies in the South* (Washington: Acropolis Books, 1976); Virginia D. Nordin and Turner L. Williams, "More than Segregation Academies: The Growing Protestant Fundamentalist Schools," *Phi Delta Kappan* 61 (February 1980): 391–394; William J. Reese, "Soldiers of Christ in the Army of God: The Christian School Movement in America," *Educational Theory* 35 (Spring 1985): 175–194.

21. Quoted in Berniece B. Seiferth, "A Critical Review of the New Christian Schools," *High School Journal* 68 (December 1984–January 1985): 70–74. See also Dan B. Fleming and Thomas C. Hunt, "The World as Seen by Students in Accelerated Christian Education Schools," and Ronald E. Johnson, "ACE Responds," *Phi Delta Kappan* 68 (March 1987): 518–521.

22. Patricia M. Lines, "An Overview of Home Instruction," *Phi Delta Kappan* 68 (March 1987): 510–517. See also Kirsten Goldberg, "Pressure Pays Off for Home-Schooling Families," *Education Week* (September 30, 1987), pp. 11–12.

23. Erickson, "Choice and Private Schools," pp. 90–91.

24. Alan N. Grover, *Ohio's Trojan Horse: A Warning to Christian Schools Everywhere* (Greenville, SC: Bob Jones University Press, 1977). The very existence of secular humanism is highly controversial, with People for the American Way, the American Civil Liberties Union, and similar groups charging that the concept is a smoke

screen, a catch-all for anything that fundamentalists dislike. See "Conservative Christians Again Take Issue of Religion in Schools to Courts" and "Secular Humanism: Meaning Varies with Political Stance," *New York Times* (February 28, 1986), p. 11.

25. Kenneth P. Nuger, "The Religion of Secular Humanism in Public Schools: *Smith v. Board of School Commissioners*," *West's Education Law Reporter* 38 (June 25, 1987): 871–879.

26. Quoted in "Freedom of Religion," *School Law Reporter* 28 (December 1987): 2.

27. "A Reprise of Scopes," *Newsweek* (July 28, 1986); Kenneth P. Nuger, "Accommodating Religious Objections to State Reading Programs: *Mozert v. Hawkins County Public Schools*," *West's Education Law Reporter* 36 (February 19, 1987): 255–265.

28. Quoted in "Textbook Religious Matters," *School Law Reporter* 28 (December 1987): 3. For discussions of both *Smith* and *Mozert*, see Kenneth P. Nuger, "Judicial Responses to Religious Challenges Concerning Humanistic Public Education: The Free Exercise and Establishment Debate Continues," *Alabama Law Review* 39 (Fall 1987): 73–101, and Perry A. Zirkel, "The Textbook Cases: Secularism on Appeal," *Phi Delta Kappan* 69 (December 1987): 308–310.

29. Patricia M. Lines, "State Regulation of Private Education," *Phi Delta Kappan* 63 (October 1982): 119–123; Phyllis L. Blaustein, "Public and Nonpublic Schools: Finding Ways to Work Together," *Phi Delta Kappan* 67 (January 1986): 368–372.

30. Ibid.

31. James C. Carper and Neal E. Devins give these arguments a favorable review in "Rendering unto Caesar: State Regulation of Christian Day Schools," *Journal of Thought* 20 (Winter 1985): 99–113.

32. Michael D. Baker takes the side of the state officials in "Regulation of Fundamentalist Christian Schools: Free Exercise of Religion v. the State's Interest in Quality Education," *Kentucky Law Journal* 67 (1978–79): 415–429; Goldberg, "Pressure Pays Off," p. 11.

33. Ralph D. Mawdsley and Steven P. Permuth, "State Regulation of Religious Schools," *NOLPE School Law Journal* 11 (1983): 55–64; Goldberg, "Pressure Pays Off."

34. Mark K. Kutner, Joel D. Sherman, and Mary F. Williams, "Federal Policies for Private Schools," in Levy, ed., *Private Education*, ch. 2.

35. For a discussion of the arguments on tuition tax credits, see Thomas M. James and Henry M. Levin, eds., *Public Dollars for Private Schools: The Case of Tuition Tax Credits* (Philadelphia: Temple University Press, 1983).

36. Martha M. McCarthy, "Tuition Tax Credits and the First Amendment," *Issues in Education* 1 (1983): 88–105.

37. Ibid: Kirsten Goldberg, "Lawmakers Adopt Income-Tax Credits for Tuition in Iowa," *Education Week* (May 20, 1987), pp. 1, 18.

38. John E. Coons and Stephen B. Sugarman, *Education by Choice—The Case for Family Control* (Berkeley: University of California Press, 1978).

39. For a debate on vouchers, see R. Freeman Butts, "Educational Vouchers: The Private Pursuit of the Public Purse," and John E. Coons, "Of Family Choice and 'Public' Education," *Phi Delta Kappan* 61 (September 1979): 7–13. See also Chris Pipho, "Student Choice: The Return of the Voucher," *Phi Delta Kappan* 66 (March 1985): 461–462.

Index